A Peculiar People

The Rediscovery of Primitive Christianity

BY JOSEPH JOHN GURNEY

Richmond, Indiana • www.fum.org

Copyright © 1979 by Friends United Press

All rights reserved. No portion of this book may be reproduced, stored in electronic retrieval system or transmitted in any form or by means—electronic, mechanical, photocopy, recording or other—except for brief quotations in printed reviews, without the prior permission of the publisher.

Original Printing 1979
Reprinted 2008

Friends United Press
101 Quaker Hill Drive
Richmond IN 47374
friendspress@fum.org
www.fum.org

Cover design by Shari Pickett Veach

Library of Congress Cataloging-in-Publication Data

Gurney, Joseph John, 1788-1847
A Peculiar People
   Includes footnotes.
   ISBN 0-913408-48-4
   ISBN 978-0-913408-48-3

79-50100

INTRODUCTION TO
A PECULIAR PEOPLE:
THE REDISCOVERY OF
PRIMITIVE CHRISTIANITY

Joseph John Gurney was born in 1788 near Norwich, England. The Gurney family had long been associated with the Society of Friends (Quakers) and were influential members of the East Anglia community. The Gurneys lived in Earlham Hall, a rambling but magnificent estate located a few miles outside Norwich from which the present Earlham College (Indiana) derives its name.

Joseph John was the tenth child in a family of eleven. Elizabeth Gurney Fry, one of his sisters, was to become an outstanding social activist in the early nineteenth century, known principally for her work in bettering the lot of women and children and in prison reform. The Gurney household was visited by hosts of gentry and nobility including the frequent stays of the Duke of Gloucester. Thus Gurney's childhood contributed to a social openness and receptivity in his later life which was somewhat uncharacteristic of Friends in his day.

His education took him to Oxford where because of his dissenting church status he was denied membership and a degree. This was no obstacle, however, to his learning for he attended the lectures and immersed himself in the resources of the university nonetheless. Under his tutor, John Rogers, young Gurney developed skills in Latin, Greek, Hebrew and French. He was learned in the classics and became something of an authority in his own day in the Rabbinical and Patristic writings. Gurney was foremost a Bible scholar, versed in the Vulgate and Syriac Peschito as much as in the Testaments in their original languages. A banker by vocation, he remained a disciplined student and throughout his lifetime continued the habit of early rising to devote blocks of time to scholarship. Gurney published over 50 books, tracts, and articles ranging on subjects from Biblical studies and labor relations to geology.

Perhaps more important than this to us today was the tremendous impact his ministry had upon Friends of his day and subsequent generations. Joseph John Gurney is in many respects one of the greatest enigmas of the Quaker past. Some see him as a prophet who called a languid, Laodicean-type sect out of the spiritual myopia of Quietism to a fresh baptism of the Spirit. Others see Gurney as a brash interloper whose thought was at the foundation of "Friendly" schisms.

Gurney came to a full surrender of his life to the leadership of Christ at the age of 24. He mentions the significance of this viz. a viz. his birthright place among Quakers in the "Preface" which follows. He first spoke as a minister in 1816 and was recorded in 1818. His thirty years of active ministry spanned one of the most critical eras in Quaker history, of which he is a central figure. Gurney travelled extensively, often in the company of Elizabeth Fry. Ireland, Scotland, Canada, America, the West Indies, and most of the nations of the European continent were stops in his itinerary. His influence extended far beyond the tiny society in which he belonged. Hundreds, even thousands in the Americas, were attracted to public meetings called at his coming. Sometimes hastily printed broadsides nailed up the night before were all that was needed to fill a hall or Quaker meeting-house to hear Gurney. Young people especially responded to his ministry and teaching.

It was primarily for this latter group that the *Observations on the Distinguishing Views and Practices of the Society of Friends*[1] was written. This work went through 10 editions in Britain and America and was translated into German. With George Fox two centuries earlier, Gurney believed Quakerism to be nothing more or less than primitive New Testament Christianity without diminution or addition. Gurney was unwilling for his faith to be an antiquarian relic. "One great reason", he wrote in 1824, "why the religious principles of Friends are not found to take a more rapid and extended course in the church and in the world, is probably this — that so many of us fail, in various respects, from properly regulating our practice according to those principles." Gurney longed for the emergence of vital Christianity as it was experienced by the early church. He believed that the youth and seekers of his day would find this in the purified, ancient faith and practice of Friends. He labored in actualizing this conviction until his death in 1847. For this reason, I have chosen to retitle his book as I have. The edition that is reprinted here is significant because of the addition of an introductory chapter and a concluding essay on corporate Christian disciple.[2]

The Society of Friends has produced so far only two systematic thinkers — distantly related to each other — Robert Barclay and Joseph John Gurney. While much has been done in analyzing the contribution of the former, very little has been attempted in the case of Gurney. I believe that the time is right for reevaluating the wholistic thrust of Gurney's theology. Christ is all and all for him. His emphases on simplicity, personal and corporate discipline, the universal ministry, the equipping of the Holy Spirit and divine guidance are as contemporary today as is the New Testament itself. The integrative character of his presentation highlights the unity and depth of his insights.

The church, as a sojourning community, is called to be a peculiar people (I Peter 2:9), transforming the world as a redemptive body but not of it. Joseph John Gurney is a strong voice from the past encouraging our effort under the direction of the Spirit of Christ.

DONALD A. GREEN

FOOTNOTES

[1] This book was originally published as *Observations on the Religious Peculiarities of the Society of Friends* in 1824. In his introduction to the seventh edition which is included in the present volume, Gurney explains that the retitling was occasioned by "frequent complaints" about his choice of terms in the original.

[2] These appeared first in the seventh edition.

PREFACE.

AMONG the arguments employed in the course of the following Observations, there are some which are urged upon the attention of such persons, *exclusively*, as already possess an intimate knowledge of the character and circumstances of the Society of Friends.

The present volume is, in fact, intended chiefly for the use of the junior members of that Society. To these the essays contained in it may be considered to be addressed. I am persuaded that there are not a few of them who, although brought up in the Society, are not sufficiently informed respecting the religious principles by which it is distinguished; and who, perhaps, have seldom reflected, *with accuracy*, on the Christian and scriptural grounds of our several distinguishing views.

It has fallen to my lot to be brought into familiar acquaintance with serious Christians of several denominations; and, although I enjoyed a birthright in the Society, my situation, after I had arrived at years of discretion, was of that nature which rendered it, in rather an unusual degree, incumbent upon me *to make my own choice of a particular religious course*. Under these circumstances, I was led, partly by research, but chiefly, I trust, by a better guidance, to a settled preference, on my own account, of the religious profession of Friends. Nor ought I to hesitate in expressing a heartfelt gratitude to the "Shepherd of Israel," who has bestowed upon me a resting-place in this department of his fold: for although, in some degree, aware how much there is of vital Christianity in other societies, I may acknowledge that I have found the situation thus provided for myself, to be one of true safety, and attended by many substantial advantages.

Since such has been my experience, and since, in reference to this selection of a religious profession, I have been, at various times, engaged in much reflection and in some scriptural investigation, I am inclined to submit to the candid attention of my young friends the grounds on which I was originally led more closely to attach myself to Friends, and on which I have since been confirmed in the persuasion that I was right in so doing.

Although, however, these essays are addressed principally to the junior members of our own body, I confess that I have also had in view a number of individuals who do not actually belong to us, but who have an intimate connexion with us, and appear to be brought, in various degrees, under the same religious peculiar administration.

Should the younger members of our Society, receive, from this humble endeavour to serve them, any instruction, or any encouragement to persevere in that restricted path which Providence has cast up for them—and should the individuals before alluded to be confirmed, by any of the arguments here adduced, in the choice which they appear to be making of the same restricted path—my object in publishing the following statement of thought and sentiment will be answered, and I shall rest satisfied in the comforting persuasion, that my labour (which I trust has been a labour of love) has not been in vain in the Lord.

Here it may be proper for me to remark, that, while the various subjects considered in the present work are discussed in distinct dissertations, and while it may be hoped that these, when separately read, will be found intelligible, it has been my endeavour to maintain, throughout the work, one continued train of reflection and argument; and to do this in such a manner as that the several parts of the series might be closely connected with each other, and that all might tend in harmony to the same general conclusion. Such having been my plan, I may now venture to request the reader to abstain from forming a final judgment of any particular section or chapter, until the whole volume shall have passed under his review.

Since, lastly, the views which I have attempted to unfold are of a nature entirely *religious,* it has, of course, been necessary for me largely to refer to that sacred Book, to the test of which all religious opinions are rightly brought, since it was given by inspiration of God, and contains a divinely-authorized record, both of the doctrines which we ought to believe, and of the duties which we are required to practise. In thus referring to the Holy Scriptures, I have often found occasion, on critical points, to appeal to the decisions of various commentators, both ancient and modern. While, however, I have not hesitated thus to avail myself of the well-applied learning and useful researches of these writers, I wish to take the present opportunity of expressing my conviction, that, for the *most important* practical purposes, the common English version of the Bible may be understood with sufficient precision, without the aid of the critic or the annotator. Above all, may it ever be remembered, that if the Scriptures of truth are to make us "wise unto salvation, through faith which is in Christ Jesus," that spiritual eye must be open in us, which alone is capable of a just and efficacious perception of their divine contents: for it remains to be an incontrovertible truth, that as no man knoweth the things of a man, save the spirit of man which is in him, "*even so the things of God knoweth no man, but the Spirit of God.*"

CONTENTS.

                                                                PAGE

INTRODUCTORY CHAPTER TO THE SEVENTH EDITION 1

CHAP. 1.—ON THE GROUNDS OF RELIGIOUS UNION WHICH SUBSIST AMONG MANKIND IN GENERAL, AND MORE ESPECIALLY AMONG TRUE CHRISTIANS 21

    ADDENDUM, ON UNIVERSAL LIGHT 49

CHAP. 2.—ON DISTINGUISHING RELIGIOUS VIEWS. GENERAL REMARKS ON THOSE OF THE SOCIETY OF FRIENDS . . . 68

CHAP. 3.—ON THE PERCEPTIBLE INFLUENCE AND GUIDANCE OF THE SPIRIT OF TRUTH 75

CHAP. 4.—ON THE DISUSE OF ALL TYPICAL RITES IN THE WORSHIP OF GOD 99

    ADDENDUM, ON BAPTISM AND THE SUPPER 169

CHAP. 5.—ON THE NATURE AND CHARACTER OF THE CHRISTIAN MINISTRY 176

CHAP. 6.—ON THE SELECTION, PREPARATION, AND APPOINTMENT OF THE MINISTERS OF THE GOSPEL 204

CHAP. 7.—ON THE OBJECTIONS ENTERTAINED BY FRIENDS TO THE PECUNIARY REMUNERATION OF THE MINISTERS OF THE GOSPEL 237

CHAP. 8.—ON THE MINISTRY OF WOMEN 261

    ADDENDUM, ON RELIGIOUS INSTRUCTION, PRAYER, &C. . 274

CHAP. 9.—ON SILENT WORSHIP 291

    ADDENDUM, PRACTICAL REMARKS AND ADVICES ON SILENT WORSHIP 306

CHAP. 10.—ON OATHS 317

CHAP. 11.—ON WAR 342

    ADDENDUM ON WAR.   374

CHAP. 12.—ON THE MORAL VIEWS OF FRIENDS. PLAINNESS OF SPEECH, BEHAVIOUR AND APPAREL 376

    ADDENDUM, ON PLAINNESS 426

CONCLUSION 433

ESSAY ON THE DISCIPLINE OF THE PRIMITIVE CHRISTIANS, AND ON THAT OF THE SOCIETY OF FRIENDS 453

INTRODUCTORY CHAPTER

TO THE

Seventh Edition.

In presenting to my young friends and the public at large, a new edition of the " Observations," I wish to make a few preliminary remarks on its contents, as well as on some subjects with which they are connected, and which I deem to be of vital importance to the welfare of our religious body.

First, with respect to the language and style of the volume— I have endeavoured to simplify many of the sentences, and have exchanged a number of long words of foreign origin, for others which are at once shorter and plainer. The experience of more than ten years, since the work was first published, has convinced me of the importance of aiming, as far as possible, at a simple style, that the meaning of the writer may be clear to all men; and especially to a large class of readers, who have not enjoyed the opportunity of much mental cultivation, but to whom religious truth, in all its branches, is, I trust, increasingly precious.

Frequent complaints having been made to me of the title of the work, I have ventured in the present edition to take the somewhat unusual step of changing it; and for the term "Peculiarities" in the title page, I have substituted "Distinguishing Views and Practices."

The reader will observe that in the present edition, I have added some new passages and notes, which I have marked with a double asterisk. These are the results of farther reflection and observation; and will, I trust, be found to strengthen the several arguments to which they are attached. I propose also to add, as an appendix to the volume, a brief essay on one part of our system, which, although it is of considerable importance, I have not hitherto noticed—I mean the nature, origin, and effect, of our *Christian Discipline*. I am persuaded that the more diligently our young friends inquire into the subject, the more they will find cause to believe, that our plan of discipline was very wisely formed, and that its provisions, in their scope and intention, truly agree with the order of the gospel. May they be led to place a right value on its wholesome checks, and to account the protection which it affords them, one of their most valuable privileges!

In confining my attention, in the present work, chiefly to those points in religion, by which Friends are *distinguished* from other bodies of true Christian believers, nothing can be farther from me than any desire to throw into the shade those fundamental doctrines, in which all such believers agree. To unfold these doctrines, and to prove their truth from Scripture, is, in some other works, the sole object which I have pursued; and to maintain them fully and freely (as ability is afforded) in the presence of all men, I deem to be both my first duty, and my dearest right. When we reflect on the unutterable importance of eternity, on the value of never-dying souls, on the pains of hell, and on the joys of heaven, we cannot deny that to dwell on essential, saving, truth, is the main business of every religious teacher.

Dearly ought we to prize the many noble testimonies which have been borne by the Society of Friends, not only in the present day, but from its earliest rise, to the truth and importance of the doctrines of the New Testament. *Christ* has been the centre around which they have delighted to gather; and those who have quitted that centre have never failed to lose, in a spiritual sense at least, their unity with the body.

Since the Holy Scriptures contain a *divinely* authorised standard of revealed truth, and *are fully sufficient for their purpose*, Friends have always refused to bind themselves by any other written creed. Nevertheless, in every period of the Society's history, the acknowledged faith of the body has been sound and unquestionable. Repeatedly have they confessed their belief in one ever-living God, all-wise, almighty, omnipresent, the Creator and Ruler of the universe, holy, just, true and merciful; in the immortality of the soul; in the resurrection of the dead; in the eternity of future rewards and punishments; in the mysterious union and distinction of the Father, the Word, and the Holy Spirit; in the deity of our Lord Jesus Christ; in his incarnation and birth of the virgin Mary; in his sinless human nature; in his meritorious obedience, sufferings, and death; in his resurrection and ascension; in his supreme and universal reign; in his spiritual presence with his people; and in his glorious future coming to judge the quick and the dead.

They are well aware of the fatal effects of the transgression of our first parents—that man is a fallen creature, by nature the child of wrath, prone to iniquity, and absolutely incapable of true holiness and happiness, unless he be born again of the Spirit; and they have been among the foremost to proclaim the power and devices of Satan, our tempter and accuser, who rules, in every age of the world, over the children of disobedience.

They know that " all have sinned and come short of the glory of God," and have often declared in the most explicit manner, that it is only through the precious blood of Jesus Christ, shed for us on the cross, that our " iniquity is forgiven," and our " sin covered." This awful sacrifice they have always regarded as ordained in the eternal counsels of the Father, and as the highest proof both of his holiness and his love; and boldly have they asserted that it was made for *all men;* Christ was " the propitiation for our sins, and not for ours only, but for the sins of the whole world."

I conceive that the views of our Society on this

subject are remarkably comprehensive, and not more comprehensive than just. While Friends have at all times ascribed the forgiveness of sin to the free mercy of God in Christ Jesus; they also believe that the sacrifice of Christ (ordained before the foundation of the world, and accomplished in due season) was the means of procuring for fallen man the gift of the Holy Spirit; and that CHRIST HIMSELF, manifested by his Spirit in the heart, is that "true light which lighteth every man that cometh into the world."

Our frequent declaration of the Christian principle, that without holiness none can see the Lord, or enter into his kingdom, has led some persons to imagine that our Society underrates the importance and necessity of *faith*. Yet there is probably no truth on which Friends have been more accustomed to dwell, than the Scripture doctrine, that the "just shall live by faith." They freely acknowledge that *faith* is essential to man's salvation; and that as is the light bestowed upon us, so is the *belief* required of us. They rejoice in the assurance of Scripture, that "God was in Christ, *reconciling* the world unto himself, not imputing their trespasses unto them;"[1] that "we are justified freely by his grace, through the redemption which is in Christ Jesus,"[2] and that whosoever *believeth* in the Son of God, shall "not perish," but shall "have everlasting life."[3]

But Friends have not failed to declare their persuasion, that the faith by *which we are saved*, is not the

[1] 2 Cor. v, 19. [2] Rom. iii, 24. [3] John iii, 16, 36.

result of learning, or the mere conviction of the human understanding, but a divine gift — an effect of the Spirit—infallibly productive of a life of righteousness, —as a tree produces its natural fruit. Neither do they allow that even a saving faith is anything more than the *instrument* of our justification—the *hand* by which the penitent sinner, made sensible of the terrors of the law, and *turned away from his iniquities*, is enabled to put on the robe of the righteousness of Christ. They have ever held that, under the pardoning love of the Father, the procuring cause of our acceptance with God, and of our final salvation, is CHRIST ALONE, received into the heart of the believer as the sole object of his confidence, and ruling thereby His Spirit.[4]

We plainly learn from Scripture that the Mosaic priesthood with all its ceremonial rites, was in point of authority abolished by the death of Christ; and that, under the dispensation of the gospel, the glorified Jesus *alone* is invested with the sacerdotal office. Not only has he offered once for all a sacrifice for the sins of mankind, but now he " appears in the presence of God for us," pleads our cause, rebukes our enemy, destroys his works, and intercedes with the Father, on our behalf. He is the " minister of the sanctuary, and of the true tabernacle which the Lord pitched, and not man ;"[5] and " in that he himself hath suffered being tempted, he is able to succour them that are tempted."[6] Now I conceive that among the various classes of true Christians, there are none who have

[4] Rom. iv, 25 ; Gal. iv, 19.
[5] Heb. viii, 2.   [6] Heb. ii, 18.

more faithfully maintained these truths than the Society of Friends. It has always been with them a point of leading importance, that Christ is the *only* High Priest of our profession; the *sole* Mediator between God and man, on whom the Christian believer may place his reliance. How often has it been proclaimed within our borders, that Christ "is able to save them to the uttermost who come unto God by him; seeing he ever liveth to make intercession for them;" and that " such an high priest became us, who is holy, harmless, undefiled, separate from sinners, and made higher than the heavens!"[7]

It was part of the office of the high priest of the Israelites, to conduct the worship of the people, to preside over their religious assemblies, and to bless them in the name of the Lord. Friends have always been strongly attached to the corresponding features in the priesthood of our Redeemer. They delight in the assurance that he still condescends to preside over the solemn meetings of Christian believers, to hallow their worship, and to spread over them the peaceful canopy of his presence. Long have they been accustomed to realise that ancient prophecy—"In that day shall the Lord of Hosts be for a crown of glory, and for a diadem of beauty to the residue of his people; and for a spirit of judgment to him that sitteth in judgment, and for strength to them that turn the battle to the gate."[8]

What a comprehensive view did our forefathers take of the doctrine of the Holy Spirit! They were bold

[7] Heb. vii, 25, 26. [8] Isa. xxviii, 5, 6.

to assert, that as on the one hand, Christ died for all men, so on the other, all are made partakers of a measure of the light, life, power, and spirit, of the Redeemer of men—that there is not a man born into the world who has not his day of visitation—that a law is written with the finger of God, on the hearts of all men, by which, in *various degrees*, the natural conscience is enlightened and guided.

They knew indeed that this light is often very faint in the children of ignorance and idolatry; that it shines " in a dark place," and that the darkness comprehends it not; but they also knew that it is pure and unchanging in its character. Never did they dare to consider it as a part of fallen man's corrupt nature; never did they hesitate to ascribe it to the free and universal grace of God, through Christ Jesus our Lord.

The view which our early Friends took of this great doctrine, appears never to have suggested to them a single doubt of the importance of spreading a knowledge of the gospel of our Lord Jesus Christ. On the contrary many of them were diligently engaged in this work, and laboured for the diffusion of true Christianity, not only in their own land, but when they ran to and fro in the earth, and in the distant isles of the sea. George Fox in particular, was a zealous promoter of the knowledge of Christ, and laboured for its dissemination among the negroes of the West Indies. The same faithful elder fervently exhorted his friends in North America to teach the native Indians in that country, that Christ had tasted death for every man; and he freely told them, that the gospel of life and salvation must be preached to every creature under heaven.[9]

It is, indeed, only the abuse of the doctrine of a universal light, which could lead any man to set at nought any Christian effort for so holy a purpose. The doctrine itself affords a delightful encouragement to all such labours of love. Who that is engaged in preaching the gospel either at home or abroad, can deny the advantage of being able to appeal to the light of God's law appearing in the hearts of his hearers? Such an appeal may, through the influence of the Holy Spirit, be the means of convincing them of sin, and may thus prepare the way of Christ; and although this light may not always shine brightly, yet *according to its measure*, it will still be a sure ally to the word preached; it will be found *invariably* on the side of truth, and holiness, and God.

That there is a vast difference in point of morals and religion, between the condition of the heathen world and that of Christian nations, no well-informed person will pretend to deny; and the more we are aware of our superior advantages in these respects, the more zealous we ought to be in diffusing the benefits which we ourselves enjoy, among our benighted fellow-men. But of what permanent use to *us* will be the knowledge of the gospel, if we do not give way to the influence of that divine Spirit, who *strives*, in much long-suffering, with unregenerate man?[1]

There is a work of God upon the soul, which precedes conversion, as well as one which follows it; and

---

[9] Epistles 1679.   [1] See Gen. vi, 3.

the former, though sometimes rapid, or even sudden, is, for the most part, like the latter, extremely gradual. This *preparatory* work of the Spirit, especially in the minds of young people, when he visits them at unexpected moments, reproves them for sin, brings them into tenderness, and allures them into the love and fear of God, is one branch of the great plan of redemption, on which Friends have at all times loved to dwell. They strongly insist on the necessity of obedience to the still small voice of the inward Teacher; and they have always maintained that this obedience is of primary importance to a right knowledge of the truth. The more use we make of the light bestowed upon us, the more will that light be increased; it will set our sins in order before us; it will humble us in a clear view of our own unworthiness; it will lead us to the foot of the Saviour's cross. It is the influence of the Spirit of the Father, operating on the willing soul, which can alone bring us to a real and practical acquaintance with the Son of his love.

Yet nothing could be farther from the minds of our early Friends, than so to misapply this truth, as in any degree to justify the disuse of the Holy Scriptures. They were themselves diligent readers of the Bible; and they gave no countenance whatsoever to the neglect of this blessed means appointed by Providence for our instruction.

There is probably no body of Christians who have taken more pains than Friends have done, to enjoin upon their members a frequent perusal of the Scriptures of Truth. It is one of those duties which is annually brought home to us by a public inquiry addressed to all our inferior meetings; and it has been the subject of many a warm exhortation, and many a strong advice, issued by our yearly meeting itself. Nothing can have been more clear than the testimony of the Society to the divine origin of the book. Friends have always asserted that it was given by inspiration of God; and when our forefathers were defamed by their adversaries, and falsely accused of unsound principles, they always appealed to Scripture as the ONLY authoritative written testimony by which their sentiments could be tried. They boldly invited their hearers and readers to imitate the example of the noble Beræans—to search the Scriptures daily that they might know " whether these things were so."

On this important subject I apprehend that the views of Friends are in accordance with those of other sound and reflecting Christians, although there may prevail between them and ourselves some difference in *phraseology*. If we object to call the Scriptures the Word, or the Word of God, it is not because we entertain the smallest doubt that they are given by inspiration of God; it is only because the Scriptures themselves teach us that this name, *considered as a title of pre-eminence*, properly belongs to our Lord Jesus Christ. If we assert the essential superiority of the Holy Spirit, it is not that we regard the sacred writings as fallible, or do not truly reverence them; but only that we are anxious to distinguish between that which is produced, and the power which produces it; between the work which we can see, and handle, and *its divine, unchangeable Author*.

That the Holy Scriptures, like other ancient writings, have in some degree suffered by passing through the hands of men, is evident from the numerous various readings, both in the Hebrew Bible, and in the Greek Testament. But although the sacred volume thus partakes of the imperfection which attaches to all material objects, Friends have ever been ready, in unison with their fellow-christians, to adore that especial providence which has so signally preserved it from *essential* harm. They joyfully confess that the lapse of time, and the carelessness of transcribers, have not been permitted to deprive the Scriptures of a single doctrinal truth, or a single moral principle; that the wisdom, richness, and harmony of their contents, afford abundant proof that they came from God; and that as the original record of all religious truth, they stand, and ever must stand, unrivalled and alone.

Many of the early members of the society were persons of considerable learning, and they freely made use of their literature, for the elucidation of religious subjects—a remark which applies with peculiar force to Barclay the apologist. Certainly there is nothing in our genuine principles which need discourage any one from a critical study of the Bible in a humble and teachable spirit. It is surely both a duty and a privilege, as opportunity is afforded, to make use of those various sources of information, from which so much light has been thrown, not merely on its historical and descriptive parts, but even on its doctrines and precepts. Yet Friends have always regarded it as an especial duty to insist on the great principle, that "the things of God knoweth no man, but the Spirit of God;" and that we cannot possibly obtain a saving knowledge of the truths revealed in the Bible, except by the gracious aid of its omnipotent Author.

Often have they been led to exhort one another, earnestly to seek for that divine influence, in the perusal of Scripture, which can alone present its precious contents in their true light to the understanding, and impress them with power on the heart. It has been well said by a learned and pious man, that to the spiritually minded reader, and to him alone, the Bible is a book full of illuminated characters. But even when the book is not before us, how often does the good Remembrancer remind us of passages suited to the various turns of our experience, and arrayed for the occasion in new brightness and beauty!

Having offered these remarks on the views of Friends respecting the sacred volume, I must revert, for a short time, to the doctrine of the Spirit. I conceive that there is nothing to which the Scriptures bear a stronger testimony, than the divine character and unfettered influences of the Holy Ghost. As it is by the Spirit alone that we are brought to Christ, and become, through living faith in the Saviour, the reconciled children of God; so the Spirit alone can lead us onwards in the way of holiness, cleanse the inward recesses of our hearts, and prepare us for an entrance into perfect purity. Thus it is, as Friends have always believed, that "the path of the just is as the shining light, that shineth more and more unto the *perfect* day"[2]—thus only that we can obey the

[2] Prov. iv, 18.

awful precept—" Be ye therefore *perfect*, even as your Father, which is in heaven, is *perfect*."[3]

The pre-eminent grace, and peculiar office, of the Holy Spirit *in believers*, as well as his general and preparatory influences, are indeed subjects which have always been prominent in the religious views of Friends. From their first rise as a society, they were led to testify of the utter vanity of the most orthodox creed, without the *possession* of the *life* which is in Christ; and while they spake with deep reverence of the atoning blood of the Lamb, they assured their hearers that it would be impossible for them to partake of its benefit, unless their hearts were given up to the cleansing work, and inward government, of the Spirit of their Redeemer. They boldly declared that justification by faith in Christ crucified, and sanctification by his Spirit, went hand in hand, and could never be separated. Christ " gave himself for us that he might redeem us *from* all iniquity, and purify unto himself a peculiar people, zealous of good works."[4] He " bare our sins in his own body on the tree, that we being dead to sins, should live unto righteousness."[5]

The comprehensive nature of the promises of God respecting the Holy Spirit, is a point to which the attention of our religious society has always been directed with peculiar force. They believe them to be addressed to the *whole* church of Christ *in all ages*, for they read that the Comforter was to continue with the disciples of Jesus " for ever "[6]—that His influence was to be bestowed not merely on the earliest con-

[3] Matt. v, 48.   [4] Titus ii, 14.   [5] 1 Peter ii, 24.
[6] John xiv, xv, and xvi.

verts to Christianity, but on their children also, and on all that are afar off, even "as many" as the Lord our God should "call."[7]

And what are these promises? Large and various indeed! That the Spirit should be poured forth from on high, and convert the wilderness into a fruitful field; so that the work of righteousness should be peace, and the effect thereof quietness and assurance for ever;[8] that God should write his law on the hearts of his people, and that all should know him, from the least to the greatest;[9] that he should sprinkle clean water upon them, give them new hearts and new spirits, and cleanse them from *all* their filthiness and *all* their idolatry;[1] that he should pour forth his Spirit upon *all* flesh, and that the sons and the daughters, the servants and the handmaidens, should prophesy;[2] that *all* the children of Zion should be taught of the Lord, and that great should be their peace;[3]—that Jesus exalted very high, "should sprinkle many nations;"[4] that he should lead captivity captive, and receive gifts for men, even for the rebellious;[5] that he should sit as a refiner and purifier of silver, and purify the sons of Levi;[6] that he should baptize his followers with the Holy Ghost and with fire, and thoroughly cleanse them from sin;[7] that he should send the Comforter unto them from the Father, and that the Father should send the same Comforter in the name of Christ;[8]—that

[7] Acts ii, 39.   [8] Isa. xxxii, 15—17.   [9] Jer. xxxi, 33.
[1] Ezek. xxxvi, 25.   [2] Joel ii, 28, 29.   [3] Isa. liv, 13.
[4] Isa. lii, 15.   [5] Ps. lxviii, 18.   [6] Mal. iii, 3.
[7] Mat. iii, 11.   [8] John xiv, 26; xv, 26.

the Holy Spirit should convince the world of sin, of righteousness, and of judgment;[9] that he should testify of Christ;[1] that he should receive of the things of Christ, and show them to his disciples;[2] that he should teach them all things, and bring all things to their remembrance whatsoever Christ has said unto them;[3] that he should be in them, and dwell in them;[4] that he should show them things to come;[5] finally, that he should GUIDE THEM INTO ALL TRUTH.[5]

Paul bears testimony to the fulfilment of these predictions when he declares, in reference to the gospel dispensation, that the law of the Spirit of life in Christ Jesus had made him free from the law of sin and death;[6] that as many as are led by the Spirit of God, they are the sons of God;[7] that Christians are "the temple of the Holy Ghost" which is *in* them, which they " have of God;[8] and that they are " baptized by one Spirit into one body;"[9]—Peter, when he writes of the baptism which now saves us,[1] and of the Spirit of glory and of God resting on believers;[2]—James, when he tells us of the pure and peaceable wisdom which cometh from above;[3]—and John, when he proclaims the sovereign efficacy of the Lord's anointing, " Ye have an unction from the Holy one, and ye know all things............the anointing which ye have received of him (i. e. of Christ) abideth in you, and *ye need not that any man teach you ;* but as the same anointing

[9] John xvi, 8.   [1] John xv, 26.
[2] John xvi, 14.   [3] John xiv, 26.   [4] John xiv, 17.
[5] John xvi, 13.   [6] Rom. viii, 2.   [7] Rom. viii, 14.
[8] 1 Cor. vi, 19.   [9] 1 Cor. xii, 13.   [1] 1 Pet. iii, 21.
[2] 1 Peter iv, 14.   [3] James iii, 17.

teacheth you of all things, and is truth and no lie, and even as it hath taught you, ye shall abide in Him."[4]

There is probably no body of Christians by whom these precious truths have been more clearly advanced, than by the Society of Friends. It has always appeared to them, that the free and immediate teaching of the Spirit of Christ is the main characteristic of that new covenant which was established in the world by his propitiatory death. It seems, indeed, to have been the chief service intrusted to them, in the church of Christ, to wean men from an undue reliance on an outward ministry, and from all merely human systems in religion, and to lead them to the feet of Jesus. Rightly have they deemed it to be the highest privilege of the Christian believer to draw near to the Father of mercies, through his beloved Son, to wait on God in the silence of all flesh, and to be guided and governed in ALL THINGS, by his Holy Spirit.

It is under this guidance, as Friends have always believed, that the disciples of Jesus are enabled to apply to *particular* occasions, the *general* rules of God's law; and that even in temporal matters which, more or less, involve their spiritual interest, they may be led along in a path of safety. Christ, their divine teacher, cannot be removed into a corner—his light shines in their consciences. If they patiently wait upon him, and pray for his Spirit, he will, from time to time, arise for their help; he will guide them with his " counsel," and make *his* " *way* " straight before their face.

But if this be true respecting our common course of life and duty, who shall deny that it is also true in

[4] 1 John ii, 20—27.

relation to the particular services into which we may be called for the benefit of the church? It is on scriptural authority, that Friends have always asserted, that no voice can lawfully call into these services, but the voice of the Holy Spirit; and that nothing can truly qualify for the performance of them, but the *Lord's anointing.*

I wish to take the present opportunity of expressing my continued conviction of the immense importance of this Christian principle, which appears to me to have been far too much neglected in the professing church of Christ. I am, indeed, well aware that we have no reason in the present day to expect either *miracles,* or those extraordinary measures of inspiration, which were bestowed on the apostles; for these probably have already served their purpose in the establishment of Christianity in the world. But we are surely authorized in expecting the enlivening visitations of an omnipresent Saviour, the perceptible guidance of his Spirit in the path of duty, and the pouring forth of that divine influence, which can alone prepare us for the Lord's service, and rightly direct the ministry of the gospel.

Through the efficacy of this principle our society first arose; and if we would continue as a people, to live and grow in the truth, we must adhere to it with unalterable firmness. "The anointing" will yet do wonders for us, if we are but faithful to its monitions, and submissive to the various crosses and mortifications into which it leads.

Nor are we left without an adequate motive to such a course of faithfulness and obedience. The *love of*

Christ constraineth us; we are bound by every tie of duty, honour, and gratitude, to devote ourselves to the service of that adorable Redeemer, whose we are, because he has bought us with *his own blood.*

Here I must be allowed to express my belief, that a humble reliance on the teaching of the Spirit, and a diligent use of the sacred Scriptures, were the means of leading our forefathers into all those distinguishing views and practices which are described in the present volume. If this be true—and we have surely abundant reason for believing it to be so—what ought to be our course?

Shall we turn our backs on our high Christian views of the spirituality of true worship? Shall we return to ceremonial and figurative rites? Shall we make way in our meetings for a ministry, which one man may prepare, and another appoint? Shall we cease from our testimony against all pecuniary corruption in the church? Shall we forget the sweetness and solemnity of true silent waiting on the Lord? Shall we surrender our Saviour's standard of the yea and the nay, and no longer refuse an oath when expediency is supposed to demand it? Shall we, after all our peaceable professions, recur to the warfare of the world? Shall we forsake our simplicity in dress and language, and break down a hedge which so usefully protects many of our beloved young people from the vanities of the world? In short, shall we renounce that *unbending* adherence to the rule of right, by which our forefathers were distinguished? Shall we exchange a child-like obedience to the Shepherd's voice, for the disposition which is ever ready to criticise and to argue?

If such, through the wiles of Satan, should be our course, how awful and affecting must be the consequence! The gracious purposes for which we were raised up to be a people, will be frustrated through our want of faithfulness; and by forsaking our own place and sphere of duty in the fold of Christ, it is but too probable that we may, in the end, fall from Christ himself, and become wanderers in the barren wastes of an empty profession. But if, on the contrary, we are bold in the Lord to answer these questions in the negative—if we resign ourselves, through every loss and cross, to the disposal of our Holy Head, and diligently endeavour to "keep" *all* his "testimonies;" if we resolve to follow the Lord's Spirit in *all things*—we may reverently believe that he will preserve us unhurt. The humble hope may then arise, that his own eternal power will again be known to abound amongst us; and that many living witnesses to the truth will yet be raised up, within our borders, to the praise of his glorious name.

In conclusion, I would express an earnest desire that we may be enabled more and more to commend our religious Society, in secret and fervent prayer to God. Let us pray that we may be taught of him, to open our hearts and understandings to the *whole* truth as it is in Jesus—that we may stand with immoveable steadfastness on the foundation of the apostles and prophets, Jesus Christ himself being the chief corner stone—and that we may be built up a spiritual temple, which shall ever bear the inscription of HOLINESS UNTO THE LORD.

CHAPTER I.

ON THE GROUNDS OF RELIGIOUS UNION WHICH SUBSIST AMONG MANKIND IN GENERAL, AND MORE ESPECIALLY AMONG TRUE CHRISTIANS.

To a series of observations on the tenets and peculiar religious advantages (as I deem them) of a comparatively small body of persons, I know of no introduction more salutary than a survey of those grounds of union in matters of religion which subsist, first, among mankind in general; and secondly, among the true members of the visible church of Christ. Such a survey will, I trust, produce the effect of warming our hearts with the love of our neighbour, and will prepare us for a calm and charitable discussion of those particulars which belong, more or less exclusively, to our own religious situation in the world and in the church.

I. Let us, then, in the first place, endeavour to form some estimate of the breadth of that ground in religion, on which we are standing in common with mankind in general. God is the Creator and merciful

Father of us all. Christ died for us all. A measure of the influence of the Holy Spirit enlightens, and, if obeyed, would save us all. Upon these successive positions I will venture to offer a few remarks, and will adduce a selection of scriptural declarations, by which they appear to me to be severally established.

1. God, to whom alone can be ascribed the existence of the universe, and of every thing which it contains—" from whom, and through whom, and unto whom, are all things"—is the Creator of all men. Now, it is expressly asserted in Scripture, of this omnipotent Author of our being, that he is " Love;"[1] and again, the character in which he proclaimed himself to his servant Moses was that of " the Lord God, merciful and gracious, long-suffering, and abundant in goodness and truth."[2] Hence we can scarcely fail to conclude, that as the Father of the whole family of man, he extends over them *all* the wing of his paternal care, and graciously offers to them *all* his help, his protection, and his mercy. The royal psalmist, after describing Jehovah as " merciful and gracious, slow to anger and plenteous in mercy," calls upon " *all* his works, in *all* places of his dominion, to bless his holy name."[3] And again, on another occasion, he expressly declares that " the Lord is good to all, and his tender mercies are over *all his works.*"[4] The attributes of the Creator were admirably unfolded by the apostle Paul, in his address to the philosophical Athenians : " God" said he " that made the world and all things therein,

---

[1] 1 John iv, 8.   [2] Exod. xxxiv, 6.   [3] Ps. ciii, 22.   [4] Ps. cxlv, 9.

seeing that he is Lord of heaven and earth, dwelleth not in temples made with hands; neither is worshipped with men's hands, as though he needed anything, seeing he giveth to all life, and breath and all things; and hath made of one blood all nations of men for to dwell on all the face of the earth, and hath determined the times before appointed, and the bounds of their habitation; *that they should seek the Lord, if haply they might feel after him and find him, though he be not far from every one of us;* for in him we live, and move, and have our being; as certain also of your own poets have said, *for we are also his offspring.*"[5]

Let it not be imagined that God is the merciful Father of all mankind, only because he makes his rain to fall and his sun to shine, and bestows upon them all a variety of outward and temporal benefits. The Scriptures plainly declare that he wills for them a happiness of a far more exalted and enduring nature. Fallen and corrupt as they are, and separated by their iniquities from the *Holy* One of Israel, "he is long-suffering," "not willing that any should perish, but that *all* should come to repentance."[6] And to all mankind he proclaims the same invitation : " Let the wicked forsake his way, and the unrighteous man his thoughts, and let him return unto the Lord, and he will have mercy upon him; and to our God, for he will abundantly pardon."[7] The apostle Paul expressly assures us, that " the grace of God that bringeth salvation hath appeared to *all men ;*"[8] that God our Saviour

[5] Acts xvii, 24—28. [6] 2 Pet. iii, 9. [7] Isa. lv, 7. [8] Tit. ii, 11.

would "have *all* men to be saved and to come unto the knowledge of the truth."[9] "Look unto me, and be ye saved, *all the ends of the earth*," said Jehovah himself, " for I am God, and there is none else."[1] Nor are these expressions to be understood as being of a merely general and undefined character. He who offers deliverance to all men, has appointed for all men a way of escape: he who would have all men to be saved, has provided for all men the means of salvation. " God was in Christ reconciling *the world* unto himself, not imputing their trespasses unto them."[2] "God sent not his Son into the world to condemn the world; but that *the world* through him might be saved.[3]

2. This concluding observation naturally leads to my second proposition, that *Christ died for all;* and in order to prove this truth, I need only cite the explicit declarations of inspired writers. " My little children," says the apostle John in his general epistle, " these things write I unto you, that ye sin not. And if any man sin we have an advocate with the Father, Jesus Christ the righteous. And he is the propitiation for our sins, and not for ours only (that is, not only for the sins of Christians, to the whole company of whom this epistle was probably addressed,[4]) but *also for the sins of the whole world.*"[5] The same doctrine is affirmed by Paul: " There is one God," says he in his first epistle to Timothy, " and one mediator between God and men, the man Christ Jesus; *who gave himself a ransom for all*, to be testified in due time;"[6]

[9] 1 Tim ii, 4.   [1] Isa. xlv, 22.   [2] 2 Cor. v, 19.   [3] John iii, 17.
[4] See *Michaelis, Introd. N. T. by Marsh*, vol. iii, ch. 30.
[5] 1 John ii, 1, 2.   [6] Chap. ii, 5, 6.

and again to the Corinthians, he plainly states that "Christ died for all."[7] We may presume it is the same apostle who writes as follows in the epistle to the Hebrews, " we see Jesus, who was made a little lower than the angels, for the suffering of death, crowned with glory and honour; that he by the grace of God *should taste death for every man.*"[8] Lastly, in his epistle to the Romans, Paul declares that we are " reconciled unto God by the death of his Son," and, in drawing the comparison between Adam, in whom man fell, and Christ by whom he is recovered, he argues as follows: " Therefore as by the offence of one [judgment came] upon *all men* to condemnation; even so by the righteousness of one [the free gift came] upon *all men* unto justification of life; for as by one man's disobedience many (or, as in the Greek, " *the many*"[9]) were made sinners, so by the obedience of one shall the many be made righteous. Moreover, the law entered, that the offence might abound; but where sin abounded, grace did much more abound; that as sin hath reigned unto death, even so might grace reign through righteousness unto eternal life, by Jesus Christ our Lord."[1] The complete parallel here maintained, between the effects of Adam's transgression, on the one part, and those of the righteousness of Christ on the other, appears to afford a satisfactory evidence of the comprehensive nature of the plan of Christian redemption. The two things are described as being in their operation upon mankind absolutely co-extensive; and as it is true, without

---

[7] 2 Cor. v, 14, 15.   [8] Chap ii, 9.   [9] οἱ πολλοί.   [1] Chap. v, 18—21.

limit or exception, that all men are exposed to death through the sin of Adam, so it is true, without limit or exception, that all men may obtain eternal life through the righteousness of Christ. Multitudes there are, undoubtedly, by whom this free gift "unto justification of life" is despised, disregarded, and rejected. Nevertheless, among the children of men there are *none* " upon" whom it has not "come"—none to whom it is not freely offered. " God was in Christ reconciling the *world* unto himself."[2]

3. Since Christ died for all men, and has thus placed within their reach the free gift of justification unto life; since such is the natural proneness of mankind to sin, that none can avail themselves of the benefits of the death of Christ, or receive the free gift of God, except through the influence of the Holy Spirit; and since it cannot, without great irreverence, be imagined that the mercy of God in Christ, thus freely offered, should in any instances be merely nominal, and nugatory in point of fact; I cannot but draw the conclusion, that a measure of this divine influence is bestowed upon all men, by which they are enlightened, and by which they may be saved.

Christians can have no difficulty in acceding to the doctrine of Elihu, that " there is a spirit in man," and that the " inspiration of the Almighty giveth them understanding;"[3] nor will they fail to form a just estimate of the words of Wisdom, as recorded in the book of Proverbs, " I will *pour out my Spirit* unto you; I will make known my words unto you."[4] It will not

---

[2] 2 Cor. v. 19.   [3] Job. xxxii, 8.   [4] Chap. i, 23.

be disputed by any impartial student of Scripture, that the Holy Spirit was the true enlightener and sanctifier of men, *before* as well as *after* the coming of Christ in the flesh; and that many, in ancient times, who had only very partial and indistinct views of the Messiah, were delivered by the influence of this Spirit from the power of sin, and fitted for eternal life. Hence it seems a very reasonable inference, that the outward knowledge of Christ is not absolutely indispensable to salvation, and that other persons, who are *completely destitute* of that knowledge, may *also* be saved from sin, and from the penalties which are attached to it, through the secret operations of divine grace.

To this argument from analogy may be added another of considerable weight. Between the effects of Adam's sin and those of the obedience of Christ, there is, in various respects, a perfect coincidence. The universality of the plan of redemption has already been deduced, on the authority of the apostle Paul, from the universality of the fall; and it appears to have been provided by the mercy and *equity* of God, that in both the *extent* and manner of their operation there should still be a correspondence between the disease and the remedy. Now, as men partake in the disease arising from the sin of Adam, who are quite ignorant of its original cause, so we may with reason infer that men may also partake in the remedy arising from the obedience of Christ, who have received no outward revelation respecting that obedience.

This inference derives substantial confirmation from certain passages in the New Testament. Although Cornelius, the Roman centurion, previously to his intercourse with Peter, might have been aware of the events recorded in the gospel histories, it is obviously improbable that he knew Jesus Christ as the *Redeemer of men;* yet, that he had received the gift of the Spirit of grace is indisputable, for he was a *just man, living in the fear of God.*[5] And what was the remark suggested by the case of Cornelius to the apostle Peter?—" Of a truth I perceive," said he, " that God is no respecter of persons; *but in every nation he that feareth him, and worketh righteousness, is accepted with him.*"[6] When the apostle used these words, the truth which he contemplated appears to have been this: that among the nations of the Gentile world, ignorant as they generally were, both of the institutions of the Jews, and of the offices of the Messiah, there were individuals who, like Cornelius, feared God and worked righteousness[7]—who had experienced, therefore, in some degree, the sanctifying influence of the Holy Spirit—and that such individuals were accepted by the Father of mercies, who is no respecter of persons. It is true that the mercy of God towards Cornelius was displayed after a particular manner, in his being brought to the outward knowledge of his Saviour; but before he obtained

---

[5] Acts x, 22.   [6] Ver. 34, 35.

[7] "ὁ φοβούμενος αὐτὸν, καὶ ἐργαζόμενος δικαιοσύνην. *Colens eum, et exercens virtutem,* pro modulo cognitionis primæ, ex lumine naturæ haustæ. Etiam inter paganos fuerunt, qui recte de Deo ejusque providentiâ et regimene statuerent. Ἐργαζόμενος δικαιοσύνην, *recte agens, secundum legem naturæ:* Rom. ii, 13—27." *Rosenmüller Schol.* in Acts x, 35.

Chap. 1.] *with our Fellow-men and Christians.* 29

that knowledge, he was accepted of the Father; and had he died in his condition of comparative ignorance, we can scarcely doubt that he would have received, with all the children of God, his eternal inheritance, through the merits and mediation of Christ. And such also we may believe to have been the happy experience of all those Gentiles whom the apostle was considering, who might be so influenced by the power of the Lord's Spirit as to *live in the fear of God, and to work righteousness.*

That this was, to a considerable extent, the character of some of the more virtuous of the ancient Gentile philosophers, their recorded sentiments and known history afford us strong reasons to believe; and that it was the character of many others also, who were destitute of an outward revelation, we may learn without difficulty from the apostle Paul. "Not the hearers of the law are just before God," says this inspired writer, "but the doers of the law shall be justified. For when the Gentiles, which have not the law, do by nature the things contained in the law, these, having not the law, are a law unto themselves; which show the work of the law written in their hearts, their conscience also bearing witness, and their thoughts the meanwhile accusing or else excusing one another."[8] Upon this clear and striking passage of Scripture, it may be observed, first, that the law here mentioned is not the ceremonial law, as the whole tenor of the apostle's argument plainly shews; but the moral law of God, which was revealed to the Jews, and was with still greater completeness unfolded under the Christian

[8] Rom. ii, 13—15.

dispensation: secondly, that the Gentiles here brought into a comparison with the Jews, were not the converts to Christianity; (for, of these it could not, with any truth, be asserted that they *had not the law ;)* but they were persons, who had received no outward revelation of the moral law of God; thirdly, that the work of the law was nevertheless written on their hearts, and that many of them (according to the apostle's obvious supposition) were thereby actually enabled to become doers of the law; and, lastly, that these persons were justified or accepted of the Father.[9]

[9] A curious exemplification of the apostle's doctrine respecting the practical excellence of some of those Gentiles, who are destitute of any knowledge either of the Jewish law or of the Christian revelation, will be found in the following extract from an account of the *Sauds,* a moral sect of the Hindoos, who dwell in the north-western part of Hindoostan. It has been kindly communicated to me by W. H. Trant, a gentleman of great respectability, who once occupied an important post in the civil service of the East India Company, and who personally visited this singular people.

"In March, 1816, I went with two other gentlemen from Futtehgurgh, on the invitation of the principal persons of the Saud sect, to witness an assemblage of them for the purpose of religious worship in the city of Furrakhabad; the general meeting of the sect being held that year in that city. The assembly took place within the court yard (dalen) of a large house. The number of men, women, and children, was considerable: we were received with great attention, and chairs were placed for us in the front of the *deorkee* or hall. After some time, when the place was quite full of people, the worship commenced. It consisted solely in the chanting of a hymn: this being the only mode of public worship used by the Sauds.

" The Sauds utterly reject and abhor all kinds of idolatry; and the Ganges is considered by them with no greater veneration than by Christians; although the converts are made chiefly, if not entirely, from among the Hindoos, whom they resemble in outward

CHAP. 1.]   *with our Fellow-men and Christians.*   31

Those who accede to this view of the passage before us (and such a view is surely just and reasonable) will probably find no difficulty in admitting another point—namely, that the work of the law written on

appearance. Their name for God is *Sutgar;* and *Saud,* the appellation of the sect, means servant of God; they are pure theists, and their form of worship is most simple, as I have already stated.

"The Sauds resemble the Quakers in their customs, to a remarkable degree. Ornaments and gay apparel of every kind are strictly prohibited; their dress is always white; they never make any obeisance or *salam;* they will not take an oath, and they are exempted in the courts of justice,—their asseveration, as that of the Quakers, being considered equivalent. The Sauds profess to abstain from all luxuries, such as tobacco, pawn, opium, and wine; they never have *nautches* or dances. All attack on man or beast is forbidden; but in self-defence resistance is allowable. Industry is strongly enjoined. The Sauds, like the Quakers, take great care of their poor and infirm people; to receive assistance out of the punt or tribe would be reckoned disgraceful, and render the offender liable to excommunication. All parade of worship is forbidden; secret prayer is commended; alms should be unostentatious; they are not to be done that they should be seen of men. The due regulation of the tongue is a principal duty.

"The chief seats of the Saud sect are Delhi, Agra, Jypoor, and Furrukhabad; but there are several of the sect scattered over the country. An annual meeting takes place at one or other of the cities above mentioned, at which the concerns of the sect are settled.

"The magistrate of Furrukhabad informed me that he had found the Sauds an orderly and well-conducted people. They are chiefly engaged in trade.

"Bhuivanee Dos (one of their leaders) was anxious to become acquainted with the Christian religion, and I gave him some copies of the New Testament in Persian and Hindoostanee, which he said he had read and shown to his people, and much approved. I had no copy of the Old Testament in any language which he understood well; but, as he expressed a strong desire to know the account of the creation, as given in it, I explained it to him from

the hearts of these Gentiles, through which they were thus enabled to bear the fruits of righteousness, was nothing less than the inward operation of the Spirit of truth; for Christianity plainly teaches us, that, without such an influence, there can be no acceptable obedience to the moral law of God.[1] Here it

an Arabic version of which he knew a little. I promised to procure him a Persian or Hindoostanee Old Testament, if possible. I am of opinion that the Sauds are a very interesting people, and that some intelligent and zealous missionary would find great facility in communicating with them. *(Signed)*
" *Calcutta*, 2 *Aug.* 1819. " W. H. TRANT."

W. H. Trant informs me that, previously to the adoption of their present views, the Sauds do not appear to have received any Christian instruction. The head of their tribe assured him that they knew nothing of Christianity.

[1] This consideration is strong and palpable enough in itself, to afford a sufficient evidence that, when the apostle makes mention of their performing the works of righteousness "*by nature*" he cannot be understood as alluding to *nature unassisted by divine grace.* The fruits of the flesh—that is, of the carnal and unregenerate state of man—are not righteousness; but, as the apostle himself declares, " adultery, fornication, uncleanness, lasciviousness, idolatry," &c., Gal. v, 19; and when speaking of men in their fallen condition, without grace, he expressly asserts that they are the " children of wrath," Eph. ii, 3 ; "that there is none that doeth good, no not one :" Rom. iii, 12. Besides, after using this expression, he goes on to attribute the righteousness of the Gentiles, not to their natural reason or acquired wisdom, but to the " law written in their hearts." Now this law of God written in the heart can be nothing less than a divine illumination; and the larger measures of such illumination are described *in the very same terms*, as one of the choicest blessings of the Christian dispensation : Jer. xxxi, 33. The word φύσει appears to refer to that natural condition of the Gentiles, by which they were distinguished from the Jews— a condition of comparative darkness, and one in which they did not enjoy the superadded help of a written law, or outward revelation. Not having a law, they performed the works of righteous-

may be observed that this inward work of the Spirit ought not to be confounded with the operation of the *conscience*. The two things are separately mentioned by the apostle; and I would submit that they are, in fact, totally distinct. The law written on the heart is a divine illumination; the conscience is a natural faculty, by which a man judges of his own conduct. It is *through* the conscience that the law operates. The law *informs* the conscience. The law is the *light;* the conscience is the *eye*. The light reveals the beauty of any given object: the eye "bears witness" to that beauty; it beholds and approves. The light is of a uniform character; for, when not interrupted, it never fails to make things manifest *as they really are;* but the eye may be obscured or destroyed by disease, or it may be deceived by the influence of surrounding substances. So the law written on the heart, although capable of being hindered in its operation, is of an unchangeable nature, and would guide *invariably* into righteousness and truth; but the conscience may be darkened by ignorance, deadened by sin, or perverted by a wrong education. The conscience, indeed, like every other natural faculty of the human mind, is *prone* to perversion, and the law written on the heart is given not only to enlighten but to rectify it. Those only have "a good conscience" who obey that law.

ness *by nature*, i.e. "without the law." Just on the same principles, in verse 27, the uncircumcised Gentile, *in his natural condition*, and fulfilling the law, is compared with the Jew, who *possesses the letter and the external rite*, and nevertheless infringes the law. In both passages, the state of nature is placed in opposition, not to a state of grace, but only to one of outward light and instruction.

As the Gentiles to whom the apostle was here alluding were, according to their measure of light, sanctified through the Spirit, and when sanctified accepted, so, I think, every Christian must allow that they were accepted, not because of their own righteousness, but through the sacrifice and mediation of the Son of God. Now the benefit of that sacrifice and mediation is offered, according to the declarations of Scripture, only to those who believe; for "without faith it is impossible to please God." The doctrine that we are justified by faith, and that without faith none can obtain salvation, is to be freely admitted as a truth revealed to mankind on the authority of God himself. Let it, however, be carefully kept in view, that God is *equal*. It is unquestionably true, in great as well as in little things, that "if there be first a willing mind, it is accepted according to that a man hath, and not according to that he hath not." [2] The extent of faith required in man, in order that he may be accepted with the Supreme Being, will ever be proportioned to the extent of light communicated. Those to whom the incarnation and atonement of the Son of God are made known, are plainly required to believe in these essential doctrines. Those from whom the plan of redemption is hidden, and to whom the Deity is manifested only by his creative works and by his law written on the heart, may nevertheless so believe in God that it shall be counted to them "for righteousness."

The reader will observe that I have already inferred

[2] Cor. viii, 12.

the universality of a moral and spiritual light from the declarations of Scripture that God's tender mercies are over *all* his works, and that Christ died for *all* men. The most plausible objection to this inference arises from the notion, so prevalent amongst some Christians, that the Spirit of God operates on the heart of man *only* in connexion with the outward knowledge of the Scriptures and of Christ, and that consequently, such outward knowledge is indispensable to salvation. Having therefore, endeavoured to remove this objection, and to show, on apostolic authority, that there were individuals in the Gentile world who had no acquaintance with the truths of religion, as they are revealed in the Holy Scriptures, but who were nevertheless enabled to fear God and work righteousness, I consider there is nothing in the way to prevent our coming to a sound conclusion, that as, on the one hand, God is merciful to *all* men, and Christ was a sacrifice for *all* men, so, on the other hand, *all* men have received *a measure* of that divine influence, through which alone they can permanently enjoy the mercy of God, or partake in the benefits of the death of Christ.

In confirmation of this conclusion, it remains for me to adduce the apostle's memorable declaration that the Son or Word of God, was "*the true light which lighteth every man that cometh into the world.*"[3] In order to perceive the true force of these expressions, it will be desirable to cite the entire passage of which it forms part. 1. "In the beginning," says the inspired apostle, "was the Word, and the Word

[3] John i, 9.

was with God, and the Word was God. 2. The same was in the beginning with God. 3. All things were made by him; and without him was not any thing made that was made. 4. *In him was life, and the life was the light of men.* 5. And the light shineth in darkness, and the darkness comprehended (or received) it not. 6. There was a man sent from God, whose name was John. 7. The same came for a witness, to bear witness of the light, that all men through him might believe. 8. He was not that light, but was sent to bear witness of that light. 9. *That was the true light, which lighteth every man that cometh into the world.* 10. He was in the world, and the world was made by him, and the world knew him not. 11. He came unto his own, and his own received him not. 12. But as many as received him, to them gave he power to become the sons of God, even to them that believe (or believed) on his name. 13. Which were born, not of blood, nor of the will of the flesh, nor of the will of man, but of God. 14. And the Word was made flesh and dwelt among us (and we beheld his glory, the glory as of the only-begotten of the Father,) full of grace and truth."

In this solemn and emphatic preface to his gospel history, John has unfolded the character and attributes of the Word of God; that is, of the Son in his *original and divine nature.* That this is the true meaning of that title, is almost universally allowed by Christian commentators, both ancient and modern; and is, in my opinion, amply proved by the known theology of the Jews, at the time when the apostle wrote. At the conclusion of the passage we are informed that this divine Word was made flesh (i. e. *man,*) and dwelt amongst us: and that so his glory, the glory as of the only-begotten Son of God, became *visible*. But the order in which the apostle has treated his subject, plainly leads us to suppose that, in the previous verses, he is speaking of Christ in his condition of pre-existence, or at least solely with reference to his *original and divine nature*. I would suggest that the declarations respecting the word contained in verses 10 and 11, that he was "in the world" and "came unto his own," form no exception to this observation; for these declarations may very properly be explained of the appearances and visitations of the Son of God (whether visible or merely spiritual) before his coming in the flesh. But, even if we interpret these verses as connected with verse 14, and as forming a part of the apostle's account of the incarnation, it certainly appears most probable, that the preceding doctrine respecting Christ, relates to his operations *only* in that glorious and unchangeable character, *in which he was with God in the beginning, and in which he was God.*

Accordingly, it is declared, first, that by him *all things were made;* and, secondly, that *in him (or by him) was life, and that the life was the light of men.* Let us then inquire in what sense the eternal Word of God was thus described as the author or medium of *life* and *light*. Since all things were made by him, he is undoubtedly the origin of their natural life, and the bountiful giver of those intellectual faculties by which man is distinguished from the inferior animals; but those who take a comprehensive view of the writings of the apostle John, can scarcely suppose that he is here speaking of the natural life and of the light of reason. The " life," of which in every part of his works he makes such frequent mention, is that of which they only lay hold who are the true children of God—the spiritual life, in the first place, by which the souls of men are quickened in this world, and the eternal life, in the second place, which is reserved for them in the world to come.[4] That such is here the apostle's meaning is confirmed by a comparison with the opening passage of his first epistle, in which Jesus Christ, in reference to his pre-existence, is expressly denominated that *" eternal life"* (*i. e.* that *source of eternal life*) " which was with the Father." So, also, the word *light* is no where used by this apostle to designate the intellectual faculty, or the light of reason. With him it denotes spiritual light—the light which is enjoyed by those who come to a real knowledge of the truth—the light in which the children of God walk before their Father.[5] I conceive, therefore, that the apostle's doctrine, declared in the fourth verse of his Gospel, is precisely this—that the Son, or Word of God, or the Messiah, in his original and divine character, was the giver of eternal life, and the spiritual *quickener and illuminator* of the children of men. And this inference is strengthened by the consideration that " the life" here mentioned *was* " the light;" for it is the peculiar characteristic of the Spirit of Christ, that it quickens and enlightens at the same time.

[4] See John iii, 15 ; v, 24, 40 ; vi, 33, 63 ; viii, 12 ; xiv, 6 ; &c.
[5] See John iii, 19 ; ix, 5 ; 1 John, i, 7 ; ii, 8 ; &c.

CHAP. I.] *with our Fellow-men and Christians.* 39

That very Spirit which illuminates our darkness, raises our souls from the death of sin, and springs up within us unto everlasting life.

Since such appears to be the true meaning of verse 4, we cannot reasonably hesitate in our interpretation of verse 9. In the former, the light is said to be *in* or *by* the Word; in the latter, according to a very usual figure of speech, the Word being the source of the light, is himself denominated "light." The *light*, in either case, must be of the same character; and if there be any correctness in the view we have now taken of the whole passage, it can be no other *than the light of the Spirit of the Son of God*. Hence, therefore, I conclude, on the authority of the apostle John, that a measure of *the light of the Spirit of the Son of God* "lighteth every man that cometh into the world."[6]

---

[6] JOHN i, 9. ῀Ην τὸ φῶς τὸ ἀληθινὸν ὃ φωτίζει πάντα ἄνθρωπον ἐρχόμενον εἰς τὸν κόσμον. "That was the true light which lighteth every man that cometh into the world." "It was observed by Augustine, *De Peccatorum Meritis et Remiss.* lib. i, § 38) and the suggestion has been adopted by many modern critics, that the words ἐρχόμενον εἰς τὸν κόσμον, in this passage, are *capable* of being construed in connexion with φῶς, "the light," instead of with πάντα ἄνθωρπον, "every man;" in which case the sentence must be rendered as follows: "That was the true light, which, coming into the world, lighteth every man." Now, it ought to be remarked that the term "every man" is in itself very strong and precise. It denotes *every individual man*; and, since there is nothing in the context to limit its signification, it must be considered as signifying the *whole of mankind*. Were we, therefore, to adopt such a construction and translation of the passage, there would still be good reasons for interpreting it, not of that outward knowledge of Christianity which is enjoyed by a comparatively small number of human beings, but of an internal light bestowed universally on

Such, according to my apprehension of scriptural truth, are the religious advantages which may be deemed the common allotment of mankind in general. God is their equal Judge and compassionate Father: the Son of God, when clothed with humanity, gave his life a ransom for them all; and lastly, through the operation of his Holy Spirit, a manifestation of the divine law, accompanied with a portion of quickening and purifying power, is bestowed upon them universally. Here, then, we may perceive grounds of union and brotherly kindness co-extensive with the whole world; and whilst we cultivate a sense of these animating truths, we shall be disposed neither to think too highly of ourselves, nor to despise others. On the contrary, a feeling of true charity towards our neighbour, of whatever colour or country, will spread in our hearts; and a lively disposition will arise in us to labour for the happiness of that universal family, who

---

man. It is, however, obvious that the commonly adopted construction of this sentence is more agreeable to the order of the apostle's words, and therefore more consistent with the general simplicity and perspicuity of his style. That construction is, moreover, confirmed by the consideration that John has here adopted a phrase well known amongst the Jews, in its *usual* sense. With that people, "to come into the world" was a common expression, signifying "to be born;" and "all men who come into the world" was a customary description of "all mankind:" Vide *Lightfoot, Hor. Heb.* in loc. The ancient fathers in general appeared to have construed this passage in the same manner as the authors of our English version. See, for example, *Tertullian, adv. Prax.* cap. 12, Ed. Semler, ii, 214; *Theodotus, Epitom. in Ed. Bened. Clement. Alex.* p. 979; *Origen, in Lib. Judicum Homil.* Ed. Bened. ii, 460. See also *the two Syriac, Æthiopic, Persic, and Vulgate versions.*

not only owe their existence to the same Creator, but are the common objects of his fatherly regard and of his redeeming love.

While I am persuaded of the existence of these broad grounds of union; and am well satisfied, that there is bestowed upon all men a *measure* of the enlightening and quickening influence of the Holy Spirit, I am very far from forming a low estimate of the sinfulness and misery of the heathen world. It is impossible to deny the melancholy fact, that although universally visited by a moral light, mankind have yielded themselves a prey to the depravity of their own hearts. How great are the multitudes, among those who have not enjoyed the benefit of an outward revelation, who "when they knew God, glorified him not as God, neither were thankful, but became vain in their imaginations, and their foolish heart was darkened!" "Professing themselves to be wise, they became fools, and changed the glory of the incorruptible God into an image made like to corruptible man, and to birds, and four-footed beasts, and creeping things."[7] Hence hath he given them over to "uncleanness through the lusts of their own hearts," and hence may be applied to them that awful description used by the apostle—"Gentiles in the flesh,' "aliens from the commonwealth of Israel, and strangers from the covenants of promise, having no hope, and without God in the world."[8]

We are not to forget that the same apostle who has drawn this affecting picture of the Gentile world, has

[7] Rom. i, 21, 23.   [8] Eph. ii, 11, 12.

declared that the Jews, on whom was bestowed the written law, were "not better than they,"[9]—that all will be judged by a perfectly equitable Being, according to their *own* demerits, the Gentiles "without the law," the Jews "by the law,"[1] and finally, that God "hath concluded them all in unbelief, that *he might have mercy upon all.*"[2]

It is also worthy of remark, that many of the tribes of idolators, which have been visited by modern travellers, are in a state of extreme intellectual degradation. Hence their apprehension of moral truth, is often found to be peculiarly weak and limited; and we may reverently trust that the principle is, in a great degree, applicable to them, that they who know not their master's will and who "commit things worthy of stripes," *shall be* "*beaten with few.*" Nevertheless, a contemplation of their wretched state may serve to convince us of the unutterable advantages of that outward revelation by which are so clearly made known to us the glorious attributes of the one true God, the awful realities of an eternal world, and the offices of that divine Saviour, who is made unto us of the Father, "wisdom, righteousness, sanctification, and redemption." This consideration naturally leads to the second branch of my present subject, and will fitly introduce a brief view of those religious advantages which are not bestowed upon the world in general, but are common to all true Christians.

II. The visible church of Christ, upon earth, may be regarded, either in its most extensive character, as

---

[9] Rom. iii, 9.   [1] Rom. ii, 12.   [2] Rom. xi, 32.

consisting of the whole of that proportion of mankind who *profess* Christianity; or in that narrower, yet more accurate, point of view, in which none can be looked upon as its members, except those persons who really love and serve their Redeemer, and who evince by their conduct and conversation, that they are brought under the influence of vital religion.

It is to such as these alone, that my present observations will be directed. Merely nominal Christians may indeed be considered as partaking in the religious advantages of the church of Christ, so far as they receive their share of benefit from that *general* improvement in the moral views and habits of mankind which has in a remarkable manner, been effected by the introduction of Christianity. But from the more important, substantial, and enduring, privileges of the followers of Jesus, the careless and disobedient hearers of the truth are plainly excluded. Nothing, indeed, can be more fraught with danger than the condition of those persons who, whilst they profess to believe in Jesus, and are called by his name, are nevertheless the servants of sin, and are living to the "lusts of the world, the lusts of the flesh, and the pride of life." The light of the Sun of righteousness has risen upon them; but they hide themselves from its beams. They love "darkness rather than light, because their deeds are evil." In despite of those awful truths which, on the authority of their Creator himself, have been proclaimed in their hearing, they pursue without interruption, the mad career of vice and dissipation. If there is any class amongst mankind, by whom, above others, the punishment of "many stripes" may justly be expected, it is surely that class who profess Christianity, without practising it. "And every one," said our Lord Jesus, "that heareth these sayings of mine, and doeth them not, shall be likened unto a foolish man which built his house upon the sand; and the rain descended, and the floods came, and the winds blew, and beat upon that house; and it fell; and *great was the fall of it*."[3]

Let us therefore direct our regards to that scattered flock of Christ, comprehending various kindreds and classes, who, have received revealed religion in the love of it; who have been made willing in the day of the Lord's power, to follow and obey him; and who, with earnestness and honest determination, are fighting the good fight of faith, and laying hold of eternal life.

The religious privileges which are common to the whole of this family of true believers in Christ are unspeakably valuable. At some of the principal of them we may now shortly glance.

1. *They are brought out of darkness into marvellous light.* "Ye are a chosen generation," said the apostle Peter to some of the early Christians, "a royal priesthood, a holy nation, a peculiar people; that ye should shew forth the praises of him who hath called you out of *darkness into his marvellous light.*"[4] Furnished with full and satisfactory evidences of the truth and divine authority of Christianity, they have found in that holy religion, as it is recorded in the Scriptures,

[3] Matt. vii, 26, 27. [4] 1 Peter ii, 9.

CHAP. 1.]   *with our Fellow-menand Christians.*   45

a plain statement of all those truths which relate to man's salvation—a clear account of his fall and depravity—of the attributes of God—of the future life—of eternal rewards and punishments; and more especially of that divine Saviour, the incarnate Son of God, who died for our sins, and rose again for our justification. The outward knowledge, which has been thus graciously communicated to them, may truly be called a "*marvellous light.*" Yet these expressions are more properly applicable to that spiritual illumination, by which the humble followers of Jesus are enabled to form a right *estimate* of the things of God. True Christians may be described as persons whose moral sight is rectified. God has given them the spirit of "a sound mind." Every thing connected with religion appears to them (so far as is consistent with the narrow limits of the apprehension of mortals) in its real dimensions. From the secret illumination of the Lord's Holy Spirit, and by means of the outward revelation of divine truth, they are enabled to form a comparatively just view of themselves, as corrupt and fallen creatures—of their Creator, as a being of perfect holiness—of virtue and vice—of the world and eternity—of heaven and hell—and more particularly of Jesus Christ, as their Mediator with the Father, as their divine and all powerful Redeemer. Such persons can acknowledge, with humble gratitude, that "the darkness is past," and that "the true light now shineth."[5]

2. The religion, respecting the truths of which

[5] 1 John ii. 8.

Christians are thus enlightened is a *powerful* religion. In other words, it is the medium through which the power of God operates upon them, for the great purposes of sanctification and salvation. Thus the apostle Paul expressly asserts that the Gospel of Christ is " the *power* of God unto salvation."[6] Again, he says, " The preaching of the cross is, to them that perish, foolishness; but, unto us which are saved, it is the *power* of God;"[7] and, in addressing his Ephesian converts, he makes particular mention of the " *exceeding* greatness" of the "*power*" of God " *to us-ward who believe*, according to the working of his mighty power which he wrought in Christ, when he raised him from the dead, and set him at his own right hand in the heavenly places."[8]

Faith in the Son of God is not the mere assent of the understanding to the mission and divinity of Jesus. *It is a practical aud operative principle of wonderful energy.* Those who live by this faith enjoy an access unto the Father by a new and living way, which Christ hath " consecrated for them through the veil, that is to say, his flesh." Their dependence is placed, not upon their own strength and wisdom, but upon that Great High Priest of their profession, who " ever liveth to make intercession" for them—who " is able also to save them to the uttermost that come unto God by him;"[9] and at his gracious hands, they receive that more abundant effusion of the Holy Spirit, by which they are enabled, in a distinguished degree to mortify the deeds of the flesh, and to be-

---

[6] Rom. i, 16.   [7] Cor. i, 18.   [8] Eph. i, 19, 20.   [9] Heb. vii, 25.

come conformed to the will of a righteous and Holy God. Thus do they experience, that, "if any man be in Christ, he is a new creature; old things are passed away; behold, all things are become new."¹

3. The followers of Jesus Christ being enlightened in their darkness, and strengthened in their weakness, are animated during the varied course of their earthly pilgrimage, with the *clear hope of immortal joy*. Their treasure, their conversation, are in heaven; their desire is fixed on that " city which hath foundations, whose builder and maker is God." They are seeking "a better country, that is, a heavenly." Often indeed are they cast down under a humbling sense of their great infirmities and many transgressions; and are at times scarcely able to entertain the belief that they shall "be counted worthy of the kingdom of God." Yet, as their hope and trust remain steadily fixed on that Saviour who died for their sins, and rose again, and is their advocate with the Father; as they are "kept by the power of God, through faith;" they are seldom permitted to sink into despondence, or finally to lose a peaceful expectation of that inheritance which is "reserved for them in heaven"—" an inheritance incorruptible, and undefiled, and that fadeth not away." ²

4. Lastly.—They are, "baptized by one Spirit into one body." How delightful is the union which subsists among the numerous members of this holy family! It is true that they are ranged under various

¹ 2 Cor. v, 17.   ² 1 Pet. i, 4.

banners, and are called by many different names.—It is true, also, that they do not all possess the same measure of light; and that the sentiments of some among them are of a more spiritual character than those of others. Nevertheless their ground of accordance is at once wide and substantial. Their footing is placed on the same Rock of ages; and that Rock is Christ. They enjoy a true fellowship one with another, even because their fellowship is "with the Father, and with his Son Jesus Christ." Love is the blessed principle by which they are united, and which animates them in the prosecution of joint efforts, conducted on common principles, in support of the same cause.

Such, then, are the religious privileges which appear to distinguish, from mankind in general, the members of the true visible church of Christ; and which, as it relates to *them*, are universal. They are in a peculiar manner brought out of darkness into marvellous light —they experience the *exceeding* greatness of the power of God revealed in Christ for their salvation—they are cheered by the prospect of immortal joy, clearly manifested to them by the Gospel; and they are brought into spiritual fellowship one with another. May the love which cements together the varied members of this mystical body of Christ more and more abound; may the barriers which ignorance and prejudice have reared among them, be broken through and demolished; may Christians be enabled increasingly to *strive together* for the hope of the Gospel; and, while they individually draw nearer to the Fountain of all good, may they be taught of their common Master to keep the " unity of the Spirit in the bond of peace !"

ADDENDUM TO CHAPTER I.

A.D. 1834.

ON UNIVERSAL LIGHT.

" If ye were blind," said our Saviour to the Pharisees, " ye should have no sin."[1] This is a most equitable principle, and it is plain that the apostle Paul kept it steadily in view, when he declared the sinfulness of the Gentile world. " For the wrath of God is revealed from heaven against all ungodliness and unrighteousness of men, who hold (or restrain)[2] *the truth* in unrighteousness. *Because that which may be known of God is manifest in them ;* for *God hath showed it unto them.* For the invisible things of him from the foundation of the world are clearly seen, being understood by the things that are made, even his eternal power and godhead, so that they are without excuse. Because that when they knew God, they glorified him not as God, neither were thankful; but became vain in their imaginations, and their foolish heart was darkened. Professing themselves to be wise, they became fools; and changed the glory of

[1] John ix, 41.
[2] κατεχόντων. So Schleusner, Rosenmüller, Beza, Castalio, Hammond, Doddridge, &c. The verb κατέχω has the same sense in Luke iv, 42 ; 2 Thess. ii, 7.

the incorruptible God, into an image made like to corruptible man, &c."[3]

It is evident that the " ungodliness" of the Gentiles is here condemned on the ground that some knowledge of divine truth was bestowed upon them. Not only were they furnished with a visible evidence, in the outward creation, of the eternal power and godhead of Jehovah, but " that which may be known of God was manifest in them." They were not left without some sense of his holiness, and of their responsibility to him, as the righteous governor of the world. Thus it appears that their guilt consisted in *restraining the truth*, by their unrighteousness. Graciously provided as they were, not only with outward proofs of the omnipotence of God, but with a measure of light respecting his moral government, they nevertheless followed the corrupt desires and devices of their own hearts. They held the truth in bondage, not yielding to its influence, so that it was suppressed in their hearts, and did not rise into dominion.

Having thus convicted the Gentiles of sin, in the breach of that part of the divine law which relates to the worship of God, the apostle proceeds to describe their dissolute and wicked practices—and especially those fearful transgressions against their fellow-men, which were the inevitable consequence of their falling from God—" being filled with all unrighteousness, fornication, wickedness, covetousness, maliciousness; full of envy, murder, debate, deceit, malignity, &c." Here again their guilt was inseparably connected with

---

[3] Rom. i, 18—23.

CHAP. 1.] *On Universal Light.* 51

their knowledge of the divine law—"knowing the judgment (or rather the *righteous rule)* [4] of God, that they which commit such things are worthy of death, they not only do the same, but have pleasure in them that do them." [5]

Now it may be freely allowed that some scattered rays of information respecting the supremacy of God, and respecting this *righteous rule* by which he governs mankind, might have descended to the Gentiles, in the apostle's days, from original revelation, by means of tradition. It is probable also that some of their more inquisitive philosophers may have obtained a little knowledge on these subjects, indirectly from the Jews. But it is sufficiently obvious, that the apostle's argument mainly rests on a far stronger and wider basis—even on that of *an inward and universal light.*

That he alluded to an inward light, we may in the first place learn from his declaration respecting the Gentiles, that the truth of God was "*manifest in them;*" that God "had shewed it unto them." For although the outward creation afforded them an evidence of the omnipotence of the Deity, their knowledge of God, as a *moral governor*, which the apostle's argument obviously includes, must have arisen chiefly from what passed in their own minds. Such is the view of the passage taken by the generality of commentators. "Much of the nature and properties of God," says Burkitt, "may be known by the light of nature. His infinite power, wisdom, and goodness,

[4] τὸ δικαίωμα.   [5] Rom. i, 29—32.

are *manifest in the minds and consciences of men*, for God both showed it unto them *partly by imprinting these notions of himself on the hearts of all men*, and partly by the book of creation, &c." "There are some things," says Dr. Gill on this passage, "which may be known of God without a revelation .... as that he is all powerful, wise, good, and righteous; and this (knowledge of God) is *manifest in them* or *to them*, by the light that is given them; it is light by which that which may be known of God is manifest; and this is the light of nature [6] which every man has that comes into the world; and this is internal, it is in him, in his mind and conscience, and is communicated to him by God, and that by infusion or inspiration;[7] for " *God hath shewed it unto them ;*" i.e. what may be known of him by that light; and which is assisted and may be improved by a consideration of the works of creation and providence."[8] Again, that the "*righteous rule*" which the apostle describes the Gentiles as knowing, was a rule inwardly revealed to them, is evident from ch. ii, 14, 15, in which passage he speaks of some of them as doers of the law, and as showing the work of it "*written in their hearts*"—" their conscience also bearing witness ; and their thoughts the meanwhile, accusing or else excusing one another."

Secondly, that the light alluded to by the apostle was *universal*, we may learn from the doctrine so plainly declared in chap. iii, that both Jews and Gen-

[6] Although Dr. Gill calls this light the "light of nature," he goes on to describe it as a work of the Spirit.

[7] See Job xxxii, 8.

[8] See also Beza, Whitby and Pool, *in loc.*

tiles are *all* proved " to be under sin,"—that *all* have sinned and fallen short of the glory of God. Soon after pronouncing his verdict against the *whole world* as guilty before the Lord, he states, in the most explicit manner, that sin is not imputed where there is no law —" that where no law is there is no transgression." Hence it appears that according to the views of this inspired writer, the sinfulness of men, and the knowlege of the divine law are absolutely co-extensive; and since *all men* are sinners, it inevitably follows, that all men have *some* knowledge of the law.

Now I conceive that it forms no exception to the universality of this divine law, as the gift of God to man, or to that of the conscience as one of the faculties of our nature, that the former is not perceived, and that the latter does not operate, when the intellect is not developed. Our moral faculties are bestowed upon us as rational beings; and wherever reason is dormant, they will of necessity be dormant also. Such is the case with infants, with idiots, and to a considerable extent, with some of the most degraded tribes of uncultivated men. Who can deny that in these respective classes of human beings, there is the *germ* of conscience—with its corresponding measure of light; although to our superficial observation, both are nearly latent? With respect to all such persons, it may be emphatically said, that the *light shines in darkness, and that the darkness comprehends it not.*

But no sooner do we rise a little higher in the scale of reason, than the moral faculties begin to display themselves. The North American Indians, notwithstanding their rude and often savage habits, plainly recognise the distinction between right and wrong, and recognise it with direct reference to the One Great Spirit. Notwithstanding all the debasement of their idolatry, the crafty Hindoos recognise it also. A baptist missionary was preaching one day, to a company of these people, on the subject of *sin*. "But what is sin?" cried a Hindoo out of the crowd, as the missionary himself informed me. "Sin," said the preacher, "is the transgression of the law." "But what law do you mean?" replied the idolater—"for I do not admit your shaster (or sacred book) neither do you admit mine." "Brother," said the missionary "I will explain myself. When you go to the fair or to the market, and lie, cheat, or steal, you feel something in yourself which condemns you for your deeds. There is a law written on your heart, which compels you to acknowledge that these things are wrong. This is the law of which I am speaking. Sin is the transgression of *this* law." "Brother," exclaimed the Hindoo, "you are right; I now accept your definition."

But although the knowledge of this holy law is bestowed upon us as rational creatures, it is not a matter of reason; it is instinctive—the immediate gift of God. The law itself shines in the soul by its own uncreated light, and bears its own evidence. Like the axioms in mathematics, or the first truths in natural philosophy, it neither requires proof, nor admits of it; it consists of intuitive and unchanging principles. "The first principles of morals," says Dr. Reid, "are immediate dictates of the moral faculty...... The supreme Being has given us this light within to direct our moral conduct. It is the candle of the Lord set up within us to guide our steps." "The mind," says Dr. Watts, " contains in it the plain and general principles of morality, not explicitly in propositions, but only as native principles, by which it judges, and cannot but judge virtue to be fit, and vice unfit." " It is altogether absurd and unintelligible," says another writer on ethics, "to suppose that the first perceptions of right and wrong can be derived from reason. These perceptions cannot be the object of reason but of immediate sense and feeling." "The light of truth," says Plutarch, " is a law not written on tables or in books, but dwelling in the mind, which never permits the soul to be destitute of an interior guide."[9]

Many passages of a similar import might be selected from the works of moral philosophers, both ancient and modern; but it will be sufficient to cite, in addition, the following sentences from Cicero, which are so luminous, that Lactantius, who quoted them A.D. 303, was almost ready to ascribe them to a temporary inspiration. "There is indeed a true law, a right reason, diffused among all men, agreeable to nature; which calls to duty by its commands, and deters from crime by its prohibitions. For this law nothing may be substituted; from it nothing may be abstracted; neither can it, as a whole, be abrogated. We can be absolved from its obligation neither by the senate, nor by the people; and we are to seek for no explainer, or interpreter of it, besides itself. Nor will it be one

---

[9] These passages are quoted, with others of the same description, by Jonathan Dymond, in his section on the Moral Sense: see *Principles of Morality*, vol. i, p. 84.

thing at Rome, another at Athens, another now, another hereafter; but the same unchanging and immortal law must comprehend all nations, in all ages; and that God who formed and enacted it, and who judges according to it is the one common Preceptor (as it were) and Ruler of all men. The man who will not obey him must fly from himself, and disregard the nature of man, by which very thing he will be most severely punished; even if he should escape those inflictions, which are usually regarded as punishments."[1]

It is a remarkable proof of the inaccuracy of our moral philosophers, that while they so generally admit the universality of this moral light, they confound it in terms, with the faculty of conscience; whereas it is evident that the two things are no more identical, than is the law of the land, with the *judge* on the bench, who administers it.

The conscience, which in the court of every man's soul, sits as a judge, must be regarded as one of the original faculties of human nature; and, like our other faculties, it is miserably degraded through the fall. Who can doubt that, in our first parents, before they sinned, Conscience held undisputed sway, was infallible in her decisions, and never failed to be

---

[1] "Est quidem vera lex, recta ratio, naturæ, congruens, diffusa, in omnes, constans sempiterna; quæ, vocet ad officium jubendo, vetando a fraude deterreat.....Huic legi nec abrogari fas est, neque, derogari ex hac aliquid licet, neque tota abrogari potest. Nec vero aut per senatum, aut per populum, solvi hac lege possumus, Neque est quærendus explorator aut interpres ejus alius. Nec erit alia lex Romæ, alia Athenis alia nunc, alia posthac : sed et omnes

heard in every moment of temptation? But, alas! how different is our condition now! " How is the gold become dim! how is the most fine gold changed!" The effect of the fall of man upon this ruling faculty, is chiefly observable in three respects. In the first place, Conscience is often dislodged from her supremacy, and deprived of her power, by the strength and violence of the passions. In the second place, she is so prone to be deluded by the false light of superstition, that she is frequently found to decide erroneously, and to declare good actions to be bad, and bad actions to be good. And lastly, when rebellion against her is become inveterate, and sin obtains its full mastery, she sometimes appears to throw up her functions in despair, and her voice which had long been growing fainter and fainter, ceases to be heard at all.

But, notwithstanding the effects which human corruption thus produces on the judge, the law continues unchanged and unchangeable; and in none of the three cases now described, are we left without clear marks of the universality of its manifestations. In the first place, although our restless appetites may often dislodge Conscience from her seat of power, the divine decree which establishes her authority,

---

gentes, et omni tempore, una lex et sempiterna et immortalis continebit : unusque erit communis quasi Magister et Imperator omnium Deus ; ille legis hujus inventor, disceptator, lator ; cui qui non parebit, ipse se fugiet, ac naturam hominis aspernabitur, atque hoc ipso luet maximas pœnas, etiam si cætera supplicia, quæ putantur, effugerit :" *De Repub.* lib. iii *a fragment quoted by Lactantius, de vero Cultu,* lib. vi, § 7.

is still known to be in force. We can never dispossess ourselves of a feeling that, through all, her sway is a rightful one, and that she ought to govern both our bodies and souls.

Secondly, in the midst of those perversions, which sometimes induce Conscience to call evil actions good, and good actions evil, the light of God's law continues to be so far manifest to her, that she is compelled to acknowledge its essential principles. She is incapable of approving vice, or of condemning virtue, *for their own sakes;* but, under the influence of a bad education, she falsely imagines that there are certain elements in the actions in question, which reconcile her decisions respecting them to the rule of right. If, for example, she approves of the sacrifice of the Hindoo widow, it is not because of its cruelty, or because it is self-murder, but because she has been taught to believe that it is a needful mark of allegiance from a wife to a husband. When the "work of the law written on the heart" becomes truly influential, Conscience is rectified—her corrupt estimate of facts is gradually corrected.

Lastly, when this presiding judge is silenced in the heart of any individual, it is not that such a one has never known the law; it is that he has obstinately refused to obey it, and has trampled on all its sanctions. The same law still shines in the hearts of his neighbours, and although he has ceased to condemn himself, it is with a perfect unanimity that *they* condemn him. Moreover, in such cases, it often happens that under the pressure of some peculiar exigence, the law of God again shines upon Conscience, and awakens her from her slumbers. Then she summons all her scorpions, and inflicts a double vengeance on the transgressor—an awful foretaste, except he repent, of the "worm" which "dieth not," and of the "fire" which "never shall be quenched."

The reality and universality of the *law*, or in other words, of the *light* being allowed, I would ask, What is it, and whence does it come? Is it, as Lord Bacon imagines, a "sparkle of the purity of man's first estate," or is it a work of the Spirit—an especial gift bestowed on the fallen children of Adam, through the redemption which is in Christ Jesus? I am persuaded, that the principal reason why Bishop Butler and other *Christian* philosophers have ascribed this light to our own nature is, that they have confounded it with the conscience; which must, of course, be regarded as one of our natural faculties. Distinguish the law from the conscience—the pure infallible guide from the fallible and often perverted judge—and we at once perceive, that an enlightening principle, which varies in *degree* indeed, but never in *character*—unchangeably holy, heavenly, divine—without any mixture of error or taint of sin—cannot possibly be inherent by *nature* in the dark and corrupt mind of man. On the broadest scriptural principles, we must trace it *immediately* to God—to the Holy Spirit as the author of true moral illumination—to the Son as the Mediator through whom all spiritual blessings flow—to the Father as the true fountain and origin of every perfect gift. Between the declaration of Paul, that Christ gave himself "*a ransom for all*," and that of John, that he "*lighteth every man that cometh into the world*," there is surely a most satisfactory and delightful accordance.

But as an additional evidence of this truth, we must remember that the law of God, written on the heart, is *light accompanied by power*. In Christ "was *life;* and the *life* was the light of men."[2] This truth, like the existence of the law itself, may be inferred from the Scripture doctrine, that all men are "sinners," and "guilty" in the sight of God. For as they could not be accounted sinners, were there no law made known to them, so they could not be "guilty in the sight of God" were there no capacity bestowed upon them, by which they might obey the law. That the Gentiles who shewed the work of the law written on their hearts were, in fact, gifted with this capacity, is evident from the mention which the apostle makes of some of them, as actual doers of "the things contained in the law,"[3] and even as justified persons, which they could not possibly have been without faith in God, and without a measure of divine grace. The same truth is apparent from the apostle Peter's assertion, that "in every nation, he that feareth God and worketh righteousness, is accepted with him."

[2] John i, 4.

[3] "For not the hearers of the law are just before God, but the doers of the law shall be justified. For when the Gentiles, which have not the law, do by nature the things contained in the law, these, having not the law, are a law unto themselves: which shew the work of the law written in their hearts, their conscience also bearing witness, and their thoughts the mean while accusing or else excusing one another;" Rom. ii, 13—15.

CHAP. 1.] *On Universal Light.* 61

When a tribe of North American Indians, who had long been engaged in scenes of bloodshed, were brought, in a solemn convention, to open penitence, sacrificed a spotless white dog, as an atonement for their sins, and then threw their tomahawks into the lake—who can doubt that they were under an immediate visitation of the power of that Spirit, which is as the wind blowing where it listeth? When Socrates, as compared with his fellow-countrymen, attained to an eminent degree of disinterestedness, integrity, justice, and charity; when he obeyed the counsels of that unknown monitor who so frequently checked him in the hour of temptation; when he bore so clear a testimony to virtue, as to be persecuted to death for virtue's sake—on what Scriptural grounds can any man deny that he was made a partaker, to a certain degree, of a divine influence?[4]

[4] "Perhaps," said Socrates, in his public defence before the judges, "it may, to some persons, appear improper, that I should communicate my advices in private, going about from house to house, and busying myself in other people's matters; but I dare not join in your assemblies, and publicly counsel the state. The cause of my not doing this, you have often heard me mention—it is that a voice speaks to me—something divine and supernatural—the very thing for which Melitus has ridiculed me in his comedies. Now this voice has followed me ever since I was a child; and when it comes, it is always as *a check* against something which I am about to do—never as an incentive. This it is which opposes and hinders me, *when I would meddle with politics:*" *Apol. Soc.* § 19. This passage (which might be instructive to many in the present day) affords a specimen of the manner in which this virtuous philosopher was accustomed to make mention of his inward monitor.

It was a rule with Socrates, that every man ought to conform himself, in his outward practice, to the religion of his country.

These may be regarded as rare instances; but they are far from being solitary ones. They may at least serve the purpose of shewing the nature and origin of that law by which the natural consciences of men are illuminated, and by which they *may be* rectified. It appears to be a doctrine truly consistent with the scope and tenor of Scripture, and with the *breadth* of that foundation which is laid in Zion—even the foundation of Jesus Christ and him crucified—that as every man born into the world receives a measure of moral light, so every man born into the world, has his *day* of spiritual visitation.

I conceive that the Christian church at large is much indebted to George Fox and his brethren, for the bold, clear, and steadfast manner in which they maintained these important views; but here it ought

This rule—objectionable as it was—affords an explanation of his frequent allusion to "the gods," and of his commanding, even after he had drunk the poison, that a cock should be sacrificed to Esculapius. He *played* with idolatry, and was very culpable in doing so; but there are passages in his dialogues, which afford a sufficient evidence, that he acknowledged and worshipped One Supreme God. The testimonies borne to his many virtues are at once numerous and clear; and the aspersions which some writers have since attempted to cast upon his moral character, are, in my opinion, wholly undeserving of notice.

The gravest charge of this description was advanced, six hundred years after his death, by Tertullian—incidentally, and in the heat of an argument. The only ground on which the charge is made, is the well-known fact, that he was arraigned before the Athenian judges as a corruptor of the public morals. But it is equally well known, that he triumphantly rebutted the accusations preferred against him; and certainly the persecution which he suffered from a superstitious and dissolute people, can be regarded only as an evidence of his good conduct: See *Tertullian, Apol. adversus Gentes*, cap. 46.

CHAP. 1.] On *Universal Light.* 63

to be observed, that the doctrine of the universality of divine grace is very far from being peculiar to ourselves. Happily, it is held by a large, and I believe very increasing proportion of Christian believers. The late William Wilberforce, so well known as an evangelical member of the church of England, emphatically expressed to me, on two occasions, his full conviction that an "*effective offer* of salvation" is made to "every man born into the world;" and how can such an offer be made, except by a visitation of the Holy Spirit? The sentiments of the Wesleyan Methodists, on this subject, may be regarded as affording one explanation of the remarkable extent to which their gospel labours have been blessed. These sentiments may be safely inferred from the following remarkable passage in the creed of the late Dr. Adam Clarke.

"The *free will* of man is a necessary constituent of his rational soul, without which he must be a mere *machine*—either the sport of blind chance, or the mere patient of an *irresistible necessity ;* and consequently not accountable for any acts which were predetermined, and to which he was irresistibly compelled. Every human being has this *freedom of will*, with a sufficiency of light and power to direct its operations; but this powerful light is not inherent in any man's nature, but is graciously *bestowed* by him who is *the true light, that lighteth every man that cometh into the world.*[5]

---

[5] This proposition affords a clear proof, that the term "*free will*" is used by Adam Clarke, in contradistinction to the doctrine of *unconditional decrees*—not to that of *divine grace.*

"Jesus Christ has made his one offering on the cross, a sufficient sacrifice, oblation, and atonement for the sins of the whole world; and his gracious Spirit strives with, and enlightens all men; thus putting them into a salvable state; therefore every human soul may be saved, if it be not his own fault."[6]

Between the Scripture doctrine of *election* " according to the foreknowledge of God," and that of *universal grace*, there may appear, to our weak apprehensions, a want of agreement; but can we dare to doubt, that in point of fact, they are perfectly reconcilable; and form two distinct parts of one harmonious system of truth. Let us apply them, in all humility, to their respective practical purposes; and for further light on the subject, let us quietly wait for the day, when we "shall know, even as we are known!"

I cannot easily refrain from now quoting a passage, in which *one of our best practical theologians* has expressed, in vivid poetry, the same views as those of George Fox, Robert Barclay, and Adam Clarke.

> "Is virtue then, unless of Christian growth,
> Mere fallacy, or foolishness, or both?
> Ten thousand sages lost in endless woe,
> For ignorance of what they could not know?
> That speech betrays at once a bigot's tongue;
> Charge not a God with such outrageous wrong.
> Truly not I—the partial light men have,
> My creed persuades me, well employed, may save;
> While he that scorns the noon-day beam, perverse,
> Shall find the blessing, unimproved, a curse.

[6] See *Life of Dr. A. Clarke*, vol. i, p. 176.

Let heathen worthies, whose exalted mind
Left sensuality and dross behind,
Possess for me their undisputed lot,
And take unenvied the reward they sought.
But still, in virtue of a Saviour's plea,
Not blind by choice, but destined not to see.
*Their fortitude and wisdom were a flame
Celestial,* though they knew not whence it came;
*Derived from the same source of light and grace,
That guides the Christian in his swifter race;*
Their *judge* was conscience, and her *rule* their law;
That rule, pursued with reverence and awe,
Led them, however faltering, faint and slow,
From what they knew, to what they wished to know.
*But let not him that shares a brighter day,
Traduce the splendour of a noon-tide ray;
Prefer the twilight of a darker time,
And deem his base stupidity no crime.
The wretch who slights the bounties of the skies,
And sinks, while favoured with the means to rise,
Shall find them rated at their full amount;
The good he scorned all carried to account.*"[7]

COWPER.

With these sentiments of the Christian poet, I cordially concur, and especially solicit the attention of my young friends to the cautionary lines with which he concludes.

Every doctrine of religion must be held in its just proportion, and kept in its right place; otherwise it will be sure to invade, and perhaps displace, some other truth, which equally belongs to the revelation of God. While I have no doubt that the ancient heathen enjoyed some light, independently of all outward information, and while I believe this light to have been of a nature and origin truly divine, I would

---

[7] *Truth*, line 515.

on no account exaggerate either its brightness or magnitude. The early twilight, and the blaze of noon, equally proceed from the sun; but could they be contrasted, it would be *almost* like the comparison of night and day. Just such is the difference between the degrees of moral and religious light bestowed upon Plato, Aristotle, and Cicero, on the one hand, and upon the prophets, the evangelists, and the apostles, on the other.

The contrast between the mental condition of the wretched idolators of modern times, and that of Christians who are acquainted with the Holy Scriptures, is perhaps still more palpable. In contemplating these differences, we ought always to remember, that God deals with all his rational children after a rule of perfect equity; and that in exact proportion to the measure of light bestowed upon them, is their moral responsibility. Where the law of God shines very faintly, the guilt of transgressing it is, in the nature of things, comparatively small. On the other hand, how awful will be our condition, if we neglect or despise the *noon-tide ray*, with which we are so mercifully blessed in the gospel of our Redeemer! The law of Christ is pre-eminently a law of love; let us then be willing diligently to labour for the diffusion of the gospel among our fellow-men; *and let us, at the same time, dearly prize our own privileges.* Let us be diligent in the daily perusal of the Holy Scriptures. Let us come to Christ in simple faith, not only for the forgiveness of our sins, but for those more abundant measures of the light and influence of the Comforter, as they are bestowed on believers, which shall guide us into all truth, and sanctify us wholly " in body, soul, and spirit!"

With these precautions, we need fear no danger in the Christian doctrine of *universal light and grace*. On the contrary, a hearty acceptance of it will be one important means of enlarging our hearts and understandings, and of animating and increasing our love both to God and man. Happy shall we be, if we *individually* discover, from our *own* experience, the benefit and importance of this precious truth!

CHAPTER II.

ON DISTINGUISHING RELIGIOUS VIEWS—GENERAL REMARKS ON THOSE OF THE SOCIETY OF FRIENDS.

UNITED as are the living members of the universal church of Christ, in the fundamental principles of "repentance toward God, and faith toward our Lord Jesus Christ," they are often distinguished, one from another, by different and sometimes even opposite views, on points of a less important character.

When we consider the infirmity and deceitfulness of the heart of man, and remember how often the power of habit and prejudice is found to interfere with a just and enlightened apprehension of truth, it is no matter of wonder that such a result should have taken place. Nor ought we, in tracing the causes of these differences, by any means to forget that, on many points of a secondary nature—those particularly which relate to *modes* of worship and of church government—there is to be found, in the divinely authorized records of the Christian revelation, very little of precise direction; and thus is there obviously left, in reference to such points, a considerable scope for the formation of different views.

While indeed these differences afford many humbling proofs of weakness and imperfection, and, in some instances, of degeneracy from the strength and purity of truth, we ought to acknowledge that they are, in some respects, *overruled* for good. The existence of different opinions, respecting minor points, entails on us the necessity of a careful selection of our own particular course, and thus operates indirectly as a stimulus, by which we are induced to bestow a closer attention on religion in general. Such a difference of sentiment brings with it, moreover, a course of *moral discipline*: for many occasions arise from this source, which call for the exercise of Christian charity—of mutual liberality, meekness, and forbearance: nor is it unreasonable to suppose that, as we rightly avail ourselves of this discipline, it will be one means of preparing us for a perfect unanimity in a better state of being. Lastly, it may perhaps be allowed that, in that variety of administration, through which the saving principles of religion are for the present permitted to pass, there is much of a real adaptation to a corresponding variety of mental condition. Well, therefore, may we bow with thankfulness before that unsearchable Being, who in all our weakness *follows us with his love*, and who, through the diversified mediums of religion, to which the several classes of Christians are respectively accustomed, is still pleased to reveal to them all *the same* crucified Redeemer, and to direct their footsteps into the way of holiness.

Here, however, I wish explicitly to declare my

conviction that were Christians of every name and class more simply influenced by the Holy Spirit, and were they, at the same time, less prone to mix up the traditions and opinions of men with the records of Scripture—they would be brought to a condition of far greater simplicity and unity than is generally known amongst them at present. Errors, both doctrinal and practical, would be gradually dispersed by the light of truth; and the religion of Jesus would be restored to its primitive purity, beauty, and force.

To promote this blessed end has been the marked desire and intention of Friends, from their first rise as a religious body to the present day; but before we proceed to discuss their distinguishing views and practices, it may be well to advert to two excellent rules laid down by the apostle Paul, on the subject of secondary differences in matters of religion.

The first of these rules enjoins that Christians, united in the great fundamentals of doctrine and practice, but differing on minor points, should abstain from all harsh judgments one of another. " Let not him that eateth despise him that eateth not; and let not him which eateth not judge him that eateth; for God hath received him. Who art thou that judgest another man's servant? To his own master he standeth or falleth. Yea, he shall be holden up: for God is able to make him stand."[1]

The differences of opinion and conduct, to which Paul was here alluding, were indeed of less magnitude,

[1] Rom. xiv, 3, 4.

Chap. 2.] *Religious Peculiarities.* 71

and related of matters of less practical importance, than many of those which now exist within the *more extended* borders of the church of Christ; but whatever change may have taken place in this respect in the circumstances of Christians, it is plain that the apostle's principle of <u>mutual liberality</u> still holds good. While in our various allotments within the church we are severally endeavouring to "live unto the Lord," it is our unquestionable duty to <u>refrain from accusing and condemning each other.</u> Had this principle been uniformly observed among those who call themselves Christians, where would have been the vexatious disputes, the polemical severity, and, above all, the cruel persecutions, which have retarded the progress, and disgraced the profession, of a pure and peaceable religion.

The apostle's second rule, respecting the different views maintained by Christians in his own time, is applicable, with an increased degree of force, to those more important religious peculiarities, by which in the present day the church <u>is divided into classes.</u> "Let every man," says he, "be fully persuaded in his own mind"—a rule to which may be added his emphatic remark, "happy is he that condemneth not himself in that thing which he alloweth."[2] In order to obtain that "full persuasion" to which we are thus exhorted, it is plainly necessary for us to comply with another precept of the same inspired writer—"*prove all things.*"[3] It will not be disputed by persons of good sense, candour, and liberality, that it is very

[2] Rom. xiv, 5, 22.   [3] 1 Thess. v. 21.

generally desirable for Christians, who are arrived at years of sound discretion, to *prove* those peculiar religious principles in which they had been educated— to examine the foundation on which they rest—to try them by the test of Scripture and experience—and, more especially, with all humility and devotion of heart, to seek the counsel of God respecting them. Such a course seems to be prescribed, not only by the rule already cited, but by the exhortation of the apostle Peter: " Add to your faith virtue; and to virtue *knowledge;*"[4] an exhortation which coincides with the injunction of Paul: " Brethren, be not children in understanding: howbeit in malice be ye children, *but in understanding be men.*"[5]

This careful and devout examination might, in various instances, lead to the discarding of views and practices which are useless and irrelevant, and which have no favourable influence in promoting the cause of vital and practical religion. On the other hand, should any Christian be led, by such a proving of his peculiar principles, to a *"full persuasion,"* that being founded on the law of God, they are calculated to edify himself, and to promote the spiritual welfare of the church in general, it becomes him again to obey the dictate of the apostle, and to " *hold fast that which is good.*"[6]

Having premised these general remarks, I shall proceed, in pursuance of my main object, to apply them to the distinguishing views and practices of that society of Christians, of which I am myself a member.

[4] 2 Peter i, 5. [5] 1 Cor. xiv, 20. [6] 1 Thess. v, 21.

There are, I believe, few persons accustomed to a comprehensive view of the militant church, and of the course which true religion is taking amongst mankind, who will be disposed to deny, that the situation occupied in the body by the Society of Friends, is one of considerable importance to the cause of righteousness. My own observation has indeed led me to believe, that there are some spiritually-minded persons, not immediately connected with Friends, who go still farther; and who even *rejoice* in the consideration that, among the various classes of the Christian church, there is numbered one fraternity who bear a plain and decisive testimony against warfare in all its forms—against oaths under any pretext—and against all hiring or paying of the ministers of the Gospel: a fraternity, whose practice and history afford a sufficient evidence that God *may* be acceptably and profitably worshipped without the intervention of a single typical ceremony, and without the necessary or constant aid of any human ministry. Although these persons may differ from us in the precise view of these very subjects, they appear to be aware that the *tendency* of our peculiarities is good, and they will allow that Christianity, in its progress through the world, may derive no trifling advantage from the circumstance that these religious principles are, by *some*, at least, among the followers of Jesus, plainly and resolutely upheld.

That such an apprehension is well founded—that the consistent and religious part of the Society of Friends are actually occupying an important and useful station in the mystical body of Christ—that their peculiar principles are of an edifying tendency, and are calculated to promote the spiritual welfare, not only of Friends themselves, but of the Church in general—is the deliberate conviction of my own mind; and it is probable that the persons for whose use this work is principally intended, will generally unite with me in that conviction.

If such be the case, I would remind them that no religious views or practices can be salutary in the long run, or truly promote the spiritual progress of the militant church, which are the mere creatures of human reason and imagination, and which do not arise directly or indirectly out of the essential principles of the *law of God*. I may with humility acknowledge my own conviction, that the distinguishing views and practices of the Society of Friends are indeed derived from those principles; and to the proof of this point my future observations respecting them will be chiefly, if not exclusively, directed. In the first place, however, I must invite the reader's attention to an important doctrine of religion, which, although by no means peculiar to Friends, is certainly promulgated among them with remarkable earnestness, and which lies at the root of all their particular views and practices—the doctrine of the *perceptible influence and guidance of the Spirit of Truth.*

CHAPTER III.

ON THE PERCEPTIBLE INFLUENCE AND GUIDANCE OF THE SPIRIT OF TRUTH.

It is generally allowed, among the professors of Christianity, that in us, that is in our "flesh" or *natural man*, "dwelleth no good thing;" that we are unable of ourselves to fulfil the law of righteousness, or to serve the Lord with acceptance; and that the fountain of all true moral excellence, in mankind, is the Spirit of God. The serious and enlightened Christian of every name, will readily confess that it is only through the influence of this Holy Spirit, that he is enabled rightly to apprehend God, to know himself, and to accept Jesus Christ as his all-sufficient Saviour —that it is only through such an influence that he is converted in the first place, and afterwards sanctified and prepared for his heavenly inheritance.

The differences of sentiment which exist in the church, on this great subject, have respect, not to the question whether the Holy Spirit does or does not operate on the heart of man, (for on this question all true Christians are agreed,) but principally, if not entirely, to the *mode* in which that Spirit operates.

On this point there appears to exist, among the professors of Christianity, and even among serious Christians, a considerable diversity of opinion. Some persons conceive that the Spirit of God does not influence the heart of man *directly*, but only through the means of certain appointed instruments; such as the Holy Scriptures and the word preached. Many others who allow the direct and independent influences of the Spirit, and deem them absolutely essential to the formation of the Christian character, refuse to admit that they are perceptible to the mind; but consider them to be hidden in their actions, and revealed only in their fruits. Now, with Friends (and probably with many persons under other names) it is a leading principle in religion, that the work of the Holy Spirit in the soul is not only immediate and direct, but perceptible. We believe that we are all furnished with an inward Guide or Monitor, who makes his voice known to us, and who, if faithfully obeyed and closely followed, will infallibly conduct us into true virtue and happiness, because he leads us into a real conformity with the will of God.

That our sentiments, on this important subject are well founded—that the principle in question forms a part of the unchangeable truth of God—is satisfactorily evinced, according to our apprehension, by various declarations contained in the Holy Scriptures.

In a former chapter I have called the attention of the reader to the doctrine, that a measure of the Spirit of the Son of God is bestowed upon all mankind: and I have endeavoured to show it to be in reference to his spiritual appearance in the hearts of

CHAP. 3.] *and Guidance of the Spirit.* 77

his creatures, that Christ is styled " the *true light* which lighteth every man that cometh into the world." Now, it is certain that nothing can justly be called *light* which does not *make manifest.* " All things that are reproved," says the apostle Paul, " are made manifest by the light; for *whatsoever doth make manifest, is light:*"[1] since, then, the Spirit of Christ appearing in the soul of man, is *light*, it is plain that this Spirit *makes manifest*—communicates an actual moral sense—teaches what is right and what is wrong, in a perceptible or intelligible manner. Thus the Psalmist prayed as follows: "O send out thy light and thy truth; let them lead me; let them bring me to thy holy hill and to thy tabernacles."[2] The light and the truth, for which he thus offered up his petitions, could not be the written law of which he was already in possession: the expressions are rather to be understood of the light of God's countenance, and the truth revealed by his Spirit: and these, according to the views of the Psalmist, were at once perceptible and powerful; for they were to *lead* him in the way of righteousness, and to *bring* him to the holy hill and tabernacles of God.

Under the Christian dispensation, the Holy Spirit is poured forth in pre-eminent abundance, as has been already observed, and as the Scriptures testify, *on the souls of true believers in Jesus Christ.* Of the operations of divine grace, under this new covenant, none of the inspired writers appear to have enjoyed a clearer view than the apostle Paul. Often was he led to expatiate on the Spirit who " dwells" in the children of

[1] Eph. v, 13.   [2] Ps. xliii, 3.

God, and who enables them, on the one hand, to mortify their carnal affections, and, on the other, to bear the peaceable fruits of righteousness. It is *in* or *after* this Spirit, that the apostle commands us to *walk :* "If we live in the Spirit, let us also *walk* in the Spirit;"³ and again to the Romans, he says, "there is therefore now no commendation to them which are in Christ Jesus, *who walk not after the flesh, but after the Spirit.*"⁴ Now, to walk in or after the Spirit, who dwells in us, can be nothing less than to conform our life and conversation to his dictates; and this we could not do, unless those dictates were perceptible to the mind. On the same principles the apostle has, on two occasions, described Christians as persons who are led by the Spirit. "If ye be *led* of the Spirit, ye are not under the law."⁵ "For as many as are *led* by the Spirit of God, they are the sons of God."⁶ Any one, who impartially examines the two chapters from which these quotations are derived, will easily perceive that the *leading*, of which Paul is here speaking, is not the instruction derived from inspired preaching, or from divinely authorized Scripture, but an internal work carried on by the Spirit in the soul of man. If, then, there be given to us an internal communication of the Spirit of Truth, by which we are to be *led*, it is surely very plain that such communication must be made manifest to our mental perception, or otherwise we could not follow it.

The Spirit, whose practical influence the apostle

³ Gal. v, 25.   ⁴ Rom. viii, 1.   ⁵ Gal. v, 18.
⁶ Rom. viii, 14.

thus describes, is the Spirit of Christ. With this inspired writer the declarations, *that the Spirit is in us,* and *that Christ is in us,* appear to be equivalent. " But ye," says he, " are not in the flesh, but in the Spirit, if so be that the Spirit of God dwell in you. Now, if any man have not the *Spirit of Christ,* he is none of his. And if *Christ* be in you, the body is dead, because of (or as it relates to) sin; but the Spirit is Life, because of (or as it relates to) righteousness."[7] Since, then, the apostle teaches us that we are to be led by the Spirit, and that the Spirit, by whom we are to be led, is the Spirit of Christ, we may, without difficulty, understand the principle on which Christ is denominated the " Shepherd and Bishop of souls."[8]

The character of Jesus, as the Shepherd of his people, was unfolded in very touching expressions by our Lord himself. " I am the good Shepherd," said he, "and know my sheep, and am known of mine...other sheep I have, which are not of this fold: them also I must bring, and they shall hear my voice, and there shall be one fold and one Shepherd."—"My sheep hear my voice, and I know them, and they follow me; and I give unto them eternal life; and they shall never perish, neither shall any man pluck them out of my hand."[9] The disciples of Jesus who were gathered to him during his short abode upon the earth, undoubtedly enjoyed the privilege of being instructed by his outward voice; but the voice of Christ, which was to be afterwards heard by his sheep, who were not of the Jewish fold, and which is

[7] Rom. viii, 9, 10.   [8] 1 Peter, ii, 25.   [9] John x, 14, 16, 27, 28.

still heard by his faithful followers, whom he leads "in the way of righteousness," we may conclude to be the voice of his Spirit—a voice inwardly communicated to the soul of man. Such a view of our Lord's pastoral office, and of the method by which it is conducted, is perfectly accordant with the promise which he made to his disciples on a subsequent occasion;— "I will pray the Father, and he shall give you another Comforter, that he may abide with you for ever; even the Spirit of Truth; whom the world cannot receive, because it seeth him not, neither knoweth him; but ye know him; for he *dwelleth with you, and shall be in you.*"...."But the Comforter, which is the Holy Ghost, whom the Father will send in my name, he shall *teach you all things, and bring all things to your remembrance,* whatsoever I have said unto you."[1] "Howbeit, when he the Spirit of Truth is come, he will *guide you into all truth;* for he shall not speak of himself; but whatsoever he shall hear, that shall he speak; and he shall shew you things to come. He shall glorify me; for he shall receive of mine, and *shall shew it unto you.*"[2]

These passages contain a plain description of the perceptible guidance of the Spirit of Christ; and the same doctrine was declared, with equal clearness, by the apostle John, at a period when the promises thus made by the Lord Jesus had been graciously fulfilled in the experience of his disciples. "But ye," says the apostle, "have an unction from the Holy One, and ye *know* all things."......"The *anointing* which ye have

---

[1] John xiv, 16, 17, 26.   [2] John xvi, 13, 14.

received of him *abideth in you,* and ye need not that any man teach you; but *as the same anointing teacheth you of all things, and is truth, and is no lie,* and even as it hath taught you, ye shall abide in him."[3]

It may indeed be remarked, that the disciples who personally received these promises, and many of those primitive Christians whom the apostle was thus addressing, were endowed, for special purposes, with miraculous powers, and with a corresponding *extraordinary* measure of the Holy Spirit; but it cannot, I think, with any reason, be denied, that the promise of the Holy Ghost, the fulfilment of which is described in this passage of the apostle John, was addressed to *all who might believe in all ages of the church of Christ.* " He that believeth on me," said the Saviour, " out of his belly shall flow rivers of living water;"[4] this spake he of the Spirit; and in a passage already cited, he expressly declared that the Comforter, whom he thus promised to believers, should abide with them *"forever."* " Repent," cried the apostle Peter to the listening multitude, " and be baptized every one of you, in the name of Jesus Christ, for the remission of sins, and ye shall receive the gift of the Holy Ghost. *For the promise is unto you and to your children, and to all that are afar off, even as many as the Lord our God shall call.*"[5] Hence, therefore, it follows that the true believers in Jesus, of every description, and in all ages, are, in a peculiar manner, visited and guided by the Comforter. No longer are they to depend on the teaching of their fellow-creatures; for the anointing which they have

---

[3] 1 John ii, 20, 27.   [4] John vii, 38.   [5] Acts ii, 38, 39.

[margin note: Confirmation]
[margin note: When we begin to hear & serve God]

received of Christ *abideth in them, and teacheth them of all things, and is truth, and no lie.*

Such was indeed one of the most striking characteristics of that new dispensation, under which all real Christians are living; and I cannot better conclude this selection of scriptural evidences on the perceptible guidance of the Holy Ghost, than by citing a well-known prophetical description of that dispensation:—
" Behold, the days come, saith the Lord, that I will make a new covenant with the house of Israel and with the house of Judah; not according to the covenant that I made with their fathers in the day that I took them by the hand to bring them out of the land of Egypt; which my covenant they brake, though I was an husband unto them, saith the Lord; but this shall be the covenant that I will make with the house of Israel; after those days saith the Lord, *I will put my law in their inward parts, and write it in their hearts;* and will be their God, and they shall be my people. *And they shall teach no more every man his neighbour, and every man his brother, saying, Know the Lord: for they shall all know me, from the least of them unto the greatest of them,* saith the Lord; for I will forgive their iniquity, and I will remember their sin no more."[6]

Thus explicit are the declarations contained both in the Old and New Testaments, respecting the actual illumination of divine grace—the intelligible voice of the true Shepherd—the perceptible guidance and instruction of the Spirit of Truth in the souls of men

[6] Jer. xxxi, 31—34; *comp.* Heb. viii, 8—13.

CHAP. 3.]   *and Guidance of the Spirit.*   83

While it may be hoped that the spiritually-minded Christian will readily admit the force of these scriptural evidences, and will cheerfully embrace that profitable truth which they so clearly unfold; it is not to be forgotten, that *the human imagination is very active and delusive,* and that persons who are superficial in religion, or who are not sufficiently watchful, may sometimes mistake the unauthorized dictates of their own minds, for the voice of a divine and unerring guide. That errors of this description have on many occasions occurred, must be freely allowed; and that, under particular circumstances, they may probably continue to occur, will not be denied by those who are sufficiently aware of the infirmity and deceitfulness of the heart of man. It appears therefore, on the one hand, that the inward illumination of the Spirit of God is mercifully bestowed on us as a perceptible guide to righteousness, and on the other that we are exceedingly liable to be led about by the dictates of our own imagination. Such a view of the subject naturally leads to the inquiry, by what characteristics the voice of the Lord's Spirit and that of the human imagination, in matters of religion, may be distinguished from each other.

The least reflection may serve to convince us, that the two influences of which I have spoken, the true guide and the false guide, are in reality absolutely distinct, different, and sometimes even opposite. The true guide is "the day-spring from on high," and comes immediately from God, in whom there is no mixture of evil, and who is the original and unfailing source of all good. The false guide is the creature of human infirmity and misapprehension; and frequently the source from which it arises is positively evil and corrupt. Those who are faithfully following the true guide, are the dedicated children of a holy God. Those who are following only the false guide, have constructed for themselves an *unsound* religion, and are mere enthusiasts.

As the voice of the true Shepherd and that of the stranger are thus really distinct, and in fact, opposite, so I believe, the sincere and humble Christian, who has been taught the lesson of waiting upon God, and whose religion is of no shallow character, will be enabled by divine grace to discern the one from the other. He will find that they are clearly distinguished; first, by the mode of their operation; and secondly, by the fruits which they produce.

First, with respect to the mode of their operation; the human imagination, when applied to matters of religion, may often be justly described as working in the whirlwind. It is violent in its impulses: it lays hold of us, and leads us astray when we are in a condition of restlessness and temporary confusion, and when the disquietude in which we find ourselves affords a sufficient evidence, to any candid mind, that *self* is predominant. On the other hand, the voice of Christ in the heart is not more pure than *gentle.* Justly may it be styled, the " *still small voice,*" and clearly is the mode of its operation, as distinguished from the work of mere imagination, *illustrated* by that part of the history of the prophet Elijah, from which these expressions are borrowed. When Elijah stood before the Lord on Mount Horeb, we read, that " the Lord passed by, and a great and strong wind rent the mountains, and brake in pieces the rocks before the Lord; but *the Lord was not in the wind:* and after the wind an earthquake; *but the Lord was not in the earthquake:* and after the earthquake a fire; *but the Lord was not in the fire:* and after the fire *a still small voice!*"[7] When the pride of the heart is laid low, when the activity of human reasoning is quieted, when the soul is reduced to a state of silent subjection in the presence of its Creator, then is this "still small voice" intelligibly heard, and the word of the Lord, as it is inwardly revealed to us, becomes "a lamp" unto our "feet" and "a light" unto our "paths." Here I would remark that, in order to maintain this state of humble and quiet dependence upon God, the habit of a frequent retirement from the common occupations of life is of great use and importance. Nevertheless, such a frame of mind may be preserved, even when we are engaged in the pursuits of business. Watchful Christians are taught to live with a heart subjected before the Lord, and with an eye ever directed towards him in real simplicity. While such is their condition, the true guide to peace will not forsake them. When they turn to the right hand, or when they turn to the left, a voice shall still be found to follow them, saying, "*This is the way; walk ye in it.*" If, however, there are persons (as I believe there are) of real piety, who sincerely desire to follow the guidance of their Lord and Master, and yet have not learned to distinguish, as they would wish to do, the internal manifestations of his Holy Spirit, let them not be unprofitably

[7] 1 Kings xix, 11, 12.

discouraged. Let them rather pursue their course, in humble reliance on the mercy of God; and let them cultivate the animating hope that, as they are preserved in dedication to the divine will, and grow in grace, they will gradually become better acquainted with the word of the Lord within them, and will be comforted in a greater degree with the light of his countenance.[8]

Secondly, with regard to the fruits which these opposite influences respectively produce: the suggestions of the human imagination, in matters of religion, as they prevail over us when we are in a state of restlessness and confusion, so when they are followed, confirm and aggravate that condition. While they tend only to the elevation of self, and to the gratification of the eager desires of the unsubdued mind, they may indeed inflame us with a false zeal; but they can never soften the obdurate heart, bring the restless mind into stillness, or truly pacify the troubled conscience. On the contrary, the sure effect of obedience to the " still small voice" of our Divine Master in the soul, is quietness, tenderness, humility, soundness of mind, and substantial peace.

But we may extend our views further, and consider the consequences of these respective influences, not only on the inward frame of the mind, but on the outward conduct of the man. Here the difference between the fruits of two distinct and even opposite principles, become completely manifest. The imaginations of the heart of man, when not subdued and rectified by the power of divine grace, are continually

[8] See Isaiah l, 10.

CHAP. 3.]   *and Guidance of the Spirit.*   87

prone to evil; and although Satan may transform himself into an "angel of light," and conceal his operations under the cover of a religious profession, and even a sincere enthusiasm, his fruits will still be those of darkness and unrighteousness. Persons who, in the heat of their own spirits, commit themselves, without reserve, to so delusive and perilous a guidance, will not fail to make shipwreck, in many particulars, of the great moral principles of the Gospel of Christ. Again and again will they be found breaking the law of their Redeemer—the law of kindness, charity, order, submission, gentleness, integrity, purity, and peace. And, truly, the end of such a course is sorrow. "Behold, all ye that kindle a fire, that compass yourselves about with sparks, walk in the light of your fire, and in the sparks that ye have kindled. This shall ye have of mine hand; *ye shall lie down in sorrow.*"[9]

On the other hand, those who follow the Lord's Spirit will assuredly be found to bear the *fruits* of the Spirit, which are "love, joy, peace, long-suffering, gentleness, goodness, faith, meekness, temperance. Against such there is no law."[1] That there are very many persons, not of our religious body, who are endeavouring to follow the Spirit as a *perceptible guide*, there can be little doubt. Nevertheless there will, I trust, be no impropriety in my making an appeal, in connexion with the present branch of my argument, to the observation of those persons to whom this work is principally addressed. Although discouragement may often overtake us, through the misconduct

[9] Isaiah 1, 11.   [1] Gal. v, 22, 23.

of unsound brethren, my young friends, with myself, have enjoyed many opportunities of watching the demeanour and conduct of experienced persons, who profess that obedience to the dictates of the Spirit of Truth, in the soul, is their *main rule in life;* and who, by a long course of patience and self-denial, have fully evinced the sincerity of their profession. Now, we are certainly well aware, and we need not fear to acknowledge, that the character and deportment of such persons are distinguished for sobriety and substantial excellence, and that, however various may be their situations, their talents, and their gifts, they resemble one another in this main characteristic —that they are fulfilling the law of love, and living a life of piety and usefulness.

Our observation of others may suffice to convince us that, when the great principle of religion, to which I am now adverting, is conscientiously maintained, these pure and lovely fruits are invariably produced. And so far as we ourselves also, who are younger in religious growth, have been enabled to order our conversation by the same rule, and to "mind the same thing," our own experience will oblige us to confess that the Shepherd of Israel, as he is *thus* followed, is an unerring guide. We *know* that he would never fail to lead us away from the snares of the enemy, from the sinful pleasures of the world, and from the pride of life, into humility, charity, and pure morality. Finally, may we not with gratitude acknowledge, that in observing the latter days and death of many faithful servants of the Lord, who once occupied a place among us, we have been furnished with ample evidence that the end of a life passed in obedience to the inward monitions of the Spirit, as well as in reliance on Christ as our all-sufficient Saviour, is *quietness* and *peace?*

That God is *able* to illuminate the souls of men with the immediate visitations of spiritual light, the most incredulous metaphysician will not venture to deny. On the other hand, we may readily accede to the principle laid down by Locke, that we can entertain no reasonable confidence in any supposed spiritual illumination, further than as we are furnished with evidence that it proceeds from God.[2] Now, that the perceptible influence of the Holy Spirit on the soul proceeds from God, the Christian enjoys satisfactory evidence—first in the declarations of Scripture, that such an influence shall be bestowed upon him—and secondly, in the practical results into which it leads. " He that believeth on the Son of God hath the witness in himself."[3] He brings his own sensations to the test of experience. *He knows the tree by its fruits.*

This general argument will be found to derive confirmation from a view which we may now briefly take of some practical particulars in this perceptible guidance. In discussing those characteristics, I must of course be understood as appealing to the experience of my readers; and happy should I be, were my observations to serve as way-marks to any of them, by which they may learn more clearly to distinguish the Spirit of Truth from the Spirit of error.

[2] See *Essay on the Human Understanding,* book iii, ch. 19.
[3] 1 John, v, 10.

1. The light of the Spirit of Christ in the heart *tends to the humiliation of man;* for, in the first place, it reveals to him his many iniquities, and affords him the clearest evidence that he is fallen, corrupt, and prone to evil; and in the second place, as he endeavours to follow this light, he is again and again instructed in the lesson that his own strength is utter weakness, and that he can do no good thing of himself. Besides, it is ever to be remembered, that divine grace in the soul is not only light, but power. It softens all that is hard, and levels, as with the dust, all that is lofty within us. Those persons, therefore, who are truly subject to it, will, of necessity, become *tender, contrite, and lowly of heart.* The operation of the same principle tends, moreover, to the *exaltation of Christ.* That light and that power, which convince us of our own iniquities, lead us also to form a right estimate of the character and merits of our Lord. While, in our endeavours to follow his guidance, we are brought to the humbling discovery of our own weakness and worthlessness, we are taught that, in this weakness, the strength of Christ is made perfect; and we cannot but extol that Saviour, who supports us in every difficulty, arms us against every temptation, restores our souls, and leads us in the paths of righteousness for his name's sake.

2. Since fallen man is corrupt and perverse; since his natural inclinations, if not checked, will infallibly lead him, under some form or other, into the vanities of the world and the sins of the flesh; and since it is the great purpose of the Christian system to recover him from this lost condition, and to bring him into

CHAP. 3.] *and Guidance of the Spirit.* 91

conformity with the will of God, we may rest assured that the true voice of Christ in the heart will conduct us in the path of *daily self-denial.* And such undoubtedly is the experience of all those persons who have committed themselves to the guidance of this inward Monitor. They find that he leads them through the " straight gate," and by the " narrow way," and that, in order to follow him, it is indispensably necessary for them to resist their own desires, and to mortify those perverted selfish principles which constitute the character of the natural man.

When our Lord declared that, if any man would come after him, he *must take up his cross* and follow him—(the cross being the instrument employed for the infliction of capital punishment)—he might perhaps intend to press upon his immediate followers, that, in order to be *his* disciples, they must be willing even to die for his name's sake. Such a doctrine was well adapted to the circumstances in which these persons were placed: but, in that spiritual sense of which our Lord's words are obviously capable, it will be found to coincide with the experience of every real Christian. None can " follow the Lamb whithersoever he goeth," without being conformed to his sufferings—without bearing about in the body the dying of the Lord Jesus—without dying themselves to the lusts of the world, the sins of the flesh, and the pride of life. " We are buried with Christ by baptism *unto death*, that, like as Christ was raised up from the dead by the glory of the Father, even so we also should walk in newness of life."[4] But let us not fear

[4] Rom. vi, 4.

this death, or shrink from the cross of Christ: He who imposes it in order to our highest good, will render it more than tolerable; and it is the enemy of our souls who magnifies in our view the pain and difficulty of bearing it. To the dependent, simple, yet decided Christian, the yoke of Jesus becomes easy and his burden light.

3. Those who resist and grieve their heavenly Guide, and quench that delicate flame of light with which he condescends to visit them, gradually envelop themselves in gross darkness. They become incapable of perceiving the instructions of their Divine Monitor, and thus they continually form a lower and a lower standard respecting right and wrong. On the contrary, the Spirit of Christ, as it is closely followed and scrupulously obeyed, rectifies and quickens the faculties of the conscience. Our perceptions of good and evil become more and more just and lively; and, at the same time, our apprehension of spiritual things is enlarged and strengthened. Thus is accomplished in the experience of his followers, the promise of the Lord Jesus, that "unto every one that hath shall be given."[5] "The path of the just is as the shining light, that shineth more and more unto the perfect day."[6]

4. Since the inward manifestations of divine light in the soul, if attended to, lead invariably into the practice of Christian graces; and since those graces are clearly described and enjoined in the Holy Scriptures, (especially in the New Testament,) it is plain that these two practical guides to righteousness will

[5] Matt. xxv, 29. [6] Prov. iv, 18.

ever be found in accordance with each other. The law written in the book, and the law written on the heart, have proceeded from the same Author; the only standard of both of them is the will of God; and therefore they can never fail to correspond. Scripture is a divinely authorized *test*, by which we must try not only all our sentiments on matters of doctrine; but all our notions and opinions respecting right and wrong. "To the law and to the testimony; if they speak not according to this word, it is because there is no light in them."[7] It ought, however, to be remarked, that the written law, for the most part, consists in *general directions.* Now, the inward manifestations of the Holy Spirit, while they *confirm* the principles on which those general directions are founded, will instruct us how to apply them in our daily walk, and under all the various circumstances and exigencies of life. For example, the written law declares, "Thou shalt love thy neighbour as thyself." The Spirit of Christ will not only inculcate the same rule, but will point out to his obedient followers in what manner, and on what occasions, this love is to be brought into action.

5. It is worthy, in the last place, of particular observation, that the monitions of the Holy Spirit within us direct an *exact, comprehensive,* and *unmixed* obedience to the will of God. How imperfect is the obedience of those persons, who acknowledge only the written law, and who, in the application of that law to the various occasions of human life, are accustomed to seek no other direction than that of their

[7] Isaiah viii, 20.

own reason, and to depend upon no other strength than that of their own wills! While in the secret of their hearts there dwells a spirit of rebellion against that Lord who would lead them into self mortification; how readily can they plead excuses, and urge the doctrine of expediency, in opposition to the dictates of truth? Notwithstanding their professed regard to the Scriptures, they neglect to seek that guidance of the Holy Spirit of which the Scriptures so plainly testify. And what is the consequence? Their moral sense degenerates, and they presently learn to "call evil good, and good evil;" to "put darkness for light, and light for darkness;" to "put bitter for sweet, and sweet for bitter."[8] In such unsound professors of religion there is no full coming out—no effectual emancipation—from that which is evil in the sight of God.

May not a degree of the same kind of imperfection be detected in the experience even of seriously-minded Christians, who, while their dependence is mainly placed on the grace of God, are not fully believing in the light of Christ, *as it is inwardly revealed to the soul?* I am, in some measure, aware of the depth of human iniquity, and I well know how difficult it is to escape from its secret influence; but I believe that Christians would not be so much perplexed as they often are, with a sense of imperfection and sin in the performance of their various religious duties, were that performance less of themselves, and more of God; were it less dictated by the activity of their own minds, and derived with greater simplicity from the

[8] Isaiah v, 20.

CHAP. 3.]   *and Guidance of the Spirit.*   95

Fountain of all good. Great as is our own infirmity; deep as is our natural defilement; it is certain that the inward Guide, of whom we are speaking is *entirely holy*, and he still upholds to his followers the very highest standard of action—" *Be ye therefore perfect even as your Father which is in heaven is perfect.*" He commands them to be of clean hands, and to refrain completely from every thing which his own light has made manifest to be evil. He admits of no excuses; he sacrifices his law to no apparent expediency; he is satisfied with no mixed obedience; and when he calls us into active duties, and more especially into religious services, he is ever ready to assist us in our humble endeavour to offer unto the Lord an " offering in righteousness"—even a *pure* offering.

Such are the tests, and such are the fruits, of the perceptible guidance of the Holy Spirit in the soul. The reader will recollect, that the doctrine of such perceptible guidance rests upon the authority of Scripture; being clearly declared by the prophet Jeremiah, by the apostles John and Paul, and by our Lord himself—that the dictates of the Spirit, which lead into truth, are totally distinct from those of the human imagination, which lead into enthusiasm; that the two influences are to be distinguished, first, by the mode of their operation, and, secondly, by the fruits which they produce—that the influence of the Spirit operates in a *gentle* manner on the waiting and prostrate soul—that the fruits which it produces are the " peaceable fruits of righteousness"—that these afford a substantial evidence of the divine origin of that guiding principle which leads to them—and, lastly, that this general ·argument is greatly strengthened, when we come to trace some particular features in the practical operation of the principle in question: for as it is closely followed, it is ever found to lead to the humiliation of men, and to the exaltation of Christ; to the denial of self, and to the bearing of the cross; to the increase of moral and spiritual light; to the confirmation and right application of the divine law, as it is recorded in the Holy Scriptures, and to an *exact* fulfilment of that law.

Before I dismiss the subject of the perceptible guidance of the Spirit, it is necessary for me, somewhat more distinctly than I have hitherto done, to advert to the practical religious points which distinguish the Society of Friends. The principal of them may be enumerated as follows:—their disuse of all typical observances in the worship of God: their refusal to recognize any ministry in connexion with divine worship, which they do not conceive to be dictated by the immediate influence of the Holy Spirit: their acceptance of the public ministry of females; their objection to the human ordination, and also to the paying or hiring of preachers: their custom of silent worship: their abstaining from all warfare, both offensive and defensive, and from the use of oaths: their plainness in speech, behaviour, and apparel. In the preceding chapter has been advanced the sentiment (which I believe to be held by many persons without, as well as within, the pale of the Society) that these peculiarities are of an edifying *tendency,* and that the maintenance of them by Friends is calculated to promote the spiritual welfare of the church at large. It has also been observed, that this can be true only in so much as they arise out of the principles of the divine law: and I have already stated my intention, in the future discussion of them, to direct my remarks chiefly to the proof of this very point—*that they arise out of the principles of the divine law.*

Now, the first argument to be adduced, in support of this position, is immediately connected with the doctrine unfolded in the present chapter. If the question be addressed to us, why we consider it to be our duty to adopt our several religious peculiarities, we may answer, *because we believe we have been led into them by the Spirit of Truth.* The casual observer may indeed, attribute our maintenance of them to the mere force of habit and education; and certainly, there is much reason to apprehend that, with too many amongst us, they rest upon no better foundation. Nevertheless, you whom I am now addressing can scarcely fail to be aware, that, with *real* Friends, the adoption and punctual observance of such a line of conduct are not only matters of honest principle, but are truly the consequences of obedience to their *inward Guide.* It is a fact which the world can scarcely be expected to notice, but which is well known to every experienced Quaker, and will not be denied by any persons who possess an intimate knowledge of the Society, that the *very same guiding and governing principle, which leads the sincere-hearted and serious among Friends into the practice of universally acknowledged Christian virtues, leads them also into these peculiarities.* Such, therefore, being our experience, we cannot but derive from it a strong and satisfactory conviction, that our religious peculiarities belong to the law of God; for it is certain, that the Spirit of Truth, by whose influence alone men are made truly righteous, and brought into conformity with the divine will, would never lead the followers of Jesus into a course of conduct which is not founded on the principles of that law. The inward manifestations of the Spirit are, in themselves, <u>the law of God written on the heart.</u>

I may now proceed to confirm this general argument by more particular observations on the several peculiarities already enumerated; and, in endeavouring to trace the connexion of each of them with the law of God, I shall appeal to the principles of that law as they are unfolded in the New Testament. For I consider that it is only under the new and more spiritual dispensation, that the <u>divine law is revealed to us in all its purity, and in all its completeness.</u>

CHAPTER IV.

ON THE DISUSE OF ALL TYPICAL RITES IN THE WORSHIP OF GOD.

THOUGH it is almost universally allowed among Christians, that, when the New Covenant was established in the world, by the death of Christ, the ceremonies of the Jewish law were abolished, there are two religious rites of a very similar description, the maintenance of which is still very generally insisted upon, as necessary to the edification, and true order, of the church of Christ. These rites are *baptism with water*, and that participation of bread and wine, which is usually called the *sacrament of the Lord's supper*. So great is the virtue and efficacy ascribed to these ceremonies, that they are considered, by very many Christians, to be especial means of grace, or mediums through which grace is conveyed to the soul; and not a few theologians, both ancient and modern, appear to have entertained the extraordinary opinion that the rite of baptism, more especially, is indispensable to salvation.

On the other hand, I am informed that, in some parts of the continent of Europe, there are small societies of pious Christians, by whom water-baptism and the ceremony of the Lord's supper are entirely disused;[1] and that such is the fact in the Society of Friends is generally understood. It is our belief that we have been led out of the practice of these rites by the Spirit of Truth; that we could not recur to them without grieving our heavenly Monitor; and that, in fact, they are not in accordance with the entire spirituality of the Gospel dispensation.

In order to explain our principle on the subject, I must remark, *in limine*, that the ceremonies in question, as now practised among Christians, must be considered as forming a part of *their system of worship:* for they are, in the first place, in the strictest sense of the terms, *religious rites* performed in supposed obedience to the command of the Almighty; and, secondly, they are employed in immediate connexion with the more direct, and generally with the public, acts of divine worship. Such being the state of the case, the objection of Friends to the use of these ordinances will be perceived to have its foundation in a principle of acknowledged importance, and one which is clearly revealed in the New Testament, that, under the Christian dispensation, the worship of God is not to be formal, ceremonial, or typical, but, simply spiritual.

This principle was declared in a clear and forcible manner by Jesus Christ himself. When the woman of Samaria, with whom he condescended to converse

---

[1] This is the case, as I understand, with the Inspirés in Germany, and with the Malakans in South Russia.

by the well of Sychar, spake to him of the worship observed by the Jews at Jerusalem, and by the Samaritans on Mount Gerizin, our Lord answered, "Woman, believe me, the hour cometh when ye shall neither in this mountain, nor yet at Jerusalem, worship the Father ...... The hour cometh, and now is, when the true worshippers shall worship the Father *in spirit and in truth;* for the Father seeketh such to worship him. God is a spirit: and they that worship him must worship him in spirit and in truth."[2] In this passage of our Lord's discourse, there is an evident allusion to two separate and distinct systems of worship, belonging to two different dispensations; and it is equally clear that the change was then about to take place from one of these to the other; that the one was about to be abolished—the other to be established. The system of worship about to be abolished was that which the Jews were accustomed to practise at Jerusalem, and which the Samaritans had endeavoured to imitate on their favourite mountain. Now, every one who is acquainted with the records of the Old Testament, must be aware that this was a system of worship chiefly consisting in outward ceremonies, in figurative or typical ordinances. The greatest nicety of divine direction accompanied the institution of these various rites, which were a "figure for the time then present," and "which stood only in meats and drinks, and divers washings, and carnal ordinances, imposed" on the Israelites "*until the time of reformation.*"[3] But now that *time of reformation* was at

[2] John iv, 21—24.   [3] Heb. ix, 10.

hand, and the law was pronounced by the great Mediator of the New Covenant, that men were henceforward to worship the Father in spirit and in truth. The new worship which was thus to distinguish Christianity was to be *in spirit;* because it was to consist, not in outward rites of a formal and ceremonial nature, but in services dictated by the Spirit of the Lord, and in direct communion of the soul with its Creator. It was to be *in truth;* not simply as arising from a sincere heart—a description which might apply with equal force to the abolished worship of the Jews —but because it was to consist in substantial realities. It was to be carried on, not through the old medium of types and figures, but by the application to the heart of the great and essential truths of the Gospel; for the type was now to be exchanged for the antitype, the figure for the thing figured, the shadow for the substance.[4] Such then, and such only, is the true character of Christian worship.

We ought by no means to disparage the forms and ceremonies of the Jewish law, as connected with the covenant to which they appertained. We cannot forget that this ministration of worship was appointed by the Almighty himself; nor can we refuse to, acknowledge that it was, in its own time, glorious. For, although these ceremonies could not make him that did the service perfect, as pertaining to the conscience, yet was the whole system, of which they formed

---

[4] A similar explanation of our Lord's expressions, respecting Christian worship, will be found in the Commentaries of the following biblical critics :—Theophylact, Calvin, Jac. Cappellus, Grotius, Rosenmüller, Whitby, Gill, Scott, and Doddrige.

Chap. 4.]   *in the Worship of God.*   103

a part, perfectly adapted, by Divine Wisdom, to the condition of the Israelites; and the ritual law served a purpose of high importance to the ultimate promotion of the cause of righteousness. To that purpose we have already alluded: it was to typify, prefigure, and *introduce*, the better, purer, and *more* glorious, ministration of the Gospel: for it is precisely in reference to these ceremonies, that the apostle describes the Jewish law as being "a figure for the time then present;" and as "having a *shadow of good things to come.*"[5]

But, important as was the purpose thus answered by the establishment and maintenance of the ceremonial law, it was one of a merely temporary nature. When the Messiah was come—when he had revealed the spiritual character of his own dispensation—when he had died for our sins—when he had risen again for our justification—when he had shed forth on his disciples the gifts and graces of the Holy Spirit—then were all the types fulfilled; *then was the law of types abolished.* "There is verily," saith the apostle, "a disannulling of the commandment going before, for the weakness and unprofitableness thereof; for the law made nothing perfect, but the bringing in of a better hope did, by the which we draw nigh unto God."[6] Again, "Wherefore, when he cometh into the world, he saith, sacrifice and offering thou wouldst not, but a body hast thou prepared *me:* in burnt-offerings and (sacrifices) for sin thou hast had no pleasure: then said I, Lo! I come, (in the volume of the book it is

[5] Heb. ix, 9; x, 1.   [6] Heb. vii, 18, 19.

written of me,) to do thy will, O God. Above, when he said sacrifice and offering, and burnt-offerings, and (offering) for sin, thou wouldest not, neither hadst pleasure therein; which are offered by the law; then said he, Lo! I come to do thy will, O God. *He taketh away the first, that he may establish the second.*"[7]

The system of types and sacrificial ordinances, therefore, being "taken away," and the spiritual system being, by the coming of Christ, established, we are no longer to worship the Father through the intervention of a human priesthood, of formal ceremonies, or of typical institutions, but *solely* through the mediation of the High Priest of our profession, and under the immediate and all-sufficient influences of the Holy Ghost. Although the shadows of the old law formed an essential part of the *Jewish* dispensation, they were no sooner imposed upon Christians than they became *unlawful*, and assumed the character of an unrighteous bondage and of "beggarly elements."[8] "Wherefore, if ye be dead with Christ, from the rudiments of the world," says the apostle Paul to his Colossian converts, "why, as though living in the world, *are ye subject to ordinances.*"[9]

Having thus endeavoured to unfold the nature of that spiritual worship of God which the Lord Jesus enjoined on his followers, and to show how clearly it was distinguished from the old ceremonial worship practised among the Jews, I may now take up the more particular consideration of the rites of Baptism,

---

[7] Heb. x. 5—9.   [8] Gal. iv, 9.
[9] Col. ii, 20, *comp.* 14, Eph. ii, 14—16.

Chap. 4.]   *in the Worship of God.*   105

and the Lord's Supper. These rites have both received the name of "sacraments"—a word which properly signifies *oaths*, and formerly designated more especially the oaths of allegiance required of Roman soldiers; but which, as applied to these religious ceremonies, may be considered as denoting "sacred and binding ordinances."

It is imagined by many persons, that the ordinances, thus held as sacred in the church, are but little connected with those Jewish institutions, which are, on all hands, allowed to have been abolished by the coming and sacrifice of the Messiah; that they are, on the contrary (with the single exception of the baptism of John,) of an origin exclusively Christian. On the supposition of the correctness of this opinion, it is, nevertheless, undeniable, that these rites, as they are now observed, are of *precisely the same nature* as the ceremonies of the ancient Jews. They are actions indifferent in themselves, employed as religious forms, and as a constituent part of a system of divine worship; and like those Jewish ceremonies, they are mere types or shadows, representing, in a figurative manner, certain great particulars of Christian truth. It is plain, therefore, that the *principle* on which these practices are founded, appertains to the old covenant; and equally plain (in the opinion of Friends) that such practices do not consist with that spiritual worship, which is described as so distinguishing a feature of the dispensation of the Gospel.

Although, however, the rites of Baptism and the Supper have been so generally adopted, as belonging to their own religious system, by the professors of faith in Jesus, I cannot consider it true, in any accurate sense of the terms, that they are of Christian origin. On the contrary there is every reason to believe that before the coming of Christ, these practices actually formed a part of the customary Jewish ritual.

First, with respect to <u>baptism in water</u>. It is notorious, that, according to the ceremonial law of the Jews, there could be no removal of uncleanness, no purification either of things or persons, without ablution in water. On various occasions the performance of that ceremony was appointed by the divine law: and on many others, it was observed on the authority of Rabbinical tradition. Now, these " divers washings," to which the Jews were so much accustomed as a ritual means of purification, are, in the Greek Testament, described as <u>baptisms</u>;[1] and it is certain that the principal of them were effected by dipping or immersion. Before going into the temple to minister or officiate, the priests of the Jews were accustomed to dip their whole body in water, and the house in which this ceremony was performed was called " <u>the house of baptism.</u>"[2] Persons of every description, who had contracted any bodily pollution, were strictly enjoined by the law to wash or *bathe* their flesh;[3] and the learned Jews determine that, if the least part of the surface of the body was not wetted by the dipping, the purification was incomplete. In the Greek original of the book of Ecclesiasticus, a person purified, after

---

[1] Heb. ix, 10 ; Mark vii, 4 ; Luke xi, 38..
[2] *Cod. Joma.* cap. 3, *quoted by Hammond on* Matt. iii.
[3] See Levit. xv, 5, 8, 11.

Chap. 4.] *in the Worship of God.* 107

touching a dead body, is described as one *dipped* or *baptized*.[4] Judith, when on the point of performing an action which she erroneously deemed to be of a highly religious nature, " washed (or, as in the Greek, baptized) herself in a fountain of water."[5] Now, although the baptism practised by John and by the apostles did not, in all its circumstances, resemble those Jewish washings to which I have now adverted, yet it was precisely similar to them in that main particular of *immersion in water ;* and, in all these instances, this immersion was typical of one and the same thing—that is to say, of *a change from a condition of uncleanness to one of purity*. But the Jewish dipping, from which the baptism, first, of John, and afterwards, of the apostles, principally took its rise, and of which those baptisms may, indeed, be considered as mere instances, was the *dipping on conversion*. We read in the book of Exodus, that three days before the delivery of the law, " the Lord said unto Moses, Go unto the people, and sanctify them to-day and to-morrow, and let them *wash their clothes ;*" in pursuance of which command, we are afterwards informed that " Moses went down from the mount unto the people, and sanctified the people; and *they washed their clothes.*"[6] From the comparison of other similar passages, it appears probable that the washing of clothes here mentioned was a baptism or immersion in water of the whole body, together with the apparel.[7] Such is the express judgment of the Rab-

---

[4] Chap. xxxiv, 25.   [5] Chap. xii, 7.   [6] Exod. xix, 10, 14.
[7] *Compare* Levit. xi, 25 ; xiv, 47 ; xv, 5, &c.

binical writers; and they further determine that this baptism was commanded and observed, on the principle that the Israelites were then about to be introduced to a new religious covenant or dispensation;—that, in other words, it was a *baptism of conversion*, to a purer and more excellent system of worship, faith, and conduct, than that to which they had hitherto been accustomed.[8]

Hence, as it is declared by Maimonides and other Jewish writers, arose the *baptism of proselytes*, or of the Gentile converts to the religion of the Jews.[9] It was a principle well understood among that people, that *as it was with the Israelite, so should it be with the proselyte;*[1] and accordingly, as the Israelites had entered into their covenant by "circumcision, baptism, and sacrifice," the same introductory rites were considered indispensable for every true convert to their religion.[2]

---

[8] *Maimonides, Issure Biah*, cap. 13. Lightfoot, *Hor. Heb. in* Matt. iii, 6.

[9] The proselytes were of two descriptions: *proselytes of the gate*, who forsook Idolatry and worshipped the true God, but did not conform to the Jewish law; and *proselytes of justice*, who went further, and embraced the whole legal and ceremonial system. It was the latter only who were baptized.

[1] See Num. xv, 15.

[2] According to the traditions of the Rabbins, circumcision, baptism, and sacrifice, were enjoined on every male, and the two latter on every female convert from heathenism to the Jewish faith. It was a trite axiom, as Lightfoot informs us, that no man could be a proselyte until he was circumcised and baptised. In the Babylonish Gemara, (part of the Talmud) we find the following disputation. "The proselyte who is circumcised and not baptized, what are we to say of him? Rabbi Eliezer says, Behold he is a proselyte; for so we find it was with our fathers (the Patriarchs,)

Maimonides, who was a man of extraordinary sense and learning, and was deeply versed in the laws and customs of the ancient Jews, has stated a variety of particulars respecting the baptism of proselytes. It appears that, about three days after circumcision, the convert to Judaism was conducted, during the daytime, to a confluence of waters, whether natural or artificial, sufficiently deep to admit of entire immersion. Having been placed in the water, he was instructed in various particulars of the Jewish law, by three scribes of learning and authority, who presided over the whole ceremony; and, when these doctors had received his promises of a faithful adherence to the Jewish institutions, and had fully satisfied themselves respecting his motives and condition of mind, he completed the immersion of his whole person, by dipping his head. He then ascended from the water, offered his sacrifice to the Lord, and was thenceforward considered as a complete Jew, and as a new or regenerate man.[3]

I am aware that the existence of the rite of proselyte baptism, before the Christian era, is disputed by some of the learned, on the ground that such a rite is not specifically mentioned either in the Old Testa-

---

that they were circumcised and not baptized. He that is baptized and not circumcised, what are we to say of him? Rabbi Joshua says, Behold he is a proselyte; for so we find it is with females. *But the wise men say*, Is he baptized and not circumcised? or, is he circumcised and not baptised? *He is no proselyte until he be circumcised and baptized.* Jevahmoth, fol. 46, 2. Lightfoot, Hor. Heb. in Matt iii, 6.

[3] *Issure Biah*, cap. 13, 14. *Wall on Infant Baptism*, p. xliv. Selden de Synedriis, lib. i, cap. 3.

ment or in the most ancient uninspired writings of the Jews; but this omission is very far from being sufficient to prove the negative; and the doubt which it occasions appears to be greatly out-balanced by positive evidences in favour of the antiquity of the practice. It seems necessary shortly to glance at these evidences.

1. The Jewish writers, who make mention of the baptism of proselytes, expressly describe it as an ordinance practised among their countrymen at a date long prior to the Christian era. Thus, it is said in the Talmud, that Jethro, the father-in-law of Moses, was baptized as a proselyte.[4] From Maimonides we learn that the baptism of proselytes was practised *from age to age*,[5] after the Israelites themselves had been admitted into their covenant in the days of Moses; and, again, he makes mention of the proselytes in the time of David and Solomon, as of persons *who had been baptized.*[6]

2. There was a marked resemblance in several leading particulars between the baptism of proselytes, as described in the Talmud and by Maimonides, and the baptism practised by John and the early teachers of Christianity. The baptism of the proselytes was a complete immersion, and was appointed to take place in a *confluence of waters.* The baptism of John and of the Christians is generally allowed to have been of the same character. "John baptized in Ænon, near to Salim, because *there was much water there ;*"[7]

---

[4] Tract. Repudii, Hammond on Matt. iii. [5] לדורות
[6] Issure Biah, cap. 13. [7] John iii, 23.

and when the Ethiopian was to be baptised, we read that he and Philip went down or " *des. ended into* the water," and afterwards that they " *came up out of* the water."[8] It has, indeed, been remarked that, as the proselyte dipped his own head, he might be considered as baptizing himself, whereas the convert to Christianity was baptized by some minister; and the disciples of John were baptized by that prophet. But, I apprehend, the supposed difference in this respect is merely imaginary; for, although the proselyte plunged his own head in conclusion of the rite, he might properly be described as being baptized by the persons who placed him in the water, and who arranged the whole ceremony. Accordingly, I observe that the Jews speak of "*baptizing*" their proselytes, just as Christians make mention of "*baptizing*" their converts.[9] Again—during thè act of baptism, the proselyte was instructed, and made to stipulate for himself by the scribes;[1] that the same circumstances now attend the rite of baptism, as practised among Christians, is well known; and that they have been, from very early times, the accompaniments of that ceremony, is generally allowed.[2] Again—when the proselyte was baptised, the rite was frequently adminis-

---

[8] Acts viii, 38, 39.

[9] Even as they circumcise and *baptize* proselytes, so do they circumcise and *baptize* servants who are received from Gentiles, &c.: *Maim. Issure Biah,* cap. 13. When a proselyte is received, he must be circumcised, and when he is cured, they *baptize* him in the presence of two wise men, &c. *Talmud Babyl. Mass. Jevamoth,* fol. 47.

[1] *Selden de Syned.* lib. 1, cap. iii, p. 785.

[2] See *Macknight and others on* 1 Peter iii, 21.

tered, not only to himself, but to his family. So also it appears to have been with the early baptism of the Christians: we read, that Lydia was baptized *with her household;* that Paul baptized " the *household* of Stephanas; and that, when the jailer at Philippi became convinced of the truth of Christianity, he and " all his" partook together of the same ceremony.[3] Again—the proselyte, who had entered into covenant by circumcision, baptism, and sacrifice, was considered as a new man; or, to adopt the language of the Jews, as " a child new born;"[4] and of this new birth, or introduction to a better and purer faith, *immersion in water was evidently used as the expressive sign.* So it is notorious, that the genuine convert to the faith of Christ is ever represented, in the New Testament, as one regenerate, or born again; and baptism, as employed by John and the apostles, was a figure of this regeneration. These points of resemblance between the Jewish proselyte baptism, and that of the Christians, are so important and so striking, as to render it nearly indisputable that the one baptism was borrowed from the other. Since, therefore, it is altogether incredible that the Jews should borrow one of their leading ceremonies from the Christians, whom they despised and hated, there can be little reasonable doubt that the baptism of John and the Christians was derived from the proselyte baptism of

---

[3] Acts xvi, 15, 33 ; 1 Cor. i, 16. *Gemara Babyl. Chetub,* cap. i, fol. 11, &c. *Wall,* p. xlix.

[4] *Gemara, Jevamoth,* cap. iv, fol. 62, 1. *Maim. Issurc Biah,* cap. 14 ; *Wall,* p. lvii.

[CHAP. 4.] *in the Worship of God.* 113

the Jews; and that, of course, the latter was of a date prior to Christianity.

3. Our Saviour's discourse with Nicodemus is considered (and I think with justice) to contain an allusion to the baptism of proselytes; for he there describes *conversion* under the figure of a second birth—a birth of "*water* and of the Spirit." Here there is a precise accordance with the known Jewish doctrine respecting proselytism; and, after having thus treated of that doctrine, and applied it in a spiritual sense, our Lord adverts to the want of intelligence displayed by Nicodemus on the subject, as to a surprising circumstance: "*Art thou a master in Israel, and knowest not these things.*"

4. Although the baptism of proselytes is no where expressly mentioned in the Old Testament, it was the natural, and indeed necessary, consequence of the admitted principle of the Jewish law, *that unclean persons of every description were to be purified by washing in water*, and of the custom, which so generally prevailed among the ancient Jews, of effecting this washing by *immersion*. On whatever occasion the rite of baptism was employed—whether as a preparation for religious service, or for the removal of uncleanness, or as a type of conversion to a holier faith —whether it was enjoined on the High Priest, or on the leper, or on the proselyte from heathenism, or on the disciple of John, or on the convert of the apostles, —it was, in all cases, a *rite of purification*.

Thus we find, that the baptism of John excited a dispute between him and the Jews, on the subject of *purifying* :[5] thus Paul was exhorted by Ananias to be

[5] John iii, 25.

baptized (or, as in the Greek, to baptize himself) and *to wash away his sins :*[6] and thus, in apparent allusion (although in a spiritual sense) to the rite of baptism, the same apostle describes his own converts, as *washed and sanctified,*[7] &c. Now, it is certain that, at the Christian era, the Jews considered the Gentiles to be *unclean* persons, so that they were not permitted to associate with them, or to eat in their company.[8] Hence, therefore, it must have followed, *as a matter of course*, that no Gentile could become a Jew—could become clean himself, or fitted to unite with a clean people—*without undergoing the rite of baptism.*

Such are the positive evidences and plain reasons which appear to prove, in a very satisfactory manner, the antiquity of the Jewish rite of *baptism on conversion*, and which confirm the opinion of Hammond, Selden, Lightfoot, Wall, and other learned writers, that this ceremony was perfectly familiar to the Jews, before the incarnation of our Lord. Accordingly, we may observe that, when John " baptized in the wilderness, and preached the baptism of repentance (or conversion) for the remission of sins," his doctrine was very far from being strange or surprising to his hearers; nor did they evince the least difficulty in submitting themselves to the ordinance. On the contrary multitudes pressed around him for the purpose : " And there went out unto him," says the evangelist, " all the land of Judea, and they of Jerusalem, and were all baptized of him in the river of Jordan, confessing their sins."[9]

---

[6] Acts xxii, 16.
[7] 1 Cor. vi, 11 ; *comp.* Eph. v, 26 ; Heb. x, 22, &c.
[8] See Acts x, 28 ; *comp.* John iv. 9, &c.   [9] Mark i, 4, 5.

It was the office of the Baptist to proclaim the approach of that heavenly kingdom—that purer dispensation—for which the pious among the Jews were so anxiously looking: and the faith, into the profession of which he baptized, was faith in the coming Messiah, the long-expected ruler of restored and renovated Israel. "John, verily," said Paul, "baptized with the baptism of repentance, saying unto the people, that *they should believe on him which should come after him*, that is, on Christ Jesus."[1] On the ground of his being either the Christ himself, or Elias, the expected forerunner of the Christ, no objection could be taken to his baptism, by the Pharisees who came to dispute with him; for, in either of these characters, he would be the authorised minister of a new and purer faith, and, as a matter of course, a *baptizer*. It was because of the declaration of John, that he was *not* the Christ—that he was *not* Elias—that he was *not* that prophet—and for that reason only, that the Pharisees addressed the question to him, "Why baptizest thou then?"[2]

And so it was also with the disciples of Jesus. As John baptized on conversion to a faith in the Messiah to come, so they baptized on conversion to a faith that Jesus was the Messiah. Both John and the apostles were engaged in the work of converting—in making disciples to a new system of faith and conduct, to a holier law, and to a more spiritual dispensation—and, therefore, on a well-known Jewish principle and in conformity with a common Jewish practice, *they respectively baptized their converts in water*.

[1] Acts xix, 4. [2] John i, 25.

Secondly, with respect to the "*Lord's Supper*," I conceive that as it was observed by the primitive Christians, it could not justly be considered as a direct ceremonial ordinance. But upon the supposition that the apostles and their companions, like more modern Christians, were accustomed to practise it only as a religious rite, and as a part of their system of divine worship, such an institution must be regarded as immediately connected with the Jewish Passover. The lamb eaten at the Passover, and the bread broken and wine poured forth in the Christian Eucharist, were equally intended as types; and they were types of the same event—the death and sacrifice of Christ. The two ceremonies, therefore, may be looked upon as the same *in point of principle*. But, it is more especially to our present purpose to remark, that the breaking of the bread, and the pouring forth of the wine, together with the blessing and giving of thanks, which distinguish the ceremony of the Eucharist, actually formed a part of the *ritual order* to which the ancient Jews were accustomed, in celebrating the supper of the Passover. This fact is sufficiently evident from the narrations contained in the Gospels, of our Lord's last paschal meal with his disciples; and is fully substantiated on the authority of the Rabbinical writers, who in their minute statements respecting the right method of conducting that ceremonial Jewish supper, have explicitly directed the observance of all these particulars.[3]

---

[3] See *Extracts from the Talmud and Maimonides, in Lightfoot, Hor. Heb. in* Matt. xxiv.

CHAP. 4.]　　*in the Worship of God.*　　117

Before we draw a conclusion from the facts now stated, it may be desirable briefly to review the former part of the argument. In explaining that great law of the New Covenant, that God, who is a spirit, must be worshipped in *spirit and in truth*, I have adverted to the comparison so evidently instituted by Jesus Christ when he pronounced the law in question, between the spiritual and substantial worship thus enjoined on his own followers, and that which was customary among the ancient Samaritans and Jews. The two systems of worship are described as completely distinct; the one was about to die away, the other to be established. The old worship consisted principally in the performance of typical rites. The new worship was of a precisely opposite character. The ordinance was to cease; the shadow was to be discontinued; the substance was to be enjoyed; and, in the total disuse of ancient ceremonial ordinances, communion was now to take place between the Father and the souls of his people, only through the mediation of Jesus Christ, and under the direct influences of the Spirit of Truth. On the supposition, therefore, that water-baptism and the Eucharist were not of Jewish origin, yet, being shadows and types, and nothing more, they perfectly resemble the ordinances of the law, and plainly appertain to the principle of the Old Covenant. But, further—on a fair examination of the history of these ceremonies, we find that they not only belong to the *principle* of the Old Covenant, but were practices observed on that principle by the Jews themselves, before the introduction of the Christian revelation. Thus, then, it appears, that they actually formed a part of the ritual system of Judaism itself; and since it is, on all hands allowed that the whole of that ritual system, although observed for many years after the death of Jesus by most of his immediate disciples, is nevertheless null and void under the Christian dispensation, we appear to be brought to a sound conclusion, that, in connexion with the worship of Christians, *the ceremonies in question are rightly disused.*

It will scarcely be denied by any persons who are awakened to a sense of the spirituality of true religion, that in this view of the subject there is much which is reasonable, and consistent with the leading characteristics of Christianity. But, on the other hand, it is pleaded, that the New Testament contains certain passages, in which the practice of these rites is not only justified, but enforced; and, which, in fact render such practice binding upon all the followers of Christ.

In order to form a sound judgment whether this notion is correct or erroneous, it will be necessary for us to enter into a somewhat detailed examination of the passages in question, and of several others in which baptism and the dominical supper are either alluded to, or directly mentioned. Previously, however, to entering on such an examination, I may venture upon one general observation; namely, that if any such passages be found fairly to admit of either a literal or a spiritual interpretation, and if it be allowed (as I think it must be, for the general reasons already stated,) that the latter is far more in harmony than the former with the nature of the Chris-

CHAP. 4.] *in the Worship of God.* 119

tian dispensation—in such case, we are justified, by the soundest laws of biblical criticism, in adopting the spiritual, and in dropping the literal, interpretation.

We may commence with *Baptism.*

The first passage to be considered, in reference to this subject, is that in which the apostle John has described our Lord's conversation with Nicodemus, on the doctrine of regeneration. " Verily, verily, I say unto thee, except a man be born again, he cannot see the kingdom of God."............" Verily, verily, I say unto thee, except a man be born *of water and of the Spirit*, he cannot enter into the kingdom of God."[4] I cannot deny that, when our Lord thus spake of being born of water, his words contained an allusion to the rite of purification.— It has been already remarked, that the doctrine on which he thus insisted, in a spiritual sense, and respecting which he adverted so pointedly to the ignorance of Nicodemus, was one which, in its merely external bearings, was perfectly familiar to the Jews. The proselyte, who had forsaken heathenism, and adopted the Jewish religion, was considered as one *new-born;* and of this new birth his immersion in water appears to have been the appointed sign. The new birth of the true Christian—that indispensable preparation for his entrance into the kingdom—is therefore fitly illustrated by the circumstances of the baptized proselyte. But, though it is sufficiently evident that our Lord alluded, in this passage, to the Jewish rite of baptism on conversion, it appears to be equally clear that he made that allusion in a merely figurative and spiritual sense.

[4] John iii, 3—5.

Those who would prove, that to " be born of water" in this passage literally signifies to be *outwardly baptized*, defeat their own purposes by attempting to prove too much. If the *possibility* of an entrance into the kingdom of heaven, which a multitude of moral sins does not preclude, is precluded by the infraction of a merely positive precept, and by the omission of a rite, *in itself* indifferent, it may almost be asserted that the system of Christianity is overturned, and that the Gospel falls to the ground. To impose on an obscure and ambiguous expression a sense which thus contradicts so many general declarations made by the sacred writers, and which is directly opposed to the fundamental doctrines of the New Testament, is obviously very inconsistent with the laws of a just and comprehensive criticism. Nothing, one would think, but absolute necessity, would compel any reasonable critic to the adoption of such an alternative.

But, in point of fact, the expressions thus employed by Jesus are capable of being otherwise interpreted with the greatest propriety. Numerous passages might be adduced, from both the Old and New Testament, in which the carnal washings or baptisms of the Jews are alluded to in a merely spiritual sense, and in which more particularly, we find the grace of the Spirit—that sacred influence given to men for their conversion and sanctification—described under the figure of " water."[5] According, therefore, to this known scriptural phraseology, " to be born of

---

[5] See Psa. li, 2, 7 ; Isaiah i, 16 ; Jer. iv, 14 ; Ezek. xxxvi, 25 ; John iv, 10 ; vii, 38 ; 1 Cor. vi, 11 ; Eph. v, 26.

CHAP. 4.]   *in the Worship of God.*   121

water" may be properly understood as signifying *to be converted, cleansed, and introduced to newness of life, by the Spirit of God.* Such is the interpretation of these words, which is adopted not only by Friends, but by various pious writers and commentators on Scripture, who have no connexion with that Society.[6] This interpretation is by no means precluded by the addition—" *and* of the Spirit:" for our Lord's words may here be understood, not as relating to two things, but as representing one thing, first by means of a figure, and afterwards without that figure. Such a mode of expression is not unusual in the sacred writings. Just in the same manner the apostle Paul describes his own converts, first as "*washed*" and immediately afterwards as "*sanctified*" by the Spirit of God;[7] and when John the Baptist declared that Jesus, who was coming after him, should "baptize with the Holy Ghost and with fire," he probably employed *both* those terms to represent *one* internal and purifying influence.

That spiritual interpretation of our Lord's expressions which is thus plainly admissible, is moreover confirmed by the immediate context. Jesus says to Nicodemus (according to the common English version) "Except a man be born *again*, he cannot see the kingdom of God;" and again he says, " Except a man be born of water and of the Spirit, he cannot enter into the kingdom of God." It is obvious, that the latter of these sayings is nothing more than an *explanatory repetition* of the former, and that, in point of meaning, they are to be regarded as equivalent.

[6] See *Scott, A. Clarke, Gill, &c.*   [7] 1 Cor. vi, 11.

Now, from the comparison of the other passages in the writings of this apostle, in which the same adverb is used, it appears that the term rendered *born again*, although denoting that birth which was in fact a second one, ought rather to be rendered " born *from above*."[8] It follows, therefore, that to be " born from above" and " to be born of water and the Spirit" are expressions which have the same meaning. But " *to be born from above*" can surely signify nothing less than to undergo that true regeneration—that real change of heart, which is indeed " from above," because it is effected only by the Spirit and power of the Almighty. Again, after speaking of this heavenly birth " of water and the Spirit," our Lord immediately drops his figurative allusion to water, and contrasts the *moral* change, of which alone he is speaking, with the birth of the flesh, " That which is born of the flesh, is flesh : and *that which is born of the Spirit, is spirit*."[9]

When the apostle Paul described the Corinthian Christians as persons who were " washed," " sanctified," and " justified, in the name of the Lord Jesus, and by the Spirit of our God;" and when, on another occasion, he made mention of the whole church as sanctified and cleansed " with the washing of water by the word;"[1] he probably derived his figurative language from the well-known Jewish custom of purification by water ; and yet the impartial critic will scarcely

---

[8] John iii, 3, 31; xix, 11, 23; *comp.* Matt. xxvii, 51; Mark xv, 38; James i, 17; iii, 15, 17. So *Schleusner in Lex.*
[9] John iii, 6.   [1] Eph. v, 26.

deny related *solely* to the operations of divine grace. The same remark applies to another passage in the writings of this apostle, which, while it plainly illustrates our Lord's doctrine respecting a birth " of *Titus* water and of the Spirit," affords additional information on the subject of true Christian baptism. " For we ourselves also," says the apostle to Titus, " were sometimes foolish, disobedient, deceived, serving divers lusts and pleasures, living in malice and envy, hateful, and hating one another. But, after that the kindness and love of God our Saviour toward man appeared, *not by works of righteousness which we have done*, but according to his mercy he saved us, by the *washing of regeneration, and renewing of the Holy Ghost*, which he shed on us abundantly, through Jesus Christ our Saviour."[2] Where is the enlightened Christian who will refuse to allow that, under these expressions, the apostle is promulgating a doctrine entirely spiritual? The " washing of regeneration" which is here distinguished from all our own works of righteousness, attributed solely to the merciful interposition of God our Saviour, and described as a *divine operation*, effectual for the salvation of souls, can surely be nothing else than the baptism of the Spirit, or, to adopt the apostle's own words of added explanation—" *the renewing of the Holy Ghost.*"

Another passage of similar import, is found in the epistle to the Hebrews; which I deem to *Hebrews* be rightly ascribed to the same inspired author.— " Having, therefore, boldness," says the apostle, " to

[2] Titus iii, 3—6.

enter into the holiest by the blood of Jesus, by a new and living way which he hath consecrated for us, through the veil, that is to say, his flesh; and having a High Priest over the House of God; let us draw near with a true heart, in full assurance of faith, having our hearts sprinkled from an evil conscience, and our bodies *washed with pure water*."[3] The " pure water" mentioned in this passage is explained by some critics as signifying the water of an outward baptism; but a little examination may serve to convince the candid inquirer, that such an interpretation is inconsistent with the whole scope of the apostle's argument. Every one who attentively peruses the ninth and tenth chapters of this admirable epistle, will observe that Paul is there unfolding the great doctrines of the Christian dispensation, as they were prefigured by the circumstances of the Jewish ceremonial law. The ritual appointed to be observed on the great day of atonement, as described in Lev. xvi, is that part of the Jewish institution to which he is particularly adverting. On that day, the High Priest was accustomed to enter into the Holy of holies, or inner sanctuary of the temple, after a careful washing or bathing of his own body. After this purification he offered up a bullock and a goat, as an atonement for sin, and sprinkled the blood of the victims on the mercy-seat and on the altar. These and similar ceremonies (among which he particularly mentions "divers baptisms") are treated of by the apostle as denoting the spiritual realities of the New Covenant; and when he proceeds to describe those realities, it is from the ordi-

[3] Chap. x, 19—22.

CHAP. 4.]   *in the Worship of God.*   125

nances of Judaism that he borrows his figures. As the mercy-seat and the altar, on the great day of atonement, and the people themselves on other occasions, were sprinkled with the blood of bulls and of goats, so are the hearts of Christians to be sprinkled from an evil conscience by the blood of Christ; and as the flesh of the priest, of the unclean person, or of the proselyte, was bathed in pure water, so is the natural man, to be cleansed and renewed by the purifying influence of the Holy Ghost. The " sprinkling of the heart" and the " washing of the body" are expressions equally metaphorical. The one denotes our deliverance from guilt; the other our purification from sin. The one is the application of the sacrifice of Christ; the other is the baptism of his Spirit.[4]

Such are the passages in the New Testament which contain indirect allusions to purification by water, and in which the circumstances of that rite are figuratively adverted to, in descriptions relating *exclusively* to the work of grace. We may now proceed to consider certain other passages of the same general import, in which the verb " baptize," or the substantive " baptism," are actually introduced. In the passages already cited, the baptism of the Spirit is represented by its characteristic circumstances. In those to which I am now about to invite the reader's attention, it is called by its name; it is described as a *baptism*.

The first passages to be adduced, of this description, are those which contain the declarations of John, the forerunner of Jesus, respecting the baptism of the Messiah, as contrasted with his own: one of these

[4] So *Calvin, Gill, and other Commentators.*

declarations is recorded by Matthew, Mark, and Luke, and the other by the apostle John. " I indeed baptize you with water unto repentance," cried the Baptist to the Pharisees and Sadducees, and to the whole multitude by whom he was surrounded;[5] " but he that cometh after me is mightier than I, whose shoes I am not worthy to bear: *he shall baptize you with the Holy Ghost and with fire:* whose fan is in his hand, and he will throughly purge his floor, and gather his wheat into the garner; but he will burn up the chaff with unquenchable fire."[6] Luke has recited the Baptist's declaration, in nearly the same words;[7] and Mark records it simply as follows: " John preached, saying, There cometh one mightier than I after me, the latchet of whose shoes I am not worthy to stoop down and unloose. I indeed have baptized you with water; but he shall baptize you with the Holy Ghost."[8] The manner in which *the baptism with fire*, mentioned in Matt. iii, 11, and Luke iii, 16, is introduced to notice, in immediate connexion with that of the Holy Ghost, affords strong reason to believe that it represents the enlightening, cleansing, refining operation of the Spirit upon the hearts of men. *One* thing is described, as Grotius observes on Matt. iii, 11, by two different modes of expression—an observation which derives confirmation from Mark i, 8, in which passage, the baptism ascribed to Christ, is only that with the Holy Ghost.[9] The other

---

[5] *Comp.* Luke iii, 16.   [6] Matt. iii, 11, 12.   [7] Chap. iii, 16, 17.
   [8] Chap. i, 7, 8.
   [9] Such is the view taken of the " fiery baptism" here mentioned, by many learned and able critics : for example, Munster, Erasmus,

CHAP. 4.] *in the Worship of God.* 127

declaration made by the Baptist to the same effect, is related by the apostle John, as follows: " And John bare record, saying, I saw the Spirit descending from heaven like a dove, and it abode upon him, and I knew him not: but he that sent me to baptize with water, the same said unto me, Upon whom thou shalt see the Spirit descending and remaining on him, the same is he *which baptizeth with the Holy Ghost.* And I saw and bare record that this is the Son of God."[1] Such is the contrast drawn by John between his own baptism and that of Christ. The one is with water, merely external; the other is with the Spirit and fire, internal and powerful. The one is the work of man, and like the minister who practised it, is " of the earth, *earthly,*" the other is *divine,* the work of the Son of God, who came from heaven, and " is above all."[2]

A precisely similar comparison was afterwards made by our Saviour himself. When he was on the point of quitting this lower world, the sphere of his humiliation, and was about to shed forth upon his disciples, in freshness and abundance, the gifts and graces of the Holy Spirit, he commanded them not to depart from Jerusalem, but to wait there for the " promise of the Father;" for " John truly," said he, " *baptized with water;* but ye shall be *baptized with the Holy Ghost* not many days hence."[3] Although the immediate

---

Vatablus, Clarius, Lud. Cappellus, and Calvin; Grotius I have already mentioned: See *Critic. Sacr. in loc.* An excellent exposition of Matt. iii. 11, will be found in the well-known and justly-valued commentaries of the late Thomas Scott.

[1] Chap. i, 32—34.   [2] John iii, 31.   [3] Acts i, 5.

disciples of Christ were endowed with a very unusual measure of the divine influence, it is always to be remembered that the promise of the Father was to all, in every age, who should truly believe in Jesus:[4] we may conclude, therefore, that all, in every age, who should believe in Jesus, were to receive, as well as the apostles themselves, the baptism of the Holy Ghost. Such, it is expressly declared, was the case with Cornelius and his family:[5] and such undoubtedly, must be the case with every Christian, whether more or less *gifted*, who is converted and sanctified by the influence of divine *grace*. Now, the general doctrine to be deduced from the declarations thus made both by the Baptist and by our Saviour, may be explicitly stated in a few words. It is, first, that the baptism which properly belonged to the dispensation of John, and which *distinguished it from Christianity*, was *the baptism with water;* and secondly, that the baptism which properly belongs to Christianity, and which distinguishes it from the dispensation of John, is the *baptism of the Spirit*.

The baptism of the Spirit is expressly mentioned by the apostle Paul. When describing the union which subsists among all the living members of the church of Christ, he writes as follows:—" For as the body is one, and hath many members, and all the members of that one body, being many, are one body; so also is Christ. *For by one Spirit are we all baptised into one body*, whether we be Jews or Gentiles, whether we be bond or free; and have been all made

---

[4] Acts ii, 39.   [5] Acts xi, 15, 16.

to drink into one Spirit."⁶ Baptism with water, as adopted among the early Christians, was nothing more than a sign of that conversion which introduced into the church of Christ. The baptism of the Spirit, here mentioned by the apostle, is that powerful and divine operation, which really effects such an introduction, and by which, therefore, all the believers in Christ are brought together and united as fellow-members of the same body.

Since this apostle has so frequently alluded to the work of the Spirit on the heart, *under the figure of washing in water ;*⁷ and since, in the passage now cited, he has plainly used the verb *baptize* in reference solely to that internal work, we are fully warranted in attributing to him a similar meaning on other occasions, when he makes use of the same verb, or its derivative substantive, in a manner somewhat less precise and defined. The examples to which I allude are as follows:—" Know ye not that so many of us as were baptized into Jesus Christ were baptized into his death? Therefore we are buried with him *by baptism* into death : that, like as Christ was raised up from the dead by the glory of the Father, even so we also should walk in newness of life."⁸ " In whom (that is, in Christ) ye are circumcised with the circumcision made without hands, in putting off the body of the sins of the flesh by the circumcision of Christ: buried with him *in baptism*, wherein also ye are risen with him through the faith of the opera-

⁶ 1 Cor. xii, 12, 13.
⁷ As in 1 Cor. vi, 11 ; Eph. v, 26 ; Tit. iii, 5 ; Heb. x, 22.
⁸ Rom. vi, 3, 4.

tion of God, who hath raised him from the dead."⁹ "For as many of you as *have been baptized into Christ* have put on Christ. There is neither Jew nor Greek, there is neither bond nor free, there is neither male nor female: for ye are all one in Christ Jesus."¹ That we are *correct* in the spiritual interpretation of these passages, they will severally be found, on examination, to afford a strong internal evidence. In Rom. vi, 4, baptism appears to be described as the *efficacious means* of our dying to sin and of our walking in newness of life. In Col. ii, 11, 12, to be buried with Christ by baptism, and to rise with him therein, are mentioned in immediate connexion, and apparently represented as the same, with being spiritually circumcised *in putting off the body of the sins of the flesh;* and it is moreover declared that the good effects of this baptism—this purifying influence, are produced in us by the *faith of the operation of God.* In Gal. iii, 27, those only are described as baptized into Christ who have actually "*put on* Christ,"² or who, in other words, are clothed with his righteousness, and are truly made one in him. Now, all these descriptions apply with the greatest accuracy to that baptism of the Spirit, to which Paul in other parts of his epistles has so frequently adverted; and they are, as completely inapplicable to the outward rite of immersion in water. On a general view, therefore, of the passages in which the apostle makes any doctrinal allusion to this

⁹ Col. ii, 11, 12.
¹ Gal. iii, 27, 21, *comp.* 1 Cor. xii, 12, 13.
² *Comp.* Rom. xiii, 14; Eph. iv, 24.

subject, we may fairly conclude that the only baptism of importance, in his view, was that of the Spirit; and that it was only to this inward work that he intended to direct the attention of his readers, when he expressed himself as follows:—"There is one body, and one Spirit, even as ye are called in one hope of your calling; one Lord, one faith, ONE BAPTISM."[3]

A very lucid declaration on the same subject may be found in the writings of the apostle Peter. After adverting to the events which happened in the days of Noah—"while the ark was a preparing, wherein few, that is, eight souls, were saved by water"—that apostle continues, "the *like figure* whereunto *even baptism* doth also now save us (not the putting away of the filth of the flesh, but the answer of a good conscience toward God,) by the resurrection of Jesus Christ."[4] The common English version of the first part of this verse is calculated to produce an erroneous impression of the apostle's meaning. There is nothing in the original Greek which conveys the idea that Christian baptism is a "*figure.*" The word rendered "the like *figure*" signifies, as is justly remarked by Schleusner, nothing more than that which is *similar* or *corresponding.* So Archbishop Newcome renders the apostle's words, "*And what answereth to this* (even) baptism doth now save us." I apprehend,

[3] Eph. iv, 4, 5.

[3**] There is one Lord, even Jesus Christ; one faith, even that of which *he* is the object; one baptism, even that of which *he* is the author; *comp.* Matt. iii, 11, 12.

[4] 1 Pet. iii, 21.

however, that the Greek would be still more accurately rendered, "A corresponding baptism whereunto doth now save us."[5] We are informed by the apostle Paul that the Israelites, who were led by the cloud, and passed through the sea, "were all *baptized* unto Moses in the cloud and in the sea."[6] On a similar principle, I conceive Peter to insinuate that Noah and his family, who were saved in the ark "by water," underwent a baptism of their own. By that baptism their natural lives were saved: and Christians enjoy a *corresponding* baptism which effects the salvation of their immortal souls. After drawing this comparison between the baptism of Noah, by which the life of the body was preserved, and the baptism of Christians, by which eternal life is secured for the soul, the apostle proceeds still further to determine his meaning by adding a definition, first, of that which this saving Christian baptism *is not*, and secondly, of that which *it is*. Accordingly, he informs us that it *is not* the putting away of the filth of the flesh—or, in other words, not the washing of the body in the water; and that it *is* the answer of a good conscience towards God. Now this answer or stipulation of a good conscience is the result of a moral change, of a real *regeneration*. This is the baptism which the apostle here describes as distinguishing Christianity, and as saving the soul of the believer. Nor is it like the baptism of water, the work of *man*. Peter expressly informs us that it, is "by the resurrection of Jesus Christ." It is effected by the power of that Saviour who is risen from the dead—"who is gone into heaven,

[5] ᾧ καὶ ἡμᾶς ἀντίτυπον νῦν σώζει βάπτισμα. [6] 1 Cor. x, 2.

CHAP. 4.]   *in the Worship of God*   133

and is on the right hand of God; angels and authorities and powers being made subject unto him."[7]

[7]** It is a satisfactory circumstance when we find persons who are wholly unconnected with Friends, and have probably but little knowledge either of the habits or principles of our Society, imbibing a truly spiritual view of Christian baptism. It has been my lot to meet with a few remarkable instances of this description in ministers of the Church of England; and a public example of the same kind, is afforded us by Thomas Stratten of Sunderland, the enlightened author of the "Book of the Priesthood." This author appears to have no hesitation in adopting a spiritual interpretation of many of the passages which have now been cited from the epistles of Paul and Peter, on the subject of Baptism. "The Minister of the gospel," says he "may baptize with water in the name of the Father, and of the Son, and of the Holy Ghost; but it is Christ's own prerogative, which he exercises in answer to the prayer of those who call upon him, to baptize with the Holy Ghost *into his death,* that being buried with him, by baptism, into death, we may also like him be raised up from the dead, to walk in newness of life;" see Rom. vi, 3, 4. *Book of Priesthood,* p. 198.

The following passage, on the same subject, is very luminous:

"We have found, in a quotation from the apostle Paul, a distinction made between the circumcision which was outward in the flesh, and that which was inward in the heart: we have also noticed evident indications of a corresponding distinction in the case of baptism, the visible application of water by the hand of man, and the invisible communication of the Holy Spirit's grace, from the hand of the exalted Redeemer. The passage in which this distinction is most specifically made, and by which this part of our subject is brought into close connexion with the work of our atoning and interceding Priest, has yet to be adduced. The waters of the deluge once saved the feeble remnant of the righteous, sweeping away in their flood the hosts of the ungodly, by which they were encompassed, and raising them to a new life of security, and separation from the wicked, in the ark into which they had retired. 'The like figure,' (says Peter) 'whereunto even baptism doth also now save us, *not* the putting away of the filth of the flesh,' (that is, the outward affusion of water upon the flesh) 'but the answer of a good conscience toward God, by the resurrection

With the exception of Mark xvi, 16, (a text presently to be cited) I believe we have now examined the *whole* of the passages in the New Testament which contain any *doctrinal* statement on the subject of bap-

of Jesus Christ: who is gone into heaven, and is on the right hand of God.'* The nature of that answer, and consequently of the baptism to which Peter refers, Paul illustrates, when surveying the marshalled legions of the Christian's foes, he defies the power of the whole, and triumphantly declares the ground on which security is enjoyed: 'Who shall lay anything to the charge of God's elect? It is God that justifieth. Who is he that condemneth? It is Christ that died, yea rather, that is risen again, who is even at the right hand of God, who also maketh intercession for us.'† The heart is sprinkled from an evil conscience, that is, a conscience uneasy and disturbed by a sense of its guilt before God, by the application of the blood of sprinkling, which speaketh better things than that of Abel. The answer of such a conscience is : I am safe, not because I have kept my baptismal vow, (for that no individual, who, either by his own lips, or by the lips of others appointed for him, has come under the obligation of a vow, has ever perfectly performed ;) but I am safe, because Jesus died for my sins, and rose again for my justification ; because I have fled for refuge to lay hold of the hope which is set before me in the gospel ; because I am baptized by the power of his Spirit, applying to my conscience the blood which cleanseth from all sin.

"This is the baptism, which, like the circumcision of the heart, rises so far in importance above ritual observances, that they may not with propriety be compared with it. Of the baptism which is administered by the hand of man, when compared with this, we may say, as the apostle did of circumcision, Neither is *that baptism* which is outward on the flesh. Whatever instruction and encouragement may be afforded by its administration, it has in it no inherent efficacy ; it conveys no grace, it is not essential to salvation. The things which accompany salvation, work 'that one and the selfsame Spirit.' 'For by one Spirit are we all baptized into one body, whether we be Jews or Gentiles, whether we be bond or

---

* 1 Peter iii, 21, 22. † Rom. viii, 33, 34.

tism. Now, the reader will probably recollect that, in the epistle to the Hebrews, which contains so noble an exposition of the spirituality of the Christian religion the " doctrine of baptisms " is mentioned as one of those rudiments of truth, which were familiar even to the babes in Christ.[7] Of the nature and principal features of that doctrine, the information of which we are in possession respecting the old baptisms of the Jews, together with the several passages of the New Testament which have now been considered, will enable us to form a sound and satisfactory estimate. Judging from the documents before me, I should say that this well known " doctrine of baptisms " must have been nearly as follows. That, under the legal dispensation, " divers carnal baptisms " were observed by the Jews as rites of purification ;[8] that among those rites was numbered the *baptism on conversion*, a ceremony to which the Israelites themselves submitted on their original entrance into the covenant of the law ;[9]

free ; and have all been made to drink into one Spirit.'[*] And this passage clearly and closely connects the subject with the interesting summary of essentials, which is given in another epistle written by the same apostle ; redeeming it from hands employed in ceremonies of human invention, by which it has been confused, perverted, and debased, and presenting it in harmony with the vital principles of the Gospel, which it has been our endeavour to unfold and establish. 'There is one body, and one Spirit, even as ye are called in one hope of your calling ; one Lord, one faith, *one baptism*, (by the one Spirit into the one body) one God and Father of all, who is above all, and through all, and in you all :'"[†] p. 205—208.

[7] Heb. v, 13, 14 ; vi, 2.   [8] Heb. ix, 10.   [9] Exod. xix, 14.

[*] 1 Cor. xii, 13.   [†] Eph. iv, 4—6.

and which was afterwards invariably practised in the admission of the proselytes of justice to the character and privileges of the native Jew;[1] that, under divine authority, this *baptism on conversion* was applied by John to the peculiar purposes of his own ministry;[2] that these ancient Jewish baptisms were severally effected by washing or immersion in *water*, that they were all figures of another and a better baptism, by which Christianity was distinguished from every preparatory dispensation— a baptism of which Christ is the author, and his disciples, in every age and country, the objects; that this true Christian baptism is applied not to the body, but to the soul, and is effected entirely by the power of the Holy Ghost; that by it we are regenerated or converted, sanctified and saved from sin; and, finally, that without it no man can find an entrance into the mansions of eternal glory.

We cannot fail to observe, that the "doctrine of baptisms," as it is thus unfolded on the authority of Scripture, perfectly consists with that great principle of the divine law, to which, in the preceding part of this chapter, we have so particularly adverted; namely that, under the last or Christian dispensation, God is no longer to be worshipped through the old medium of ceremonies, shadows, and types, but *in spirit and in truth.*

We may now proceed to consider another passage of the New Testament, in which it is very generally imagined that the practice of water-baptism is instituted as a Christian ordinance, and enjoined on the ministers of Christ. Matthew concludes his Gospel

[1] John iii, 5, 10.   [2] John i, 32—34.

CHAP. 4.] *in the Worship of God.* 137

with the following narration of our Lord's last address to his eleven apostles: and Jesus came and spake unto them, saying, All power is given unto me in heaven and in earth. Go ye, therefore, and teach all nations (or, as in the Greek, " Going therefore, make disciples of all nations") *baptizing them in* (or rather " into") *the name of the Father, and of the Son, and of the Holy Ghost:* teaching them to observe all things whatsoever I have commanded you; and, lo, I am with you alway, even unto the end of the world. Amen."[3]

That persons who have long been accustomed to regard water-baptism as sacred, should understand this passage as relating to it, is a circumstance which need not surprise us. Nevertheless, it ought to be observed that there is no mention made in the passage of *water*, or any thing whatsoever in the terms used, which renders such literal interpretation imperative upon us. On the contrary, I am persuaded that an impartial consideration of the collateral points which throw light on the true meaning of our Lord's injunction, will lead us to a very different view of that meaning.

Jesus commands his apostles to make disciples of all nations; and, in executing that high commission, it was to be their duty, as we learn from his subsequent words, to baptize the persons whom they taught, *into the name of the Father, and of the Son, and of the Holy Ghost.* Now, the peculiar solemnity of that parting moment, and the apparent improbability that, on *such* an occasion, a merely external ceremony

[3] Matt. xxviii, 18—20.

should be so prominently brought forward—the method so often employed by Jesus, of conveying instruction and precept, concerning spiritual things, in words which bore an outward allusion to the flesh[4]—the frequent occurrence of the terms " baptize" and " baptism" in the New Testament, and particularly in the discourses of Christ himself, in a sense purely metaphorical—the abolition, under the new dispensation, of the whole Jewish ritual, and the substitution of a spiritual worship—the evidence derived from so many other explicit passages of Scripture, in favour of the doctrine that the baptism of Christianity is the work of the Spirit only—the pointed manner in which Jesus himself, in a preceding part, as is most probable, of this very conversation, contrasted that powerful influence, which was the privilege of his own followers, with the water-baptism of John[5]—all these are collateral circumstances which bear, with no slight degree of force, on the passage before us, and which, when considered as a whole, appear to afford substantial evidence that the baptism here referred to by the Redeemer of men, was simply a *spiritual baptism.*

It is, indeed, true that the baptism of the Spirit is elsewhere attributed to Christ himself. Undoubtedly it is a *divine* work; but, originating, as it ever must do, with our divine Master, this baptism might nevertheless *be administered* by the instrumentality of his servants. In as much as the apostles of Jesus Christ were enabled, through the efficacy of an inspired ministry, to turn away their hearers from idolatry and

[4] See, for example, John iv, 14, 32 ; vii, 38.
[5] Acts i, 5.

Chap. 4.]   *in the Worship of God.*   139

other sins, to introduce them to a state of comparative purity, and to convert them to the true faith; in so much did they possess the power to baptize, in a spiritual sense, into the name of the Father, and of the Son, and of the Holy Ghost. It appears to be on the same principle that Christ is described by the apostle Paul as applying to his own church the baptism of the Spirit—as sanctifying and cleansing it " with the washing of water"—" *by the word*,"[6] that is, probably, by the ministry of the Gospel.[7] " The preaching of the cross," when prompted and dictated by the Holy Spirit, is often found to be " the power of God."[8] The ministers of the Gospel ought, however, always to remember, that they can administer the baptism of the Spirit only through the power of their Lord and Saviour; and in their humble efforts to perform so sacred a duty, they must derive their encouragement from that gracious promise—" *Lo, I am with you alway, even unto the end of the world.*"

Upon the present point it only remains to be observed, that the observations now offered on Matt. xxviii, 19, 20, will be found to derive material support from the parallel passage in the Gospel of Mark; " Go ye into all the world, and preach the gospel to every creature. *He that believeth and is baptized shall be saved*, &c.[9] Here the baptism, to which our Lord is described as adverting, is classed with that faith which is essential to our salvation. *It is the baptism which saves.* Now,

[6] The expression in the original Greek is not λόγος, which sometimes signifies the essential Word of God, and is applied as a title to the Son himself, but 'ῥῆμα.

[7] Eph. v, 26; *comp.* Rom. x, 17.   [8] 1 Cor. i, 18.
[9] Mark xvi, 15, 16.

we are assured that the baptism which saves is " not the putting away of the filth of the flesh," or any work of righteousness which we can perform for ourselves;[1] it is that birth of water and the Spirit, which is " from above," and which prepares us for an entrance into the kingdom of heaven:[2] it is " the answer of a good conscience toward God, by the resurrection of Jesus Christ;[3] it is " the washing of regeneration, and renewing of the Holy Ghost."[4]

On a review of the various passages cited in the present chapter, my readers will probably agree with me in the sentiment, that there is no part of the New Testament, in which the observance of baptism *in water* is either *commanded or declared to be necessary.* Such being the case, I know of nothing which remains to be pleaded in support of that ceremony as a part of the religious service of Christians, but *the example of the apostles.* That many of the apostles were accustomed, both before and after the ascension of Jesus, to baptize their converts in water, is indeed rendered indisputable by certain passages in the Gospel of John and in the book of Acts. But this fact by no means affords any sufficient evidence that the practice of a similar rite is universally imperative on the ministers of Christianity. The spirituality of the new dispensation—the great principle, that God was no longer to be served by the intervention of sacerdotal and typical institutions, but only through the mediation of the Son, and under the influence of the Holy Spirit, was very gradually unfolded to these servants of the Lord.

[1] Titus iii, 5.   [2] John iii, 5.   [3] 1 Peter iii, 21.
[4] Titus iii, 5.

CHAP. 4.] *in the Worship of God.* 141

It is notorious that many of them adhered with strictness to a great part of the Jewish ritual, long after it was abrogated by the death of Christ; and, even on the Gentile converts, they enjoined an abstinence from things strangled and from blood, (that is, from the blood of animals,) no less imperatively than from the sin of fornication.[5] It is true that, after they had ceased to recommend circumcision to the Gentiles, they continued to baptize them in water. But the reason of this distinction is plain: namely, that circumcision was the sign of an entrance into the covenant of the law, but that baptism, although a Jewish practice, and observed on the principles of Judaism, was the type of conversion to Christianity itself, and was, therefore, very naturally considered by the apostles as appropriate to the specific purposes of their own ministry. As long as they observed the ceremonies of Judaism in their own persons; as long as they continued unprepared for a full reception of the doctrine, that the ordinances and shadows of the law were now to be disused, and that God was to be worshipped spiritually: so long would they, *as a matter of course*, persevere in the practice of baptizing their converts *in water*. Neither are we to imagine that, in this respect, the apostles acted in opposition to the will of their divine Master, who appears to have imposed upon them no sudden change of conduct respecting ritual observances, but simply to have left them in possession of those great principles of spiritual religion, the tendency of which was to undermine these practices at the foun-

[5] Acts xv, 29.

dation, and thus, in a gradual manner, to effect their abolition.

But there is another reason why the example of the earliest Christian teachers affords no valid evidence, that the practice of water-baptism is still incumbent on the ministers of the gospel of Christ—namely, that this example is not uniform. Its uniformity is known to have been interrupted by two exceptions of peculiar weight and importance. The exception which I shall first notice is that of the apostle Paul. That eminent individual—who was not "a whit behind the chiefest apostles," and who had formerly been a "Pharisee of the Pharisees," and a zealot in the support of the Jewish law—when he was once converted to the Christian faith, was the first to throw off the bondage of that law, and he presently excelled his brethren in his views of the spirituality of the gospel dispensation. Accordingly, we find that baptism with water was, in his judgment, by no means indispensable, or inseparably connected with the duties of a Christian minister. Although it is probable that his converts were generally baptized in water, a large proportion of them received no such baptism at the hands of the apostle. He expressly asserts that, among the whole multitude of the Corinthians who had been converted by his ministry, he baptized *none* save Crispus and Gaius, and the household of Stephanas.[6] It is not, however, merely the apostle's personal abstinence from the use of the rite which claims our attention in reference to the present argument: it is rather the ground and

---

[6] 1 Cor. i, 14—16.

principle on which he declares that he abstained from it. The practice of this ceremony in the Christian church is supported chiefly by the generally received opinion that Christ commanded his apostles, when they made disciples of all nations, to baptize them with water; and that from the apostles this duty has descended to all rightly-authorized ministers who, like them, are engaged in the promulgation of Christian truth. But Paul, highly favoured as he was, as a minister of the gospel, and engaged far more extensively than any of his brethren in the work of making disciples of all nations, abstained, to a very great extent, from the act of baptizing with water; and for this express reason—*that he had received no commission to perform it:*—" For Christ," said he, " sent me not to baptize but to preach the gospel.[7]

The other exception alluded to, is one of still greater moment: it is that of the divine founder of our religion. The Lord Jesus Christ rendered, in his own person, a complete obedience to all righteousness, as it was observed under the law; and therefore he submitted to the baptism of John. But his own converts, who belonged to that spiritual institution which he so frequently denominates the " kingdom of heaven,"[8] he *baptized not*. Although he permitted his disciples to practise the ceremony, he abstained from it himself. This fact is noticed by the apostle John, who, after stating that " the Pharisees heard that Jesus made and baptized more disciples than John," carefully adds, (for the prevention of error, no doubt,

[7] Verse 17.   [8] See Matt. xi. 11, &c.

on so interesting a subject,) "though (or howbeit) *Jesus himself baptized not*, but his disciples."[9] Those preachers of the gospel, therefore, who consider it their duty, in conformity with the great fundamental law of Christian worship, to abstain from the practice of baptizing their converts in water, have the consolation to know that, in adopting such a line of conduct, they are following the example of him who afforded us a *perfect* pattern.

Since, therefore, water baptism was a Jewish ceremonial or typical observance; since, under the new dispensation, the plan of divine worship is changed, and all such observances are, by a general law, abolished; since, in precise conformity with that law, " the doctrine of baptisms," as unfolded in various passages of the New Testament, appears to attribute to Christianity *only* the baptism of the Spirit; since that particular passage in which the outward rite is supposed to be enjoined upon Christians may, with the truest critical propriety, be otherwise explained: and since the example of the first preachers of Christianity, in favour of that ceremony, arose out of peculiar circumstances, and was interrupted by two overpowering exceptions—I cannot but deem it undeniable that Friends are fully justified in their disuse of water baptism.

I may now proceed to the consideration of those parts of the New Testament which relate to the practice called the *Lord's Supper*.

[9] John iv. 1, 2.

CHAP. 4.] *in the Worship of God.* 145

In order to clear our ground respecting its nature and character, it is desirable, in the first place, to direct our attention to the tenth chapter of the First Epistle of Paul to the Corinthians—a chapter which contains a remarkable allusion to the Lord's supper, as it was observed by the early Christians. It appears that some of the Corinthian converts had so far sacrificed their religious consistency, as to join the banquets of their heathen neighbours, and to feast with them upon meats which had been previously offered to idols. Such was the unchristian practice which suggested to the apostle Paul the following reproof and exhortation: " I speak as to wise men: judge ye what I say. The cup of blessing which we bless, (or for which we give thanks,) is it not a *joint participation (Eng. Trans.* " the communion ") of the blood of Christ? The bread which we break, is it not a *joint participation (Eng, Trans.* " the communion ") of the body of Christ? For we being many are one bread, and one body: for we are all partakers of that one (or that same) bread. Behold Israel after the flesh: are not they which eat of the sacrifices *(joint) partakers* of the altar? What say I then? that the idol is any thing, or that which is offered in sacrifice to idols is any thing? But I say, that the things which the Gentiles sacrifice, they sacrifice to devils, and not to God: and I would not that ye should *be joint partakers in (Eng. Trans,* " have fellowship with") devils. Ye cannot drink the cup of the Lord and the cup of devils: ye cannot be partakers of the Lord's table and of the table of devils. Do we provoke the Lord to jealousy? Are we stronger than he?"[1] In reciting this passage, I have ventured upon some slight alteration of the common English version. The word "communion" is properly defined by Johnson, "a participation of something in common," and this, no doubt, is the sense in which it was here employed by our translators. I have exchanged that word for "*joint participation*," merely for the purpose of showing the manner in which the true meaning of the original expression,[2] as it is here applied, is fixed by the use, in two other parts of the same passage, of the corresponding noun, rendered, *joint partakers*.[3]

On a comparison with certain parts of the following chapter, (hereafter to be noticed,) it must, in all fairness, be allowed that the bread and wine, which the apostle here declares to be a "joint participation in the body and blood of Christ," are those which were eaten and drunk, in a literal sense, at the supper called by the apostle himself, *the Lord's supper*.[4] It appears, then, that those who ate and drank together of that bread and wine, were joint partakers of the body and blood of Christ, on the same principle, and in the same sense, that the Jews, who ate together of the sacrifices ordained by the law, were joint partakers of the altar; and the Christians, who united with idolators in the eating of meats offered to false gods were joint partakers with them in *devils*. It is plain, therefore, that the Christian communicants are not here represented as *feeding on the body and blood of Christ*, any more than the Jews are described as feeding on the altar; but only as jointly partaking in

---

[1] 1 Cor. x, 15—22. [2] κοινωνία.
[3] κοινωνοί. [4] Chap. xi, 20.

those things which *had respect to* the body and blood of Christ.

I have entered into this examination of the passage before us, not so much for the purpose of disproving the Roman Catholic doctrine of transubstantiation, as in order to show that the apostle's words give no real countenance to the notion, so generally entertained among Protestants, that those who rightly communicate in the rite of the Lord's supper *do thereby feed together, in a spiritual sense, on the body and blood of Christ.*

The declarations of this doctrine, unfounded as it appears to be on the authority of Scripture, are in the communion service of the Church of England, both frequent and striking. The "sacrament of the Lord's supper" is there denominated a "*holy mystery,*" and a "*banquet of most heavenly food.*" Thanksgiving is enjoined unto God, "for that he hath given his Son our Saviour Jesus Christ, not only to die for us, but *also to be our spiritual food and sustenance* in that holy sacrament;" and, on another occasion, this service states that, when "we receive that holy sacrament, then we spiritually eat the flesh of Jesus Christ and drink his blood; then we dwell in Christ and Christ in us: we are one with Christ and Christ with us."

By such language a mystical importance is attached to the rite, which appears to have no foundation in its original use as a memorial of the death of Jesus. In these days of increasing light and spirituality, as we may justly esteem them, it is necessary to say but very little on this branch of our subject.

Although Christians, while they are partaking of the bread and wine, may sometimes be permitted to "eat the flesh and drink the blood of the Son of man," no arguments need now be advanced to prove that this spiritual eating and drinking has no necessary or even peculiar connexion with any external ceremony; and that, in every time and place, it may be the privilege of the humble Christian, who lives by faith in the Son of God, and whose soul is subjected to the purifying, yet sustaining influence of his Holy Spirit.[5] Neither will it be any longer disputed that, when persons of such a character meet in companies for the solemn purpose of worshipping the Father, they may, without any use of the outward ordinance, *feed together, in a spiritual sense, on the body and blood of Christ*, and experience the truest communion with their Holy Head, and with one another *in Him*.[6]

Having premised these remarks on the apostle's description of the Lord's supper, we may henceforward consider it in that more simple light in which alone I believe it to be regarded, in the present day, by many of those persons who observe it; namely, as an *outward ceremony, constituting part of divine worship, and intended typically to represent, and thus to bring into remembrance, the death and sacrifice of Christ;* and we may proceed to examine those passages of the New Testament which have given rise to the opinion, so generally entertained, that such a rite was ordained by our Saviour, and that the practice of it is universally obligatory on believers in Christ. The passages to which I have to refer, under this head

---

[5] See John vi, 53, 58, 63. [6] See Matt. xviii, 20.

CHAP. 4.] *in the Worship of God.* 149

are only two in number. The first is in the Gospel of Luke, who, in describing the last paschal supper which Jesus ate with his disciples shortly before his crucifixion, writes as follows: " And he (Jesus) took bread and gave thanks, and brake it, and gave unto them, saying, This is my body which is given for you: *this do in remembrance of me.* Likewise, also, the cup after supper, saying, This cup is the new testament in my blood, which is shed for you."[7]

The second passage alluded to, contains a declaration of the apostle Paul, which fully confirms the particulars related by Luke. It appears that the Corinthian converts had so greatly abused the practice to which the injunction of Christ had given rise, that when they met together for the purpose of eating the Lord's supper in company, there was found among them a total want of order and harmony; and many of them availed themselves of such occasions, for the intemperate indulgence of their carnal appetites; " For, in eating," says the apostle, " every one taketh before other his own supper; and one is hungry and another is drunken." In order to correct habits of so disgraceful a character, Paul sharply reproves these Corinthians, and calls to their recollection the origin and object of the observance. " For I have received of the Lord," says he, " that which also I delivered unto you, That the Lord Jesus, the same night in which he was betrayed, took bread: and when he had given thanks, he brake it, and said, Take, eat; this is my body, which is broken for you; *this do in remembrance of me.* After the same manner also he took the cup,

[7] Luke xxii, 19, 20.

when he had supped, saying, This cup is the new testament in my blood; this do ye, as oft as ye drink it, in remembrance of me. For as often," adds the apostle, " as ye eat this bread, and drink this cup, ye do show the Lord's death till he come. Wherefore whosoever shall eat this bread, and drink this cup of the Lord, unworthily, shall be guilty of the body and blood of the Lord. But let a man examine himself, and *so* let him eat of that bread, and drink of that cup. For he that eateth and drinketh unworthily, eateth and drinketh condemnation to himself, not discerning the Lord's body."[8]

It will be observed that, in this address to the Corinthians, the apostle is not *enjoining* upon them the practice of observing the Lord's supper. The passage contains no *command* of the apostle's to that effect: it was intended solely to warn them against the abuse of that practice, and to explain to them its origin and true purpose. Accordingly, he briefly recites the circumstances which had given rise to it. The knowledge of these circumstances, it appears, he had " received of the Lord;"[9] and the apostle's statement,

[8] 1 Cor. xi, 23—29.

[9] *For I have received of the Lord.* Ἐγὼ γὰρ παρέλαβον ἀπὸ του Κυρίου. That commentators are by no means unanimous in the opinion that an immediate revelation is here intended, will be sufficiently evinced by the following short abstract, given in Pool's Synopsis, of the remarks made on this passage by certain eminent critics, and particularly by Beza. "It may be doubted whether the apostle learned these things *mediately* from those who were eye and ear witnesses, on the narration of the other apostles, or immediately by revelation. He learned them *of the Lord;* that is as proceeding from the Lord ; the information being given to him by Ananias, or the other disciples, or else of the Lord by revela-

CHAP. 4.] *in the Worship of God.* 151

founded on the instruction thus given to him on the subject, substantially accords with the narration of Luke. We are, therefore, to consider it as a fact resting on *confirmed* evidence, that, when our Lord, at his last paschal supper, invited his disciples to take and eat the bread which he had broken, he added, " *This do in remembrance of me:*" and, further, we learn from the apostle that, after Jesus had handed to them the cup to drink, he repeated a similar command, —" *This do ye, as oft as ye drink it, in remembrance of me.*"

Persons who have been long habituated to associate these expressions of our Lord with the rite of the Eucharist, *as they themselves observe it*, are naturally led to explain the former by the latter: and thus, with respect to the passages now quoted, they lose sight of those simple principles of interpretation, which they would, of course, apply to any other part of the sacred volume. I confess, I see no other way of accounting for the sentiment, still so prevalent among Christians, that when our Lord, after partaking with his disciples in the Passover supper, said to them, " Do this in remembrance of me," he instituted a religious cere-

tion. In the latter case, however, he would not have said ἀπό but παρά, according to the usage of Greek authors in general, of the writers of the New Testament in particular, and more especially of Paul himself." Other commentators understand the passage in a still more general sense, as implying only that the matters which Paul communicated to the Corinthians, respecting the Lord's supper, were no invention of his own, but rested on divine authority. So Camero and Calvin. Rosenmüller, one of the most able and impartial of modern biblical critics, expresses a clear judgment that no direct revelation was here alluded to by the apostle : Vide *Schol. in N. T. in loc.*

mony, which was thenceforward to form an essential part of worship; and which, in that point of view, was to be binding, in all ages, on the believers in Jesus. That the words of Christ, when tried by the test of common rules, and explained by the circumstances under which they were spoken, *do not appear, and cannot be proved, to have been fraught with so extensive a meaning*, will probably be allowed by the candid and considerate critic; and I would suggest that no such meaning can justly be applied to them, for two reasons.

That our Lord's words, in the first place, are not rightly interpreted as relating to a *typical ceremony in connexion with Christian worship*, there arises a strong presumption, on this general ground—that such an interpretation is directly at variance with the acknowledged fact, that the old Jewish system of types was then about to be abrogated by the death of Christ; and with our Saviour's own law, that the Father was now to be worshipped, not according to the shadowy ritual of the Jews and Samaritans, but in spirit and in truth.

Secondly, it is to be observed that the command of Jesus respecting the bread and wine was addressed only to twelve persons, and was of a nature simply *positive*. It is true that all the precepts of Jesus were addressed to those persons who were in his company at the time when they were uttered, and many of them probably to his apostles only; but there is an excellent reason why the bulk of them are to be received as of universal obligation—namely that they are *moral* in their nature, and belong to that unchangeable law of God which, when revealed, demands the obedience of all men at all times. But a merely positive precept has no connexion with that unchangeable law, and does nothing more than enjoin, for some specific purpose, a practice *in itself* indifferent. Such a precept, therefore, appears to contain no sufficient *internal* evidence of its being binding on any persons, except those to whom it was actually addressed, and others who were placed under the same peculiar circumstances. I would suggest that a universal obligation, on the followers of any *moral* lawgiver, to obey a precept of the nature now described, cannot be rightly admitted, unless it be by such lawgiver expressly declared; and that its not being so declared, affords an indication that no such universality was intended.

The present argument may be fitly illustrated by another example of a similar nature. On the very same affecting occasion, when Jesus directed his apostles to observe the practice now under consideration, he also enjoined them to *wash one another's feet.* We read in the Gospel of John that, after that last paschal supper, Jesus rose from the table, took a towel, girded himself, poured water into a basin, and "began to wash his disciples' feet, and to wipe them with the towel wherewith he was girded." After thus evincing the lowliness of his mind, he said to his disciples, " Know ye what I have done unto you? Ye call me Master and Lord, and ye say well; for so I am. If I then, your Lord and Master, have washed your feet, *ye ought also to wash one another's feet; for I have given you an example, that ye should do as I have done to you.*" Here was an injunction conveyed to the apostles, in words fully as explicit, and with accompaniments equally striking, as was the preceding command respecting the bread and wine. Yet, since that injunction was simply positive, relating to an act of no moral importance in itself, and one which was connected with the peculiar habits of the persons thus addressed—no one supposes that an obedience to such an injunction is necessary for Christians of every age and country. Undoubtedly, that mutual respect and benevolence, of which the washing of one another's feet was thus enjoined on some of his servants as an instance and a sign, is incumbent on all the followers of Jesus. Universally incumbent upon them, also, is that love and allegiance towards their Saviour, and that dependence upon his atoning death, which the apostles were accustomed to express by their commemorative supper. But, in both cases, according to the view of Friends on the subject, the outward circumstance may be omitted, without any infraction of the revealed will of God.

In confirmation of these arguments, the reader's attention may now be called to a very striking fact; namely, that, in the Gospel of Matthew, which was written by an eye witness, and at an earlier date than that of Luke, and which contains a very exact description of our Lord's last supper with his disciples, of the breaking of the bread, of the handing of the cup, and of the comparison made by Jesus of the one with his body and of the other with his blood; the words upon which *alone* could have been founded the institution of this supposed Christian rite—" Do this in remembrance of me"—*are omitted.* We are not to conclude from this omission that those words were not spoken. That they were spoken, on the contrary, is certain, on the authority of both Luke and Paul. But, since Matthew describes all the circumstances of the occasion, and gives the whole of our Lord's address, with the single exception of these words, we can hardly suppose him to have understood that the precept of Jesus was of that *very leading* importance which is generally imagined; or, that our Lord then instituted a rite which was, in every age of the church, to form an essential part of Christian worship. Precisely the same observation applies to the Gospel of Mark, which is supposed to have been written under the immediate superintendence of the apostle Peter.

What, then, may be deemed a fair and reasonable interpretation of our Lord's very simple precept? and in what signification would the twelve apostles, to whom these words were addressed, naturally understand them? In order to give a satisfactory answer to this inquiry, we may, in the first instance, observe, that the apostles were all Jews or Galileans; that they had long been accustomed to observe the rites of the supper of the Passover, and that among those rites were numbered (as has been already stated) the breaking of the bread, and the handing of the cup, with the blessing and giving of thanks. As they had already been habituated to these customs, so was the Lord Jesus well aware that they would still maintain them: for, as it has been already remarked, the apostles continued in the practice of parts of the Jewish ritual, long after the crucifixion of our Lord; and, although that ritual was abolished by his death, the sudden disuse of it does not appear to have been enjoined upon them by their divine Master. Having these facts in our view, we may reasonably interpret the words of Jesus as commanding nothing more than that his apostles should call *him* to their recollection when they met to celebrate the supper of the Passover. " This cup," said Jesus, "is the new testament in my blood." Now, it was not every cup of wine which represented the new testament in the blood of Christ: it was the cup of wine drunk at the supper of the Passover—an institution which they were then celebrating, and which, in some of its circumstances, was expressly typical of the death of the Messiah. It appears, then, by no means very improbable, that it was to the cup of the passover exclusively that our Saviour's injunction applied—"This do ye, *as oft as ye drink it*, in remembrance of me;" that is, as often as ye meet together to celebrate the supper of the Passover, and to drink of that cup, which represents the new testament in my blood, take care that ye forget not the true purport of the ceremony—do it in remembrance of *me*.

Such appears to be an easy and natural interpretation of our Lord's words. Nevertheless, it cannot be denied that they are capable of a sense somewhat more extensive. Although the breaking of the bread, the handing of the wine, &c., formed a part of the Jewish ceremonial order of the Passover supper, there is reason to believe that a similar method was observed in those more common meals, of which the Jews were accustomed to partake in one another's company.

Thus, when Jesus, on a subsequent occasion, "sat at meat" with the two disciples at Emmaus, we again find him blessing, breaking, and distributing the bread;[1] and when Paul had induced his companions, on the voyage, to unite with him in taking the needful food, we read that "he took bread, and gave thanks to God in the presence of them all: and when he had broken it, he began to eat."[2] Such being the common practice of the Jews, it is very probable that the apostles might understand our Lord's injunction as not confined to the Passover supper, but as extending to other more familiar occasions, when they might be gathered together to partake of a common meal. On these occasions, as well as at the Passover supper, they might consider it a duty laid upon them by their beloved Master, to break their bread, and to drink of their cup, not only for the satisfaction of their natural appetites, but in commemoration of the body which was broken, and of the blood which was shed, for their sakes.

That the Lord Jesus was thus understood by some of his hearers, may be collected from the known practice of the church, at the very earliest period of its history. Of those numerous persons who were converted by means of the ministry of Peter, on the day of Pentecost, we read that "they continued stedfastly in the apostles' doctrine and fellowship, and in breaking of bread, and in prayers."[3] Since the "breaking of bread" is here mentioned among other signs of religious communion, it probably signifies (according to the general opinion of biblical critics) *that* break-

---
[1] Luke xxiv, 30.   [2] Acts xxvii. 35.   [3] Acts ii, 42.

ing of bread which was introduced as a memorial of the death of Christ. Nevertheless, that the practice in question was observed as a part of the social meal, is evident from the immediate context. " And all that believed," adds the historian, " were together, and had all things common......and they, continuing daily with one accord in the temple, and *breaking bread from house to house, did eat their meat with gladness and singleness of heart.*"[4] On another occasion, when we are informed that, " on the first day of the week," the disciples at Troas " came together to break bread ;"[5] there is no reason to suppose that they met for the purpose of performing a religious ceremony. It appears, rather, that they came together to partake of a brotherly repast, of which it is probable that *one* particular object was the joint commemoration of the death of their Lord. After Paul had taken the opportunity, afforded him by this meeting, of preaching at length to the disciples, it is obvious that he brake bread with them for the refreshment of his body, and for the satisfaction of the demands of nature. " When he, therefore, was come up again," says Luke, " and *had broken bread, and eaten*, and talked a long while, even till break of day, so he departed."[6]

Lastly, the same fact is evident from the description given by Paul of the abuses which had crept in among his Corinthian converts in their method of conducting these common repasts. " When ye come together, therefore, into one place, this is not to eat the Lord's supper. For, in eating, every one taketh before other his own supper; and one is hungry, and

[4] Ver. 44, 46.   [5] Acts xx, 7.   [6] Ver. 11.

another is drunken. What? have ye not houses to eat and to drink in? or despise ye the church (or assembly) of God, and shame them that have not? What shall I say to you? shall I praise you in this? I praise you not."[7] After thus reproving them, and after explaining to them, in a passage already cited, the origin and true object of the observance which they had thus abused, the apostle, zealous as he was for the right order of this Christian meal, concludes with the following exhortation; " Wherefore, my brethren, *when ye come together to eat*, tarry one for another; and if any man hunger,[8] let him eat at home, that ye come not together unto condemnation."

The supper, which the apostle here describes as the Lord's supper, which the Corinthians had so shamefully misconducted, and during the course of which the bread was broken, and the wine handed about, in commemoration of the death of Christ, was probably the same as was otherwise called " love," or the " supper of love." " Their coming together," says Theophylact, on 1 Cor. xi, 20, (or rather Chrysostom, from whom his commentaries were borrowed,) " was intended as a sign of love and fellowship; and he *denominates this social banquet the Lord's supper*, because it was the imitation of that awful supper which the Lord ate with his disciples."[9] These sup-

[7] 1 Cor. xi, 20—22.
[8] Vide *Grotii Comm. in loc.* " Est χλευασμὸς *(irrisio acerba.)* Loquitur, enim tanquam pueris qui ita solent esse ὀξύπεινοι *(famelici)* ut quidvis arripiant, nec alios, ad partem vocent, neque velint σῦκα μερίζειν *(ficus partiri.)*"
[9] So Grotius, Estius, Justinian, and others—see Poli Synopsis.

pers of love, or " love-feasts," are alluded to by the apostles Peter[1] and Jude;[2] and are described by Pliny,[3] as well as by Tertullian[4] and other early fathers.[5] It appears that they were frugal public repasts, of which the poor and the rich, in the early Christian churches, partook together, and which were regarded both as the symbols and pledges of brotherly love. Such, then, was the " Lord's supper" of the primitive Christians; such were the occasions on which they were accustomed to break their bread, and drink their wine, as a memorial of the body and blood of Christ.[6]

To the simple practice which thus prevailed among these primitive Christians (if preserved within proper

[1] 2 Peter ii, 13.   [2] Ver. 12.   [3] *Epin.* lib. x, 97.
[4] *Apol. adv. Gentes,* cap. 39.
[5] *Clem. Alex. Pæd.* lib. ii, cap. 1, *Constit. Apostol.* lib. ii, cap. 28, &c.
[6] Vide *Schleusner Lex. in loc.* ἀγάπη, No. 7. "'Αγάπαι, agapæ, (love-feats,) faerunt convivia publica in conventibus Christianorum sacris instituta, conjuncta in primitiva et apostolica ecclesia cum celebratione festiva cœnæ Dominicæ, ita dicta quod Christianæ charitatis symbola essent et tesseræ," &c. The celebration of the Eucharist, and that of the *love-feast,* appear to be mentioned by Ignatius (A.D. 101) as identical. " Let that be considered," says the ancient father, "a *valid Eucharist,* which is under the care of a bishop, and in which he takes a part. Where the bishop appears, there let the people attend. It is unlawful either to baptize or to celebrate the *love-feast* without the bishop." *Ep. ad Smyrn. ch.* 8, So we are informed by Tertullian (A.D. 200,) that, even in his day, the Eucharist was received by Christians in connection with their meals : " Eucharistiæ sacramentum *et in tempore victus,* et omnibus mandatum a Domino, etiam antelucanis cœtibus, nec de aliorum manu quam præsidentium sumimus." *De Coron. Milit. cap.* 3. *Ed. Semleri,* iv, 341. See also *Grotius and Whitby, on* 1 Cor. x and xi.

bounds) there appears to be nothing which can fairly be objected. It was a practice which might be classed rather under the head of pious customs than under that of direct religious ceremonies. It was, perhaps, little more than giving to one of the common occasions of life a specific direction of an edifying character; and under the peculiar circumstances of these early disciples, it might be considered no inconsistent result of that general law, that, whether we eat or drink, or whatsoever we do, all is to be done to the glory of God, and in the *name of the Lord Jesus.* But, appropriate as these feasts of charity might be to the condition of the infant church, when the believers were comparatively few in number, and in a considerable degree possessed all things in common, they would evidently be much less adapted for the use of those vast multitudes of persons, very slightly connected with each other, who profess Christianity in modern times. As the numbers increased in any church, who would, as members of it, possess a right to attend the *love-feasts,* there would necessarily arise a great danger of abuse in such a practice; and that this abuse actually took place in the church of Corinth, to an alarming and disgraceful degree, we have already noticed on the authority of the apostle Paul.

On the one hand, therefore, we may allow that those persons who continue the observance of the Lord's supper, not as a religious ceremony constituting a necessary part of divine worship, but *on the simple system of the primitive Christians,* are not without their warrant, for the adoption of such a course. On the other hand, it is no less evident that the apparent unsuitableness of the custom to the present condition of the visible church, its known liability to abuse, and, more especially, its close *affinity* with the abolished ritual of the Jews, appear to afford sufficient reasons for its discontinuance.

That there is nothing in the history of the origin of that custom which precludes, under so obvious a change of circumstances, *the liberty of its disuse*, the reader will probably allow, for reasons already stated. Here, however, it appears necessary to notice an expression of the apostle Paul's, from which many persons have derived an opinion that this practice is binding on believers in Jesus, *until the end of the world*. "For as oft as ye eat this bread, and drink this cup," says the apostle, in a passage already cited, "*ye do show the Lord's death till he come.*" The inference deduced from these words respecting the *necessary* permanence of the rite of the Lord's supper appears to be ill founded. For, in the first place, they contain no *command* to the Corinthians to continue the practice in question until the Lord's coming: and in the second place, it is evident, from the context, that it was not here the apostle's object to impress upon his friends the *duration* of the custom, but rather its *meaning* or *direction*. The stress of his declaration plainly lies upon the words, "*Ye do show the Lord's death.*" The words "*till he come*" appear to be added, as a kind of reservation, for the purpose of conveying the idea that, when the Lord himself should come, such a memorial of his death would be obsolete and unnecessary. It is the belief of Friends that the *principle* on which this reservation is made, substantially agrees with their own sentiment, that the spiritual presence of the Lord Jesus with his disciples, and the direct communion with him, which they are even now permitted to enjoy, virtually abrogate any practice in his service, which is of a merely symbolical character.

The view now taken of the apostle's doctrine will fitly introduce a concluding remark—that, while Friends consider it to be their duty to abstain from that ritual participation in bread and wine, so usually observed among their fellow Christians, there are no persons who insist more strongly than they do on that which they deem to be the only needful *supper of the Lord.* That supper, according to their apprehension, is of a spiritual nature. Now, it is a circumstance which strongly confirms this general view, that our Lord availed himself of the very occasion which has given rise among Christians to the rite of the Eucharist, in order to direct the attention of his disciples to the supper now alluded to—a repast of a totally different description, and one which may be enjoyed by the disciples of Christ independently of every outward ordinance. " With desire I have desired," said Jesus to his apostles, " to eat this Passover with you before I suffer; for *I say unto you, I will not any more eat thereof, until it be fulfilled in the kingdom of God.*"[7] Again, " This is my blood of the new testament, which is shed for many, for the remission of sins. *But I say unto you, I will not drink henceforth of this fruit of the vine, until that day when I drink it new with you in my Father's kingdom.*"[8]

[7] Luke xxii, 15, 16. [8] Matt. xxvi, 28, 29.

Again, " Ye are they which have continued with me in my temptations. And I appoint unto you a kingdom, as my Father hath appointed unto me; that *ye may eat and drink at my table in my king!om.*"[9]

We may, indeed, believe that these gracious declarations are accomplished *in all their fulness*, only in the heavenly state of happiness and glory; but it is sufficiently evident, and is allowed by various commentators, that our Lord's expressions, now cited, cannot be considered as relating exclusively to the world to come. When Jesus Christ had died on the cross, a sacrifice for the sins of the whole world, the type of the Passover had received its fulfilment in the kingdom of God. When his blood had been shed for many, for the remission of sins, and when he had ascended to the right hand of the Father Almighty, that kingdom or reign, conducted through the mediation of the Messiah, was established in the earth. Then, therefore, did the day arrive, as we may fairly deduce from these impressive passages, when Jesus was again to eat the Passover with his disciples, and to drink the new wine in their company: according to his own declaration, on a subsequent occasion, " Behold, I stand at the door and knock; if any man hear my voice, and open the door, I will *come in to him, and will sup with him, and he with me.*"[1] When the faithful disciples of our glorified Redeemer open the door of the heart at the voice of his Holy Spirit; when, more especially, they are engaged in rendering unto him their joint and willing service, and are worshipping God in unison; he is often pleased to come

[9] Luke xxii, 28—30.   [1] Rev. iii, 20.

in among them, to sup with them, and to permit them to sup with him. Then does he bring them into a holy fellowship with the Father, with himself, and one with another; breaks for them the bread of life, and gives them to drink of his most precious blood; and thus, while their souls are refreshed, nourished, and comforted, they are brought, in a living and effective manner, to the remembrance of that crucified Lord who is their strength, their joy, and their salvation.

While Friends believe it best to abstain from that outward ceremony, which their Christian brethren have adopted, may they ever be partakers of the true supper of the Lord! May they ever remember the indispensable necessity of that living and abiding faith in Christ crucified, by which alone they can enjoy the communion of his body and blood! " Verily, verily, I say unto you, Except ye eat the flesh of the Son of man, and drink his blood, ye have no life in you. Whoso eateth my flesh, and drinketh my blood, hath eternal life, and I will raise him up at the last day. For my flesh is meat indeed, and my blood is drink indeed. He that eateth my flesh, and drinketh my blood, dwelleth in me, and I in him. As the living Father hath sent me, and I live by the Father; so he that eateth me, even he shall live by me. This is that bread which came down from heaven; not as your fathers did eat manna, and are dead; he that eateth of this bread shall live for ever."[2]

On a general review, then, of the particular passages of the New Testament which relate to the ob-

[2] John vi, 53—58.

servance of the Lord's supper, I may venture to recapitulate my own sentiments, that such a practice has no proper or necessary connexion with a spiritual feeding on the body and blood of Christ—that the history of our Lord's last paschal supper with his disciples affords no reason for believing that he then instituted a religious ceremony, which was thenceforth to form an essential part of the worship of Christians—that his injunction, on that occasion, may be understood, either as relating solely to the rites of the Passover, or as intended to give a religious direction to the more common social repasts of his disciples— that it was in connexion with such repasts, and particularly with their love-feasts, that the primitive Christians were accustomed to commemorate the death of Christ-- that the custom of those love-feasts, however appropriate to the circumstances of the earliest disciples, soon fell into abuse as the number of believers increased, and appears to be, in a great degree inapplicable to the present condition of the Christian world—and, lastly, that under the influence of the spiritual manifestations of our Redeemer, we may, without the bread and wine, participate in that *true* supper of the Lord, which he has himself so clearly upheld to the expectation of his disciples, and which alone is indispensable for the edification, consolation, and salvation of his people.

Although, for the reasons detailed in the present disquisition, it may fairly be concluded that the practices of water-baptism and the Lord's supper are by no means needful, it is certain that these practices have been very generally observed by the professors of the Christian name. This fact is easily explained, not only by the known power of example and tradition, but also by that principle in our nature, which leads us so commonly to place our dependence upon outward and visible things. Man is naturally prone to trust in any thing rather than in the invisible Creator; and he is ever ready to make the formal ordinance a part of his religious system, because he can rely upon it with ease to himself, and may often find in it a plausible substitute for the mortification of his own will. Now, I would suggest that the ceremonies which we have been considering, so far from being like the moral law of God, *universally* salutary, are evidently fraught with no little danger, as occasions by which this deceitful disposition in the human heart is naturally excited and brought into action. And here our appeal may be made, not only to theory, but to facts; for, it is indisputable that the outward rites of baptism and the supper, as observed among the professors of Christianity, have been the means of leading multitudes into gross superstition. How many thousands of persons are there, as every spiritually-minded Christian will allow, who place upon these outward rites a reliance which is warranted neither by reason nor by Scripture, and which, so far from bringing them nearer to God—so far from reminding them of Christ—operates in the most palpable manner as a *diversion* from a true and living faith in their Creator and Redeemer! How often has the ignorant sinner, even in the hour of death, depended on the "sacrament" of the Lord's supper as upon a saving ordinance! And how many a learned theologian, both ancient and modern, has been found to insist on the dangerous tenet, that the rite of baptism is *regeneration!*

While the Society of Friends believe that ordinances which are so peculiarly liable to abuse, and which have been the means of exciting, not only the superstitions now alluded to, but endless divisions and contentions, and many cruel persecutions in the church, cannot truly appertain to the law of God; while they are persuaded, on the contrary, that the spirituality of that law is opposed to the continued observance of any typical religious rite; and while, on these grounds they consider themselves amply justified in the omission of such practices; they entertain, I trust, no disposition whatsoever to judge their fellow believers who conscientiously make use of these ceremonies. There are, as I believe, many persons who avail themselves of the rites in question, on principles which cannot be deemed superstitious; and who even derive, through these *signs and memorials*, some real instruction and edification. Such instances may serve to convince us that God continues to accept the sincere heart, and that he is still pleased to bless a variety of means to a variety of conditions. Nevertheless, I cannot but deem it probable, that as serious Christians, not of our profession, draw yet nearer in spirit to an omnipresent Deity, they will be permitted to find, in *the disuse of all types*, "a more excellent way."

ADDENDUM TO CHAPTER IV.

A.D. 1834.

It has not been without pain and conflict to myself that I have pleaded, or at least apologized for the disuse of practices, which many sincere Christians would seem to value like the apple of their eye. Yet the feelings which are thus entertained on the subject by so large a proportion of the followers of Christ, may be one reason why Friends have been *led* to uphold a more spiritual standard; nor could we, in my opinion, forsake the high ground which we have hitherto occupied, respecting forms and ceremonies in worship, without inflicting a serious injury on the cause of truth; and therefore on the whole church of our Lord Jesus Christ.

After a lapse of more than ten years since this work was published, and after many a review of the points here discussed, I do not find that I have any thing material to alter in the foregoing chapter. It may not, however, be amiss, even at the risk of repetition, now to state, in a concentrated manner, the views of baptism and the Lord's supper, which continue to be satisfactory to my own mind, and on which it seems graciously permitted to repose. For this purpose I beg to offer to the attention of the reader the following propositions, which I wish to be regarded not in the light of dogmatic *assertions*—for these I can have no right to make—but as the plain expression of my own deliberate sentiments.

I. Under the gospel dispensation, the worship of God is at once simple and spiritual; it is the communion of the soul of man with his Creator, under the direct influence of the Spirit, and through the sole mediation of our Lord Jesus Christ.

II. Consistently with this truth, all observances in worship which are of a purely ceremonial nature, all mere types and shadows, are at once fulfilled and abrogated by the great realities of the gospel of Christ.

III. The rite of water-baptism exactly answers to this description. It is in its nature *wholly* ceremonial; it is a *mere* shadow or figure, and therefore, unless some peculiar and sufficient cause be shown to the contrary, it can have no permanent place in the system of *Christianity*.

IV. The history of the rite affords no evidence that it is an exception to the general rule: but rather the contrary. Washing or dipping in water, under various forms, was ordained as a part of the Mosaic ritual, and was often practised as a figure of purification. In that peculiar mode in which John the Baptist and the apostles used it, it was employed by the Jews, both before and after the Christian era, on the admission of proselytes into the church; and in all these cases, it was the obvious type of repentance and conversion. John, who lived under the law, baptized by divine authority; and Jesus himself submitted to his baptism as part of the righteousness *which then was*. The apostles observed the rite, as they did a variety of

CHAP. 4.]   *in the Worship of God.*   171

other Jewish ceremonies; and having connected it in their practice with conversion to Christianity, they applied it even to the Gentiles. But Christ himself, as the Institutor of the gospel dispensation, baptized not; and Paul, who to a great extent personally abstained from the use of this ceremony, declares that he had received no commission from Christ to perform it.

V. Shortly before his ascension, the Lord Jesus commanded his apostles to go and make disciples of all nations, " baptizing them *into* the name of the Father, and of the Son, and of the Holy Ghost." That the use made by the apostles of water-baptism is not to be ascribed to this command, is clear from the fact that they employed the rite before the command was issued. That the command is to be understood only in a spiritual sense—as indicating " the washing of water *by the word* "—may be inferred from the figurative use which our Lord has elsewhere made of the word baptize, from his own doctrine respecting the spirituality of true worship, and from the distinction which he so clearly drew between the water-baptism of *John*, and Christian baptism by the Spirit. It may also be inferred from the declaration of Paul—an undoubted partaker in the apostolic commission—that the Lord Jesus did *not* send him to baptize with water, but to preach the gospel.

Had a typical ceremony thus binding on the church been here instituted, the analogy of the Jewish law would lead us to expect the most precise directions, as to the persons who should perform it, and as to the manner, times, and circumstances, in which it should be performed. But no such directions are given, and Christians who admit the continued authority of the rite, are left, in reference to these particulars, in a state of irremediable doubt and dispute.

VI. In the mean time Christianity has a baptism of its own, of which our Lord and his apostles made frequent mention, without attaching to it the condition or accompaniment of any outward ceremony. It is that of Christ himself, " with the Holy Ghost and with fire;" and is productive of a new birth, by the Spirit. It is the baptism which " now saveth us," and which brings the " answer of a good conscience towards God, by the resurrection of Jesus Christ;" it is " the washing of regeneration and renewing of the Holy Ghost." This baptism properly agrees with the nature and character of Christianity, and coincides with that worship of God, which is " in spirit and in truth." Without it, the sinner cannot be converted, or joined in fellowship with the church; without it the soul of the believer can never be prepared for an entrance into heaven.

VII. Whatsoever opinion therefore they may entertain respecting the ceremonial rite, *this* is the baptism on which Christians of every denomination ought chiefly to insist, and in so doing, they will not fail to experience " the unity of the spirit in the bond of peace."

I. When the Lord Jesus celebrated his last Passover-supper with his disciples, " he took bread, and when he had given thanks, he brake it, and said, Take, eat; this is my body which is broken for you; this do in remembrance of me. After the same manner also he took the cup, when he had supped, saying, This cup is the new testament in my blood: this do ye, as oft as ye drink it, in remembrance of me."

II. The words used by our Lord on this solemn occasion, afford no more evidence that the bread which he brake was *itself* his body, than they do, that the cup which he held in his hand, was *itself* the new testament in his blood. The bread was distinct and separate from his body, occupying a different part of space, and could not *possibly* be the same with it. But the bread represented his body, which was about to be broken for many; and the wine in the cup was a symbol of his blood which was about to be shed for many, for the remission of sins.

III. It was at an actual meal, intended for bodily refreshment, that our Saviour thus addressed his disciples; and when, in conformity with his command, the earliest Christians partook of "the Lord's supper," there was no mystery in the observance; much less was any miraculous change wrought upon their food. Convened from time to time, *at their social repasts*, they brake their bread and handed round their cup of wine, in the sweet fellowship of the gospel of Christ, and in solemn remembrance of his death.

IV. The Scriptures do not appear to afford us any sufficient proof that the command on which this custom was founded, was intended for the whole church of Christ in all ages, any more than our Lord's injunction to his disciples to wash one another's feet. There is nothing however in the practice itself, as it was thus observed by the primitive believers, inconsistent with the general law, that all mere types and figures in worship are abolished under the gospel. Let Christians, when they eat their meat together " with gladness and singleness of heart," still be reminded *by their very food*, of the Lord who bought them. Let them, more often than the day, gratefully recollect their divine Master, " who bare our sins in *his own body*, on the tree," and whose *precious blood* was shed for all mankind.

V. But no sooner was this practice changed from its original simple character, employed as a part of the public worship of God, and converted into a purely ceremonial right, than the state of the case was entirely altered. The great principle that God is to be worshipped in spirit and in truth, was infringed; and, as far as relates to this particular, a return took place to the old legal system of *forms* and *shadows*.

VI. It is probably in consequence of this change— the invention and contrivance of man—that an ordinance, of which the sole purpose was the thankful remembrance of the death of Jesus, has been abused to an astonishing extent. Nothing among professing Christians has been perverted into an occasion of so much superstition; few things have been the means of staining the annals of the church with so much blood.

VII. " *It is the Spirit that quickeneth*," as our Saviour himself has taught us, " *the flesh profiteth nothing ;*" and Christianity is distinguished by a *spiritual* supper, as well as baptism. To partake of *this* supper is essential to our salvation. We can never have a claim on the hopes and joys set before us in the gospel, unless we feed, by a living faith, on the bread which came down from heaven, and giveth life to the world—unless we " eat the flesh of the Son of man, and drink his blood." Now they who partake of this celestial food, are fellow members of one body; they are joined together by a social compact of the dearest and holiest character, because they all commune with the same glorious Head. They are *one in Christ Jesus ;* and when they meet in solemn worship —Christ himself being present—they are guests, even here, at the table of their Lord, and drink the wine ". new," with him " in his kingdom."

May this be the happy experience of all who read this volume, whether they use or disuse what is called the sacrament of the supper!

CHAPTER V.

ON THE NATURE AND CHARACTER OF THE CHRISTIAN MINISTRY.

THE influences of the Holy Spirit on the hearts of men are both general and extraordinary. By the general influences of the Spirit I mean the work of *grace*—a work essential to the salvation of the soul: by which alone we are turned from our evil ways, enabled to serve God out of a pure heart, and preserved alive, as members of the body of Christ. " The grace of God that bringeth salvation," says the apostle Paul, " hath appeared to all men, teaching us that, denying ungodliness and worldly lusts we should live soberly, righteously, and godly, in this present world."[1] Again, he says, " By grace are ye *saved* through faith; and that not of yourselves; it is the gift of God."[2] The *extraordinary* influences of the Spirit are those which qualify individuals for particular religious services; they are by no means indispensable to salvation; neither are they, *as a whole*, the common allotment of all the living members of the true church, but are variously bestowed—one upon one person, and another upon another.

[1] Titus ii, 11, 12. [2] Eph. ii, 8.

CHAP. 5.] *of the Christian Ministry.* 177

These extraordinary influences are usually denominated the *gifts* of the Spirit. " To one," says Paul, " is given, by the Spirit, the word of wisdom; to another the word of knowledge, by the same Spirit; to another faith, by the same Spirit; (that is, probably, such faith as qualified for the execution of some peculiarly important service;) to another the gifts of healing, by the same Spirit; to another the working of miracles; to another prophecy; to another discerning of spirits; to another divers kinds of tongues; to another the interpretation of tongues: but all these worketh that one and the self-same Spirit, dividing to every man severally as he will."[3]

This apostolic description of the distribution of divine gifts in the church is introduced by the declaration that " the manifestation of the Spirit is given to every man[4] to profit withal;" or, as in the Greek, *in order to that which is profitable or useful.*[5] And, as every member of the natural body contributes, by the exercise of its own functions, to the welfare of the whole body; so it may be presumed that there is no real Christian who is not, sooner or later, endowed with some particular spiritual capacity for usefulness in the church, and called to the performance of some specific services, in the great cause of truth and righteousness. When, however, we consider any one gift of the Spirit, we plainly perceive that it is not bestowed generally, but is the portion of those individuals only, upon whom is laid that peculiar office in the church, to the exercise of which such gift is directed. Now the gift to which I am about to advert

[3] 1 Cor. xii, 8—11 [4] ἑκάστῳ. [5] πρὸς τὸ συμφέρον.

is pre-eminent, above all others, as a means of general usefulness—of conversion, instruction, and consolation; it is that which is now generally denominated the gift of "ministry," but which, in the Scriptures, is sometimes described as the gift of "prophecy."[6] Undoubtedly, there have existed, at various periods, and for particular purposes, other gifts of the Spirit, which require a higher degree of supernatural influence; such as those of "miracles" and of "tongues:" but the gift by means of which divine truth is outwardly communicated and applied, is of constant and therefore of primary use; and, when we take into our view the weakness and imperfection of human nature, we may consider it as equally important, in every age, to the maintenance, edification, and enlargement of the militant church.

I believe it to be allowed, among the plurality of Christians, that none can be true ministers of the gospel, who are not called to the exercise of that office by the Holy Ghost; and, consequently, that the faculty of ministry is still to be considered a *gift of the Spirit*. But, although this doctrine is generally admitted, it is very far indeed from being consistently or universally carried into practice. Many rush into the ministerial office, and enjoy the temporal privileges with which it is usually connected, whose whole deportment evinces in the plainest manner, that they are destitute of qualification for any such undertaking. Others, whose views are of a somewhat more serious complexion, and who are actuated by a general desire to perform their duty, are obviously depending, in their ministry, not upon that Spirit who can alone qualify

[6] 1 Cor. xiv, 3.

for the exercise of his own gifts, but upon human learning and merely intellectual exertion. Their discourses are so far from being prompted by a divine influence, that they are the mere produce of their own reflections and industry—unless indeed they are borrowed, as is too frequently the case, from the reflections and industry of others. Such discourses may be the word of the preacher, or they may be the word of his neighbour; but they cannot, with any degree of strictness or propriety, be described as "the word of the Lord."

Happily, there is still another class of ministers, among various denominations of Christians, (as I can testify from my own observation,) whose views on the present subject are of a much more spiritual character. In the first place, they enter on the work of the ministry under very decided impressions of duty, and in the humble, yet full persuasion, that they are called into this field of service by the great Head of the church. And, in the second place, when invested, according to their own apprehension, with the office in question, they exercise its important functions, not only with zeal and fidelity, but with a real feeling of dependence upon the divine Spirit. Such persons are evidently the servants of the Lord Jesus Christ; and we can scarcely fail to observe how frequently their labours are blessed to the conversion and edification of the people. Nevertheless, I conceive that even *these* preachers of the gospel do not consider it necessary that their ministry should be the *unmixed* offspring of the Lord's Spirit. The principle upon which they generally (I will not say universally) conduct their religious services, appears to be this—that, having been called to the work, and invested with the office of preachers, they are constantly to seek for the assistance of divine power in the exercise of its functions; nevertheless, that the discourses which they actually utter are not to be immediately prompted of the Lord; but, under the more general and indirect influences of the Holy Spirit, are to be the produce of their own minds, and mostly of previous study, research, and reflection.

Little as I am inclined to cast any blame upon others who are evidently accepted and assisted by their " own Master," I conceive it to be a duty plainly laid upon the Society of Friends, to hold up a still higher and purer standard respecting the Christian ministry. It is a principle generally understood and admitted by the members of that Society, that this ministry is a gift of the Spirit, which cannot be rightly exercised *otherwise than under the direct and immediate influence of that Spirit.* Friends are not, therefore, satisfied with any general impression that it is their duty to preach the gospel; nor do they venture, under such impression, either to employ their own intellectual exertions as a preparation for the service, or to select their own time for performing it. If it be the divine will that they should minister, they believe it will be manifested to them, by the divine Spirit, when they are to speak, whom they are to address, and what things they are to express. In the exercise of so high and sacred a function, they dare not depend, either in a greater or less degree, upon their own strength or wisdom; but they feel constrained to place their *sole* reliance upon him who "searcheth the reins and the hearts;" upon him who "hath the key of David;" who "openeth and no man shutteth, and shutteth and no man openeth."[7]

The individual who, according to the apprehension of Friends, is a true minister of the gospel, (and there may be many such persons in a single congregation,) avails himself, with strict regularity, of the opportunities provided amongst us, as in every religious society, for the purpose of divine worship. In company with his brethern and sisters, he waits, in public, upon Him who is alone the author of every good and perfect gift. His soul is humbled in true prostration before God; and, while he continues in this condition, he is often sensible, not only of a general desire for the spiritual welfare of his friends, but of a strong, yet hidden exercise of mind on their account. Now, as he patiently waits in reverent dependence upon Christ, the great Minister of the sanctuary, this exercise of mind often assumes an explicit direction; and, when he apprehends that the secret command has gone forth towards him, either to address the congregation in preaching, or *vocally* to call on the Almighty in prayer, he obeys the mandate of his Lord, and speaks as the Spirit gives him utterance. When he has been enabled to discharge himself of the burden which has thus rested upon him, he returns to a state of reverential silence, and is often permitted to experience a consoling feeling of relief and tranquillity. The quietness and true ease which then prevail in his mind afford him an evidence

[7] Rev, iii. 7.

which he may with humble gratitude accept, that in thus exercising his gift, he has been following, not the imagintions of his own heart, but the voice of the true Shepherd.

Here I would observe that, with every humble and devoted minister who acts on these principles, and who carefully maintains the watch, the internal operations of the Spirit will not only prompt to a right exercise of the gift, but will afford a constant check upon its abuse. There will be found, in those internal operations, a secret discipline, a salutary correction, for those who exceed the limits of their calling, and stretch their gift beyond its true measure. If, however, in any persons, who have received the gift of the ministry, a watchful dependence upon God is not maintained, and thus their services degenerate into the use of words without life, the spiritually-minded hearer will not fail to observe the change; and thus, while the members of a religious society are " subject one to another in love," and a right Christian oversight is preserved among them, it will not, for the most part, be found a difficult matter to prevent the continuance, in any congregation, of a *spurious* ministry.

The Christian ministry, whether in preaching or in prayer, and whether exercised in larger or smaller assemblies, is immediately connected with the worship of God. The sentiments of Friends, therefore, on this subject, like those on the rites of baptism and the supper, arise out of that part of the divine law, as revealed under the new covenant, which declares that God is a Spirit, and must be worshipped, by his followers, *in spirit and in truth.*

CHAP. 5.] *of the Christian Ministry.* 183

They conceive that true worship consists in the immediate communion of the soul with its Creator; and they apprehend that no verbal administrations properly accord with it, but those which spring from the influence of the Holy Spirit. They believe that God can be rightly praised only by his *own works.* Now, among those works may be reckoned the spiritual ministry of which I am speaking; for although it may be affected in a greater or less degree by the infirmity of the instrument through which it passes, it is nevertheless called into exercise, ordered, and directed to its right object, by the Lord himself.

These remarks apply with especial force to those solemn occasions, when the church is publicly assembled to worship the Deity. It is then, in a peculiar manner, that the Almighty Saviour of men is present with his people. The sacred canopy of their heavenly Father's love is spread over them; nor can they worship him aright, unless the reasonings and imaginations of their own minds are brought into subjection. At such times the mandate is proclaimed to the spiritual worshipper: "Be silent, O all flesh, before the Lord; for he is raised up out of his holy habitation."[8] If incense is then to be offered unto him, its sweet savour must arise from no "strange fire."[9] If the ark of the covenant is to be uplifted among the people, none may touch it, to whom the command is not given.[1] If the pure temple of the Lord is to be built up, he must himself prepare the materials, "and neither hammer nor axe, nor any tool of iron"—

[8] Zech. ii, 13.   [9] Lev. x, 1.   [1] 2 Sam. vi, 6.

nothing of the *unauthorized* instrumentality of man—must be "heard in the house."[2]

In offering this description of the nature and operation of that which we deem to be the true ministry, I have not forgotten our own infirmities and deficiencies; and it has been very far indeed from my intention to convey the idea that we are found universally to maintain in *practice* this high, yet simple, standard. I am remarking only, that this is our *principle*, and that it is a principle which evidently appertains to the divine law, and accords with its holiness and perfection.

There is another point of view, in which the present subject requires to be considered.

Although the object for which Christians meet in congregations, is the worship of the Deity, and although it is by means of a direct communion between God and the soul that the worshipper is *chiefly* edified, the "Master of assemblies" is pleased to appoint the outward ministration of preaching, in immediate connexion with the service thus offered to himself, for the purposes of *conversion*, *edification*, and *comfort*. It is obvious that, in an assembly of persons, there is always a great variety of internal condition; and the mental state, even of a single individual, is varied, from time to time, by circumstances known only to himself and to his Creator. In order then, to be useful to its fullest extent, the ministry of the gospel ought to consist, not only in the declaration of scriptural truths, but in a right experimental application

[2] 1 Kings vi, 7.

of them to all *this variety of internal condition.* Now, although the preacher, from his own observation, may form some opinion respecting the states of his hearers, he cannot penetrate the secrets of the heart; and his judgment never fails to be obscure, uncertain, and imperfect. Thus his administrations may or *may not* be fitted to those persons for whom they are intended. But the Minister of ministers *searches the hearts of men;* and, under the immediate influence of *his* Spirit, the preacher of the gospel is enabled to unfold the condition of individuals, and rightly to apply to their several wants the word of consolation, reproof, or instruction. The light of the Holy Spirit in their hearts, bears witness to the truth of that which is spoken. Such was the character of that prophesying, or preaching of which we read in the epistles of Paul. "If all prophesy," says he, "and there come in one who believeth not, or one unlearned, he is convinced of all, he is judged of all: *and thus are the secrets of his heart made manifest; and so, falling down on his face, he will worship God, and report that God is in you of a truth.*"[3]

So, also, in public prayer, the minister speaks as the representative of the congregation, and the minds of the hearers are supposed to accompany the words of the speaker. If he utter the written prayer, and the congregation follow him in the same words, it is sufficiently obvious that the expression of the lip, and the feeling of the heart, will often be in total dissonance. The obdurate sinner may be found addressing an omnipresent Deity in the language of contrition—

[3] 1 Cor. xiv, 24, 25.

the sorrowful and desponding spirit, in the voice of praise and thanksgiving—the happy and rejoicing believer, in the words of mourning and woe! Nor can it be considered that a less inconsistency prevails, when the prayer of the minister is extemporaneous, and proceeds not from the Spirit of the Lord, but from his own powers of invention and composition. The words which, under such circumstances, he may express, although satisfactory to his own mind, may often be in absolute discordance with the feelings and condition of his hearers. Were we, in our public assemblies for worship, to use addresses either to the people or to the Almighty, not prompted by his Spirit, but either previously written, or in our own strength composed on the occasion, we should *with our views of the subject*, consider ourselves, not as honouring the God of our fathers, but as making an improper use of his holy name. And we are persuaded, from long experience, that such practices would greatly injure the *life*, and as greatly lessen the *true efficacy*, of our Christian worship.

In confirmation of the principles which have been stated, and as a further proof that they rest on divine authority, I have now to appeal to the numerous and plain examples of inspired ministry recorded in the Bible.

Various instances are given in that sacred volume, of ministry uttered either publicly or on private occasions of importance; and the prayers, praises, and sermons, thus spoken, bear the character not of compositions prepared beforehand through the exertions of human intellect, but of spontaneous effusions from that divine Spirit, who animated and impelled the speakers. When Joseph interpreted the dream of Pharaoh; when the dying Jacob pronounced his blessing on his children and grand-children; when Moses sang aloud his song of rejoicing, and when he recited to the people the marvellous dealings of God with them; when Joshua also recounted the mercies of the Lord, and exhorted the Israelites to obedience; when Deborah and Barak uttered their triumphant hymn; when Hannah, in the temple, vocally poured forth her thanksgiving; when Samuel declared the word of the Lord to Eli, and, on another occasion, pleaded the cause of God with the people; when David sang his psalms of penitence, prophecy, and praise;[4] and when his successor uttered his proverbs of wisdom, and his thousand songs;[5] when Solomon, when Hezekiah, and when Ezra, lifted

[4] From various statements, contained in the recorded history of David, it may be collected that he sometimes uttered his prayers and psalms, before they were committed to writing : see 2 Sam. vii, 18 —29; xxii; xxiii, 2—5. Nor can we doubt that the Spirit often led him, in the first instance, to write that sacred poetry which was *afterwards* sung both by himself and others. While, however, it is evident that psalmody prevailed among the ancient Hebrews to a great extent, it is to be remembered that the songs which they introduced into their worship were the songs of prophets and *originated* in direct inspiration.

The psalms to which the earliest Christians were accustomed, I conceive to have been often uttered without premeditation, and under the immediate influence of the Holy Ghost. In two of his epistles, Paul describes them as "spiritual songs," (Eph. v, 19 ; Col. iii, 16,) and, on another occasion, he numbers the "psalm" among those inspired administrations which distinguished the public worship of primitive times, 1 Cor. xiv, 26.

[5] 1 Kings iv, 32.

up their voices, in audible supplication, before the assembled multitudes; when Elizabeth addressed the mother of her Lord, and when Mary responded with the voice of thanksgiving; when Zacharias praised the Lord, who had " visited and redeemed his people;" when John the Baptist proclaimed the personal presence and approaching reign of the Messiah; when all these and many other individuals thus exercised the gift of ministry, as it would now be denominated, there is every reason to believe (and in some of the instances alluded to, it is expressly declared) that they spake as they were moved by the Holy Ghost.

Among the ancient Israelites, the duty which properly corresponds with that of the Christian minister did not necessarily devolve on the priests and Levites, whose office it was to perform the service practised in the temple, and to offer the sacrifices appointed by the law. It rather appertained to the prophets, who, at various periods of the Israelitish history, were a numerous body of men; and were distinguished from their countrymen, not by hereditary dignity or official appointment, but, simply, by the gifts of the Holy Spirit. These persons, as we find from a multitude of passages in their written works, were by no means exclusively engaged in predicting events to come, but were often sent forth to proclaim the judgments and mercies of the Lord, to warn the people, and to exhort them to faith, obedience, and holiness. The gift of " prophecy," therefore, during the more ancient periods of sacred history, frequently assumed the same character as in the days of the apostle Paul, who described it as identical with that of preaching.[6] Now, whether the prophets exercised their gift in predicting or in exhorting, it is, on all hands, allowed that their words were uttered under the direct influence of the Spirit of God. They delivered, not the productions of their own invention, but the messages of Jehovah. It was not they who spake; it was the Lord who spake by them.

Very similar to the case of the prophets was that of the apostles of Jesus Christ. All Christians allow that the ministry of these servants of God was immediately inspired of the Holy Ghost. When our Lord sent forth his disciples to heal the sick and to preach the gospel, he said to them, " Ye shall be brought before governors and kings for my sake, for a testimony against them and the Gentiles. But when they deliver you up, take no thought how or what ye shall speak, for it shall be given you, in that same hour, what ye shall speak. For it is not ye that speak, but the Spirit of your Father which speaketh in you."[7] On a subsequent occasion, immediately before his ascension, we read that Jesus opened the understanding of the apostles " that they might understand the Scriptures;" when he addressed them in the following manner— " Thus it is written, and thus it behoved Christ to suffer, and to rise from the dead the third day ; and that repentance and remission of sins should be preached in his name, among all nations, beginning at Jerusalem. *And ye are witnesses of these things. And, behold, I send the promise of my Father upon you;* (i. e. the Spirit;) but tarry ye in the city of Jerusalem,

[6] 1 Cor. xiv, 3.   [7] Matt. x, 18—20.

until ye be endued with power from on high."⁸ In pursuance of this declaration, the apostles, when gathered together on the day of Pentecost, were "*filled with the Holy Ghost*, and began to speak with other tongues, as the *Spirit gave them utterance.*"⁹ Paul, in a particular manner, has explained the nature, and declared the authority of his own preaching. " And I was with you," says he to the Corinthians, " in weakness, and in fear, and in much trembling. And my speech and my preaching were not with enticing words of man's wisdom, but in demonstration of the Spirit and of power; that your faith should not stand in the wisdom of men, but in the power of God."......Again, " Now we have received, not the spirit of the world, but the spirit which is of God; that we might know the things that are freely given to us of God; which things also we speak, *not in the words which man's wisdom teacheth, but which the Holy Ghost teacheth.*"¹

But the immediate operation of the Spirit, as productive of ministry, was by no means confined, under the gospel dispensation, to the apostles of Jesus Christ. There are, in the book of Acts, a variety of passages, which prove that the gifts of the Holy Ghost were poured out, in great abundance, upon others also. On that memorable day of Pentecost, more especially, the Spirit descended from above, not only on the apostles, but on the whole company of their followers. Then, according to the express declaration of Peter, was accomplished the prophecy of Joel; " And it shall come to pass in the last days (saith God) I will pour out my Spirit upon all flesh; and your sons and your

⁸ Luke xxiv, 46—49.   ⁹ Acts ii, 4.   ¹ 1 Cor. ii, 3—5, 12, 13.

daughters shall prophecy, and your young men shall see visions, and your old men shall dream dreams: and on my servants and on my hand-maidens I will pour out in those days of my Spirit, and they shall prophecy."[2]

The same truth may, without difficulty, be collected from various passages of Paul's epistles; for he often mentions the gifts of direct inspiration, with which his own converts were endowed by the Lord Jesus. On one occasion, particularly, he reproves the Corinthians for their misuse of the gift of tongues; and gives them very explicit directions respecting the manner in which that gift, and others of a similar nature, were to be exercised. " *If, therefore, the whole church be come together into one place,* and all speak with tongues, and there come in those that are unlearned, or unbelievers, will they not say that ye are mad? But, if all *prophecy,* and there come in one that believeth not, or one unlearned, he is convinced of all, he is judged (or discerned) of all. And thus are the secrets of his heart made manifest; and so, falling down on his face, he will worship God, and report that God is in you of a truth. How is it, then, brethren? *When ye come together,* every one of you hath a psalm, hath a doctrine, hath a tongue, hath a revelation, hath an interpretation. Let all things be done unto edifying. If any man speak in an unknown tongue, let it be by two, or, at the most, by three, and that by course; and let one interpret. But if there be no interpreter, let him keep silence in the church; and let him speak to himself, and to God. Let the prophets speak two or three,

[2] Joel ii, 28, 29; Acts ii, 16—18.

and let the others judge. If any thing *be revealed* to another that sitteth by, let the first hold his peace. For ye may all prophecy, one by one, that all may learn and all may be comforted. And the spirits of the prophets are subject to the prophets; for God is not the author of confusion, but of peace, as in all churches of the saints."[3]

This remarkable passage of Scripture, as well as the whole chapter of which it forms a part, plainly relates, as is universally allowed by commentators, to the conduct of the early Christian converts in their public assemblies for worship; nor does there, I believe, exist any other document which throws the same degree of light upon that interesting topic. The passage naturally suggests a few remarks.

It is to be observed, in the first place, that the ministry, which the apostle describes as exercised on these occasions, was not prepared or premeditated, but was the direct effect of the impulses of the Spirit. That this was the character of the gift of tongues, or of ministry in foreign languages, by which the original preachers of the gospel were *miraculously* enabled to promulgate the truth among all nations, cannot be denied. Nor is it less clear that the *prophesying*, which the apostle so much commends as profitable for comfort, conviction, and edification, and which comprehended not merely predicting, but, more especially, preaching, praying, and singing praises, was uttered under the direct and extraordinary influences of the Holy Ghost: for, it is because of those very influences that public ministry is thus named by the apostle. It

[3] 1 Cor. xiv, 23—33.

CHAP. 5.]   *of the Christian Ministry.*   193

was " prophecy" for no other reason than because it was directly inspired.[4] Koppius, a learned biblical critic, remarks that this word, as employed by the apostle, describes a faculty possessed " by a certain description of Christians in the apostolic church, who, being in a singular manner affected by divine power, were accustomed to speak publicly in their assemblies for worship; uttered prophecies; laid open the secret designs of men; prayed with a remarkable impetus and fervour of mind; rose up, *under the impulse of the Holy Spirit,* to teach, exhort, and console; and sang hymns which bore the stamp of a divine origin."[5]

It appears, in the second place, that these gifts of the Holy Spirit, although truly of a divine origin, were capable, through unwatchfulness or perverseness,

[4] " *Prophecy* was another spiritual gift, which St. Paul hath defined (1 Cor. xiv, 3) to be 'a speaking unto men for edification, and exhortation, and comfort.'

" I have never found *prophesying* used, in the Old or New Testament, for mere explaining the Scriptures, or teaching *without inspiration.* But it appeareth to me, to be always meant of speaking or acting *by inspiration.* Sometimes it is to be understood of foretelling future events, such as no human sagacity could have foreseen. But this is not always its signification.

" In Scripture, *prophesying* is sometimes to be understood as a *delivering by inspiration of some doctrine, direction, or exhortation,* more peculiarly suited to the state of that church, or of some parts of it. At other times, *praying by inspiration,* or singing *psalms* and *hymns,* and *spiritual songs,* come under the general name of *prophesying.* For, all these were performed in the primitive church *by inspiration,* and were a speaking, not only unto God, but unto men also; and that for edification, or exhortation, or comfort."
See *Benson's Essay on the Public Worship of the first Christians, in his Work on the Epistles,* 4to. Ed. vol. i, p. 609.

[5] See *Excurs.* iii, *in Epist. ad Ephes.* So, also, *Schleusner in voc., Grotius,* and *other commentators.*

O

of being misapplied or abused; and that they were, in some measure, placed under the control of the persons on whom they were bestowed. The " spirits of the prophets" were " subject to the prophets;" and, to preserve a right order in the use of their ministry, it was necessary for them to cultivate individually a sound and enlightened judgment, and a tender regard for others. Such a state of mind could, in fact, be maintained only through a watchful dependence upon the Lord, who is the source of wisdom and of all spiritual illumination. Under *his* guidance and influence every man would find his own place; all might then prophesy, and all be edified, in their turn; and thus would it be made manifest to all the churches of the saints, that God, the inspirer of his chosen servants, " is not the author of confusion, but of peace."

Lastly, the reader cannot fail to notice that the ministry which, at that early period, was exercised in Christian assemblies for worship, was not the prayer and lecture of any appointed individual, but consisted in the spontaneous effusions of many—of all who were impelled by the Spirit, and to whom the word of the Lord was revealed on the occasion.

Such were the principles on which were conducted the preaching and praying of the earliest Christians in their assemblies for worship; *and such precisely are the principles on which, in their own religious meetings, the Society of Friends profess to regulate the ministry of the gospel.*

An opinion, I am well aware, is commonly entertained, that those extraordinary endowments of the Holy Spirit, which distinguish the period when Chris-

CHAP. 5.] *of the Christian Ministry.* 195

anity was first promulgated, have long since ceased to be enjoyed in the church of Christ; and, in order to complete the present argument, it is necessary for me to state the grounds on which I am persuaded that this opinion *in the full extent to which it has been carried*, is by no means correct.

It may, indeed, be readily allowed that several of the endowments in question, such as the gifts of healing and of tongues, were of a nature absolutely miraculous. As such, they were peculiarly adapted to the great work of *establishing* in the world a religion which was not only new to almost the whole of mankind, but was directly opposed to their favourite maxims and habits. That object being now effected, it is by no means surprising, according to my apprehension, that such gifts should be withdrawn from the church: and there does not appear to be any reason for supposing that, under the present circumstances of Christianity, they are likely to be called into action. Nor are we to forget that many of the original preachers of the gospel, on whom this work of establishing a new religion devolved, and several of whom were employed in composing those records of divine truth which are of permanent and universal authority, were gifted in a *far more eminent degree* with divine inspiration, than now appears to be the case with any of the Lord's servants. But, although these admissions are to be freely made, there are good reasons for the conviction entertained by Friends, that the immediate operations of the Spirit, as productive of ministry, continue to this very hour to be bestowed on the followers of Christ.

In the first place, there is a great probability, *a priori* that such would be the fact. Since, even under the dispensation of the law, the ministry was prompted by those immediate operations, it is altogether inconsistent with the analogy of divine truth to suppose that, under the more spiritual dispensation of the gospel, the church should be deprived of so salutary a privilege. Again, it is to be remembered that the " prophesying" of which we are speaking was intended, as the apostle declares, for the great purposes of exhortation, edification, and comfort.[6] Now, since exhortation, edification, and comfort, are required at the present day, as much as they were in the times of the apostles, and since the Great Head of the church is ever willing and able to supply the need of his servants, there are obvious reasons for our believing that the gift which was directed to these purposes, would still be permitted to operate.

The strong probability now adverted to, may be sufficient to throw the *onus probandi* upon those who *deny* the continued existence of the gift of inspired ministry. Nevertheless, it is desirable for us to remark, in the second place, that this probability is confirmed by certain plain promises contained in the Holy Scriptures. The Prediction of Joel,[7] as it is cited by the apostle Peter, declares that an abundant measure of this very gift should be poured forth on the

---

[6] 1 Cor. xiv, 3.
[7] In Joel ii, 28, we read, "And it shall come to pass *afterwards*,— Hebrew אחרי כן Kimchi, the Jewish commentator, informs us that this phrase signifies, *in the last days;* and it is well known that by " the last days" the Jews denote the times *of the Messiah.*

CHAP. 5.] *of the Christian Ministry.* 197

servants of the Lord in " the last days."[8] From the comparison of various other passages of the Bible, it appears that by " the last days" are intended the " times of Christianity"— " the times of the last dispensation" —and it will scarcely be denied that these expressions include the whole of that dispensation—its career and termination, as well as its commencement.[9] It is most probable, therefore, that the promise of the Lord, through his prophet, did not relate *exclusively* to the events of the day of Pentecost, but is rather to be interpreted as describing some of the *permanent marks* of the Christian dispensation.

Such a view of this celebrated prophecy appears to have been entertained by the apostle who cited it. After explaining to the people that the wonderful events of the day of Pentecost were effected by the Son of God, who had " received of the Father the *promise of the Holy Ghost*," *and who had shed forth that which they then saw and heard*, he proceeds to declare the continuance and universality, among believers, of the same divine influence. " Repent and be baptized, every one of you," said he ......" and ye shall receive the gift of the Holy Ghost: for, the promise is unto you, and to *your children*, and to *all that are afar off, even as many as the Lord our God shall call.*"[1] This passage has been cited, on a former occasion, to prove that the Holy Spirit was not to be withdrawn from the church as a *guide to morals.* Now, when we look at the circumstances under which these words were spoken, and consider their imme-

[8] Acts ii, 17.   [9] *Comp.* Isaiah ii, 2 ; Heb. i, 2 ; 1 Peter 1, 20 ; 1 John i, 18.   [1] Acts ii, 38, 39.

diate connexion with the prediction of Joel and with its fulfilment, we can scarcely fail to perceive the evidence which they also afford, that the Holy Ghost was not to be withdrawn from the church *as a guide to prophesying.* It was, probably, in reference both to the general and peculiar operations of the Spirit, that when our Lord promised to his disciples (who then represented his church militant) the effusion of the Holy Ghost, he declared that this divine Teacher and Monitor should abide with them "*for ever;*" that is, I presume, through the whole course of the Christian dispensation.[2]

Lastly an appeal may be safely made *to the persons addressed in this work*, when it is asserted that the sentiments of Friends, on the present subject, are confirmed by their own experience. That Society has, for more than a century and a half, been acting, with respect to the ministry, on the principles which have now been stated; and they have never found reason for considering those principles either untrue or ineffective. Although we are very far, indeed, from pretending to those *higher degrees* of inspiration which for peculiar and specific purposes were bestowed on some of the immediate followers of Jesus, we know that there are individuals amongst us who have received that gift of prophecy which is profitable for "exhortation, edification, and comfort;" that these persons cannot exercise their gift in their own strength, or at any stated periods; but that, as they are preserved in watchful dependence upon their holy Leader,

[2] John xiv, 16.

CHAP. 5.] *of the Christian Ministry.* 199

they are sometimes really anointed for the service; and that, on such occasions, their prayers and their preaching, however little adorned with the enticing words of man's wisdom, are evidently accompanied with life and power.[3]

[3] In connexion with the subject of the present section, I wish to present to the reader's attention a curious passage, selected from the Pastor of Hermas, a work probably composed during the first century after Christ, and although, in many respects, a fanciful composition, held in considerable repute among many of the early Christians.

THE ELEVENTH COMMAND.

That the Spirits and Prophets are to be tried by their works, and of a two-fold Spirit.

I. He showed me certain men sitting upon benches, and one sitting in a chair; and he said unto me, Seest thou those who sit upon the benches? Sir, said I, I see them. He answered, They are the faithful; and he who sits in the chair is an earthly spirit. For, he cometh not into the assembly of the faithful, but avoids it. But he joins himself to the doubtful and empty, and prophecies to them in corners and hidden places; and pleases them by speaking according to all the desires of their hearts. For he, placing himself among empty vessels, is not broken, but the one fitteth the other. But when he cometh into the company of just men, who are full of the Spirit of God, and they pray unto the LORD, that man is emptied, because that earthly spirit flies from him, and he is dumb, and cannot speak any thing. As if, in a storehouse, you shall stop up wine and oil; and among those vessels shall place an empty jar; and shall afterwards come to open it, you shall find it empty as you stopped it up; so those empty prophets, when they come among the spirits of the just, are found to be such as they came.

II. I said, How then shall a man be able to discern them? Consider what I am going to say, concerning both kinds of men; and as I speak unto thee, so shalt thou prove the prophet of God, and the false prophet. And, first, try the man who hath the Spirit of God; *because the Spirit which is from above is humble, and quiet; and departs from all wickedness; and from the vain*

In reviewing the principal particulars of the present chapter, the reader will observe that the influences of the Holy Spirit are both general and extraordinary— that the former effect our conversion and sanctifica-

desires of the present world ; and makes himself more humble than all men ; and answers to none when he is asked ; nor to every one singly ; for the Spirit of God doth not speak to a man when he will, but when God pleases. When, therefore, a man who hath the *Spirit of God shall come into the church of the righteous, who have the faith of God, and they pray unto the Lord; then the holy angel of God fills that man with the blessed Spirit, and he speaks in the congregation as he is moved of God.* Thus, therefore, the *Spirit of God is known, because, whosoever speaketh by the Spirit of God, speaketh as the Lord will.*

III. Hear now concerning the earthly spirit, which is empty and foolish, and without virtue. And, first of all, the man who is supposed to have the Spirit (whereas he hath not in reality) exalteth himself, and desires to have the first seat, and is wicked, and full of words; and spends his time in pleasure, and in all manner of voluptuousness ; and *receives the reward of his divination ; which if he receive not, he does not divine.* Should the Spirit of God receive reward, and divine ? It doth not become a prophet of God so to do. Thus you see the life of each of these kind of prophets. Wherefore, prove that man by his life and works who saith that he hath the Holy Spirit. And believe the Spirit which comes from God, and has power *as such.* But, believe not the earthly and empty spirit, which is from the devil, in whom there is no faith nor virtue. Hear now the similitude which I am about to speak unto thee. Take a stone, and throw it up toward the heaven ; or take a spout of water, and mount it up thitherward ; and see if thou canst reach unto heaven. Sir, said I, how can this be done ? For neither of those things which you have mentioned is possible to be done. And he answered : " Therefore, as these things cannot be done, so is the earthly spirit without virtue and without effect. Understand, yet further, the power which cometh from above, in this similitude. The grains of hail *that drop down* are exceeding small ; and yet, when they fall upon the head of a man, how do they cause pain to it ? And again : consider the droppings of a house ; how the little drops, falling upon

tion, and, as such, are essential to salvation, and common to all the Lord's children—that the latter are intended for the enlargement and edification of the church, and are variously bestowed upon various persons—that any one *gift* of the Spirit, such as that of "the ministry," appertains only to a selected few — that while the faculty of ministry (called by the apostle *prophecy*) is verbally acknowledged to be a gift of the Spirit, this doctrine is, to a great extent, practically disregarded among the professors of Christianity—that it is the principle of the Society of Friends to admit no ministry, in connexion with the worship of God, but such as is considered to spring immediately from divine influence—that their opinions on this subject, as well as those respecting typical rites, are founded upon that part of the divine law which prescribes that God, being a Spirit, should be worshipped spiritually —that, in order, moreover, to be applicable to the mental condition of the hearers, the ministry must be prompted and ordered by Him who alone " searcheth the reins and the hearts"—that the examples of preaching and public prayer recorded in the Bible, have, in general, the character of effusions flowing immediately from the Spirit of truth and righteousness—that such, more particularly, was the *prophesying* exercised, in their assemblies for worship, by the primitive Christians—finally, that Scripture and expe-

the earth, work a hollow in the stones. *So, in like manner, the least things which come from above, and fall upon the earth, have great force.* Wherefore, join thyself to the Spirit which has power; and depart from the other, which is empty. *Archbishop Wake's Version of the Apostolic Fathers,* p. 255.

rience unite in bearing evidence that the immediate influences of the Spirit, as productive of such administrations, were not to be withdrawn from the church on earth, and that they continue to operate to this very hour.

To conclude:—if the weapons, wielded by the Lord's servants, in the cause of righteousness, are to be " mighty for the pulling down of strong holds," they must be spiritual and not carnal: if the " preaching of the cross" is to be " the power of God," it must be *divine* in its origin: if the ministry of the gospel of Christ is to enliven and cleanse the recipients, it must be derived, with true simplicity, from the *Source* of life and holiness. Observation may serve to convince us that these sentiments are gradually extending their influence among true Christians. " All the minister's efforts will be vanity and worse than vanity," said a late enlightened clergyman of the Church of England, " if we have not *unction*. *Unction* must come down from heaven, and spread a savour, and relish, and feeling, over his ministry."[4] I am persuaded that there are many pious ministers, of various denominations, whose hearts will respond to such a declaration; and who are more and more convinced that, in the exercise of their gift, they must no longer rely on human learning or intellectual effort, but rather on the powerful visitations of that sacred influence which, when it is withheld, no man can command, and, when it is poured forth, no man can rightly stay. Under such circumstances, it is plainly very important, that Friends should be faithful in

[4] See *Cecil's Remains*, p. 12.

maintaining their principle on this subject, in all its vigour and all its purity; and that they should continue, without wavering, to uphold in the church the *highest* standard respecting the nature and origin of true Christian ministry. May we, therefore, on the one hand, watch unto prayer, that our preaching and praying may never degenerate into the expression of words without life; and, on the other hand, may we be diligent in the use of the gifts committed to us, and exercise a still firmer confidence in that divine anointing, which can impart, even to the foolishness of preaching, *an authority not to be gainsayed!*

CHAPTER VI.

ON THE SELECTION, PREPARATION, AND APPOINTMENT OF THE MINISTERS OF THE GOSPEL.

THE standard upheld by any body of Christians, in reference to the selection, preparation, and appointment of the ministers of the gospel, will ever be found to coincide with their standard respecting the nature and character of the ministry itself. Those who are satisfied with a ministry which requires, for its performance, nothing superior to the powers of man, will look for nothing superior to those powers, in the several steps which lead to its exercise. Those who are accustomed to regard it as the offspring, partly of the influence of the Spirit and partly of human study, will indeed consider a divine call essential to the object; but they will not, for the most part, admit such a call to be sufficient, without the addition of preparatory intellectual efforts, or without the interference of the authority of man. Those, lastly, whose principle it is to admit no ministry but such as flows immediately from the Spirit of truth, must, of necessity, leave the whole work of selection, preparation, and appointment, to the Lord himself.

CHAP. 6.]   On the Selection, &c. of Ministers.   205

In order to develop this general rule with some degree of precision, it may be desirable to examine, in the first place, how far it is exemplified by the known practices of the Anglican church, and of the generality of English protestant dissenters. I trust, however, it will be clearly understood by the reader, that, in attempting such an examination, I have no intention to throw discredit on any denomination of professing Christians. My object is simply to illustrate the subject on which I am treating, and to introduce, in a clear and explicit manner, the sentiments entertained on that subject by the Society of Friends.

When the bishop of the Anglican church ordains to the priesthood, he lays his hand on the head of the individual to be ordained, and says, " Receive the Holy Ghost, for the office and work of a priest in the church of God, now committed unto thee by the imposition of our hands." Here is an open recognition of the doctrine that the person ordained is to exercise his ministry by means of the influence of the Holy Ghost; and it is in exact coincidence with such a sentiment that the candidate for the ministry, in the same church, professes that he is " inwardly moved" to the assumption of it " by the Holy Ghost"—that he is " called" to the work " according to the will of our Lord Jesus Christ." My own knowledge of such individuals enables me freely to allow, that there are many among the ministers of this denomination who, in the exercise of their functions, really depend in great measure on a divine influence, and who would by no means have undertaken the work of the gospel, had they not believed that they were inwardly moved to it by the Holy Ghost. On the other hand, it will not be disputed that much of the ministry actually employed within the borders of the Established Church, is the production of human effort; that it is universally understood to have no other origin; and that no direct influence of the Spirit, in prompting the service, is either expected by the preacher, or required by his hearers. The multitude, who are accustomed to this low standard respecting the nature and character of the ministry itself, are habituated to a standard equally low, in relation to the steps which precede the assumption of the ministerial office. First, with respect to *selection;* the choice of the individual, who is afterwards to proclaim to others the glad tidings of salvation, is very usually understood to rest with his parents, with his friends, or with himself. Secondly, with respect to *preparation;* nothing is required, for the most part, but the passing of a few years at one of the universities, in order to the attainment of mathematical and classical literature, and of a certain moderate stock of theological knowledge. Lastly, with respect to *appointment;* the personal authority of the ordaining bishop is, for this purpose, generally deemed to be all sufficient. Were it true that, by the laying on of his hands, the bishop of modern times, like the apostle of the earliest church, was miraculously enabled to communicate to the candidate for the ministry the gift of the Holy Ghost, the most spiritual Christian could advance no objection to episcopal ordination. But, since this is not true, and since it is perfectly known not to be true, the ceremony plainly resolves itself into an appointment to the office of the ministry by the bishop only; and, with the exception of those individuals who are *really* called to the work by the inward motion of the Holy Ghost, the ministers thus ordained must be considered as undertaking the office of a preacher upon the sole authority of that appointment.

Among the generality of protestant dissenters in this country, much less of form is observed, in conducting the administrations of the gospel, than is customary in the Anglican church. The written sermon, as well as the printed liturgy, are for the most part discarded, and make way for the extempore discourse and prayer. While, however, it appears to be an opinion generally prevalent among English protestant dissenters, that the ability to preach and pray aloud is a gift of the Spirit, I believe there are few of their ministers who hesitate either to prepare themselves for the work by previous study and reflection, or to preach and pray at periods appointed by others, or fixed upon by themselves. With this mixed standard, respecting the nature of the ministry itself, the practices of these Christians, with regard to the preceding measures, will be found exactly to correspond. While the necessity of a divine call, and of the preparation of grace in the heart, are generally admitted, the first selection of the dissenting minister depends, in great measure, on the church to which he belongs. When any young person is considered as affording a sufficient evidence of suitability for the ministry, in point of conduct and talent, as well as of a general call into such a field of labour, he is mostly recommended by the church (with his own consent and that of his friends) to some preparatory academy. There his attention is directed to the acquirement of literature, and to those branches of study, more especially, which bear immediately on his great object. Thus prepared, he is invited by some congregation to come and preach the gospel among them ; and finally, when both parties are satisfied, several dissenting ministers, who have been already established in their office, unite in ordaining him as an authorized preacher, and as the minister of that congregation. This may, I believe, be considered an accurate description of the course adopted with respect to the selection, preparation, and appointment of ministers, by some of the leading bodies of dissenters in this country; and, among many others, to whom such a description will not precisely apply, the same principles are, nevertheless, allowed and enforced — namely, that a divine call and the work of grace are, in the first place, indispensable ; but that to these are to be added the application of outward means, and the interposition of human authority.

Before we proceed to consider the principles and practices of Friends in reference to the present branch of our subject, it will be well for us to examine whether any sanction is given, in the Holy Scriptures, to that practice so general among modern Christians— the human ordination of the ministers of the gospel.

That the apostles, and some others of the earliest Christians, were enabled, by the laying on of their hands, to draw down upon individuals, in a miraculous manner, the gifts of the Holy Spirit, has been already remarked.[5] But it will be allowed, by the impartial reader, that the human ordination of preachers, when connected with this extraordinary power, resolves itself, in point of fact, into a divine appointment, and affords no authority for such ordination, when the power ceases to exist. There are, however, two passages of the New Testament, in which ordination is spoken of without any allusion to such a miraculous circumstance. We are informed, in the book of Acts, that, when Paul and Barnabas revisited the churches which they had planted at Lystra, Iconium, and Antioch, they "*ordained* them elders (or presbyters) in every church;"[6] and on another occasion, Paul thus addressed himself to Titus, "For this cause left I thee in Crete, that thou shouldest set in order the things that are wanting, and *ordain* elders (or presbyters) in every city."[7]

There can be no doubt that in making these appointments, Paul and Titus acted under the immediate influence of the Holy Ghost. On the supposition, however, that their example may be safely followed in the present day, under an inferior measure of the same influence, these passages afford an authority for the human ordination or appointment of Christian *presbyters*: and, since the office of preaching is understood, among many modern Christians, to be immediately connected with the station of a presbyter, the inference is easily deduced, that the human ordination of the preachers of the gospel is authorized in the New Testament. But I apprehend that such an inference is founded upon an original error, of

[5] Acts viii, 18 ; 1 Tim. iv, 14.   [6] Acts xiv, 23.   [7] Titus i, 5.

no slight importance. In the times of primitive Christianity, there was no necessary connexion between the gift of preaching, or prophecy, and the offices of bishops, presbyters, and deacons. The fourteenth chapter of the first epistle of Paul to the Corinthians affords abundant evidence, as we have already found occasion to notice, that when the earliest Christians assembled together for the purpose of divine worship, it was not the bishop or overseer, or the presbyter or elder, or the deacon or subordinate manager, who preached and prayed, *ex officio*, in the congregation. Being, for the most part, persons of a spiritual character, they might, indeed, be frequently included in the number of those who preached and prayed in the churches; but the work of the ministry was, at that time, restricted to no appointed individuals: it devolved promiscuously upon all persons—whether men or women—whether governors or governed—to whom the word of God was revealed, and who were visited by the fresh and heavenly influences of the Spirit of prophecy.

The office of the bishops or overseers was, in the earliest Christian churches, the same as that of the presbyters or elders. The overseers were denominated elders, and the elders overseers.[8] Their situation in the body corresponded with that of the chief rulers of the ancient Jewish synagogues. " It was their duty," says Schleusner, " to rule the church of Christ,

[8] Phil. i, 1. "Paul and Timotheus, &c. . . . . . to all the saints in Christ Jesus which are at Philippi, with the bishops and deacons." Theodoret, in his note upon this passage, says, "He calls the presbyters *bishops*; for, at that period, they were called by both those names:" so also Theophylact.

but *not to teach :* more especially to preside over matters of worship; to administer the sacraments (or at least the Eucharist;) to make decrees in ecclesiastical affairs; to provide assistance for the poor and the sick; to maintain in the church integrity of doctrine and sanctity of manners, and to settle the differences which arose among Christians."[9] This able critic appears to have been somewhat hasty in excluding from the offices of the bishops and presbyters the duty of *teaching.* The gift of teaching—a gift which is sometimes distinguished from that of preaching or prophecy—does not, indeed, appear to have been universal among them; but the apostle, in his general directions respecting the character and qualifications of the bishop or overseer, nevertheless recommends that he should be "apt to teach;"[1] and, again, that he should "be able by sound doctrine (or teaching) both to exhort and to convince (or rather to refute) the gainsayers."[2] But, although the elders and overseers of early Christianity, as the spiritual guides and appointed guardians of the flock, who were to protect their followers from the encroachment of false doctrine and of every root of bitterness, were often called upon in the exercise of their Christian authority, to advise, instruct, exhort, and argue; they were not (like the bishops and presbyters of the Anglican church) necessarily ministers of the gospel. Between the *public preaching and praying, practised in assemblies for worship,* and the offices of these persons, there does

---

[9] See *Schleusner in voc.* πρεσβύτερος.

[1] 1 Tim. iii, 2.   [2] Tit. i, 9.

not appear to have been any indispensable, peculiar, or official connection.[3]

[3] In the Jewish synagogues, which were, probably, *in some respects,* the patterns of the early Christian assemblies for worship, the duty of preaching does not appear to have devolved upon any appointed officer. The officers of the synagogue were, *first,* the rulers, who corresponded with the Christian elders and bishops; they governed the church, and regulated the order of divine service. *Secondly,* the Sheliach Zibbor, or angel of the congregation, who read the forms of prayer. *Thirdly,* the Chozenim, or inspectors, who appear to have answered to the Christian deacons: it was their duty to keep every thing belonging to their place of worship in its proper order; to correct those who misread the Holy Scriptures, &c. *Fourthly,* the interpreter, who translated into vernacular Syriac the portion of Scripture, which had been previously read in Hebrew. The lessons of Scripture were divided into seven parts, and read by seven persons, most of whom were selected from the congregation at large, by one of the rulers. If the reader desired it, he was at liberty to expound: and persons who were totally destitute of office in the church were accustomed to avail themselves of the opportunity thus afforded them for preaching to the people. Such was very frequently the case with our Saviour himself, who taught in the synagogues throughout Galilee and Judea; and, also, with the apostle Paul, as is plainly recorded in the book of Acts, ch. ix, 20; xii, 5, 15; xviii, 19. Now, if there were no officers appointed for the purpose of preaching in the Jewish synagogue, it is very improbable that there should be any such officers in the early Christian assemblies for worship, which, probably, differed from the synagogues only in being conducted *on a far purer and more spiritual system.* See *Prideaux, Con.* fol. ed. i, 306.

Since the presbyters, bishops, and deacons, in the early Christian church, must have been selected as persons of an eminently spiritual character, we may presume that many of them, like Timothy and Titus, were distinguished by the gift of prophecy or preaching. And, since they were, at the same time, possessed of office and authority in the church, the erroneous doctrine might very easily arise, (as the spirituality of the church declined,) *that they alone might preach.* At how early a period the change took place, from the congregational administrations described by the

CHAP. 6.]   *and Appointment of Ministers.*   213

So, also, the *deacon* of the early Christian church was not officially a preacher. His office probably embraced a variety of subordinate services; but it is supposed to have been principally directed to the care of the sick, and to the management and distribution of the funds raised in any church, for the maintenance of the poor.[4]

On the whole, then, it may be allowed that the

apostle Paul, in 1 Cor. xiv, to the modern system of pulpit lectures, it is impossible now to ascertain. The extract given from Hermas, in a note upon the preceding chapter, may suffice to shew that the original practice of the church, in this respect, continued to be maintained in the latter part of the first century; and I observe that Polycarp, (A.D. 107,) in his description of the duties of presbyters and deacons, makes no allusion whatever to their preaching; but speaks of them only as the superintendents and managers of ecclesiastical discipline. *Ep. ad Philipp.* cap. 5 & 6. In the following curious passage of his epistle to the Philadelphians, Ignatius (A.D. 107) describes the divine origin of his own ministry. "I exhorted you, when I was with you, in a loud voice, to obey the bishop, the presbyters, and the deacons: and some persons suspected that, when I thus addressed you, I was previously aware of the divisions which existed among you. But he is my witness, for whom I am in bonds, that I knew it not from any man, but the *Spirit preached by me,* saying in this wise," &c.: cap. 7. Justin Martyr, (A.D. 133,) in his dialogue with Trypho the Jew, declares the continued existence of the gifts of prophecy, and that these gifts were exercised by both men and women: p. 308, Ed. Paris, 1636: *Benson,* vol. i, p. 624. Lastly, Irenæus, bishop of Lyons, (A.D. 178,) describes the spiritual gifts exercised, at his time, in the church, in terms which mainly accord with the accounts given to us, of the same faculties, in the epistles of Paul. "We hear many brethren in the church," says this father, "who are endued with prophetic gifts; who speak by the Spirit in all kinds of languages; who bring to light the secrets of men, for good purposes; and who declare divine mysteries." *Adv. Hæres.* lib. v, cap. 6.

[4] See *Schleusner in voc.* διάκονος.

human ordination or appointment of elders, overseers, and deacons, (provided that it be effected in reverent dependence on the guidance of the Holy Spirit,) is by no means inconsistent with the true order of the Christian church. Such officers are nominated and appointed by their brethren in the Society of Friends. But, it by no means follows, from such an allowance, that *man* is at liberty to ordain or appoint the preachers of the gospel of Christ.

Having premised these observations respecting bishops, presbyters, and deacons, we may proceed to apply the general rule, stated in the commencement of the present dissertation, to the known views and practices of the Society of Friends. In the former chapter, their sentiments respecting the true nature and character of the Christian ministry have been fully detailed; and it has been stated that it is their principle to admit no preaching or audible praying in their assemblies for worship, but such as they deem to be prompted by the immediate influence of the Holy Spirit. Since, therefore, the ministry, according to the apprehension of Friends, ought never to be brought into exercise, unless it is suggested, ordered, and directed, of the Lord; since, as far as is consistent with the infirmity of the instrument, it thus assumes, in their view, the character of a divine work; and since the influence, which alone rightly leads into such a work, is in no degree placed under their authority; it necessarily follows that they cannot interfere in any of the preceding steps—in the selection, preparation, and appointment, of the ministers of the gospel. They conceive that it is the sole prerogative of the Great

CHAP. 6.]   *and Appointment of Ministers.*   215

Head of the church himself, to choose, prepare and ordain, his own ministers. A few observations may now be offered upon each of these points.

I. SELECTION. " Before I formed thee in the belly, I knew thee; and before thou camest forth out of the womb, I sanctified thee, and I ordained thee a prophet unto the nations."[5] Such was the declaration of the Lord to Jeremiah, although the prophet *deemed himself* to be a mere child, completely incapable of the office to which he had been called. A very similar declaration was made respecting an eminent apostle of Jesus Christ. We find that Ananias, the messenger of the Lord to Paul, considered this persecutor of the Christians to be utterly unfit for the exercise of the ministry of the gospel; " but the Lord said unto him, Go thy way; for he is a *chosen vessel unto me*, to bear my name before the Gentiles, and kings, and the children of Israel."[6] Accordingly, Paul himself declares he was " *separated* unto the gospel of God;"[7] — that *God separated him, from his mother's womb, and called him, by his grace, to reveal his Son in him, that he might preach him among the heathen.*[8] As it was with Jeremiah and Paul, so, undoubtedly, it was with all the other prophets and apostles of whom we read in the Holy Scriptures. They were " witnesses chosen before of God." In the secret counsels of their heavenly Father, they were selected from among the children of men, according to his foreknowledge, for that peculiar service in the church and the world, unto which

[5] Jer. i, 5.
[6] Acts ix, 15.   [7] Rom. i, 1.   [8] Gal. i, 15, 16.

it was his good pleasure to appoint them. They were not, in general, such persons as men would have chosen for the work: they were very humble instruments in their own sight, and in the sight of others. Nevertheless, the Lord, who is alone the searcher of hearts, had selected them in his own wisdom, and for his own work. "Ye have not chosen me,"—said our Saviour to his disciples, whom he was soon to anoint with his Holy Spirit, and to send forth in the work of the gospel—"but I have chosen you, and ordained you, that ye should go and bring forth fruit, and that your fruit should remain."[9] Now there is evidently no reason why the same principle should not apply to every true minister of the gospel of Christ. Man is no adequate judge beforehand of the capacity of his brother for such a work; and often are the individuals, whom in our own wisdom, we should be prone to prefer for the purpose, passed over by the Lord. But as he is pleased, by the powerful influence of his Spirit, to anoint *some* of his servants for the work of the ministry, so it must be allowed that, in his perfect knowledge, and boundless wisdom, he *chooses* these individuals for their office in the church, before he thus anoints them in order to its execution.

Now, the selection of which we are speaking is to be regarded, not in the light of an unconditional and irresistible decree, but in that of a gracious purpose, which requires to be met with corresponding duties. This purpose may, in its operation, be disappointed by the unfaithfulness, or perverted by the activity, of man.

[9] John xv, 16.

Many an individual, doubtless, whom the Lord would have numbered among his preachers, has, through unwatchfulness and neglect of the Shepherd's voice, fallen short of the station designed for him. And many a body of Christians, also, by taking the choice of their ministers into their own hands, have imposed the sacred office upon those for whom it was not intended, and have been found, in effect, to say to the prophets of the Lord—"Prophesy not." There can be no reasonable question that, in every age of the church, the Lord chooses the individuals whom he is about to intrust with his message to man. What, then, can be the corresponding duty of his people, but to wait patiently on their divine Master, with prayer and supplication, until he shall be pleased to raise up and anoint, for their service, those whom he has chosen?

II. PREPARATION. Every Christian will allow that the prophets, apostles, and evangelists, of ancient times, who were chosen beforehand, in the divine counsels, to be the bearers of the message of their Lord, were *prepared* for their office before they were called upon to exercise its duties; and it is equally clear that this preparation, which, in some instances, appears to have been gradual and long-continued, and, in others, short and sudden, was of the Lord, and not of man. They were fitted for the exercise of the Lord's *gifts*, by the work of his *grace*. Probably, there might be occasions, when, under very peculiar circumstances, and in order to answer some extraordinary end, even the impenitent sinner might be made to prophesy. But such instances, if any such there were, can be considered only as rare exceptions to a general rule. No reasonable theologian will refuse to admit that, in general, the individuals whom the Lord raised up, among the Israelites and in the infant Christian church, to be prophets and preachers of the word— to be instruments of conversion and edification to others—were themselves previously subjected to the influence of a purifying power, and taught to live in the fear and love of God. Utterly unable would they have been to proclaim unto others, in demonstration of the Spirit, the righteousness which is by faith, had they not, in the first instance, obtained for themselves an experimental acquaintance with true religion. "Create in me a clean heart, O God," cried the Psalmist, "and renew a right spirit within me. Restore unto me the joy of thy salvation; and uphold me with thy free Spirit; *then will I teach transgressors thy ways; and sinners shall be converted unto thee.*"[1]

Friends are of the opinion that, with respect to the preparation of ministers, as well as to their original selection, no valid distinction can be drawn between the preachers of the word in ancient times, and those who are rightly authorized for the service in the present day. The latter, indeed, may receive a *far lower* degree of inspiration than the former. Nevertheless, they are gifted of the Lord according to their own measure, and minister to the people under the influence of his Spirit. We hold it, then, to be an undeniable position, that, for the right exercise of such a gift, (unless, as before mentioned, it be under

[1] Psa. li, 10, 12, 13; *comp.* 2 Tim. ii, 19—21.

very peculiar and extraordinary circumstances,) the work of divine grace in the heart, is an indispensable preparation.

Here it ought to be remarked, that this work of grace in the heart, as it is preparatory to the Christian ministry, is often found to assume a character of more than ordinary depth. The religious experience of all true Christians will, indeed, be found to accord in every main feature; for where is the living member of the church who has not some practical acquaintance with the converting and sanctifying power of the Lord; with the path of self-denial, and with a conformity to the sufferings of Christ; as well as with the refreshing and sustaining influence of his redeeming love? But those whom the Chief Shepherd of the flock is secretly preparing to minister to others, are sometimes introduced into stronger mental conflicts, and brought under more powerful spiritual visitations, than many of their brethren. It is often their lot, in no ordinary measure, to be introduced into a variety of secret trials and temptations, and to be led, as blind men, through an unknown and dreary wilderness.[2] Thus are they taught to surrender their own wills to the divine guidance, and are experimentally prepared for those duties of sympathy which are so peculiarly adapted to the office designed for them; and, when they have, at length, been permitted to experience the delivering power of their Lord, they are ready to open their mouths in his service—to utter his praise, to promulgate his law, and to proclaim his mercy.

[2] See Isa. xlii, 16.

The work of grace, which is carried forward in the hearts of his selected servants, by the Lord himself, is deemed by Friends to be at once indispensable and *sufficient*, as a preparation for the Christian ministry. The addition of literary attainment, upon which some persons are accustomed to lay so great a stress, they regard as a non-essential circumstance. Our views on this branch of the subject are justified alike by the records of Scripture, and by our own experience as a religious body. Among the prophets and preachers of ancient Israel, and the apostles and other early disciples of the Lord Jesus Christ, there were, indeed, certain individuals (for example, king Solomon, the apostle Paul, and the evangelist Luke) who were distinguished, in various degrees, by the acquirements of learning; but, in many other instances, it must be confessed that the persons who were called upon of the Lord, to become the preachers of righteousness, were destitute of these advantages. That this was the fact, in an especial degree, with most of those pre-eminently able ministers, the apostles of Jesus Christ, is universally understood and acknowledged. Nor, with the single exception of the gift of tongues, does this absence of literature appear to have been supplied by their inspiration; for this, *in general*, had no other effect than that of enlightening them respecting the great truths of Christianity, and of clothing their humble preaching with true energy, life, and authority. Even Paul, who was brought up in all the learning of the Hebrews, at the feet of Gamaliel, discarded the "enticing words of man's wisdom," visited his brethren in weakness, fear, and trembling, and determined *to*

CHAP. 6.]   *and Appointment of Ministers.*   221

know nothing among them, " save Jesus Christ and him crucified."[3]

Such are the facts recorded in Scripture respecting the preachers of the word; and our own history and experience, as a religious Society, is calculated to impress upon us a similar lesson. It is an indisputable fact that many of our most useful and convincing ministers, both in the first age of the Society and in more modern times, have been persons of very humble origin, and destitute of every thing which could fairly be described as literary attainment. Many such persons have been known to go forth from among us, and to proclaim the spirituality of the gospel dispensation, with an authority and success which have plainly evinced that, in the work carried on in their hearts by the Lord himself, they have found all that was *essential* as a preparation for their ministerial functions.

As a literary education for the specific object of the ministry, is considered by Friends to be unnecessary and improper, so the opportunity of it is precluded among them by a single consideration; namely, that, according to their sentiments, it is the Lord alone (as I have already endeavoured to explain) who selects the ministers of the gospel; and that, until the work is actually commenced, the Society is ignorant who have been selected. Those who, like Friends, allow that He only can choose his ministers, must also allow, as a necessary consequence, that He only can prepare them. The principle which excludes the interference

[3] 1 Cor. ii, 2, 3, 4.

of man in the one particular, plainly excludes it in the other also.

In bringing to a conclusion the present division of our argument, it will be desirable for me (in order to prevent erroneous impressions) to offer one or two further remarks on literary attainments, and especially on scriptural knowledge. The known opinion of Friends, that academical studies are unnecessary as a preparation for the ministry, has given rise, among some persons, to a notion that the Society avoids encouraging the general pursuit of literature. Those whom I am now addressing are well aware that such a notion has no real foundation. It is fully acknowledged by Friends, to be the duty of the Christian, as well as the privilege of the man, to avail himself of every proper opportunity for the cultivation of his mind, for the enlargement of his talents, and for the acquirement of knowledge. George Fox informs us, in one passage of his interesting journal, that he advised the institution of an academy for the children of Friends, that they might be instructed in "*whatsoever things were civil and useful in the creation;*"[4] and I am persuaded that many Friends, in the present day, entertain an earnest—I hope an *increasing*—desire that their young people may be so instructed. Whatever may be our calling in the world, or station in the church, it is unquestionable that the exercise of our intellectual faculties, and the collecting of useful knowledge, may enlarge our capacity for the service of our Great Master; and, on this principle, it is to be freely admitted, that learning may produce, *collaterally and*

[4] Fol. ed. A.D. 1765, p. 395.

subordinately, a desirable effect, even on the ministry of the gospel. Not only may the powers of the mind be strengthened for that and every other good purpose, by means of a liberal education, but occasions frequently occur, in which information upon various points may be made to subserve the great object of the Christian minister. Thus, for example, when the apostle Paul was engaged in preaching to the polite and fastidious Athenians, it probably gave him no slight advantage with his audience, that he was able to illustrate his doctrine by an apposite quotation from one of their own poets.[5]

While, however, our capacity for usefulness, as Christians, may be, in some degree, enlarged by almost every description of innocent intellectual pursuit, there is no species of mental cultivation to which this observation applies with nearly equal force as to that which has, in itself, a direct edifying tendency—the acquirement of Christian knowledge, especially through the study of the Holy Scriptures. An exact acquaintance with that divine book will be found of no little avail in the performance of almost any services which may be allotted to us in the church: for, where is the moral condition, where is the religious engagement, to which something applicable may not be discovered among the examples, the doctrines, or the precepts, recorded in the Bible? But, it must, on all hands, be allowed, that to the Christian minister, a knowledge of the Bible is of indispensable importance.

It is one of the leading excellencies of the sacred volume, and one of the practical proofs of its divine

[5] Acts xvii, 28.

origin, that it contains an inexhaustible stock of materials for the ministry of the word. The experience of Friends, in this respect, is in accordance with that of other religious bodies. Although our ministers can prescribe no limits to the diversified directions of that divine influence under which they profess to act, yet, we know that, in general, it is Scripture which supplies them with subjects for their contemplation; it is Scripture which the Spirit of truth brings to their recollection, and impresses upon their minds; it is the language of Scripture which they quote; it is the doctrine of Scripture which they unfold and apply.

Now although our religious principles prevent our instituting a course even of scriptural study, as a preparation for the office of preachers, it is to be remembered that the perusal of the sacred volume is a duty enjoined by the Society of Friends, on *all* its members; and few among them will be found more zealous in performing this duty than those whom the Lord is preparing for the office of the ministry. While he is carrying on the work of grace in their hearts, and leading them through many a secret conflict, they will be little inclined to neglect those inspired records, by means of which they may so often be strengthened in their weakness, instructed in their ignorance, and comforted in their sorrow. And thus, when, at length, they are anointed for the service, and commissioned to proclaim the gospel, they are seldom, if ever, found destitute of a useful and experimental acquaintance with Holy Writ. Lastly, after they have been acknowledged as ministers, a frequent perusal of the Bible, and a careful attention to its contents, is considered by the Society to be one of their especial duties.[6]

III. APPOINTMENT. By the appointment of a minister, I do not mean his original selection, but his actual introduction, to the office—that introduction which, in episcopal churches, is considered to be effected by the ordaining act of the bishop. In this last of the measures which are generally understood to precede the exercise of the Christian ministry, as well as in the two prior steps already considered, Friends esteem the interference of man to be needless, improper, and, on the principles which they entertain, impossible. It is needless, according to our apprehension, because the authority of that Being who really invests with the office is incapable of any augmentation. It is improper, because he has no counsellor, and no man may interrupt his designs, or interfere with his will. It is, on our principles, impossible; because, as we are ignorant who among us have been selected and prepared for the work, so are we destitute of any adequate means of judging to whom the exercise of that work may rightly be committed.

Although the gifts of the Holy Spirit were, in early times, miraculously communicated by the laying on of the hands of the Lord's inspired servants, there is nothing in Scripture, as we have already found occasion to observe, which justifies, in any degree, the merely human appointment of the preachers of the gospel. Paul declares that he was an apostle, "not of men, neither by man, but by Jesus Christ, and God

---

[6] See *Advices to Ministers and Elders—Book of Extracts.*

the Father, who raised him from the dead."[7] Such was the case with Paul; nor could it be otherwise with the apostles in general, or with their companions and associates in the work of the gospel. Whether they were, or were not, subjected to the laying on of human hands, they were really invested with their sacred office, not by their bishops—not by their churches, but by him who had already selected them for the work, and from whom alone the spirit of prophecy could ever emanate. When the one hundred and twenty persons, who were gathered together on the day of Pentecost, were all filled with the Holy Ghost, they spake with tongues, and prophesied. These persons were appointed to the office of the ministry, and invested with the powers needful for it, by an authority which precluded all interference, and which demanded nothing at the hands of the leaders of the church, but submission and praise. " Unto every one of us," says Paul to the Ephesians, " is given grace according to the measure of the gift of Christ. Wherefore he saith, When he ascended up on high, he led captivity captive, and gave gifts unto men.......And he gave some, apostles; and some, prophets; and some, evangelists; and some, pastors and teachers; for the perfecting of the saints, for the work of the ministry, for the edifying of the body of Christ."[8]

Now, although the measure of the gifts of the Holy Spirit may be found to vary in different ages of the church of Christ, yet, as long as the ministry is exercised under the immediate influence of the Spirit, so

[7] Gal. i, 1.   [8] Eph. iv, 7—12.

long the principle of ordination to such a function must continue unchanged. When the Lord Jesus has selected his ministers from among his people; when he has carried forward and completed the work of their preparation; when, finally, he has issued his gracious command that they should go forth and preach the gospel, and has anointed them for the purpose by the influences of the Holy Spirit; there is but one right and proper course for them to pursue— that of simple and unhesitating obedience. They know that man has no right to interfere with their appointment, and they dare not look to him for their warrant and authority. It is their Lord and Redeemer who has invested them with their office, and to him alone they are responsible for its execution.

Let it not, however, be imagined that, in the decision of the question, *whether or not he is truly appointed to that office*, the minister is to depend exclusively on his own judgment. Christians ought ever to be subject one to another in love; and it must, in great measure, devolve on their brethren to determine whether those who speak the word are rightly invested with their functions, or whether their communications rest on no better foundation than their own will. A *spiritual evidence* will be given to the anointed and experienced members of the church, which will enable them to distinguish the true ministers of Christ.

The generality of my readers are, probably, well aware that one of the principal duties of the elders, in our religious society, is to watch over the ministry; to guard against the encroachments of unsound doctrine; to encourage the feeble and the diffident; and to restrain the forward and hasty among the Lord's servants. Nor is the office of judging respecting the ministry confined to the elders alone. As the whole body of the church, in any place, is interested in the question respecting the authority of its ministers, so is the whole body concerned in the decision of that question. When a congregation of Christians have bestowed on the ministry of any person a due and patient attention, and know, from experience, that it is attended with the life and power of the Spirit, they are enabled to form a valid judgment that such a one is "inwardly moved" to the work "by the Holy Ghost." And then, though they have no concern with his appointment to the ministry, it is required of them, by the order of Christian discipline (and it is a practice universal in the Society of Friends), to *acknowledge* that he is a true minister of Christ, and to yield to him that station in the church, which so important a calling demands.

Before we dismiss the subject of the appointment of ministers, it will be desirable to make a few remarks on a secondary branch of it. In many Christian churches, the appointment of the minister is twofold:— the "*ordination*," by which he receives his authority to preach; and the "*institution*," by which he is intrusted with the spiritual care of a particular flock. In the Church of England, the ordination is truly the act of the bishop alone: the institution, although the official act of the bishop, depends, in reality, on the patron of the living. Upon him rests the awful responsibility (I might almost call it the divine prerogative) of assigning a flock to the shepherd, and of selecting a shepherd for the flock. Now, it may be freely allowed that this most important power is sometimes exercised with a pious care, and with an earnest solicitude, for the spiritual welfare of the parties. But, on the other hand, who is not aware that, in consequence of the prevalence of such a system, the holy things of God are often miserably profaned—that livings are bestowed and accepted for the mere purpose of temporal advantage—and that, in general, the more unfit any persons are for an authority to appoint to the care of souls, the more ready they are to exercise that authority without consideration.

Among the generality of protestant dissenters, the choice of the minister, as I have already stated, rests exclusively with the people; and his *ordination* serves the double purpose of giving an established authority to his ministerial functions, and of appointing him as the preacher to a specific congregation.

Now, with respect to this secondary appointment of the ministers of the gospel, Friends believe it to be their duty to adhere to the principles already unfolded, and to refrain altogether from any interference with the will and work of the Lord. We are thoroughly persuaded that, as he alone can bestow upon us the gifts of the Spirit, so he alone can rightly determine the line of our services, and the field of our labours. Within the compass of whatever meeting a minister is raised up in the Society, there, for the most part, he continues to reside, and to exercise the duties of his calling; nor will he, if he be rightly disposed, venture so to change his residence, as to transfer his services to another congregation, unless he can entertain the humble confidence that, in adopting such a measure, he is acting in conformity with the will of his divine Master.

As our principle, on this subject, evidently applies to the fixing of the usual residence of the minister, so does it also apply, in a very particular manner, to his travels in the work of the gospel. Every one who is acquainted with the history of the Israelitish prophets, must be aware that, in all their religious movements, they acted under the direction of "the word of the Lord;" that is, probably, of the perceptible inward communication of his Spirit. The "word of the Lord" sent them forth on their errands, and directed them to the persons for whom their message was intended, and to the places in which it was to be delivered.[9] So, also, there is every reason to believe that the proceedings of the apostles, and of the other early preachers of Christianity, although not in general described in the same manner, were, in fact regulated by the same principle. The Spirit, by whose immediate revelations they were alone enabled to preach, would not fail to direct their ministry to the right persons, and in the right places; nor can we imagine that these servants of the Lord were, in this respect, destitute of that immediate guidance, with which, in the other branches of their high duty, they were so eminently favoured. In the narration, contained in the book of Acts, of two of the apostle Paul's journeys in the work of the ministry, a clear description is given of the authority and influence

---

[9] See, for example, 1 Kings xvi, 7; xvii, 2—9; xviii, 1; xix, 15; Isaiah vii, 3; Amos vii, 14, 15; Jonah i, 2.

under which he commenced and conducted the undertaking. We read that, as the Christians at Antioch "ministered to the Lord and fasted, the Holy Ghost said, Separate me Barnabas and Saul for the work whereunto I have called them: and, when they had fasted and prayed, and laid their hands on them, they sent them away. So they, being *sent forth by the Holy Ghost, departed unto Seleucia, and from thence they sailed to Cyprus*," &c.[1] Again in the history of Paul's second journey, (when Silas was his companion,) we are informed that, " when they had gone throughout Phrygia and the region of Galatia, and were *forbidden of the Holy Ghost* to preach the word in Asia, after they were come to Mysia, they assayed to go into Bithynia; *but the Spirit suffered them not:*" and we are afterwards told, that by a special vision from the Lord, they were encouraged to cross the sea, and to go forward into Macedonia.[2]

There appears to be no good reason why that divine direction, which was thus bestowed upon the ancient prophets and apostles, should be withheld from the servants of the Lord in the present day, who accomplish their religious services under a lower degree of the same immediate influence. Accordingly, the journeys of their ministers are ever considered, in the Society of Friends, to be regulated by the perceptible guidance of the Holy Spirit; and, in adopting this principle, we conceive that we have been amply justified by a long-continued and multiplied trial of its practical operation. A short description of that

[1] Acts xiii, 2—4.
[2] Acts xvi, 6—10; *comp.* chap. viii, 26, 39.

which Friends deem to be, on such occasions, the proper experience of the minister, as well as his right method of proceeding, will, perhaps, be acceptable to such of my readers as are not, at present, well informed on the subject.

In the first place, then, it is fully acknowledged, in the Society, to be the general duty of ministers, not only to exercise their functions where they reside, but to be diligent in visiting the churches which are scattered abroad, and to be ready, when called of the Lord, to go to and fro in the earth, in order to preach the gospel. Now as the minister is preserved in humble dependence upon his divine Master, he not only feels the importance of this general calling, but is often made sensible of an impression that it is his duty to exercise it in particular places. The current of Christian love in his heart assumes a specific direction. On general grounds he can feel, with the apostle, that he is a debtor to all men—but there are certain portions of men to whom that debt is now commanded to be paid. The burden of the Lord rests upon him, and he endeavours to dwell patiently under its influence, until his views are so cleared and ripened, that he can lay them before his brethren and sisters of the meeting to which he belongs. They unite with him in the deliberate consideration of the subject; and if, on waiting in silence together on the Lord, they come to a judgment that the undertaking of the minister truly originates in the divine will, they set him at liberty for his journey; commend him to the gracious care and protection of the good Shepherd; and for the satisfaction of those persons among whom his lot may be cast, bestow upon him a certificate of their concurrence and approbation.

Thus provided with the recorded sanction of his friends, and "sent forth," as he humbly trusts, "by the Holy Ghost," to the work appointed him, the minister proceeds on his journey; and whether his labours are directed only to Friends, or also to persons of other denominations, (who, on such occasions, are frequently invited to attend our religious assemblies,) he endeavours to follow no other guidance, throughout the progress of his travels, but the secret intimations of the divine Spirit. Under this guidance he passes from place to place, and from meeting to meeting. Poor and empty in himself, and totally unprepared, by previous study, for his successive labours, he acts on a principle of simple faith in his Governor and Guide. As this faith is maintained, he finds himself again and again renewed in his spiritual strength; and, as often as the right opportunity recurs, he is revisited by the enlivening Spirit of the Lord, and anointed afresh for his service. At length, when the work assigned to him has been executed, the burden which had rested, with so much weight, upon him, is removed. He returns to his home: he restores to his friends the certificate which they had given him: and he is, for the most part, permitted to resume his usual occupations, with a remunerating and confirming sense of rest, liberty, and comfort.

In reviewing the principal contents of the present essay, the reader will recall to his remembrance the general rule laid down at its commencement; that the standard maintained by any body of Christians, respecting the steps preparatory to the ministry, will always be proportioned to their standard respecting the origin and nature of the ministry itself. He will recollect that this rule is illustrated and confirmed by the known practices of the Anglican church, and of the generality of English protestant dissenters—that the human ordination of the preachers of the gospel, so prevalent among modern Christians, derives no authority from that ordination of presbyters which is recorded in Scripture, as having taken place in primitive times; because the bishops, presbyters, and deacons, of the early church, although rulers, managers, and even teachers, were not officially the *preachers* of the word—that Friends, who allow no ministry, in connexion with worship, but such as they deem to spring from the immediate influence of the Spirit, can take no part whatever in the steps which precede the exercise of the gift; but conceive it to be their duty to leave the whole work of selection, preparation, and ordination, to the Lord himself—that Jesus Christ, according to their apprehension, chooses his own ministers beforehand, and that no man may interfere with his choice—that he prepares them for the office, by the work of his grace—that this preparation is of itself sufficient, without literary attainment; although mental cultivation and learning are, in themselves, desirable, and may produce, *collaterally*, a good effect, even on our religious services—that a practical knowledge of the Holy Scriptures is of indispensable use to the Christian preacher—that, when the Lord has chosen and prepared his ministers, he anoints them for their service, sends them forth on his own authority, and directs them in the course of their labours—that, nevertheless, the decision of the question, whether the minister be really acting under divine authority or otherwise, rests not so much with himself as with the church—finally, that the views and practices of Friends, in relation to these several particulars, are in accordance with a variety of declarations and examples recorded in Holy Writ.

Having completed my argument on the present subject, I may venture, in conclusion, to suggest to the consideration of my friends an important practical reflection. It has often and justly been observed, that every species of true excellence and virtue has its imitating and corresponding vice; and certainly it is the duty of Christians, while they earnestly endeavour to embrace the one, to be no less diligent in avoiding the other. Now, that passive course, which it is the object of the present essay to recommend — that absence of all human interference with the sole prerogative, and peculiar work of the Lord—however excellent and desirable in itself—will, I believe, be found to have its imitating and corresponding vice *in spiritual dulness and inactivity, in a real neglect of the divine call, and in the omission of required duty.* Such is our own liability to error, and such the artfulness of our spiritual enemy, that the very doctrine of our own insufficiency may be made a cover for inertness, and for a culpable and cowardly secession from the good fight of faith. The mental poverty and discouragement, also, to which even the Lord's servants are liable, may often be so fostered as to prevent their laying hold of that arm of power, which is able to support them in the most arduous conflicts, and to qualify them, notwithstanding all their weakness, for their labours in the gospel of Christ. Exposed as we are to these points of danger, and very generally placed in a condition of outward ease and security, we had need exercise a constant care, lest, while we are making a high profession of spirituality, our conduct should be marked by *indolence* in the service of our Redeemer.

Now, where is the preservative against such an indolence? Surely it will not be found in the desertion of those pure and exalted principles which it is our especial duty to uphold in the church, but rather *in watchfulness unto prayer.* Let us, then, be more diligent in seeking the animating and strengthening influence of the grace of God: let us be alive to every touch of the divine finger: let our hearts breathe the expressions of Samuel, "Speak, Lord, for thy servant heareth;" and, since " the harvest truly is plenteous " and the labourers " few," let us unite in earnest supplication to the Almighty, that he will be pleased yet more abundantly to pour forth of his Spirit upon all flesh, and thus to "*send forth labourers into his harvest.*"

CHAPTER VII.

ON THE OBJECTIONS ENTERTAINED BY FRIENDS TO THE PECUNIARY REMUNERATION OF THE MINISTERS OF THE GOSPEL.

WHEN Jesus Christ sent forth his seventy disciples to heal diseases, and to proclaim the approach of the kingdom of heaven, he forbade them to provide any stores for their journey. They were to place their confidence in the providential care of their heavenly Father; and, in the houses which they might visit, they were freely to avail themselves of the hospitality of their friends, for the supply of their bodily wants. "Into whatsoever house ye enter," said he to them, "first say, Peace be to this house. And if the son of peace be there, your peace shall rest upon it: if not, it shall turn to you again. *And in the same house remain, eating and drinking such things as they give; for the labourer is worthy of his hire.*"[1] So also the apostle Paul, when addressing his Corinthian converts, among whom he had been labouring in the gospel of Christ, asserts the claim upon them which, when so engaged, he clearly possessed, for

[1] Luke x, 5—7.

such a provision of " carnal things" as his necessities might require. " Have we not power," says he, " *to eat and to drink?* ...... or I only and Barnabas, have we not power to forbear working? Who goeth a warfare any time at his own charges? Who planteth a vineyard, and eateth not of the fruit thereof? or who feedeth a flock, and eateth not of the milk of the flock? Say I these things as a man? or saith not the law the same also? For it is written in the law of Moses, Thou shalt not muzzle the mouth of the ox that treadeth out the corn. Doth God take care for oxen? or saith he it altogether for our sakes? For our sakes, no doubt, this is written: that he that ploweth should plow in hope; and that he that thresheth in hope should be partaker of his hope. If we have sown unto you spiritual things, is it a great thing if we shall reap your carnal things?...... Do ye not know that they which minister about holy things *live* of the things of the temple? and they which wait at the altar are *partakers with the altar?* Even so hath the Lord ordained that they which preach the gospel should live of the gospel."[2]

The provision of the Mosaic law which is here cited—when regarded in its higher sense, as applying to labourers in the cause of righteousness — appears to express, in a manner at once full and simple, the *principle* on which the apostle asserts his right to a provision for his natural wants. " Thou shalt not muzzle the ox that treadeth out the corn;" or, in other words, *While the ox is treading out the corn, thou shalt not muzzle him.* When the seventy dis-

[2] 1 Cor. ix, 4—14.

ciples of Jesus forsook, for a time, all their secular employments; when they went forth, in the name of their Lord, to heal the sick, and to preach righteousness; when they were engaged in travelling from place to place, in order to publish to their countrymen the glad tidings of salvation; it is evident that their whole time was occupied in their religious services; and, deprived, as they were, during such services, of the opportunity for earning their own bread, it was right that they should cast themselves, without reserve, on the kindness of their friends. It would have been improper in the visiters to decline such assistance, and shameful in the visited to withhold it. Very similar were the circumstances of the apostle Paul, who had sacrificed his original pursuits, and knew no settled or permanent home; but moved about from place to place, according to the will of his Lord, in order to diffuse, among his fellow-men, the truths of Christianity. Since he was constantly engaged in these missionary efforts, and devoted his time and talents exclusively to the work, he possessed an undeniable moral claim on those in whose behalf he laboured, for the supply of his outward necessities.

The same rule, respecting the maintenance of the ministers of the gospel, is admitted in the Society of Friends. Occasions frequently occur, as has been remarked in the preceding chapter, when our ministers, as they apprehend, are sent forth from their homes by their divine Master. Constrained by the gentle influences of his love in their hearts, they visit the churches which are scattered abroad; and for a time devote themselves, without intermission, to the exercise of their ministerial functions. During the progress and continuance of such undertakings, they cannot be expected to provide for themselves; and it is, therefore, a practice generally prevailing in the Society, to pay the expenses of their journeys, and to maintain them during the course of their labours. Like the seventy disciples, to whom we have already alluded, they eat and drink at the houses which they visit; and if they be found true evangelists, it is universally acknowledged by their brethren, and not only acknowledged but felt—" that the labourer is worthy of his hire;" or, as the sentiment is expressed in the Gospel of Matthew, that " the workman is worthy of his meat."[3]

Although, however, Paul upholds the general rule, that the ox, when actually treading out the corn, is not to be muzzled, he was evidently very jealous of its being in any degree misapplied, or extended beyond its true bearing. Deprived as he was of any permanent home, and singularly devoted, both in mind and time, to the duties of an apostle, he might very reasonably have depended solely upon the churches for his food and raiment; but no sooner did he take up his residence in any place for a considerable length of time, than he began to apply himself to some manual labour, in order that he might earn his own bread, avoid being burdensome to his friends, and throw no impediment in the way of the gospel. "If others be partakers of this power over you," says the apostle to the same Corinthians, " are not we rather? Nevertheless, we have not used this power; but suffer all

[3] Chap. x, 10.

CHAP. 7.]   *of the Ministers of the Gospel.*   241

things, *lest we should hinder the gospel of Christ*....... What is my reward, then? Verily that, when I preach the gospel, I may make the gospel of Christ without charge, *that I abuse not my power in the gospel.*"[4] As the apostle declined receiving a maintenance from his friends at Corinth, so he observed the same line of conduct at Ephesus; where, indeed, he not only supported himself, but contributed to the support of others. Diligent as he was, during his abode in that city, in the exercise of his ministry—teaching " publicly from house to house," and warning " every one night and day with tears"—he was, nevertheless, enabled to address the Ephesian elders in the following terms: " I have coveted no man's silver, or gold, or apparel; yea, ye yourselves know that these hands have ministered unto my necessities, and *to them that were with me.*"[5] And, after thus adverting to his own conduct, he proceeded to enjoin a similar course upon those whom he was addressing: I have showed you all things, how that *so labouring* you ought to support the weak, and to remember the words of the Lord Jesus, how he said, It is more blessed to give than to receive."[6]

On the whole, therefore, while the general rule is to be admitted, that the preacher of the gospel, during the periods when his time is exclusively devoted to his ministerial functions, may properly derive his sustenance from those among whom he is thus engaged; it is quite evident that, according to the mind of the apostle Paul, any application of this rule beyond its

[4] 1 Cor. ix, 12, 18.   [5] Acts xx, 33, 34.
[6] Ver. 35.

R

true limits, is inconsistent with the purity of the divine law, and injurious to the cause of Christianity.

Now it is the opinion of Friends, that the limits of the rule are transgressed, and the rule itself dangerously perverted, in the practise, so usual among Christians, of *hiring the ministers of the gospel.* Here, I must beg my reader to understand that, in using the word " hiring," it is wholly foreign from my intention to express anything in the least degree offensive to Christian ministers of any denomination. That a considerable proportion of these persons are truly the servants of the Lord Jesus—that many of them undertake the oversight of the flock " not for filthy lucre, but of a ready mind," and are incomparably more intent upon the winning of souls than upon their own temporal advantage—I both know and am happy to acknowledge. But we are here discussing a general principle; and I use the word in question, simply because it is the only one which can properly express my meaning. It is, then, clearly the practice of many Christian societies, to *hire their ministers;* that is to say, to engage their services in consideration of pecuniary salaries. As a gentleman agrees with his servant, and a merchant with his clerk, to pay them particular sums of money, on condition of the performance of particular descriptions of work; so do these societies agree to remunerate their ministers with such and such salaries, *on condition of their preaching;* and instances sometimes occur, in which the amount of the salary given is regulated, very precisely, by the frequency of the ministry required. Whether this agreement actually takes place between the minister and his flock, as among many dissenting bodies, or whether the contract between the two parties is permanently fixed by the law of the land, as in the Anglican church —the principle which the system necessarily and universally involves, is still the same—namely, that certain work is to be performed, and pecuniary wages given for its performance.

According to our apprehension, this hiring of preachers degrades the character, and corrupts the practical operation, of the ministry of the gospel. It is evident that such a system is closely connected with the notion, that the preacher may exercise his high functions on the authority, and according to the pleasure, of *man;* and, in practice, it obviously tends, in a very injurious manner, to confirm and establish that notion. Were it true that the ministry of the gospel is properly the work of man, requiring no other sanction than *his* appointment, and no other forces than *his* exertions, no objection whatever could be made to such a method of proceeding. In that case, it would arise out of those fundamental laws of justice, which ought ever to regulate transactions *between man and man.* But, no sooner is the opposite principle allowed—no sooner is it admitted that the ministry of the gospel is the work of the Lord; that it can be rightly exercised only in virtue of his appiontment, and only through the effusions of his Spirit; and that man has no power to command, and no authority to restrain, the influence which leads into such a service—no sooner are these things understood and allowed, than the compact which binds the minister to preach, on the condition that his hearers shall pay him for his preaching, assumes the character of absolute inconsistency with the spirituality of the Christian religion. " Though I preach the gospel," says the apostle Paul, " I have nothing to glory of; *for necessity is laid upon me, yea, woe is unto me, if I preach not the gospel!* For if I do this thing willingly, I have a reward; but, if against my will, *a dispensation of the gospel is committed unto me.*"[7]

These observations will enable the reader to form a just view of the reasons which actuate the Society of Friends, when on the one hand, they accede to the doctrine that the ox, when treading out the corn, is not to be muzzled; and when, on the other hand, they totally abstain from engaging their ministers on pecuniary stipends, and from otherwise paying them for the exercise of their gift. Such pecuniary provisions would, indeed, be in total dissonance with our sentiment, that no ministry ought to be allowed, in connexion with divine worship, but such as springs from the appointment of the Lord, and is exercised under the immediate influence of his Holy Spirit. It has never been heard of, in the whole annals of sacred history, that *prophecy* has been purchased, or the *true prophets* hired: and we apprehend that, whether the immediate gifts of the Spirit operate in a higher or a lower *degree*, they are still in their nature absolutely free. No man can exercise them in pursuance of an agreement with his fellow creatures. They are delayed, withheld, withdrawn, or poured forth, according to the good pleasure of *him* who searches the reins and the heart, and who only knows the needs of

[7] 1 Cor. ix, 16, 17.

his own church. Those who preach under such an influence, do not preach because their congregation requires it of them ; but because their hearts are filled with the love of Christ, and because they are sent forth and impelled by the Spirit of the Lord, and can find no rest for their consciences, but in obedience to that Spirit. Our ministers cannot say to us, " Pay us, and we will preach ;" for a woe is upon them, if they preach not the gospel; and the same injunction is laid upon upon them as upon the servants of God in ancient times—" Freely ye have received, freely give."[8] There is not one of them, who is truly called into the work, who would *dare* to receive from the hands of men a payment for his labours, lest he should thereby sin against God, who requires of him a willing sacrifice, and should for ever prevent the effusion of that heavenly oil, by which he has been anointed; nor would his brethren *dare* to propose such a payment to him, lest a curse should come upon them—the curse of spiritual darkness and desertion—for presuming that the free gifts of God might be purchased for money.[9] In addressing our ministers, we would use the words of the apostle Peter : " As every man hath received the gift, *even so* minister the same one to another, as good stewards of the manifold grace of God. If any man speak, let him speak as the oracles of God; if any man minister, let him do it as of the ability which God giveth ; that God in all things may be glorified through Jesus Christ, to whom be praise and dominion for ever and ever;"[1] and we would add, *Cast all your care upon the Lord ; for he careth for you.*

[8] Matt. x, 8.   [9] Acts viii, 20.   [1] Peter iv, 10, 11.

In point of fact, experience has furnished the Society of Friends with ample evidence that the Great Head of the church, who calls his own servants into the work of the gospel, and who thus gently constrains them, in behalf of others, as well as on their own account, to " seek first the kingdom of God and his righteousness," adds unto them all things needful for their temporal maintenance. When they are travelling from place to place, and when their whole time is thus devoted to the work of the gospel, the necessary supply of their outward wants is not withheld from them: and when they are at home, they avail themselves, like other persons, of their own industry, and of the openings of a benevolent providence, in procuring, for themselves and for their families, an honest and respectable livelihood.

Such being the sentiments of Friends respecting the spirituality and perfect freedom of the ministry of the gospel, it evidently becomes their duty, in a clear and consistent manner, to uphold those sentiments in their practice. Not only, therefore, do they refuse to pay or hire their own ministers, but they also decline making any contributions to the paying or hiring of ministers of other denominations. Did they act otherwise, they might justly be deemed unfaithful to the light bestowed upon them, and they would, in fact, be subverting with one hand, the edifice which they are professing to erect with the other.

The reader will be aware that I am now alluding to the course, so generally pursued in our Society, in reference to tithes and other ecclesiastical imposts. It is certain that, whenever these demands are made on the true and consistent Friend, he will not fail to refuse the payment of them: not because such refusal is generally insisted on in the Society; but because the religious sentiments which he has embraced, and which have been explained in these essays, inevitably lead him, if he is faithful, into that result. He feels that it is a duty, laid upon him by his divine Master, uniformly to maintain the spirituality and freedom of the Christian ministry; nor will he venture, *by any action of his own*, to lay waste his principle, and to weaken the force of truth, with respect to so important a subject. Such an action, the voluntary payment of tithes must unquestionably be considered.

This conclusion is by no means affected by the consideration that the payment of tithes is imposed on the inhabitants of this country by the law of the land; and that, therefore, the clergy have a legal claim to such a remuneration. Faithful as Friends desire to be to the legal authorities of the state under which they live, it is evident that, as Christians, they cannot render to the law an *active* obedience, in any particular which interferes with their religious duty—that is to say, with their duty to an infinitely superior power. They cannot obey man rather than God. The only obedience to the law, which can be allowable under such circumstances, is purely passive. It is no part of the practice, and it would be quite inconsistent with the sentiments, of the Society, to *resist* the " powers that be." In those matters in which they find an active compliance with the law precluded by the dictates of conscience, Friends are, I trust, prepared to suffer the consequences, and quietly to allow the law to find its own course. While they abstain from taking any part themselves in those things which they deem to be wrong, they are ready to stand still, and abide by the consequences. On these grounds, therefore, although they refuse to pay tithes, they oppose no resistance to those legal distraints by which tithes are taken from them. It is surprising that any persons of reflection should form an opinion (not unfrequently expressed) that there is no essential distinction between these practices, and should assert that the suffering of the distraint, in a moral and religious point of view, is the same as a voluntary payment. The two courses are, in point of fact, the respective results of two opposite principles. The Friend, who voluntarily pays tithes, puts forth his hand to that which he professes to regard as an unclean thing, and actively contributes to the maintenance of a system which is directly contrary to his own religious views. The Friend, who refuses to pay tithes, but who (without involving himself in any secret compromise) quietly suffers a legal distraint for them, is clear of *any action* which contradicts his own principles. He only follows up another branch of those principles, in not opposing force to force, and in rendering a passive obedience to the law.[1]

[1] It is sometimes remarked that, in refusing to pay tithes, Friends withhold the property of their neighbour; and thus, in their endeavour not to counteract their own views on the subject of a free ministry of the gospel, involve themselves in a breach of common integrity. Now, it appears to us, that such a charge is wholly fallacious. Although, in the first place, the conscientious Friend cannot take any active part in the satisfaction of ecclesiastical demands, he opposes no obstruction to those legal operations by

It would by no means accord with that quietness of character which it is the desire of Friends to maintain, were they eager and violent in their efforts to promote their own views, or clamorous against other Christians who differ from themselves. Nevertheless, they consider it to be their duty, by the explicit, yet unobtrusive, language of conduct, to bear what they very properly call their *testimony* against such opinions and practices as they conceive to be inconsistent with the gospel dispensation. This observation is completely

which that satisfaction is, without difficulty, obtained. And, secondly, we deem the notion that any part of the produce of our lands is the property of the priest, to be destitute of any sound foundation. If it is his property, his title to it must be clear and unexceptionable. On what, then, rests the title of the priest to this supposed property? On the assumption of a *divine right* to the tithes on the part of the church, and on the recognition of that *divine right* by the British legislature. See *Statutes at large*, 29 *Hen.* VIII. ch. 20. Since almost all protestants allow that no such right exists, and since, for our own parts, we are persuaded that the assumption of it is directly opposed to some of the leading principles of Christianity, we cannot admit that the priest has any valid title whatsoever to a property in any part of the produce of our lands. His claim, however groundless in itself, is indeed sanctioned by the law of the state; and the individual who buys land, pays a smaller sum of money than he otherwise would have done for his purchase, because it is known, by both parties, that a certain proportion of that which is annually grown upon it can be legally claimed, and will be actually taken, by the ecclesiastical incumbent. Nevertheless, every particle of the land, which a man purchases, or inherits in fee, is his own property; so that he can, at all times, use it as he pleases;—crop it profitably—crop it unprofitably—or allow it to run to absolute waste and ruin. And, as every particle of the land is his own property, so also is every particle of its produce; unless, indeed, he let the land to another person, when the produce of it becomes, on certain conditions, the property of his tenant.

exemplified in their refusal to pay tithes. By such a conduct, they have exposed themselves to much expense and inconvenience; and, in former times, to very severe sufferings; but, by the course which they have thus adopted, they not only keep themselves clear of an action which they disapprove, but they plainly *express their dissent* from that system of sentiment and practice from which the institution of tithes has arisen, and with which it is still inseparably connected. A few observations, respecting some of the particulars against which Friends endeavour thus practically to testify, will enable the reader to form a complete view of the subject.

By a refusal to pay tithes, then, they express their dissent, *first*, from the practice, so prevalent in the Christain world, of hiring and paying the ministers of religion: *secondly*, from that description of ministry which is capable of being so procured—which is capable of being exercised at a man's own time, and in pursuance of an agreement with his fellow creatures: *thirdly*, from those human appointments to the ministry, originating respectively with the bishop and with the patron, by means of which the clergyman is invested with a legal claim to the tithes of any parish. On these three points, I have already endeavoured to unfold the sentiments of our Society. It only remains for me, therefore, to invite the reader's attention, somewhat more particularly, to two other branches of the same subject.

In the *fourth* place, therefore, it may be remarked that, by refusing to pay tithes, Friends express their dissent from a notion very commonly entertained—

CHAP. 7.]   *of the Ministers of the Gospel.*   251

especially among persons who have received but little religious instruction—that the priestly office is continued in the church of Christ. The institution of tithes, in the Christian church, is generally supposed to have taken place during the fourth century; or rather, the contributions made for the poor began about that period to be denominated *tithes.* By degrees these contributions were diverted from their original channel, and were applied, either in part or in whole, to the remuneration of the ministers of religion. At length, during the progress of the middle ages, and after kings, emperors, and states, had very generally fallen under the spiritual dominion of the papacy, the *tenth of the produce of the land* was boldly claimed by the clergy, as appertaining to them of *divine right;* and thus, for the partial and voluntary offerings of former days, was gradually substituted a general and compulsory tax.[2] Now, it is certain that, while these changes were taking place, the professors of the religion of Christ were quickly degenerating from the simplicity and purity of their forefathers, and were turning back, in the most obvious manner, to the ceremonial system of the old Jewish law. It is, more especially, to our purpose, to observe that, from the fourth century downwards, the ministers and bishops of the church were taught to consider their office *sacerdotal,* and to assume the obsolete titles of priests and high priests.[3] Since, therefore, under the Jewish law, tithes were appointed for the

[2] See *Rees's Cyclo. Tithes. Great Case of Tithes, by A. Pearson,* &c. &c.

[3] ἱερεῖς and ἀρχιερεῖς. See *Suiceri Thess. in voc.* ἱερεύς.

maintenance of the tribe of Levi, and for the support of the priests, (upon whom lay the duty of sacrifice and intercession, and the charge of the whole ritual, daily practised in the Lord's temple,) it is evidently probable, that the assumption of a right to tithes, by the clergy of the Christian church, arose immediately from the notion, that the priesthood—the sacerdotal office—still existed, and was still to be maintained.

This notion derives, in modern times, no little support from the ambiguity of the word *priest*, which, as it is employed in the established forms of many Christian churches, probably signifies nothing more than *presbyter;* but which is, nevertheless, generally understood to denote a person invested with the *sacerdotal office.* Now, although the total abolition of that office is asserted by many enlightened writers, it is certain that the opposite error vulgarly prevails to a great extent, and is productive of very injurious practical consequences. In Roman Catholic countries a dependence is notoriously placed on the priesthood, which can be explained or justified only on the principle that the office of the Christian minister is directly sacerdotal; nor can it be denied that remnants of the same superstition—of the same undue reliance on the authority and mediation of the priest—are very usual even in our own land.

Were it true that the priestly office is continued in the church of Christ, Friends could with no propriety refuse the payment of tithes, which were divinely appointed for its maintenance: and therefore, they consider that, in refusing to pay tithes, they plainly uphold the doctrine, that the office in question is abolished. That doctrine is allowed by the generality of well-instructed protestants; nor will the reader entertain any doubts on the subject, after an attentive perusal of the seventh, eighth, ninth, and tenth chapters of the epistle of Paul to the Hebrews. It is, indeed, an error to suppose that the duty of the *preacher* was ever necessarily connected with the office of the *priest*. In the more ancient periods of the Israelitish history, that duty lay not upon the priests who were consecrated for the service of the temple, but upon the prophets. Afterwards, in the synagogue service of the Jews, one only of the seven persons who read the Scriptures, and discoursed to the people, was required to be of the sacerdotal order; and even *his* place might be supplied, in case of need, by any other Israelite.[4] But, however the preaching of the word might be ordered among the Jews before the introduction of Christianity, it is certain that the ceremonial law, the priesthood by which it was administered, and the provision appointed for the maintenance of that priesthood, ceased in point of authority, on the death of Christ, when the whole typical and ritual system was fulfilled and abrogated. It was for the Jews of old to approach their Almighty Governor through the mediation, intercession, and sacrificial ordinances of a human priesthood: but it is the happiness of Christians to acknowledge no other Mediator than our Lord Jesus Christ, who is " made an High Priest for ever, after the order of Melchisedec;"[5] who

[4] See *Prideaux's Con.* fol. ed. vol. i. p. 306.
[5] Heb. vi, 20.

is "an High Priest over the House of God;"[6] who is "touched with the feeling of our infirmities;"[7] who, "by one offering, hath perfected for ever them that are sanctified;"[8] who is "able to save them to the uttermost that come unto God by him, seeing he ever liveth to make intercession for them."[9]

I have already found occasion to observe that the *legality* of ecclesiastical claims is no just or sufficient cause why Friends should take any active part in satisfying them. I may now advance a step further, and remark that the establishment of such claims by the law of the civil state is, in itself, one reason, among others, which renders a refusal to comply with them binding on their consciences. For, by refusing to pay tithes and other ecclesiastical demands imposed upon them by the law of the land, they express their dissent, in the *fifth and last* place, from that compulsory support of the hierarchy which originated during the darkest ages of papal superstition; and, *generally* from the interference of merely human and civil authority with the affairs of religion.

No one, who takes a just view of the condition of mankind, will deny the usefulness and importance, within their own sphere, of established forms of government, and of those various regulations by which the order of civil society is promoted and maintained; and the reader is probably well aware that Friends, as well as other Christians, consider it to be their bounden duty, in civil matters, to obey "the powers that be," and to render "unto Cæsar the things which

[6] Ch. x, 21.   [7] Ch. iv, 15.   [8] Ch. x, 14.
[9] Ch. vii, 25.

are Cæsar's."[1] We apprehend, however, that the affairs of religion appertain not to any civil polity, but to the kingdom of heaven, or, as it is otherwise described, the kingdom of God and of Christ. Although, if we are true Christians, we cannot fail to render to our earthly rulers the homage and service which are their due; yet, in those things which belong to the salvation of the soul, we profess to call no man Master, but to live under the undivided reign of Christ himself. The law which Christians are bound, in such matters, to obey, is revealed in the Holy Scriptures, and is engraven on their hearts; and we believe that their celestial Monarch exercises his dominion over them principally by an unseen and spiritual agency with which no mortal, or set of mortals, can ever possess authority to interfere. Now, this kingdom or reign of Christ is not of this world. The Head of it is Almighty; and, in the prosecution of his gracious designs for the extension, edification, and final perfection of his church, we are persuaded that he neither requires the protection, nor sanctions the interference, of the laws and governments of men.[2]

The history of the last eighteen centuries does indeed afford, in various ways, a strong evidence that the cause of true Christianity has materially suffered in the world, in consequence of the forced and arbitrary connexion between two systems, founded on such different principles, regulated by such different laws, and directed to such different objects, as those

---

[1] Matt. xxii, 21.

[2] In thus stating a very important *general* sentiment, there are two or three points which I think it desirable to guard. In the

of the *church* and the *state*. While it does not appear that the *state* has derived any real advantage from its supposed union with the church, it is probably, in a great measure, the consequence of such a union (invented and contrived as it has been by the wisdom of man) that the *church* has assumed, in almost all Christian countries, so secular a character—that Christianity has become so lamentably mixed up with the spirit, maxims, motives, and politics of a vain and evil world. Had the union in question never been attempted, pure religion might, probably, have found a freer course; the practical effects of Christianity might have been more unmixed, and extensive; and it might have spread its influence in a much more efficient manner than is now the case, even over the laws and politics of kings and nations.

It was in the reign of the emperor Constantine (A. D. 325) that the Christian religion was first estab-

---

first place, it ought to be observed, that there is nothing in that sentiment intended to be opposed to those internal regulations which are adopted, for the maintenance of its own order, by every religious society: for I conceive that, if such regulations are properly formed, and the officers, on whom it devolves to execute them, are rightly appointed, the discipline thus established in the church is so far from interfering with the government of Christ, that it is rather to be considered (according to various declarations of Scripture) as one of the means through which that government is conducted. And, in the second place, it cannot be deemed, on religious grounds, objectionable, when the civil authorities come forward, either by the exertion of prerogative, or by the enactment of law, to prevent those various breaches of *Christian* morality (including drunkenness, gaming, sabbath-breaking, &c.) which obviously interfere with the order and welfare of the body politic.

lished by law, forced into connexion with the body politic, and handled as a matter appertaining to the state. Now, though we ought not to ascribe to a single cause an effect which may have had its origin in many, we cannot but be confirmed in our view of the present subject, when we remember that, before its union with the state, our holy religion flourished with comparative incorruptness; and that afterwards it gradually declined in its purity and power, until all was nearly lost in darkness, superstition, and spiritual tyranny.

Independently, however, of these considerations, which relate to the interference of civil authority with the affairs of religion in general, there appears to be a distinct moral objection to the legal establishment, in any country, of *a particular form of Christianity*, to the disparagement of other modifications of the same essential religion. Although the provisions of such a legal establishment may have been rendered liberal, and softened down (as has been so evidently the case in Great Britain) by the powerful operation, on the legislature, of public opinion, it may reasonably be questioned, whether there must not always exist in these provisions a radical opposition to true and unbiassed religious liberty. I would, therefore, suggest, that we cannot conscientiously contribute, in an active manner, by the voluntary payment of tithes or church rates, to the maintenance of the Established Church; not only because we object to the system on which it is, in various respects, conducted, but also because it appears to be inconsistent with the rule of right that any human government should compel us, either to adopt for ourselves, or to uphold for others, *a mode of religious worship at variance with our own principles.*[3]

On a review of this essay, it will be recollected that, in the New Testament, and especially in the writings of the apostle Paul, the doctrine is clearly promulgated, that the preacher, when actually labouring in the cause of the gospel, has a claim upon those who hear him for the supply of his outward wants—that Paul, while he allowed, and even enforced, this doctrine, was exceedingly jealous (as was proved by his own conduct) of its being, in any respect, perverted or abused —that, according to the opinion of Friends, it is dangerously perverted and abused in the practice, so prevalent among Christians, of hiring the preachers of the word—that such a practice degrades the character of the Christian ministry, and is closely connected with the notion, that it may be brought into exercise according to the will of man--that, since Friends admit no preaching or public praying, but such as they deem to be offered under the immediate influence of the Spirit, they cannot pay, or otherwise remunerate, the Lord's servants, for the use of a gift which is of a nature entirely free; but they hold that, as every man has received the gift, *so* he is bound to

---

[3] It ought to be noticed that, although several observations offered in the present chapter relate specifically to *tithes,* most of them are, on general grounds, equally applicable to other ecclesiastical taxes ; such as those denominated *church rates.* *Tithes* and *church rates,* though differently applied in detail, are intended for the support of the same system : and the Friend who refuses to pay church rates, as well as he who refuses to pay tithes, *thereby expresses his dissent from that system.*

minister it—that the preachers among Friends, when travelling in the work of the gospel, are supported by their brethren; and, when resident at home, generally find no difficulty in maintaining themselves—that the same principle which prevents Friends from hiring or paying their own ministers, prevents their contributing to the hiring or paying those of other societies—that, in their refusal to comply with ecclesiastical demands, they bear a practical testimony against all such hiring and paying of preachers; against that description of ministry which is capable of being so procured; against those appointments to the sacred office which introduce to the possession of a claim on tithes; against the vulgar notion that the sacerdotal office is continued in the church; against the forced maintenance of the clergy, and the arbitrary union of church and state; and against the legal obligation to maintain, either for themselves or others, a system of religious worship inconsistent with their own views.

In concluding this dissertation, I cannot be satisfied without remarking, that our refusal to comply with ecclesiastical demands, arises from a conviction that it is our bounden duty to uphold certain principles which we deem to be both true and important, and is by no means dictated by a spirit of enmity against the particular church established by law in this country. On the contrary, we regard the members of that church with a friendly eye, and rejoice in every evidence of the extension of true religion within her borders.

While, however, we encourage a liberal and friendly feeling towards our fellow Christians *of every denomination*—while we readily make allowances for the various circumstances and conditions in which they are placed—it is certain that we cannot be too faithful in upholding our Christian testimony against the paying and hiring of preachers. For, have we not reason to believe, that the further the church of Christ on earth advances in her great career, the more generally will serious persons of every name sympathize with our solicitude, that the contrivances of man may not be allowed to interfere with the work of God; that avarice, ambition, and selfishness, may be for ever excluded from the motives which lead Christians into the professed service of their divine Master; and that the standard may be more and more exalted, of such a ministry of the gospel as shall be spiritual in its origin, and free in its operation?

CHAPTER VIII.

ON THE MINISTRY OF WOMEN.

WHILE the preaching and praying of women is strictly excluded from the public worship of the generality of Christians, Friends believe it right, freely and *equally*, to allow the ministry of both sexes. That this is indeed a necessary consequence of those sentiments which I have already endeavoured to unfold, must be evident to the reflecting reader. Since we conceive, on the one hand, that all true ministry is uttered under the immediate influence of the Spirit of Christ—and since, on the other hand, we confess that the wind bloweth where it listeth—we cannot, reasonably, do otherwise than make way for the exercise of the gift by those persons, of every description, whom the Spirit may direct into the service, and whom the Great Head of the church may be pleased to appoint as his instruments, for the performance of his own work. It is, indeed, declared that "the spirits of the prophets are subject to the prophets:" and hence it may be inferred that, in the conduct of our gifts, we ought not to neglect the dictates of a sound discretion: but we believe that we must not limit the Holy One of Israel, or oppose to the counsels of infinite wisdom our own fallible determinations. We dare not say to the modest and pious female, " Thou shalt not declare the word of the Lord," when we believe that, from an infinitely higher authority, there is issued a directly opposite injunction, " Thou shalt go to all that I shall send thee, and whatsoever I command thee, thou shalt speak."

Now, that women are often led to proclaim the word of the Lord amongst us—that it is laid upon them as an indispensable duty—that they are, from time to time, constrained, under the influence of the Spirit, to rise up in our meetings for worship, in order to instruct, exhort, convince, and console; or to kneel down and address the Most High, as the organs of the assembly; and further, that their services of this description are frequently accompanied with life and power, and greatly tend to the edification of their hearers—are facts, the truth of which long experience has taught us; and which no persons, who are intimately acquainted with our Society, will be disposed to deny.

Nor is there any thing either astonishing or novel in this particular direction of the gifts of the Spirit. Nothing astonishing, because there is no respect of persons with God; the soul of the woman, in his sight, is as the soul of the man, and both are alike capable of the extraordinary as well as the general influences of his Spirit. Nothing novel, because, in the sacred records of antiquity, there are found numerous examples of women, as well as of men, who were impelled to speak to others on matters of religion, by the direct and immediate visitations of the Holy Ghost. It was, doubtless, under such an influence, that Miriam responded to the song of Moses; that Deborah uttered her psalm of triumph; that Hannah poured forth, in the temple, her acceptable thanksgivings; that Huldah prophesied to king Josiah and his officers; that the aged Anna spake of Christ " to all them that looked for redemption in Israel;" that Elizabeth addressed the mother of her Lord; and that Mary sang praises to her God and Saviour. Of the individuals now mentioned, Miriam, Deborah, and Huldah, are expressly called prophetesses. The wife of Isaiah was a prophetess.[1] We read, also, of false prophetesses—a circumstance which plainly indicates that there were true prophetesses, who were the objects of their imitation, and from whom they were distinguished.[2]

Among the early ministers of the gospel dispensation, particular mention is made of the four daughters of Philip, who prophesied or *preached*.[3] The same office probably devolved, in a very eminent manner, on Priscilla, the wife of Aquila, *to whom all the churches of the Gentiles gave thanks*, and whom Paul expressly calls his "helper," or, as in the Greek, his *fellow labourer* in Christ."[4] Again, on another occasion, the apostle speaks of the *women* who " laboured" with him " in the gospel."[5] In order, however, to establish

[1] Isaiah viii, 3.   [2] Ezek. xiii, 17.
[3] Acts xxi, 9; *comp.* xv, 32; 1 Cor. xiv, 3.
[4] Rom. xvi, 3, 4; *comp.* Greek text of ver. 21; 2 Cor. viii, 23; Phil. ii, 25; 1 Thess. iii, 2.
[5] Phil. iv, 3.

the point now under consideration, nothing further would be necessary than a reference to the history given in the book of the Acts, of that great day of Pentecost, when the Spirit was so abundantly poured forth on the disciples of the Lord Jesus. It is recorded, in that history, that when the men and women were collected together, to the number of about one hundred and twenty, they were *all* filled with the Holy Ghost, and spake as the Spirit gave them utterance.[6] Here we have the declaration of an indisputable fact; and that fact is of the more importance, because of its agreement with the prediction of the prophet Joel. It was expressly provided and ordained, as is amply proved by that celebrated prediction, that, in the last days, or under the last dispensation, the Spirit should be poured forth " upon all flesh"—that no distinction should, in this respect, be made between the male and the female—that the *daughters* as well as the sons, the *handmaidens* as well as the servants, should receive the heavenly gift, and *prophesy*.[7]

On the other hand, however, it has often been remarked, that Paul, in one passage of his epistles, has commanded women to " *keep silence in the churches;*" and, in another, declares that he suffers them not " *to teach.*" The passages alluded to are as follows: " Let your women keep silence in the churches; for it is not permitted unto them to speak; but they are commanded to be under obedience, as also saith the law. *And, if they will learn any thing, let them ask their husbands at home;* for it is a shame for women to speak in the church."[8] Again: "I will, therefore, that

[6] Ch. i, 14, 15; ii, 1—4.   [7] Acts ii, 16—18.   [8] 1 Cor. xiv, 34, 35.

men pray every where, lifting up holy hands, without wrath and doubting. In like manner, also, that women adorn themselves in modest apparel, with shamefacedness and sobriety, &c.......Let the women learn in silence with all subjection. But I suffer not a woman *to teach*, nor to usurp authority over the man, but to be in silence; for Adam was first formed, then Eve."[9]

Now, on the comparison of these injunctions with the other passages of Scripture already cited, and especially with the prophecy of Joel, and the history of its fulfilment, the interpreter of the sacred volume appears to be driven into one of two decisions: the first, that the apostles and prophets, whose works must be ultimately traced to the same divine Author, have contradicted one another; and this on a point of considerable practical importance: the second, that the public speaking of women, so positively forbidden by Paul, was not that description of speaking which was prompted by the immediate impulses of the Holy Spirit.

Even were it impossible to throw any further light on the question, I presume there are few readers of Scripture who would hesitate in choosing the latter alternative; especially since it is quite unreasonable to suppose that the apostle would venture to forbid any ministry which was inspired, and which was therefore fully sanctioned by his *divine Master*. But, in adopting this conclusion, we are yet further confirmed by critical evidence.

In the former of these passages, the clue to the apostle's real meaning, in forbidding the public speak-

[9] 1 Tim. ii, 8—13.

ing of women, will be found in the words of ver. 35—
"*And, if they will learn anything,*" says he, "*let them ask their husbands at home.*" It has already been observed, that the whole of this chapter of the epistle to the Corinthians relates to their assemblies for divine worship, and was intended to correct certain abuses which had rendered those assemblies unprofitable and disorderly. Now, in the Jewish synagogues, after the pattern of which the meetings for worship of the earliest Christians were, probably, in some respects, regulated, *it was customary for the hearers to question the ministers on such points of their doctrine as might require further explanation;* [1] and it appears probable that a similar practice had been introduced into the church of Corinth, and that the women of that church were remarkably prone to it. Such a practice might, under peculiar circumstances, be allowed to *men,* and especially to the elders and overseers, who were possessed of authority in the body, and were the managers of the congregations; but it was, evidently, very inconsistent with that diffidence which ought ever to distinguish the character and manners of females. The apostle, therefore, enjoins them to keep silence in the church, and to restrain their eager desires for further instruction, until they could obtain it in private, from their own husbands. "In the synagogue," says the learned Benson, "any man who had a mind might ask questions of his teachers, and demand a further explanation of what had been said. And this custom was also transferred into the primitive Christian Church, and that with the approbation of St.

[1] See *Lightfoot, Hor. Heb. in loc.*

CHAP. 8.]   *On the Ministry of Women.*   267

Paul. Only, he would not permit the women to do so, as the Judaizers at Corinth would have had them. No: if they wanted to have any further instructions, they were to ask their own parents or husbands at home; and not enter into such conferences publicly in the church."² Such, then, we may conclude, was the public speaking forbidden by the apostle, and not that inspired ministry which originated in the will of Christ, and was immediately prompted by his Holy Spirit.

The second passage, above cited, is worded in a manner somewhat obscure; but appears to be best construed (according to the opinion of various commentators)³—as conveying an injunction that women, as well as men, *should pray every where*, lifting up holy hands without wrath and doubting.⁴ Having issued this injunction, together with one relating to attire, the apostle proceeds to command the women in the church of Ephesus (in conformity with his directions to those at Corinth) to "learn in silence with all subjection;" and, further, he expressly declares that he suffers them not "to teach." The verb " to teach" is one of very general import; and, together with its derivative nouns, is applied in Scripture to

---

² *On the Public Worship of the first Christians, Com. on Epist.* vol. i, p. 628.

³ See *Pool's Synopsis.*

⁴ 1 Tim. ii, 8, 9. Βούλομαι οὖν προσεύχεσθαι τοὺς ἄνδρας ἐν παντὶ τόπῳ, κ. τ. λ. Ὡσαύτως καὶ τὰς γυναῖκας ἐν καταστολῇ κοσμίῳ, μετα αἰδοῦς καὶ σωφροσύνης, κοσμεῖν ἑαυτὰς, κ. τ. λ. "I will, therefore, that men *pray every where, &c. Likewise, also, the women*, in a modest dress, *comp.* 1 Cor. xi, 5; (I would have them) adorn themselves with shamefacedness and sobriety," &c.

religious instruction of various descriptions; but, in this passage, it probably designates a specific duty or faculty in the church, which is repeatedly *distinguished* by this apostle from the gift of *prophecy* or *preaching*.[5] Now, although both these faculties, as enjoyed in the primitive church, are described as being divinely bestowed, there is reason to believe, that the impulses of the Spirit were of a far more direct and positive nature in the one case than in the other. I conceive that the *teaching*, which the apostle suffered not to be performed by women, differed from *prophesying* or *preaching*, in three respects: first, that it was dictated rather by the general impressions of Christian love and duty, than by immediate inspiration; for, had it been immediately inspired, the apostle could not have forbidden it: secondly, that, although adapted to a variety of occasions, both private and public, it was not, *like modern teaching*, employed as the ministry of the word, in assemblies for worship; for all the various administrations employed in those assemblies, appear to be described in 1 Cor. xiv, as spontaneous and divine effusions: thirdly, that, according to the hint given by the apostle in the passage before us, it involved the assumption of personal authority. This duty probably belonged, in a particular manner, to the elders and overseers, whose calling it was to exercise a spiritual superintendence over others, and who were the appointed guardians of the flock. Thus we learn from 1 Tim. iii, 2, (as already stated,) that the bishop or overseer was to be *apt to teach ;* and, from Eph. iv, 11,

[5] Rom. xii, 6, 7 ; 1 Cor. xii, 28 ; Eph. iv, 11.

that certain persons, who are there *distinguished* from the prophets or inspired ministers of the word bore the joint character of " pastors and teachers."

A very similar view of this passage is taken by Grotius. " *To teach*," says he, " was the office of the president (or bishop;) though he sometimes committed this branch of his duties to other persons, especially the elders. The apostle suffers not the women to perform such an office—that is to say, not *unless* they have, and only *while* they have, the prophetical impulse. *Prophecy is beyond the reach of positive laws.*"[5] "The apostolic rule," says Benson, " was, that, when they were under immediate inspiration, the women might pray or prophesy in the church. But, when they were under no such, inspiration, they were not to speak; i. e. neither to pray, nor read, teach, nor ask questions there."[6]

That the interpretation now given, of these passages in Paul's epistles, is substantially correct—that he had no intention to forbid that ministry of women which arose from the immediate impulses of the Holy Ghost—is rendered abundantly plain by another passage of his first epistle to the Corinthians, in which he notices the public prophesying of females, and gives particular directions respecting their conduct and appearance, during the performance of that sacred duty. " Now, I praise you, brethren," says he, " that ye remember me in all things, and keep the ordinances, as I delivered them to you. But I would have you know, that the head of every man is Christ; and the head of the woman is the man; and the head of Christ

[5] *Com. in loc.* [6] Vol. i, p. 620. See also *Locke on the Epistles.*

is God. Every man *praying or prophesying* having his head covered, dishonoureth his head. But every woman that *prayeth or prophesieth* with her head uncovered, dishonoureth her head; for that is even all one as if she were shaven. For, if the woman be not covered, let her also be shorn; but, if it be a shame for a woman to be shorn or shaven, let her be covered. . . . For this cause ought the woman to have power (or a covering) on her head, because of the angels. . . . Judge in yourselves : is it comely that a woman pray unto God uncovered ?" &c.[7] That this passage, as well as the fourteenth chapter of the same epistle, relates to the conduct of the Corinthian Christians in their assemblies for worship, is allowed by commentators, and is indeed evident from the whole tenor of the advice which is there imparted. The apostle, therefore, recognises the public prophesying of females ; and, since he gives directions respecting their dress and deportment during the performance of this service, it is plain that he had no intention to forbid the service itself. With respect to the prophesying to which Paul has here alluded, as exercised by both men and women in the churches of the saints, its nature has already been defined. The reader will remember that the gift was directed to the "edification, exhortation, and comfort," of believers, and to the convincement of unbelievers and unlearned persons ;[8] and that, in fact, it was nothing else than preaching under the immediate influences of the Holy Ghost.[9]

[7] 1 Cor. xi, 2—13.   [8] See 1 Cor. xiv, 3, 24, 25.
[9] Burton, late Professor of Divinity in the University of Oxford, in his note on 1 Cor. xi, 5, has adopted the same method of reconciling that passage with 1 Cor. xiv, 34, 35.

CHAP. 8.]   *On the Ministry of Women.*   271

Such, and such only, were the public services of women which the apostle allowed; and such was the ministry of females predicted by the prophet Joel, and described as so leading a circumstance under the gospel dispensation.

It appears, then, that the allowance of the public preaching and praying of women, in the Society of Friends, necessarily results from their principles respecting the character of all true ministry—that we dare not, in this respect more than in any other, limit the Holy One of Israel in the exercise of his own prerogatives—that our practice, in reference to the present subject, is justified by the records of Scripture respecting the effusions of the Spirit of God in times of old—that, even under the legal dispensation, many female servants of the Lord were called to the exercise of prophetical gifts—that, of the gospel times, the common participation of those gifts by men and women, was one decisive mark—and that the injunctions of the apostle Paul, against the public speaking and teaching of women, can be understood (himself being witness) only of speaking and teaching which were not inspired—which were not *prophesying*.

Such are the general sentiments entertained in the Society of Friends respecting the ministry of women —a subject which suggests, in conclusion, a few reflections of a practical nature.

When the apostle Paul said, " I suffer not a woman to teach," he added, " *nor to usurp authority over the man.*"[1] Had the women, in the church of Ephesus, after receiving this injunction, assumed the office of

[1] 1 Tim. ii, 12.

pastors; had they attempted that description of teaching, which was immediately connected with the government of the church; they would have been guilty of infringing the apostle's precept, and would have usurped an improper authority over their brethren: but, as long as their ministry was the result of the immediate influence of the Holy Spirit, and consisted in the orderly exercise of the prophetic gift, so long must they have been free from any imputation of that nature. Women who speak, in assemblies for worship, under such an influence, assume thereby no *personal authority* over others. They do not speak in their own name. They are the instruments through which divine instruction is communicated to the people; but they are only the instruments; and the doctrine which they preach derives its true weight and importance, not from the persons by whom it is uttered, but from that Being in whom it originates, and by whose Spirit it is prompted. This remark not only agrees with the doctrine of Scripture on the subject, but is confirmed, as many of my readers will be aware, by our own experience; for we well know that there are no women, among us, more generally distinguished for modesty, gentleness, order, and a right submission to their brethren, than those who have been called by their divine Master into the exercise of the Christian ministry.

Lastly, I may venture to direct the attention of my friends to a fact which I deem to be worthy of the consideration of the Society; namely, that, during the early periods of the history of Friends, the work of the ministry devolved much more largely and generally upon the men than upon the women. If, in the present day, a similar result from our religious principles does not take place; if, on the contrary, the ministry of the women is found rather to preponderate in the Society over that of the men; such a circumstance can by no means be deemed a favourable sign. Justified, as Friends appear to be, by the doctrine of Scripture, and by the powerful operations of the Spirit of truth, in equally admitting the ministry of both sexes, it is far indeed from being any indication of life and soundness in the body at large, when the stronger sex withdraws from the battles of the Lord, and leaves them to be fought by those whose physical weakness and delicacy have an obvious *tendency* to render them less fit for the combat. Were we of that stronger sex, less devoted than we now are to secular objects—were we less prone to a worldly spirit, and more diligent in seeking "*first* the kingdom of God and his righteousness"—there can be little doubt that we should be called forth, in greater numbers, into the arduous duties of the ministry of the gospel; nor would the burden of the word be found to rest, in so large a proportion as it now does, on our mothers, our sisters, and our daughters.

ADDENDUM TO CHAPTERS VI. VII. VIII.

A.D. 1834.

ON TEACHING, FAMILY AND SOCIAL RELIGIOUS DUTIES, AND PRIVATE PRAYER.

THE preceding chapters on the ministry, contain a plain statement of the sentiment of Friends, that no verbal communications consist with the solemnity of public worship, but those which directly arise from the influence of the Spirit. We should consider ourselves as departing from the due maintenance of this important principle, even were we to admit the reading of the Bible in our meetings for worship. Well do we know that Holy Scripture was given forth by divine inspiration; but we also know that it may be *read* under a different influence; and that the selection of its parts for the use of a congregation is generally matter of merely human judgment. We therefore believe it to be far more consistent with our views of worship, to leave it to the Holy Spirit to impress its contents on the minds of our ministers, to be by them delivered to the people, or to suggest them to our own minds while we are engaged in silent waiting on the Lord.

Now it is certain that there is nothing in these views which can interfere with the duty, or alter the desirableness, of the audible reading of the Bible on other occasions—in our schools, in our family and social circles, or in larger companies, when suitable opportunities occur. Neither is there any thing in the principles of Friends which precludes the exercise of the gift of *teaching*,[1] in connexion with such audible reading of the Holy Scriptures. Narrow indeed would be our notions of the varied means through which the great Head of the church condescends to minister to the needs of his children, were we to suppose that the Spirit can move in only *one channel*, and can edify the body of Christ through only *one gift*. " Now, there are diversities of gifts, but the same Spirit; and there are differences of administration, but the same Lord; and there are diversities of operation, but it is the same God who worketh all in all."[2]

I have already found occasion to observe, that to *teach* was a duty which often devolved on the overseers and elders of the earliest Christian churches; and there is reason to believe that this function was generally, if not always, connected with the reading of the Holy Scriptures— not, indeed, in meetings for divine worship, but on other occasions, whether private or public, of a somewhat more familiar character. To instruct the young and the ignorant in religious knowledge—to give them a right understanding of the written word—and to convince the gainsayers, by adducing the proofs which it contains, that Jesus is the true Messiah—was, probably, one of the leading duties of those persons who were called of the Lord both to feed and govern the flock of Christ. They were at once " pastors and *teachers*."[3]

[1] Rom. xii, 7 ; 1 Cor. xii, 28.   [2] 1 Cor. xii, 4—6
[3] Eph. iv, 11.

Still it is to be remembered, that the gift of teaching, among the early Christians, as well as that of preaching, was exercised in obedience to the will of God, and under its own required *measure* of the Lord's anointing. That neither this, nor any other gift of the Spirit, is at our command, is a truth too obvious to require a single argument for its support. But I believe that we may be prepared for the reception of it by a diligent daily perusal of Scripture, by close watchfulness, and by earnest prayer; and it is equally clear, that when it is bestowed upon us, it is our duty to wait upon it, to watch for its right occasions, and to exercise it in humility and *faith*. On the other hand, by misapplying to this branch of the subject our testimony respecting the public worship of God, and the ministry of the gospel, we may throw ourselves out of the way of some of those benefits which the Lord, in his own love and wisdom, would graciously afford us. Under mistaken notions of spirituality, we may fold our arms together, and leave both our own minds and the minds of our young people, in a state of ignorance—a state which neither comes from God, nor can ever be the means of *leading* to him.

Our understanding is bestowed upon us for wise and even holy purposes; without it we should be destitute of all capacities for our duties in life, and of all moral responsibility; and to commune with the highest intelligence, would be as impossible to us, as it is to the worm in the earth, or to the hyssop on the wall. Our intellect, therefore, must not be suffered to lie dormant—it must be cultivated not only for the purposes of life, but for those of eternity. Every one knows that this faculty is of necessity brought into use in the reading the Scriptures, as well as in every other rational pursuit. Is it not then our obvious duty, by every means within our reach, to endeavour to obtain a *right* understanding of them, and to communicate that *right* understanding to those who are placed under our care? And may we not, in reverent dependence on the Holy Spirit, exercise our own faculties for the purpose? Can we, in fact, plead any excuse for not doing so, which is likely to avail us before the judgment-seat of Him, to whom we must render an account of the use of *all* his talents?

It is a lamentable circumstance when, on conversing with young people, and even with persons of more advanced age, we find a want of common information and intelligence on the subject of religion. Such a want will, I believe, be generally found connected with a low moral and spiritual standard. The spirit of such persons will seldom soar, like the eagle, towards the centre of light and heat; it will generally be found loitering, with flagging wing, over the dust of the earth, and often in contact with its grosser pollutions.

The principles which have now been advanced, have, for many years past, been usefully in operation, both in our public and private schools. It is generally understood amongst us, to be the bounden duty of our school-masters and teachers, to endeavour to bring their pupils to a knowledge of the Bible; to unfold its contents to them; to instruct them in its history, its prophecies, and its doctrines. That the consequence of these Christian endeavours, in many of our schools, has been an increase of piety, both in the teachers and scholars, no one who is well acquainted with these institutions will venture to deny. Testimonies to that effect, of a pleasing nature, have been multiplied upon us from various quarters; and it is evident that the great Head of the church has condescended to bless the diligent use of the means afforded us in his providence, for the spreading of Christian knowledge within our borders. Yet let it not be forgotten by the preceptors of children, that religious teaching, even in its elementary parts, requires a measure of the influence of the Spirit for its right performance; and that this influence can be expected only by those who are earnest in the cause, and who reverently depend upon that divine aid, without which they " can do nothing."

But it is not only the inmates of our schools who require religious instruction; a somewhat higher description of the same kind of knowledge is equally desirable for those who are no longer children. Who can think of our numerous young people, scattered over large towns, and often exposed to a variety of dangers, without feeling an earnest solicitude for their welfare? Who would not desire that a greater number of diligent and faithful " pastors and teachers" might be raised up amongst them, who should devote both time and talent to the blessed work of cultivating their minds on the subject of religion? Alas! for the weak and inexperienced, who are now left with little protection, and less instruction—an easy prey to the temptations of the world, and the fearful aggressions of the prince of darkness!

Were I asked what is the *kind* of religious knowledge in which I think young people ought to be more instructed than many of them are at present, I would, in *the first place*, mention the external and historical evidences of the genuineness of Scripture, and of the truth of Christianity. In these days of doubt and dispute, and even of daring infidelity, it is *dangerous* to be ignorant of the *facts*, which afford a complete and satisfactory answer to the cavils of unbelievers. The study of those numerous prophecies in the Bible, which have already been fulfilled, and of the histories, whether sacred or profane, from which we may prove their fulfilment, is another interesting part of Christian knowledge. Nor must we neglect to pay some attention to the works of modern travellers, whose narratives throw a clear, though often unintended, light on the records and predictions of Scripture.

When the proofs of the divine authority of the sacred volume have thus been made clear to our minds, it becomes doubly imperative upon us to accept its contents, not in the spirit of reasoners, but in humble child-like faith. What a delightful employment, therefore, will it be, in the next place, to introduce to the attention of the young and candid mind, the evidences from Scripture, on which the main doctrines of Christianity depend! These evidences will be found to be numerous, harmonious, strong; and the more they are known, the more completely will every doubt on these all-important subjects vanish from the mind. Lastly, it is surely most desirable that our young friends should be carefully instructed in the scriptural grounds of our distinguishing views and practices; in the history of the early Christian church; and in that of the rise and progress of our own religious society.

But to bring this subject home to our firesides— Shall not the fathers and mothers of our families be pastors and teachers in their own houses? Have they not a solemn duty of this kind to perform towards their children? And have masters and mistresses no debt of Christian love to pay to their servants? I am well aware that, for want of that knowledge of Scripture, which they ought to have obtained before they settled in life, there are many parents amongst us, who feel themselves incompetent to the work of instruction—who long to be enabled to imbue their children with such a knowledge of divine things as is suitable to their tender age, but know not how to do it; and are, therefore, afraid even to make the attempt. They do, indeed, secure for their children and servants the advantage of hearing the Bible read; and most of them, I trust, perform this duty *daily;* but here their efforts for the Christian instruction of their families find both a beginning and an end.

Certainly this ought not so to be. The daily family reading of Scripture is by no means the sole duty of heads of families, as it regards Christian teaching. Children ought to be enlightened with a proper degree of Christian knowledge, even in their very early years; and as they advance towards the age when they are generally sent to school, this knowledge should be considerably extended; always, however, with a watchful care, that their minds may not be overloaded, and that their scriptural lesson may be a pleasure and a happiness—not a task. Nor will pious parents fail, by frequent precept, to direct the tender minds of their children to God, even their Father, who fills and governs all things, whom to fear is " the beginning of wisdom," whom to serve is perfect freedom. At the same time, it will be their delight to bring them to an acquaintance with that Saviour, who loved them, and gave himself a ransom for them; and they will humbly endeavour to teach them, even in childhood, to bear his yoke, and to submit to the government of his Holy Spirit.

When we read the Scriptures in our families, our servants, as well as our children, ought certainly to be assembled. The whole household, as far as circumstances will admit, should unite in showing this reasonable mark of allegiance to the King of kings; and my belief is, that heads of families, were they truly watchful and diligent in their own department of service, would sometimes be led to make remarks on what they read— to explain what may be obscure— to impress what may be peculiarly important—and to add the words of pious exhortation. Such communications, in our meetings for worship, would neither be " fitly spoken," nor " in season;" but they might be both the one and the other in our family circles; and *there*, might even be found "like apples of gold in network of silver."[4]

---

[4] It seems peculiarly desirable that a portion of the *New Testament* should be read in our families daily; and, as far as may be, in regular course, as it regards the books and chapters. The morning will, I believe, be generally found the most suitable time

"A place for every thing, and every thing in its place," is a proverb which has no better or truer application than to the various kinds of religious instruction, which the author of every good and perfect gift has graciously ordained for the use of the church, and for the benefit of his children.

Nor ought it to be forgotten, that these occasions of family union in religious matters, are, in part at least, of a devotional character. It would be well for us, were our family readings more generally preceded by a short but solemn pause; and in the time spent in silence, at the close of them, a *full* opportunity should be given to every mind present, to breathe its secret, yet earnest, supplications, in one Spirit, and through the one Mediator, to God, even our Father. Would that we might know more of "the cloud by day," and of the "brightness of a flaming fire by night," resting on our habitations, and guiding and cheering our several families, in the way and work of the Lord!"[5]

But there is something beyond the family circle which, in this point of view, demands our attention. There are the social parties—the visiting and re-visiting at each other's houses. How is it that on these occasions, the intellect is often so little fed, and the

for this purpose. At night, before we retire to rest, the reading of a psalm, or of a portion from one of the prophets, will be found a comforting close to our family intercourse for the day.

[5] I trust that Friends are almost universally in the practice of observing a silent pause before meat, and that it is increasingly our desire, during that short period of time, gratefully to acknowledge, in secret, the bounty of our God. It may, however, be right to observe, that a similar pause, after the meal is finished, is almost equally desirable; and is often accompanied with peculiar solemnity.

religious mind, above all, so seldom cultivated? Were professing Christians more alive both to their natural dignity, and to their religious duties, their hours of social intercourse would be spent in a manner far more interesting to young people, and abundantly more profitable for wise and worthy purposes, than is now, too generally, the case. Their conversation would be more intelligent; it would be less on *persons*, and more on *things;* they would unite in useful and agreeable reading; their time would be occupied to the advantage of the *mind.* Above all, they would often be led, as I believe, to recur to topics of a directly edifying tendency; and, on suitable occasions, to the social reading of the sacred volume.

If there be a deficiency, in these respects, in the habits of many amongst us, how is it to be supplied? Certainly not by efforts of a strained and formal nature —but by that ardent zeal for the truth, that pervading love of God, and that watchfulness over the passing hour, which would lead us to embrace every right occasion for promoting the cause of truth and righteousness. The more " richly" the " word of Christ" dwells in us, the more shall we be enabled to obey the apostolic precept—" whatsoever ye do in word or deed, do all in the name of the Lord Jesus, giving thanks to God and the Father by him."[6]

While I long to witness a higher tone of feeling, and a more worthy occupation of our mental powers, in the social intercourse of Friends, I do not forget, that in all these matters there ought to be preserved a *golden mean.* Little can be said in favour of the forced

[6] Col. iii, 17.

introduction of religious topics against the *current of the occasion;* nor ought we, by any means, to exclude familiar converse on other subjects, or innocent cheerfulness, in its season. In all matters connected with religion, a peculiar caution is required, that we do not render those subjects irksome and distasteful, which, if judiciously and seasonably handled, will afford a delightful relish even to the young. The sound of the bell, without the nourishment and sweetness of the pomegranate, will never invigorate the spiritual life. Only, let us keep our Lord and Master always in view, and cultivate a constant *readiness* to follow " the things which make for peace, and the things wherewith one may edify another.".

Although I believe that the various religious duties, which I have been endeavouring to point out, may fairly claim the increased attention of Friends, it is far from being my desire to excite an activity which is not of God. No more important lesson is to be learned in religion, than that of our own nothingness; " It is not of him that willeth, nor of him that runneth, but of God that sheweth mercy; and this mercy may flow to man either with or without our feeble instrumentality. There is indeed a sovereignty in the operations of the divine Spirit, which often sets very low the best-intentioned efforts of the creature, and thus again and again humbles him in the dust. God is still pleased to " destroy the wisdom of the wise," and to " bring to nothing the understanding of the prudent." Whatsoever therefore may be our religious exercises, whatsover our peculiar gifts or lines of ser-

CHAP. 8.] Private Prayer, &c. 285

vice, it becomes us all to walk watchfully and humbly before the Lord. Certainly it is our truest wisdom to open our hearts to the secret convictions of his Spirit, and to *dwell near* the *fountain* of light, life, and immortality.

There is another point of still greater importance than the religious intercourse of the family and social circles—I mean the devotion of the closet. " But thou, when thou prayest, enter into thy closet, and when thou hast shut thy door, pray to thy Father which is in secret; and thy Father which seeth in secret shall reward thee openly."[7]

I know of nothing which would more interrupt the solemnity of our meetings for worship, than vocal prayer uttered without the direct anointing of the Holy Spirit; whether offered in a written form, or extemporaneously composed by the speaker. But while public prayer rests on the ground of a spiritual gift, and devolves only on those who are called into the service, private prayer is a duty binding upon all men, and is as fully and frequently commanded in Scripture, as any other duty whatsoever. If we would grow in grace and in the knowledge of our Lord Jesus Christ, it must be our frequent practice—especially at the commencement and end of each day—to retire into solitude, and there to seek for ability to pour out our prayers to the Lord, with a diligent and fervent spirit.

Can we then rightly express ourselves in prayer, even in private, unless our hearts are prepared for the

[7] Matt. vi, 6.

duty? I believe not. The mere appearance of prayer, without *a mind* to pray, a dry, formal use of words, without life and feeling—can yield no glory to God, and no benefit to man. The great principle, that " God is a Spirit," and that " they who worship him must worship him in spirit and in truth," applies in all its force to our private as well as public devotions; and we learn from the apostles, that the prayers and thanksgivings of Christians ought to be " in the Spirit"[8]—" in the Holy Ghost."[9]

But our Saviour and his apostles would have us take it for granted that the spirit of supplication will certainly be bestowed upon us if we duly seek it. Otherwise our blessed Lord would never (as I believe) have promulgated the doctrine that " *men ought always to pray and not to faint,*" neither would his apostle have said, " *Pray without ceasing.*" The promise of the Spirit is given to us in Scripture as an encouragement to our heartfelt devotions. " Likewise the Spirit also helpeth our infimities, for we know not what we should pray for as we ought; but the Spirit itself maketh intercession for us,[1] with groanings which cannot be uttered."[2]

The apostle Paul commands the Ephesians to *watch unto prayer,* " with all perseverance."[3] If many of us find it difficult, in our private hours, to offer our humble yet fervent petitions to the Lord, the difficulty may probably be owing to our neglect of the *watching* which prepares for it. " Watch and pray," said our Saviour to his disciples, " for the spirit truly is willing,

---

[8] Eph. vi, 18.   [9] Jude 20.   [1] ὑπερεντυγχάνει ὑπὲρ ἡμῶν.
[2] Rom. viii, 26.   [3] Eph. vi, 18.

but the flesh is weak."[4] To watch to any particular duty, is to be *awake and alive to it;* and those only watch unto prayer, who *live* in the spirit of it.

If God be not in all our ways, if he occupy scarcely any of our thoughts and feelings, the duty of occasional prayer will surely be difficult. But if we dwell near to him in spirit, and humbly endeavour to " walk in the light, as he is in the light," our hearts will not fail to arise, from time to time, both in thanksgiving and supplication. And not only for ourselves shall we pour forth our secret prayers, but for our brethren and sisters in the Lord, for the Church universal, and even for the whole world.

May we be increasingly diligent in the performance of these sacred duties, and may we never forget the encouragement which is afforded to prayer, under the gospel dispensation, by the mediation and intercession of Jesus Christ! Through Him, we all have " access by one Spirit unto the Father."[5] " Whatsoever ye shall ask in my name, that will I do, that the Father may be glorified in the Son: if ye shall ask any thing in my name, I will do it."[6] " If ye abide in me, and my words abide in you, ye shall *ask what ye will*, and it shall be done unto you."[7] " Hitherto have ye asked nothing in my name: *ask, and ye shall receive*, that your joy may be full."[8] Here surely there is permitted to the Christian believer a delightful freedom in the exercise of prayer—a freedom inseparably connected with filial reverence and awe. " We have

---

[4] Matt xxvi, 41, *comp.* Mark xiii, 33.
[5] Eph. ii, 18.   [6] John xiv, 13, 14.   [7] John xv, 7.
[8] John xvi, 24.

not an High Priest which cannot be touched with the feeling of our infirmities, but was, in all points, tempted like as we are, yet without sin. Let us, *therefore, come boldly unto the throne of grace,* that we may obtain mercy, and find grace to help in time of need."[9] One point only remains to be mentioned in reference to this subject—*the example of Jesus Christ himself.* He who has opened an access for our supplications, and who graciously presents them to the Father, clothed in the incense of his own intercession,[1] has himself trodden the path of prayer. At night, on the mountain's side, was he accustomed virtually to exemplify his own precept to his disciples, that when they prayed, they should enter into the closet, and shut the door. In *perfect solitude*, he poured forth his soul in prayer, and communed with his Father. In this, as well as in other particulars of conduct, it is surely our bounden duty, at whatsoever distance, " *to follow his steps.*"

But prayer, although the principal religious duty, is not the only one which we ought to exercise in our hours of solitude and retirement. There is the private use of Scripture, which demands of every Christian who has the power to read, and the opportunity of reading, the daily sacrifice of a portion of his time. Nor will any parts of the day be more productive of instruction and comfort, than those which are devoted to a deep research into the treasures of Holy Writ. Such a practice, under the blessed influences of the Holy Spirit which gave the Scriptures forth, will lead us, from time to time, to the feet of our Redeemer, in whom alone is our life; it will help to wean us from

[9] Heb. iv, 15, 16. [1] Rev. viii, 3.

the dust of the earth; it will be the means of drawing our affections towards heaven.

Again, there is the duty of *self-examination*. The Christian ought to review his conduct at the close of each succeeding day, with a scrutinizing mind, as in the presence of God, and in the light of his sanctuary. Such an examination would help us to obtain the mastery over those false notions of our own righteousness, which are so apt to impede the progress of religion in our souls. Our secret faults, our presumptuous sins, would be brought in review before us. Humbled before God, under a sense of our own vileness, we should cast ourselves again and again on his free mercy in Christ Jesus; and should seek that more abundant grace, by which alone we could be delivered from *all* iniquity.

One important point still remains to be mentioned —*private, silent waiting upon God*. That this is an acceptable and profitable practice there cannot be the least question; it may be regarded as one of the deepest and purest exercises of the believing soul. Undoubtedly it is the most suitable introduction to the offering of prayer; and, when prayer has been offered, to revert to a state of silent waiting, will ever be found to have a salutary influence—a calming, quieting, confirming effect.

The subject of *silent worship* will be developed in the following chapter. In the mean time, I wish to express my belief that the Christian can enjoy no greater privilege, whether it be in the privacy of the closet, or in the family circle, or in social fellowship, or in the public congregation. May the preciousness of this privilege be more and more understood amongst us; may we be willing to avail ourselves of it from time to time, even in the midst of our converse with our friends; *may we never be ashamed of it;* and while we diligently employ every appointed means of instruction and edification, may we never for a moment forget, that the "KINGDOM OF GOD IS NOT IN WORD BUT IN POWER."

CHAPTER IX.

ON SILENT WORSHIP.

OUR profession and our desire, when we meet together to worship the Father, is to perform this sacred duty in spirit and in truth, To this end we conceive that a condition of outward silence is pre-eminently adapted. For worship in spirit and in truth consists neither in the practice of typical rites, nor in the forced or formal use of words which may or may not agree with the feelings of those who utter them, or in whose behalf they are spoken; but in the communion of the soul with God, in inward prostration before him. and in those heartfelt offerings of prayer and thanksgiving which, in order to enter into the ear of the Lord of Hosts, need not the intervention of any vocal utterance.

In order to unfold this interesting subject with some degree of clearness, it will be desirable to advert to a few of its principal particulars.

I. Were the inquiry addressed to me, What is the first and most essential qualification for a right and spiritual worship of the Almighty—for such a worship as would at once edify the creature and glorify the Creator?—I should feel but little hesitation in replying, *A deep humiliation and subjection of soul before the divine Majesty.* True worship may often be properly expressed by the services of the lip; but it is, in itself, the homage which the *soul* offers to its Maker—the reverential communion of man with his God. Now, this homage can never be acceptably offered—this communion can never take place in a right or perfect manner—until the mind of the worshipper is made in some degree sensible of the real relative situation of the two parties concerned—of himself and his God. The worshipper is the creature; the object of his worship is the Creator: the former is finite, ignorant, weak, and helpless; the latter is omniscient, eternal, and omnipotent: the former without grace, is fallen, sinful, and corrupt; the latter is of "purer eyes than to behold iniquity:" the former is capable of receiving either wrath or mercy; the latter is able either to punish or to forgive. " Surely men of low degree are vanity, and men of high degree are a lie: to be laid in the balance, they are altogether lighter than vanity."[1] " All nations before him are as nothing; and they are counted to him less than nothing, and vanity."[2] In order, therefore, to make acceptable approaches in spirit to the Almighty, it is abundantly evident that men ought to be humbled, prostrate, and in a mental condition of profound reverence and awe, under a sense of their own vileness and of his perfections—of their own unworthiness

[1] Psalm lxii, 9.   [2] Isa. xl, 17.

CHAP. 9.] On Silent Worship. 293

and of his power—of their own nothingness and of his infinity. Nor will our heavenly Father fail to regard such a state of humiliation. " The heaven is my throne, and the earth is my footstool: where is the house that ye build unto me, and where is the place of my rest? For, all those things hath mine hand made, and all those things have been, saith the Lord: but to this man will I look, even to him that is poor and of a contrite spirit, and trembleth at my word."[3]

The frame of mind which I have now attempted to describe is, indeed, in some measure, *at all times* inherent in the true Christian: but on occasions appointed for the high and especial purpose of communion with the Almighty, such a frame is peculiarly necessary; and is required to be formed in a higher degree, and with less interruption, than during the mixed and active pursuits of common life. Now, in order to this end—in order to the production of this entire humiliation, in those who are met together for divine worship—there is, perhaps, no outward condition nearly so well adapted as one of silence. The soul of man, although it may often be fraught with honest and pious intentions, is laden with many infirmities; and, on these solemn occasions, it appears to require the opportunity which silence so naturally affords, before it can find its true level—before it can be brought to entertain, with a sufficient degree of clearness, a just sense of itself and of its Creator. There is reason to fear that such a sense is often *very imperfectly* formed, and that it is sometimes materially interrupted by the use of words, which form pre-

[3] Isa. lxvi, 1, 2.

scribes, or which human imagination invents. Even sincerely religious people may draw nigh unto God with their lips, while their souls are far from being sufficiently humbled before him; and, if it is so, they worship their Creator *superficially*, and their religious exercises will ever be found unprofitable, in proportion as they are shallow. It is when the soul of the suppliant is thoroughly subjected in the presence of the Most High; when his pride and activity are subdued; when the restless imaginations of his natural mind are quieted and laid low—that he is prepared to adopt the words of the psalmist, " *Out of the depths have I cried unto thee, O Lord.*"[4]

Now, silence may be considered, not only as affording a most useful opportunity for the production of this complete prostration before God in divine worship, but as being eminently suited to that condition of mind when it is already produced; for experience may serve to convince us that it is the natural and frequent accompaniment of humiliation and subjection. As such, it is repeatedly described by the ancient Hebrew prophets. " I was *dumb with silence, I held my peace* even from good," said David, when he had been suffering under the chastisement of the Lord—" *I was dumb, I opened not my mouth*, because thou didst it."[5] " Why do we sit still?" cried the mournful Jeremiah—" assemble yourselves, and let us enter into the defenced cities, and *let us be silent there;* for the Lord our God hath *put us to silence*, and given us water of gall to drink, because we have sinned against the Lord."[6]

[4] Psa. cxxx, 1.   [5] Psa. xxxix, 2, 9.   [6] Ch. viii, 14.

CHAP. 9.]   *On Silent Worship.*   295

I know of no passages, however, which throw so much light on the point now before us, as the following verses in the prophecies of Habakkuk, and Zechariah: "The Lord is in his holy temple; let all the earth *keep silence* before him."[7] "*Be silent*, O all flesh, (i. e. mankind,) before the Lord; for he is raised up out of his holy habitation."[8] Here we ought to observe that the word rendered "temple," in the former of these passages, does not properly apply to the holy of holies—that inmost apartment, where the glory of God resided—but to the sanctuary, in which the priests performed their daily service.[9] On the other hand, the "holy habitation," *out* of which Zechariah describes the Lord as being "raised up," may be regarded as another name for the holy of holies.

The meaning of both these verses may be illustrated by a reference to that remarkable circumstance which occurred on the dedication of Solomon's temple. "And it came to pass, when the priests were come out of the holy place, that the cloud filled the house of the Lord, so that the priests could not stand to minister, because of the cloud; for the glory of the Lord had filled the house of the Lord."[1] It appears that on this memorable occasion, the cloud of glory, which for the most part dwelt in the holy of holies, burst forth into the sanctuary, and filled the whole house. And what was the consequence? The service of the priests was of necessity suspended; and all was silence, as in the immediate presence of the Lord.

[7] Hab. ii, 20.   [8] Zech. ii, 13.   [9] היכל. *See Gill in loc.*
[1] 1 Kings viii 10 11.

Now, the holy of holies was a type of heaven, God's glorious dwelling-place; and the idea conveyed in both these solemn proclamations, appears to be this—that God was come forth out of heaven, the holiest place of all, and was manifesting himself, by some remarkable dispensations of his wisdom and power, in the sanctuary—that is, in the church on earth. He is described as *visiting* his people; and, therefore, all mankind are commanded to keep silence before him. Not only the sanctuary, but the whole house, is to be filled with his glory.

With these sublime views, and with the principles on which this command is founded, the practice of silent congregational worship appears to be in full accordance. The meeting of the Lord's people for the solemn purpose of presenting themselves before God, in the name of Jesus Christ, is precisely one of those occasions on which, as we have reason to believe, God condescends, by his Spirit, to visit his sanctuary upon earth, and to be peculiarly present with his church. What then can be more desirable for us, when thus assembled, than literally to comply with the inspired precept, and in awful reverence of soul, to *keep silence* before the LORD?

II. A second particular, indispensably requisite for a true and spiritual worship, is *waiting upon God*. The worshippers of the Almighty Jehovah must not only be humbled and cast down under an awful apprehension of his divine power and majesty; they must not only feel their own vileness and wants; but they must also look upward unto God, as unto the Father of mercies, the Fountain of wisdom and

CHAP. 9.] On Silent Worship. 297

life, the Author of every good and perfect gift. Their expectation must be placed on him alone and they must learn *patiently to wait upon him*, until he shall be pleased to reveal his mercy, and to bestow upon his unworthy children " grace to help in time of need." On the subject of this important part of true worship, none of the sacred writers appears to have received a more powerful impression than the devout and afflicted David. " Unto thee lift I up mine eyes, O thou that dwellest in the heavens. Behold, as the eyes of servants (look) unto the hand of their masters, and as the eyes of a maiden unto the hand of her mistress: so our eyes (wait) upon the Lord our God, *until that he have mercy upon us.*"[2] " *My* soul, *wait thou only upon God;* for my expectation is from him."[3] " *Wait on the Lord:* be of good courage, and he shall strengthen thine heart: *wait, I say, on the Lord.*"[4]

When a person is anxiously expecting any particular benefit even from his fellow man, it is very natural for him to be *silent;* for anxious expectation and silence, even in the common affairs of life, are closely allied. Still more plainly, however, does this appear to be the case, when the blessings and benefits which he desires are of a heavenly nature, and when the great and glorious God is the Being on whom his expectation and reliance are placed. A holy silence of soul, accompanied by an outward stillness, is a condition peculiarly well suited to this waiting upon the Lord; and such a frame will, I believe, often be

[2] Ps. cxxiii, 1, 2.   [3] Ps. lxii, 5.
[4] Ps. xxvii, 14; *comp.* xxxvii, 7, 9; cxxx, 5; Isa. xxx, 18, &c.

found a very salutary *introduction* to the more active communion of the soul with its Creator—to the actual offerings, whether secret or vocal, both of confession and prayer.

Were such offerings, as they are presented on the altar of the Most High by Christian worshippers, less the product of their own efforts; were they dictated more completely by the Spirit who "maketh intercession for us with groanings that cannot be uttered;" and did they more generally arise out of that condition, which has now been described, of reverent *waiting* on the Lord; there is much reason to conclude that they would be still more acceptable than they now are to the great Searcher of hearts; as well as more effectual for the edification of those who worship him. And now it only remains for me to confirm these remarks by the additional observation, that waiting upon God, as well as prostration and subjection before his divine Majesty, is, in the Holy Scriptures, expressly described as connected with a state of *silence*. The words of the psalmist, "Rest in the Lord, and wait patiently for him," may be more literally rendered, as in the margin of the common English version, "*Be silent to the Lord*,[5] and wait patiently for him."[6]

In a highly instructive passage of the "Lamentations," the benefit of humble waiting upon God, and of the silence with which it is so properly accompanied, are described as follows: "The Lord is good unto them that *wait for him*, to the soul that seeketh him. It is good that a man should both hope and

[5] Heb. דים ליהוה. [6] Ps. xxxvii, 7.

quietly wait for (in the Hebrew, *be silent for*[7]) the salvation of the Lord. It is good for a man that he bear the yoke in his youth. He sitteth alone and *keepeth silence*, because he hath borne it upon him. He putteth his mouth in the dust, if so be there may be hope."[8] Again, in the prophecies of Isaiah, there is a sublime allusion to waiting in silence, as a preparation for *addressing* God. After declaring that " they who wait upon the Lord shall renew their strength," Jehovah, by his prophet, proclaims the following command: " Keep silence before me, O islands, and let the people renew their strength; let them draw near; *then let them speak;* let us come near together to judgment."[9]

Lastly, the vision of John affords us a noble illustration of the *silence of expectation*, united with the purest and most reverential worship of the Lord Almighty. We read, that when the Lamb had opened the seventh seal—the seal under which were hid such deep mysteries—" there was *silence in heaven* about the space of half an hour."[1] What can be more sublime than the idea, which is here presented, of the solemn stillness of the innumerable heavenly host, while they were bowed in awful prostration before God, and waited for the fresh manifestations of his glorious power? It may well be conceived that, even among saints and angels, such a silence was found to be a blessed introduction to new and living songs of thanksgiving and praise.

Thus are we furnished with abundant evidence from

[7] רימם.   [8] Lam. iii, 25—29.   [9] Ch. xli, 1.
[1] Rev. viii, 1.

Scripture, as well as from experience, that a state of humble *waiting* upon God, forms a very important part of true and spiritual worship; and that with such a state, *silence* is in natural and perfect accordance.

III. Among the choicest blessings in the expectation of which the true worshipper is taught to wait upon his Lord, and for which he is most accustomed to present his humble yet earnest petitions at the throne of grace, is the illumination and instruction of the Holy Spirit. It is the happiness of all true Christians that they are taught of the Lord. " All thy children," said the prophet to the church, " shall be *taught of the Lord*, and great shall be the peace of thy children."[2] The law of God is written in legible characters on the hearts of his followers. Under that new and spiritual dispensation, into which they have been introduced, they need not that one man should say to another, " Know the Lord;" because from the least to the greatest of them, all may know him for themselves;[3] they need not that any man teach them, because the anointing which they have received of Christ abideth in them, and teacheth them of all things, and is truth and no lie.[4] One is their teacher—even Christ.

The obedient family of God are, in all their ways, instructed and enlightened by their divine Master. Even while they are pursuing the active business of life, if they do but carefully maintain the watchful spirit and single eye towards him, they will not fail to receive, on every needful occasion, the secret, yet

[2] Isaiah liv, 13.   [3] Jer. xxxi, 34.   [4] 1 John ii, 27.

perceptible monitions of the spirit of truth. But, in an especial manner, may they expect to experience this grace, when they meet for the solemn purpose of worshipping the living God. That " Minister of the true tabernacle," who has promised to be in the midst of his disciples when they are gathered together in his name, is ever ready to carry forward his work in their souls, and to bestow upon them the teaching of his Holy Spirit; and this teaching, when received with submission and obedience, never fails to be efficacious, because it is derived, without mixture, from the source of wisdom; it is not only light, but *power*. Many are the Christians of various denominations, who can bear witness that the Lord Jesus does indeed condescend to instruct his people *himself*. It is Christ, that spiritual teacher of the children of God, who makes manifest to them their real condition; detects their iniquities, and convinces them of sin; brings them into humility, and contrition of soul; and thus prepares them for the exercise of fervent prayer for pardon and deliverance. It is Christ, also, who reveals to the soul of man the mercy of God, and secretly proclaims to his followers, the extent and efficacy of redeeming love. Thus is the penitent sinner relieved and comforted, and becomes rightly qualified to offer up, at the throne of grace, the acceptable tribute of thanksgiving and praise. Lastly, it is Christ who plainly sets before his people, as in the light of his sanctuary, the path of self-denial, obedience, and true holiness: he shows to them the beauty and excellence of that narrow way, and inspires them with an ardent desire to walk in it; and, at the same time, he invites them to rely with confidence upon the power of his grace, that, by this sacred influence, they may be strengthened in all their weakness, and enabled to take up their daily cross, and follow their Lord and Saviour. Such is a faint and general outline of the teaching of the Son of God; and where is the experienced Christian who will venture to deny that he thus instructs his people, not only by means of the ministry of his servants, but by the secret and immediate operations of his Holy Spirit?

If this point be allowed, and if it be further granted, as I think it must be by the spiritually-minded reader, that the periods appointed for the public worship of God are times when the immediate teaching of Christ may reasonably be expected; the propriety of *silence*, on such occasions, will at once be established. When any persons are receiving the instructions of a human teacher, they find that a state of silence, on their own parts, is both beneficial and indispensable. Not only is such a state the proper and natural token of submission to their instructor, and of their willingness to receive his lessons; but it is literally impossible for them to listen to his words, or to derive any benefit from those lessons, unless they keep silence. Every one who is accustomed to public worship, must know with what peculiar force these observations apply to the experience of Christians, in reference to the ministry of the Gospel. The preacher proclaims the word of truth; he declares the messages of God to the people; and he instructs them in a knowlege of the divine law. But all his efforts will be mere vanity, unless he receives from his hearers that respectful

CHAP. 9.] *On Silent Worship.* 303

attention, to which their entire silence is absolutely essential. And so it is, also, during those times, in the hours appointed for worship (and that there are such times we are well aware from our own experience) when the " Master of assemblies" calls forth no human instrument for the performance of his work; when he is pleased to take the office of teacher into his own hands, and to visit his unworthy children with the immediate illuminations of his Holy Spirit. They cannot avail themselves of this divine teaching; they cannot hear it; they cannot profit by it—unless they are silent—unless they maintain that stillness of soul which is naturally, and, under such circumstances, *necessarily,* accompanied with an outward silence. " Be still, and know that I am God," is a command which, in his character of universal Sovereign, Jehovah still addresses to his reasonable and dependent creatures; nor can there be any occasions on which an obedience to this command is more seasonable, than those which are appointed for public and congregational worship. While this true silence is preserved by Christian worshippers, they will often be permitted to hear the gentle and alluring accents of Israel's Shepherd, their guide, instructor, and comforter; and in listening to those accents with reverent submission, they will experience that renewal of strength, without which they can make no advances in the " way everlasting."

It appears, then, that Friends consider the maintenance of silence in their religious assemblies to be in perfect accordance with that divine law, that God, who is a Spirit, must be worshipped spiritually—that, in this sentiment, we are confirmed by a consideration of some of the principal constituents of true and spiritual worship, viz. humiliation before the divine Majesty, waiting upon God, and submissive attention to the immediate teaching of the Lord Jesus—that to these several duties the silent subjection of the soul is peculiarly suited, and even absolutely indispensable—and that this frame of mind is, in our judgment, most easily obtained, and most effectually preserved, through the medium of an outward silence.

Such are the reasons for the value which Friends are accustomed to attach to silence in worship: and which will, I trust, be found more and more to recommend so salutary a practice to Christians of every name and profession. In conclusion, however, it ought to be remarked, that although silence is a natural attendant of this inward state of prostration, waiting, and attention to the divine teaching, the former may often be maintained when the latter has no existence. It is easy for any man to be outwardly silent, while he allows his mind to be occupied with a thousand passing reflections which have no proper connexion with his religious duty; and, when this is unhappily the case with persons who are met together for the professed purpose of rendering a public homage to the Almighty, it must be confessed that their worship is as inefficacious, and nearly as much of a mockery, as it would be, did it consist in the use of words at total variance with the feelings of the heart.

How clearly, then, is it the duty of Friends, of every age and station, to maintain a true watchfulness and diligence of soul, that their silent worship may not be marred by the influence of worldly thoughts, and thus degenerate into a barren and lifeless form ? It may, indeed, be freely allowed, that a condition of true inward silence is one of no easy attainment. Great is our infirmity in this respect, and difficult do we sometimes find it, to stay the rapid movements of the mind, and to present ourselves, in real quietness, a living sacrifice to our God. But we do not expect to accomplish this object in our own strength. In our endeavours to worship God in spirit and in truth, we are taught to rely on him alone; and while such continues to be our reliance, experience will still enable us to testify that he is often pleased to arise for our help—that he has the will as well as the power, to bring our vain thoughts into silence—to raise our souls into holy communion with himself—and to say to the multitudinous imaginations of the natural man, *Peace, be still.*

ADDENDUM TO CHAPTER IX.

A.D. 1834.

PRACTICAL REMARKS AND ADVICES ON SILENT WORSHIP.

On a deliberate review of the arguments adduced in the foregoing chapter, I am confirmed in the sentiment, that the principles on which Friends have adopted the practice of silence in worship, are consistent both with reason and Scripture. Obvious indeed is the agreement between a state of silence, and that reverential awe, that humble waiting upon God, and that dependence on the teaching of our Lord Jesus Christ, which are main characteristics of true and living worship. Here then we may rest, without indulging an unprofitable anxiety to discover in the Holy Scriptures, any precise directions, as to *modes of worship.*

This appears to be one of the subjects on which we are left, by our Lord and his apostles, to follow up our own convictions, under the guidance, and in the *liberty,* of the Holy Spirit. Certain it is, however, that the only part of the New Testament, which describes the manner of public worship, to which the primitive disciples were accustomed, goes far to support the practices of Friends. From the 11th and 14th chapters of 1 Cor. it plainly appears, that the ministry which was employed in public worship was not the result of premeditation and study, but was poured forth under the especial influences of the Holy Ghost; and that it was not confined to the tenant of a pulpit, but devolved upon *all* those members of the church—whether male or female—whether few or numerous—who were gifted of the Lord for his service.

But although the true liberty of the Spirit was never curtailed on these occasions, it is expressly stated, that the "spirits of the prophets were subject to the prophets," and the apostle concludes his injunctions, on the whole subject, with the precept, "Let all things be done decently and in order." Now it appears to be nearly impossible, that such a system of ministry could be conducted decently and in order, except on the *basis of silence*. Without that basis, the frequent interruption one of another, must have been, through human weakness, an almost inevitable consequence. And further, if it is true (as I believe it to be) that no uninspired praying or preaching was then allowed in public worship, it obviously follows that at all times, except during the utterance of such ministry, the assembled church must have been in silence. In the absence, therefore, of all definite information on the subject, there is a strong presumption, that the primitive Christian believers were no strangers to silence in the public worship of God.

There can be no doubt that in those ancient times, the ministry of the word was poured forth in abundance, and that the number of persons of both sexes, who were intrusted with the prophetic gift, was large. Such also was the case, at the first rise, and during the early history, of our own society. The influence of the Spirit, in the production of the ministry of the gospel, was then experienced in an eminent degree; great numbers of persons—especially young men—were sent forth to bear the message of the Lord to every part of this land, as well as in many other countries; and the settled meetings of Friends appear to have been seldom held in total silence.

It is impossible to deny that our present condition is, in this respect, widely different from that of our forefathers. The number of our ministers is comparatively small, and many of our meetings—even some of a considerable size—are *generally* silent, from their commencement to their close. That this result is owing partly to the benumbing influence of the world, and to the want of spiritual life and vigour, there can be little doubt; but the administrations of the Spirit may be materially different at different times; and it is probable that a large proportion of silence in our meetings, may now be meted out by our divine Master, as the "food convenient" for us. I have sometimes observed that in little secluded meetings, in which a vocal ministry is scarcely ever heard, individuals are raised up, and strengthened of the Lord to preach to their neighbours, in the language of *example;* and it is a circumstance well worthy of remark, that few of our meetings appear to be so attractive to persons, not of our society, who are seeking the truth, as some which are mostly held in silence.

In all such matters we must endeavour to mark the hand of divine wisdom, and to submit to the ordering of infinite power. At the same time, we ought to feel a tender sympathy with such of our young friends, as may seldom enjoy the comfort and advantage of listening to a living gospel ministry; and I can hardly forbear availing myself of the present opportunity of offering to them a few practical hints, on *the right use of those important hours which they spend in their meetings for worship.*

In the first place, however, I would beseech them not to suffer any discouragement so to prevail over their minds, as to impede the due attendance of all their religious meetings. Public worship is a divinely appointed means for our highest good; an essential mark of allegiance to our God and Father; and it is a duty which requires *diligence.* None of us can reasonably expect divine help in the performance of it, unless we are punctual and faithful in putting ourselves in the way of that help. If we persevere in the attendance of our meetings, with an earnest aspiration after God, he will not fail to reward us in due season with a sense of his love; but if we fail to attend them regularly, the times of our absence may be precisely those, in which his power is most eminently manifested; and thus we may lose both our profit and our reward.

This remark applies with great force to the meetings which are held in the middle part of the week. The attendance of them may seem to involve a little sacrifice; but how many are there who can testify that no occasions have been more blessed than these to their immortal souls, as a means both of comfort and edification!

Five or six hours in the course of every week, is surely not too long a time for any man to devote to the public worship of his Creator; but may it not be feared, that even among the regular attenders of our meetings, a considerable part of this brief space of time is unprofitably spent? Have we not all abundant reason for shame and humiliation before God, in relation to this defect?

I would remind my younger readers, that good habits of mind in this, as well as in other respects, are, under divine grace, most easily formed in *early life ;* and I would, in the first place, affectionately advise them to cultivate *an awful sense of the Divine Majesty.* Let them remember, that it is no light or familiar matter, to enter upon the public worship of the Lord of the universe, who is able to save or to destroy our souls. Before we assemble for so solemn a purpose, our hearts ought to be turned to the Lord, and great care should be taken to avoid all levity or unprofitable conversation. To saunter about before the doors of a place of worship, and to converse with thoughtless companions, on worldly or trifling subjects, is a miserable preparation for bowing down in spirit before God our Maker. There is a holy order and propriety in all these matters, which cannot fail to be discerned, and ought ever to be followed, by the spiritually-minded Christian.

This remark suggests another of a more general nature—namely, that the degree of comfort and edification, which we derive from our silent meetings, will be found, in great measure, to depend on the degree of religious feeling which pervades our life and conversation; or, in other words, *on the spiritual condition of our minds.* Those who are slaves to the world during the hours of each passing day, will be slaves to the world in their religious meetings. Their souls, instead of ascending towards heaven, will, as a matter of course, be chiefly buried in the dust; their thoughts will wander in their old haunts; and, if a better light break in upon the mind, it will, alas! be only in glimpses. Is such an appearance of worship, without the great reality, any thing better than hypocrisy?

Those, on the other hand, who, amidst all their worldly occupations, are accustomed to turn their hearts towards God, and to remember him in all their ways, will approach him with reverence and fervour when they sit down in their meetings for worship. Should worldly thoughts then intrude upon them, they will not forget that God is their refuge; and as they diligently endeavour to wait upon him, *he* will strengthen them to overcome their infirmities, and to fix their souls upon himself.

Now, as our capacity for true worship in public, very much depends on the religious condition of our minds, so that condition is closely connected with *our private devotional duties.* Does any young friend who may read these lines, inquire, how he may be helped to restrain his wandering thoughts in silent meetings, and to worship God in spirit and in truth? I would address to such a one the counter-inquiry, What is thy daily practice as it relates to private devotion? Dost thou sit alone and keep silence before the Lord, bearing his yoke upon thee? Art thou accustomed, in solitude, to pour forth thy fervent prayers to Him who alone is able to keep thee from falling? Those who are the most faithful and diligent in the religious duties of the closet, will be the most edified in congregational worship. If a man who practices no such duties, fails to govern his thoughts at meeting, the defect is to be ascribed, not to our " custom of silence," but to his own sin of omission and neglect.

It is by *faith* that we draw near to God in our hours of private devotion, and it is by *faith* alone that we can acceptably worship him in public. " Without faith it is impossible to please God;" we can make no suitable approaches to him, except we believe " that he *is*, and that he is a rewarder of them that diligently seek him."[2] Nor ought we ever to forget, that in the heart of the Christian worshipper, this faith must embrace the Father, the Son, and the Holy Spirit. It is *through* Christ that we draw near, *by one Spirit*, unto *the Father*.[3] May the rising generation amongst us, become fully sensible that a firm belief in God, as *he is revealed to us in the gospel*, and a stedfast reliance on his mercy and power, are essential to the right performance of Christian worship. It will be the means of enabling them to wait upon him with the *patience of hope;* and to pray to him, through every discouragement, *without wavering*. When Jacob wrestled with the Angel of the covenant, his expressions were, " I will not let thee go, except thou bless me."[4] Faith was with him the spring of perseverance; and so it will ever be in the heart of every praying Christian.

I have sometimes met with persons of a tender and seeking mind, who have imbibed a notion, that the first point to be aimed at in order to silent worship, is a *vacuity from all ideas;* and who have been greatly

[2] Heb. xi, 6.   [3] Eph. ii, 18.   [4] Gen. xxxii, 26.

CHAP. 9.]   *on Silent Worship.*   313

discouraged by their unsuccessful efforts to attain to a state of which the waking mind of man is, by its nature, incapable. That which is *truly* required for this holy purpose, is an abstractedness from worldly thoughts, and even from religious meditations of our own devising, and a quiet fixing of the soul on God. The glorious idea of an omnipotent, omnipresent Being, will then fill our minds; and so far from our being destitute of an object to contemplate, one will be before us, of sufficient depth and magnitude to occupy the minds of saints and angels to all eternity. When we take our seats in a meeting for worship, we ought to endeavour, without delay, to draw near in spirit unto God, and to wait on him. When this is our condition, our secret prayers and praises will soon arise from the altar of the heart: and these will often occupy a large proportion of the time which we spend in silent meetings.

"Search me, O God," said the Psalmist, "and know my heart; try me, and know my thoughts; and see if there be any wicked way in me, and lead me in the way everlasting."[5] In answer to such petitions as these, our heavenly Father is often known to search the heart of the worshipper. Our secret faults, as well as our presumptuous sins, are detected by the light of the sanctuary, and are made manifest, for our humiliation, as in his holy presence. Now, this is a work with which we must endeavour, through divine help, faithfully to co-operate, and thus another proportion of our silent hours may be profitably spent, *in close*

[5] Psalms cxxxix, 23, 24.

self-examination before the Lord. Such an exercise will lead into penitence, and penitence will again be found the nurse of prayer. " The sacrifices of God are a broken spirit ; a broken and a contrite heart, O God, thou wilt not despise."[6]

There is an inseparable connexion between ceasing to do evil, and learning to do well. The same light which detects our transgressions, will make manifest to us the course of conduct which we ought to pursue: nor will our gracious Lord and Master turn a deaf ear to the petition—" Make *thy* way straight before my face." Not only will the true worshipper, in his silent waiting on the Lord, be impressed with the necessity of bearing all the fruits of righteousness, but the particular duties which lie in his own path—the sacrifices which he, as an individual, is called upon to make— will be made manifest to his mind ; and often will he find ability, while all around him is silence, to renew his covenant with the Lord—that he will " follow the Lamb whithersoever he goeth."

In thus drawing near to the Lord for the express purpose of being searched by his Spirit, reproved by the light of his law, and guided in a course of obedience, two qualities are indispensable in the Christian worshipper. The first is that *godly sincerity*, which will induce us to bring our *whole selves* to the light ; aud will lead us, without any compromise, to accept its reproofs and discoveries, respecting both our past transgressions and our present duties. The second is *a child-like reliance on the guidance and government of the Holy Spirit.* May this honest and believing

[6] Psalms li, 17.

heart more and more abound amongst us, for our own peace' sake, and for the glory of God!

The silent worshipper professes to be weaned from all undue dependence on vocal ministry, and to sit under the immediate teaching of Jesus Christ. Now it is not only by detecting their sins, and showing them their path of duty, that Christ instructs his people. He reveals his truth with power; he impresses a sense of the value of his atoning blood; he gently unfolds, by his own blessed Spirit, the secrets of redeeming love.

The doctrines which are thus made manifest to the understanding, and impressed on the heart, are already set forth in the Bible; and it is often through the words of that blessed book, that the Great Head of the church teaches his people. One passage of Scripture after another, passes before the mind of the silent worshipper, for his comfort or edification. Or more probably, after many passages have arisen in his recollection, some one in particular is fixed upon him, by a power beyond his own; and being interpreted and applied by the Spirit who gave it forth, becomes the medium both of instruction and nourishment.

How peculiarly important then to persons who are accustomed to silent worship, is the daily private perusal of the sacred volume! Were we, in dependence on the grace of God, more faithful and diligent in acquiring a knowledge of divine things, we should not so often be found presenting to the Lord, in public worship, the unworthy sacrifice of a mind enveloped in darkness. We should come to the enjoyment of something better than undefined and uncertain views of the truth as it is in Jesus. It would be revealed to us in its native simplicity, in its true proportions, in its glorious completeness; and great would be our peace and joy in the Lord.

While it is the very essence of silent worship, to cease from the activity of the natural man, and to watch for the influences of the Holy Spirit, the foregoing remarks may be sufficient to show, that *under those influences*, there is abundant occupation for us, of a most profitable kind, in our silent religious meetings.

In conclusion, however, I wish to express the deep value which I feel for a living gospel ministry; and I would ask my younger brethren and sisters, to whom we are to look for a succession of anointed servants, who shall proclaim amongst us the word of the living God. Surely it must be to themselves, many of whom —did they but faithfully bear his cross—the Lord, we may reverently believe, would call into his service, and qualify for the work. Through deep humiliation —through many a baptism—through the fire of divine judgment upon sin—through the inspiration of the Holy Ghost—they would become able ministers of "the New Testament."

May this blessed work of the Lord's anointing go nobly forward! "The harvest truly is plenteous, but the labourers are few." Let us therefore pray " the Lord of the harvest, that he will send forth labourers into his harvest!"

CHAPTER X.

ON OATHS.

IN the preceding chapters I have endeavoured to give a clear account of those religious peculiarities of the Society of Friends which belong particularly to the subject of worship, and which therefore involve duties (whether positive or negative) especially affecting our relation to the Supreme Being himself. The points still remaining for discussion have reference to our conduct in common life, and more especially towards our fellow creatures: for there are several matters of this description also, respecting which Friends entertain sentiments, and adopt practices, different from those of the bulk of their fellow Christians. Of these practical peculiarities, the first which presents itself for our consideration is, the *disuse of oaths*. Profane and irreverent appeals to the Almighty, and those conversational blasphemies which, even in Christian countries, continue to disgrace the various classes of worldly society, are indeed unanimously condemned by all true Christians: but Friends (in accordance, as I understand, with the Moravians) advance a step further, and consider it to be their bounden duty to avoid swearing of every kind, and on every occasion.

Independently of the direct prohibitions of swearing contained in the New Testament, such a line of conduct appears to be both justified and required by certain very obvious moral principles.

The first of these principles is embodied in the apostolic precept, "*Let your yea be yea, and your nay, nay, lest ye fall into condemnation,*"[1] and derives a clear confirmation from the declaration of Jesus himself, that "*whatsoever is more than these cometh of evil;*" or, as the Greek may be more accurately rendered, "*of the evil one.*"[2] Since the law of truth, in the verbal communications between man and man — a law strenuously supported even by heathen moralists, and obviously essential to the well-being of all human societies — is very frequently enjoined in the records of God's revealed will; since it is plainly of universal obligation on the followers of Jesus; and since, on the other hand, there is nothing more decisively condemned in the sacred volume than the false tongue, it follows that, with true Christians, a deliberate and serious, yet simple affirmation or negation, possesses a force so perfect in its kind, as to be incapable of any real augmentation. Hence there arises a plain moral obligation, in conformity with the precept of the apostle James, that our yea should be yea, and our nay, nay—that is to say, that our affirmations and negations should be naked and simple, and wholly unaccompanied with any form of oath. For if, on any particular occasion, a man swears, in addition to his yea or nay, in order to render them more obligatory and convincing, their force be-

---

[1] James v, 12. [2] ἐκ τοῦ πονηροῦ. Matt. v, 37.

comes comparatively weak at other times, when they receive no such confirmation. If such an one is a believer in the Lord Jesus, and especially if he is a serious professor of religion, it is plain that, by his conduct, he gives countenance to the false and dangerous notion, that the oath of the Christian is more binding upon his conscience, and *therefore more credible*, than his deliberate word; and thus he inevitably lowers the *standard* of the law of truth.

Nor is the deduction of this consequence the work of mere theory. Experience bears ample testimony to the fact, that the prevalence of oaths among men (Christians not excepted) has produced a very material and very general effect in reducing their estimate of the obligation of plain truth, in its natural and simple forms. Even the heathen philosophers of old were well aware of the hurtful results of the practice of swearing; and some of them have left on record an express condemnation of that practice.[3] Truly, then, may it be asserted, that those awful ap-

[3] Epictetus says, παραίτησαι ὅρκον εἰς ἅπαν — "Avoid swearing altogether." Plato, ὅρκος περὶ παντὸς ἀπέστω — "Let an oath be avoided on every occasion." Chærilus, ὅρκον τ' οὔτ' ἄδικον χρεὼν ἔμμεναι οὔτε δίκαιον—"No oath, whether it be a just or an unjust one, ought to be allowed." Menander, ὅρκον δὲ φεῦγε κἂν δικαίως ὀμνύῃς—"Abstain from swearing, even though it be justly." See *Grotius* on Matt. v, 34. "Stobæus, *Serm.* 3, relates that Solon said, *A good man ought to be in that estimation, that he need not an oath; because it is to be reputed a lessening of his honour, if he be forced to swear.* Pythagoras, in his oration, among other things, hath this maxim, as that which concerns the administration of the commonwealth: *Let no man call God to witness by an oath; no, not in judgment; but let every man so accustom himself to speak, that he may become worthy to be trusted, even without an oath.*" *Barclay's Apology,* prop. xv, § 12.

peals to a superior agency, by which, in every oath, the truth is supposed to be confirmed, (whatever may be the occasion on which such oath is employed,) arise out of an evil source—produce an evil consequence—and are at variance with the principles of that perfect law, to which Christians, above all others, owe an exact and universal obedience.

The true Christian cannot, indeed, be ignorant that he is in the presence of an omniscient God, who is perfectly aware both of his secret thoughts and of his open declarations. Nevertheless, the principle, to which I have now adverted, appears to afford a substantial reason why he should abstain from attempting to add to the force of his yea or nay, by making such an awful appeal to the Deity as constitutes an oath. But further: there appears to be a distinct moral objection to oaths, on the ground that, according to general usage, both ancient and modern, they clearly imply a curse—a conditional calling down upon oneself of some dreaded penalty. A man swears either by something which is dear and valuable to him, or by some personal object of his reverence and dread. In the former case, the penalty which he means to attach to himself, on the supposition that his oath is untrue, is the loss of that which he loves; and, in the latter case, it is the wrath and vengeance of him whom he fears. When the ancient Grecian, for instance, swore by his head, he professed to subject himself to the loss of his head; and when he swore by Jupiter, he cursed himself with the wrath of Jupiter, provided his oath should be false or broken. Now, it is a very affecting consideration, that the oaths in use among the professors of Christianity are unspeakably more terrible than any heathen oath; in so much as the penalty which the swearer calls down upon himself, on the supposition of his swearing falsely, is one of infinite weight and severity. It is nothing short of damnation—the destruction and eternal punishment of his immortal soul.

That such is the import of the common juridical oath of this country, is notorious. An individual, who is called upon to give evidence in an English court of justice, swears that he will tell the truth, the whole truth, and nothing but the truth; and he adds, "*So help me God;*" or, as the words were formerly recited, "*So help me God at his holy dome;*" that is to say, *Let this be the condition on which God shall help me in the day of judgment.*[4] The help of God, thus technically adverted to—the help of God in the day of his holy doom—plainly signifies that help by which alone the soul of man can be saved from eternal misery, and introduced to a state of never-ending happiness. Thus, then, the English swearer, in his appeal to an all-seeing, omnipotent Deity, voluntarily and expressly appends his own salvation to the condition of his speaking the truth, the whole truth, and nothing but the truth. On the supposition of his infringing that condition, he curses himself with the loss of God's help, and with consequent damnation.

Even were it absolutely certain that the alternative, on account of which a man calls down upon himself

[4] See *Rees's Cyclopædia,* "*Oath*".

this everlasting ruin and destruction, could by no possibility occur, the reflecting Christian, who dwells under a just sense of the judgments of the Lord, and of the unutterable importance of eternity, will scarcely fail to acknowledge that such a cursing of self is, in a high degree, rash and irreverent. But, how much more awfully dangerous is such an imprecation, when the alternative in question is far from being improbable. The senses of men frequently deceive them: their memory easily fails them: when they are surrounded with appalling circumstances, or perplexed with difficult questions, their presence of mind is very commonly disturbed or destroyed; and above all, their own hearts are corrupt and deceitful: so that, perhaps, a person, who is about to give evidence in a court of justice, can never be absolutely assured that he shall speak the truth, the whole truth, and nothing but the truth; and yet, in appealing to the omnipresent Johovah, he presumes to stake upon this frail and fallible condition the salvation of his immortal soul!

Those who are acquainted with the history of the Society of Friends must be aware how uniformly they have objected to the use of oaths; how fully persuaded they have at all times been, that they could in no case comply with the prevalent custom of swearing, without grieving and offending their heavenly Guide and Governor; and how multifarious and severe were the sufferings which the early members of that Society preferred to the infringement of their duty in this important practical particular. We need not be surprised at their steadiness and decision in this respect,

CHAP. 10.] *On Oaths.* 323

when we reflect on the weight and importance of the moral principles which have now been considered. But the main ground on which Friends have always regarded it as their bounden duty to abstain from all swearing, is the express command of our Lord Jesus himself. "Ye have heard that it hath been said by them of old time, Thou shalt not forswear thyself, but shalt perform unto the Lord thine oaths: but I say unto you, *Swear not at all;* neither by heaven, for it is God's throne; nor by the earth for it is his footstool; neither by Jerusalem, for it is the city of the Great King. Neither shalt thou swear by thy head, because thou canst not make one hair white or black. But let your communication be Yea, yea; Nay, nay; for whatsoever is more than these cometh of evil."[5] The apostle James has also adverted to the subject in forcible and explicit terms: "*But above all things,* my brethern, swear not, neither by heaven; neither by the earth; neither by any other oath: but let your yea be yea, and your nay, nay; lest ye fall into condemnation."[6]

It might have been supposed that such plain injunctions would have convinced the generality of persons, who derive their moral standard from the New Testament, that oaths, on any occasion, and under any pretext, are absolutely unlawful for the followers of Jesus. But the very common notion, that they are necessary to some important purposes of civil society, has evidently been the means of preventing this result. Many persons have, accordingly, acceded to the

[5] Matt. v, 33—37.   [6] Ch. v, 12.

glosses by which commentators endeavour to escape from the force of these passages; and that with a far greater readiness and facility than those glosses deserve. The objections which have been made to the more comprehensive interpretation of these prohibitions, centre principally in a single point; namely, that the oaths here specified, both by our Saviour and his apostles, are oaths, not by *Jehovah*, but only by his *creatures*. Since the latter oaths alone are specified, it is readily concluded that they alone, or they principally, are forbidden; and since it appears that, in their courts of justice, the Jews swore not by heaven, the earth, Jerusalem, or their own heads, but only by God himself, and that they used these inferior oaths on more familiar occasions, it is argued that the injunctions of Christ and his apostles were not directed against judicial swearing, but only against that which was common and conversational. Now, as this inference depends entirely upon the supposition that the swearing forbidden by our Lord and his apostle was *only*, or *chiefly*, swearing by the creatures, and not the oath by Jehovah; it follows, that, if that supposition be disproved, the inference itself must fall to the ground. I hope, then, to make it plain to the reader's apprehension that, in these passages, every kind of swearing is forbidden, and *especially swearing by Jehovah*.

In the first place, the terms in which our Lord expresses his new law are of the most decisive and comprehensive nature. " But I say unto you, *Swear not at all*."[7] The apostle, whose words may be

[7] μὴ ὀμόσαι ὅλως.

regarded as a sort of commentary on those of Christ, maintains and even increases the force and extent of these terms: he says, " *Above all things*, my brethren, *swear not;*" and, after specifying the oath by heaven and that by the earth, he completes the force of his sentence by the subsequent clause, " neither by *any other* oath." The negative injunction is, moreover, in both instances, elucidated and confirmed by another of a *positive* character. " Let your yea be yea, and your nay, nay," says the apostle—that is, let them be naked, simple, plain, absolutely destitute of any oath. " Let your communication (or " your speech"[8]) be yea, yea; nay, nay," says our Saviour; " for *whatsoever* is more than these"—whether it be the lesser or the greater oath, the oath by the creature or the oath by the Creator—" *whatsoever* is more than these, cometh of evil." Here our Lord has justified and explained his law by a *declaration*. Now, that declaration extends to every description of swearing; *it applies to the higher kinds of it with still greater force than to the lower;* and it must needs be understood as universal, because, whatever exception may here be imagined, none is expressed—none, even in the most distant manner, hinted at or alluded to—by Christ himself.

It is to be observed, in the second place, that oaths of a secondary kind are forbidden by our Lord on the express principle, *that they were nearly allied to more solemn oaths, and that some of these forms did in fact involve a real swearing by Jehovah;* Neither by heaven, *for it is God's throne;* neither by the earth, for it is *his footstool;* neither by Jerusalem, for it is *the city of*

[8] λόγος.

the great King;—the Lord of hosts. Those, therefore, who swore by the heaven, by the earth, or by Jerusalem, virtually swore by that divine Being who dwells in them, and uses them as his own: according to the clear doctrine of the Lord Jesus, on another occasion— " Whoso shall swear by the temple, sweareth by it, and by him that dwelleth therein; and he that shall swear by heaven, sweareth by the throne of God, and by him that sitteth thereon."[9] If, then, swearing by the creature was to be avoided, simply because of its virtual connexion with swearing by the Creator, how much more clearly objectionable was the direct and awful oath by Jehovah himself! I would suggest that our Lord's meaning may be expressed as follows:— " But I say unto you, swear not at all—on no occasion, and by no description of oaths—not even by those of a secondary form, which you are accustomed to use familiarly, and to regard as harmless and unmeaning. Such oaths are, in point of fact, fraught with solemnity, and are of the very same nature as swearing by the living God. Keep strictly, therefore, in all your speech, to the yea and nay; for whatsoever method of swearing may be employed to augment their force, it cometh of the evil one."[1]

[9] Matt. xxiii, 21, 22.

[1] " Graviter falluntur," says Grotius on this passage, " qui solam, a Christo improbari putant consuetudinem jurandi per res alias extra Deum. Nam Jacobus, optimus Christi interpres, ait, *Non jurandum, neque per cœlum, neque per terram, neque alia quavis jurandi formula.* Imo sensus Christi est, Non jurandum; *ne quidem* (not even) per cœlum, per terram, per Hyerosolyma, per caput; quod ostendit membrum oppositum: *Sit autem sermo vester, est non, non.*" The Greek particle μήτε is capable of being rendered " not even" as well as " nor:" *comp.* Mark iii, 20.

Lastly, the true import of the precept of Christ, respecting swearing, is to be gathered from that of the Jewish law, to which that precept is placed in opposition. It has already been observed that the worship prescribed to the ancient Hebrews was, in general, of a much lower and less spiritual character than that which is enjoined upon the disciples of Jesus; and, in complete coincidence with such a fact, it appears, with equal clearness, that the *moral law*—the law of practice—was less fully developed, and less properly understood, under the Mosaic, than it is under the Christian dispensation. In condescension to a state of comparative ignorance and weakness, many things were permitted, and even temporarily enjoined, which the full light of Christian truth has evinced to be now unlawful. Every reader of the New Testament is acquainted with the comparison instituted by our Lord, in his sermon on the mount, between the system of morals which the Jews had grounded on the law of Moses, and his own pure and perfect law. The law of Moses forbad murder; the law of Christ extends the prohibition to injuries and insults of every description, and enjoins us to subdue those angry and malicious feelings which are the source of overt wrongs. The law of Moses allowed of divorce on trifling occasions; the law of Christ repeals that provision, and holds up the highest standard respecting the security and completeness of the marriage union. The law of Moses was regarded by the Jews as sanctioning the principle of retaliation;[2] the law of Christ enjoins the suffering of injury, and the return of good for evil. One principle

[2] Exodus xxi, 23—25 ; Numb. xxxv, 17—21.

of the law of Moses was, love of friends and hatred of (national) enemies; that of the law of Christ is, love to all. So, also, the law of Moses, while it forbad both swearing falsely and swearing lightly,[3] allowed the use of oaths, when required by the order of civil and religious society, as it was then established: but the law of Christ goes further; it cuts off all opportunity of perjury, and of every other abuse of the oath, by the complete prohibition of swearing. "Ye have heard that it hath been said by them of old time, Thou shalt not forswear thyself; but I say unto you, *Swear not at all.* The oaths which the ancient Israelites were thus enjoined not to infringe were taken in the name of Jehovah, the living God, and were employed principally in their courts of justice, and on other occasions of seriousness and importance. Such, then, are the oaths, as well as others of a less solemn form and character, from which Christians are commanded, by their own Lawgiver, *entirely to abstain.*

For all the reasons now stated, I cannot but consider it abundantly evident that our Lord, and his apostle James, *have absolutely forbidden swearing of every description and on all occasions.* In this conclusion we are confirmed by the express judgment of the early fathers, both Greek and Latin, who have almost uniformly interpreted these passages as destitute of any limitation. "I say nothing of perjury," says Tertullian, "since swearing itself is unlawful to

---

[3] Both these meanings are considered by commentators, and especially by Jewish commentators, to be included in the injunction, "Thou shalt not take the name of the Lord thy God *in vain*." Exodus xx, 7.

Christians."[4]   " The old law," says Basil, " is satisfied with the honest keeping of the oath: but Christ cuts off the opportunity of perjury."[5]   " He who has precluded murder by taking away anger," observes Gregory of Nysse, " and who has driven away the pollution of adultery by subduing desire, has expelled from our life the curse of perjury by forbidding us to swear; for, where there is no oath, there can be no infringement of it."[6]   " Let the Christian entirely avoid oaths, in obedience to our Lord's prohibition," exclaims Chrysostom: " do not, therefore, say to me, I swear for a just purpose.   It is no longer lawful for thee to swear either justly or unjustly.   Let us preserve our mouths free from an oath."[7]   " It is our absolute duty," says Gregory Nazianzen, " strictly to attend to the commands of our king, and by all means to avoid an oath— *especially such a one as is taken in the name of God.*"[8]

Since Jesus Christ has thus forcibly, explicitly, and without limitation or exception, prohibited his followers from swearing, the corresponding duty on their part is, evidently, a *total* abstinence from the practice. By way of excuse, however, for not abstaining from

[4] *De Idol.* cap. 11, Ed. Semleri, tom. iv, 161.
[5] *In Psalm* xiv, *Hom.* Ed. Ben. tom. i, 356.
[6] *In Cant. Hom.* 13, Ed. Ben. tom. i, 657, 8.
[7] *In Gen.* ii, *Hom.* xv, Ed. Ben. tom. iv, p. 122.
[8] *Orat.* 53, Ed. Colon. A.D. 1690, tom. i, 760.   See also *Justin, Apol.* i, cap. Ed. Ben. 16, p. 53 ; *Clement. Alex. Pæd.* lib. 3, Ed. Ben. p. 259; *Strom.* lib. v, p. 707 ; *Origen, in Com.* Matt. *serie,* tract. 23, Ed. Ben. tom, 3, 842 ; *Cyprian, Testim.* lib. 3, § 12 ; *Hilary, Episc. in Matt.* v. 34, Ed. Ben. p. 628 ; *Theophylact. in Matt.* v. 33 ; *Ambrose, in Psalm* 118, *Exp.* 14, Ed. Ben. tom. i, p. 1145 ; *Jerom. in Matt.* v. 34 ; *Isidorus Pelus,* lib. i, ep 155 ; *Barclay's Apol.* prop. xv. § 12.

it, Christians may often be heard to remark that Jesus himself took a judicial oath—that Paul swore in his epistles—and that oaths are expedient for the security and welfare of society. It is impossible for me to complete the present argument, without taking some notice of these several objections.

When the Lord Jesus stood before the Jewish sanhedrim, and the false witnesses had delivered their testimony respecting him, "the high priest arose, and said unto him, Answerest thou nothing? What is it which these witness against thee? But Jesus held his peace. And the high priest answered and said unto him, *I adjure thee by the living God, that thou tell us*, whether thou be the Christ, the Son of God. Jesus said unto him, *Thou hast said.*"[9] The reply made by our Saviour, on this occasion, is generally, and I believe rightly, interpreted as an assent: and since he was *adjured* by the high priest to declare whether he was or was not the Christ, the Son of God, it is readily concluded that Jesus was here put upon his oath, and *took it*. Were this the matter of fact, it would, in my opinion, afford no sufficient reason why Christians should swear in contravention of the direct command of their divine Master. It ought to be remembered that, at the period when these circumstances happened, the Mosaic law was still in force, and obedience to that law was one of the principles which regulated the life of Jesus. Nor can there be any just comparison between the oath of one who was absolutely incapable of either falsehood or error, and that of others who are perpetually liable to both. A little investigation,

[9] Matt. xxvi, 62—64.

however, may suffice to convince the reader that Jesus, in the passage cited above, is *not* described by the evangelist as taking his oath.

When an ancient Jew was examined in a court of justice, he swore to the fact to which he might be deposing, in the following, or some equivalent terms: " Behold, I swear by the name of the Lord God of Israel, that such or such is the truth;" or otherwise he was put upon his oath, or sworn by the judges, who said, " We make thee swear by the Lord God of Israel, that such or such is the truth:" to which adjuration the deponent was accustomed to reply " Amen."[1] Now, it does not appear that, in the present instance, the Lord Jesus either swore himself, or was sworn by his judges. He was not attending the court as a witness, neither was there any fact to which he was called upon to depose. He was accused of having assumed the divine character; the evidence brought in proof of the point was of a suspicious and unsatisfactory description ; and it was evidently for the purpose of entrapping him into the repetition of his supposed crime, that the high priest *solemnly enjoined* him to declare to the sanhedrim whether he was or was not the Son of God. With this solemn injunction Jesus complied: and no sooner had he uttered his answer, than " the high priest rent his clothes, saying, He hath spoken blasphemy: what further need have we of witnesses? behold, now ye have heard his blasphemy."[2] Schleusner, in his Lexicon of the Greek Testament, expressly remarks that the verb, rendered in this passage, " I adjure,"[3] does not here signify,

[1] See *Buxtorf. Synag. p.* 682. [2] Verse 65. [3] ἐξορκίζω.

"I make to swear, or put upon oath;" but only, " I solemnly, and in the name of God, exhort, and enjoin." That this verb, in its more simple form,[4] is repeatedly employed in this latter signification, such of my readers as are accustomed to peruse the new Testament in its original language, will be well aware. Thus the evil spirit cried out to Jesus, "*I adjure thee by God*, that thou torment me not."[5] Thus Paul wrote to the Thessalonians, "*I charge (or adjure)* you by the Lord, that this epistle be read unto all the holy brethren."[6] Thus also, in Canticles ii, 7; v. 8 (passages in which we find the same verb in the Septuagint version, and a corresponding one in the Hebrew text,) the spouse exclaims, "*I charge (or adjure)* you, O ye daughters of Jerusalem, that ye stir not up my love till he please: *I charge (or adjure)* you, O ye daughters of Jerusalem, if ye find my beloved, that ye tell him I am sick of love." The comparison of these passages of Scripture with that now under consideration, appears to afford ample evidence that the Lord Jesus, when he complied with the solemn injunction of the high priest, no more took an oath than the Thessalonians did, when they read Paul's epistle unto all the holy brethren —than the daughters of Jerusalem did, when they abstained from waking the bridegroom, and when they delivered to him the message of the bride—or than our Lord himself did, when he acceded to the earnest entreaty of the evil spirit.

It is objected, in the second place, that the apostle Paul, in some parts of his epistles, has made use of oaths. "God is my witness," says he to the Romans,

[4] ὁρκίζω.   [5] Mark v, 7.   [6] 1 Thess. v, 27.

"that without ceasing I make mention of you always in my prayers."[7] And again, to the Thessalonians, he says, " Neither at any time used we flattering words — God is witness."[8] It is almost needless to observe that, in these passages, the apostle does not swear, but confines himself to the declaration of a truth which no man could dispute ; namely, that God was the witness of his secret exercises and of his plain address. Again, on another occasion, when describing to the Galatians the course which he pursued after his conversion, the apostle expresses himself in a somewhat similar manner. " Now the things which I write unto you, *behold, before God, I lie not.*"[9] Here was a solemn affirmation, made in the confessed presence of that Being who alone searches the heart; but no oath, no imprecation, no calling down upon himself of any dreaded penalty. Precisely the same remark will, I believe, be found to apply to another passage, in which Paul appeals still more directly to the Deity: " Moreover," says he to the Corinthians, " I call God for a record (or a *witness*) upon my soul, (or *of my mind*,) that, to spare you, I came not as yet unto Corinth."[1]

Although that appeal to an omniscient Deity which in the former of these passages, is implied, and, in the latter, plainly expressed, can by no means be considered as, in itself, constituting an oath, it may be freely allowed, on a principle stated in the first part of the present chapter, that such an addition to a deliberate yet simple yea or nay, in confirmation of

[7] Romans i, 9. [8] 1 Thess. ii, 5. [9] Gal. i, 20.
[1] 2 Cor. i, 23.

their truth, would be of dangerous application to the common affairs of life. But we are to remember that the apostle was an inspired man, and that, in the promulgation of the gospel, as well as in the government of the churches, he was, in a pre-eminent degree, invested with the sanctions of divine authority. That authority he was very frequently led to assert.[2] When therefore, we consider the peculiar circumstances under which he was thus placed, we may very reasonably interpret, *as instances of such assertion*, the appeals here made to that Almighty Being, by whose inspiration he was protected from error, and by whose direction his whole conduct, as an apostle, was so conspicuously regulated.

Here, however, it ought to be acknowledged, that the latter of these passages contains certain expressions which have sometimes been interpreted in such a manner as to give to the appeal there made to the Deity, the force of an oath. The expressions alluded to[3] are, in our common English version, rendered, *upon my soul*. If we take the preposition here rendered "upon" in the sense of *against*, (a sense in which it is sometimes used,) and the substantive rendered "soul" as meaning either the *natural life*, or the *immortal spirit*, we must conclude that Paul, when he declared to the Corinthians, that to spare them he came not again unto Corinth, not only called upon God as the witness of that truth, but actually staked either his natural life, or his soul, on the veracity of his assertion.

[2] Rom. i, 1 ; 1 Cor. i, 1 ; ii, 13 ; xiv, 37 ; Gal. i, 1. &c.
[3] ἐπὶ τὴν ἐμὴν ψυχήν.

On the supposition of the propriety of such an interpretation, it may be observed, in the first place, that the apostle's expressions related to a branch of his conduct, in which he was immediately directed of the Lord, and in reference to which, while he continued under the influence of inspiration, it was impossible for him to promulgate any falsehood. An oath taken by such a person, under these extraordinary circumstances, would afford no real countenance to the swearing of uninspired persons, on matters of a merely temporal nature. And secondly, though there is an obvious difficulty in reconciling the supposition that the apostle Paul has sworn in his epistles, with that comprehensive and absolute prohibition of the practice, which was issued by his divine Master, yet, I apprehend, that no reasonable Christian, in the regulation of his own conduct, would pretend to justify himself by the *example* of Paul, in the infringement of the *law* of Christ.

The signification of that law is, I would submit, far too clearly ascertained to be affected by the supposed collateral circumstance, that the apostle Paul has here made use of an oath. But now, on the other hand, it may be observed, that the very existence of such a law naturally and very properly leads us to a different interpretation of the apostle's expressions—an interpretation of which they are unquestionably capable, and which at once removes from the passage before us the true characteristic of an oath. The substantive already alluded to, as sometimes signifying the *natural life*, or the *immortal spirit*, still more frequently denotes *the mind*—the seat of the intentions, thoughts, and dispositions. The apostle, therefore, may here be understood, as is observed on the authority of two eminent critics,[4] in Pool's Synopsis, simply to appeal to the Deity as the witness of his *condition of mind*— of his real motives and intentions—that, *to spare them*, he came not again unto Corinth. "The holy apostle," says Theodoret, " wishing to persuade them of the truth of his assertions, calls in the testimony of Him who was the inspector of his *thoughts*."[5]

Before we proceed to the remaining branch of the present subject, it may be desirable briefly to notice a passage in the epistle to the Hebrews, which has sometimes been adduced in support of the practice of swearing: " For when God made promise to Abraham, because he could swear by no greater, he sware by himself, saying, Surely blessing will I bless thee, &c. *For men verily swear by the greater, and an oath for confirmation is to them an end of all strife (or all liti-*

[4] Vatablus and Castalio.

[5] It is observed by Pye Smith, in his valuable work entitled *The Scripture Testimony to the Messiah*, that Paul, in his epistles, has sworn by " Christ." Such is the interpretation given by this writer to the expression ἐν Χριστῷ, in Rom. ix, 1 ; a passage which he renders, " I speak the truth, by Christ ! I lie not :" see vol. II. part II. ch. iv, p. 637. That ἐν, followed by a dative, is sometimes used in the formula of an oath appears from Matt. v, 34 ; Rev. x, 6, &c. But surely it is altogether unnecessary to attribute to the apostle so light and irreverent a use of the name of his Saviour. The expression ἐν Χριστῷ, is of very frequent occurrence in Paul's epistles ; and in scarcely any instance is it capable, on any fair critical ground, of being thus interpreted. It appears to me that the true explanation of Rom. ix, 1, is to be found in the apostle's well-known doctrine, that whatever the Christian says or does, he is to say or do in the name of Christ—in the character of a disciple of Jesus : *comp.* 2 Cor. ii, 17 ; xii, 19.

gation:) wherein God, willing more abundantly to show unto the heirs of promise the immutability of his counsel, confirmed it by an oath."[6] On this passage it may be remarked, that although Jehovah, who is infallible, was pleased to swear by himself, it can never follow from such a fact, that men, who are fallible, are at liberty to swear by Jehovah, who has himself forbidden them, in the moral law of Christianity, to swear *at all.* Neither does the apostle speak in *commendation* of the practice of putting an end to strife by the confirmation of an oath. He only illustrates his argument by adverting to the actual prevalence of that practice among mankind.

Lastly, it is objected that oaths are, on many occasions, expedient for the purposes of civil society, and useful, more especially, in promoting the ends of justice. Now, while it is evident that no expediency can justify the infraction of a divine mandate so clear and comprehensive as the law of Christ against swearing, it may be admitted that there is an apparent fitness between the practice of judicial swearing, and that lax and imperfect morality which so grievously prevails in almost every part of the world. But, where the principles of the gospel of Christ become really influential, there the expediency of swearing entirely ceases; nor does the supposed congruity of the practice with a condition of second-rate morality, appear to furnish the true Christian with any just excuse for relinquishing the lofty ground on which he ought ever to be found standing, or for disobeying the direct commands of his divine Master. Those who are Christians in

[6] Heb. vi, 13—17.

deed, as well as in profession, ought ever to remember that it is their high and peculiar privilege to drop, in moral questions, the consideration of apparent expediency; to render to their Lord a consistent obedience; and to leave the consequences to his wisdom, love, and care. It is through the steady adherence of religious persons to their own holy principles of conduct, that practical truth may be expected to *spread* among men; it is thus that " the little leaven" will gradually extend its purifying influence, *until the whole lump be leavened.* Nor will such a course be ever attended with any substantial or permanent disadvantage to the interests of the community at large. No one pretends, for example, that those interests have suffered from the liberty allowed to Friends, of *affirming* instead of *swearing;* and as it is with Friends, in this respect, so it might be with serious Christians of every denomination. A steady and determined adherence to the law of Christ, in this important particular, would soon be the means of procuring for them a similar liberty from the governments under which they live; and that liberty would be no less harmless to the public, than beneficial to themselves.

But the utility of juridical oaths, even among those whose standard of morals is not that which is prescribed by true Christianity, is, in all probability, greatly overrated. Magistrates are ever accustomed to judge of testimony, not so much by the solemnity of the obligation, under which it is pronounced, as by the manner in which it is delivered, and by the known character of the parties who deliver it. And in persons whose moral sense is feeble and degenerate, and who have, in their own minds, little objection to the sacrifice of truth, veracity of evidence is far more likely to be obtained by the *uniform* and *speedy* infliction of punishment on the breach of an affirmation, than by the easily-disregarded influence of any form of words, however expressive, and however solemn.

In reverting to the principal heads of the present dissertation, I have again to observe that, while Christians of every denomination unite in condemning irreverent and conversational swearing, Friends decidedly object to any use of oaths whatsoever—that their objection is in full accordance with certain obvious moral principles, but is grounded chiefly on the express command of our Saviour himself—that the introduction of swearing on particular occasions plainly lowers the general standard of simple truth—that the self-imprecation essential to every oath is always presumptuous; and in juridical swearing, as practised among modern Christians, peculiarly rash and dangerous—that the precept of Christ, and that of his apostle James, against oaths, are of the most comprehensive and explicit character—that the attempt to explain those precepts, as relating exclusively to conversational swearing, is, by several plain considerations, evinced to be futile—that the notion of our Lord's having been himself sworn in a court of justice appears to be erroneous—that, were it true that Paul swore in his epistles, his example could not be safely followed in opposition to the law of his divine Master; but that, on examination, he in no case appears to have employed expressions which amount to an oath—that true Christians are far from being justified in breaking the law of Christ, because oaths may be deemed expedient for persons who are acccustomed to an inferior standard of morals—and that even this expediency is exceedingly doubtful.

Since the moral principles on which we object to oaths are of so much practical weight; and since the authority under which we act, in refusing to swear, is at once so high and so clear—we may well be encouraged to a persevering faithfulness in such a line of conduct. The steady sufferings of our forefathers have indeed been the means of earning for us, in reference to this particular, an entire ease and freedom.

I cannot but indulge the hope that, as such a faithfulness is maintained among Friends, and as their light is thus made to shine before other men, religious persons of every denomination will gradually perceive the obligation which so plainly rests upon them, to abstain from all swearing. Certainly it must, on all hands, be allowed, that the standard to which the professors of Christianity are at present accustomed, with regard to this subject, is *miserably low*. Not only are oaths, in our own enlightened country, introduced in connexion with matters of solemn import, and in promotion of the ends of justice; but they are multiplied in every direction; are required by the law, and taken by the subject, on a thousand occasions of comparatively trifling consequence; and are very generally administered in a loose, technical, and irreverent manner. Such provisions are utterly disgraceful to the Christian character of Great Britain; and demand the speedy interference of those members of our legislature, who are blessed with a deep sense of the importance of the principles of the Gospel, and who know that the real prosperity of every nation depends on the consistency of its counsels with the will of God.[7]

[7] Since the foregoing sentences were written, a great improvement has taken place in the laws of this country on the subject of oaths. A vast number of useless oaths have been cut off by act of parliament; and merchants and tradesmen can now transact their business at the custom-house without involving themselves in the awful and unchristian practice of the *conditional cursing of themselves*. These changes are doubtless the result of an increasingly enlightened public opinion. May the progress of divine truth, in every class of society, speedily lead to the entire abolition of a practice, which the Lord of nations and the Judge of all flesh, has emphatically forbidden!

CHAPTER XI.

ON WAR.

OF all the practices which disturb the tranquillity and lay waste the welfare of men, there is none which operates to so great an extent, or with so prodigious an efficacy, as *war*. Not only is this tremendous and dreadfully-prevalent scourge productive of an incalculable amount of bodily and mental suffering—so that, in point of view alone, it may be considered one of the most terrible enemies of the happiness of the human race—but it must also be regarded as a moral evil of the deepest dye. " From whence come wars and fightings among you?" said the apostle James; " come they not hence, even of your lusts which war in your members? Ye lust and have not; ye kill and desire to have, and cannot obtain; ye fight and war, yet ye have not, because ye ask not."[1] War, therefore, has its rise in the inordinate desires and corrupt passions of men; and as is its origin, so is its result. Growing out of an evil root, this tree of

[1] Chap. iv, 1, 2.

bitterness seldom fails to produce, in vast abundance, the fruits of malice, wrath, cruelty, fraud, rapine, lasciviousness, confusion, and murder.

Although there are few persons who will dispute the accuracy of this picture of war—although every one knows that such a custom is evil in itself and arises out of an evil source—and although the *general position*, that war is at variance with the principles of Christianity, has a very extensive currency among the professors of that religion—it is a singular fact, that Friends are almost the only class of Christians who hold it to be their duty to God, to their neighbour, and to themselves, entirely to abstain from that most injurious practice. While the views of Friends on the subject are thus complete, the generality of professing Christians, and many even of a reflecting and serious character, are still accustomed to make distinctions between one kind of war and another. They will condemn a war which is oppressive and unjust; and, in this respect, they advance no further than the moralists of every age, country, and religion. On the other hand, they hesitate as little in expressing their approbation of wars which are defensive, or which are otherwise undertaken in a just cause.

The main argument, of a scriptural character, by which warfare in a just cause (as it is termed) is defended, and its rectitude maintained, is *the divinely-sanctioned example of the ancient Israelites.* That the Israelites were engaged in many contests with other nations; that those contests were often of a very destructive character; and that they were carried forward, on the part of the Israelites, under the direct sanction, and often in consequence of the clear command, of the Almighty, are points which no one, who reads the history of the Old Testament, can pretend to deny. But we are not to forget that the wars of the Israelites differed from wars in general (even from those of the least exceptionable character in point of justice) in certain important and striking particulars. That very divine sanction, which is pleaded as giving to the example of that people an authority of which other nations may still avail themselves in the maintenance of a similar practice, did, in fact, distinguish their wars from all those in which any other nation is known to have been ever engaged. They were undertaken in pursuance of the express command of the Almighty Governor of mankind; and they were directed to the accomplishment of certain revealed designs of his especial providence. These designs had a twofold object: the temporal preservation and prosperity of God's peculiar people, on the one hand; and the punishment and destruction of idolatrous nations, on the other. The Israelites and their kings were, indeed, sometimes engaged in combating their neighbours, without any direction from their divine Governor, and even against his declared will; and these instances will not, of course, be pleaded as an authority for the practice of war: but such of their military operations as were sanctioned and ordered of the Lord (and these only are adduced in the argument in favour of war) assumed the character of a work of obedience and faith. They went forth to battle, from time to time, in compliance with the divine command, and in dependence upon that Being who condescended to regulate their movements, and to direct their efforts in the furtherance of his own providence. These characteristics in the divinely-sanctioned warfare of the Hebrews were attended with two consequences, of the most marked and distinguishing nature. In the first place, the conflicts in which this people were thus engaged, and which so conspicuously called into exercise their obedience and faith, were far from being attended by that destruction of moral and pious feeling which is so generally the effect of war; but, on the contrary, they were often accompanied by a condition of religious excellence in those who were thus employed in fighting the battles of the Lord—an observation very plainly suggested by the history of Joshua and his followers, of the successive judges, and of David. And secondly, the contests which were undertaken and conducted on the principles now stated, were followed by uniform success. The Lord was carrying on his own designs through certain appointed instruments; and, under such circumstances, while failure was impossible, success afforded an evidence of the divine approbation. Now, it cannot be predicted even of the wars which have the greatest appearance of justice, as they are usually carried on among the nations of the world, that they are undertaken with the revealed sanction, or by the direct command, of Jehovah—or that they are a work of obedience and faith—or that they are often accompanied with a condition of religious excellence in those who undertake them—or that they are followed by uniform success. On the supposition, therefore, that the system of Israelitish morals is still in force, without alteration and improvement, it is manifest that we cannot justly conclude, from the example of God's ancient people, that warfare, as it is generally practised, even when it bears the stamp of honour or defence, is consistent with the will of God.

In addition to the example of the Hebrews, the defenders of modern warfare are accustomed to plead the authority of John the Baptist.[2] It is recorded, in the Gospel of Luke, that, when that eminent prophet was preaching in the wilderness, various classes of persons resorted to him for advice and instruction. Among others, " the soldiers demanded of him, saying, And what shall we do? And he said unto them, Do violence to no man, neither accuse any falsely, and be content with your wages."[3] Since the precept of John to these soldiers, that *they should do violence to no man*, probably related to their behaviour among their friends and allies, it may be allowed that he did not, on this occasion, forbid the practice of fighting. On the other hand, it must be observed, that the expressions of the Baptist afford no direct encouragement to that practice. I would suggest that with reference to the present argument, his doctrine is neutral. The question whether war was, in itself, lawful or unlawful, is one which was probably placed beyond his scope, and which he obviously did not entertain. On the supposition that the soldiers would continue to be soldiers, he confined himself to recommending to them that gentle, orderly, and submissive demeanour, which was so evidently calculated to soften the asperities of their profession.

[2] See *Grotius de Jure Belli ac Pacis.* lib. 1. cap. ii. § vii, 5.
[3] Chap. iii, 14.

But, although John the Baptist was engaged in proclaiming the *approach* of the Christian dispensation —the kingdom of heaven—he did not himself appertain to that kingdom.[4] He belonged to the preceding institution; and his moral system was that of the law. Now, although, on the supposition that this system continues unchanged, it may fairly be denied, for the reasons now stated, that the example of the Hebrews, or the expressions of the Baptist, afford any valid authority for warfare, as generally practised, it ought to be clearly understood, that the objection of Friends to every description of military operation is founded principally, *on that complete revelation of the moral law of God which distinguishes the dispensation of the gospel of Christ.* We contend, and that with no slight degree of earnestness, that all warfare—whether offensive or defensive, and whatever may be its peculiar features, circumstances, or pretexts—is wholly at variance with the revealed character and known principles of the *Christian* religion.

In support of this position, I may, in the first place, adduce the testimony of the prophets; for these inspired writers, in their predictions respecting the gospel dispensation, have frequently alluded both to the superior spirituality, and to the purer morality of that system of religion, of which the law, with all its accompaniments, was only the introduction. In the second chapter of the book of Isaiah we read the following prophecy: "And it shall come to pass in the last days, that the mountain of the Lord's house shall be established in the top of the mountains, and

[4] See Matt. xi, 11.

shall be exalted above the hills; and all nations shall flow unto it; and many people shall go and say, Come ye, and let us go up to the mountain of the Lord, to the house of the God of Jacob: and he will teach us of his ways, and we will walk in his paths; for out of Zion shall go forth the law, and the word of the Lord from Jerusalem. And he shall judge among the nations, and shall rebuke many people; *and they shall beat their swords into ploughshares, and their spears into pruninghooks: nation shall not lift up sword against nation, neither shall they learn war any more.*"[5] The prophet Micah repeats the same prediction, and adds the following animating description: " But they shall sit every man under his vine and under his fig tree; and none shall make them afraid; for the mouth of the Lord of hosts hath spoken it."[6]

It is allowed, by the Jews, that the "last days," of which the prophets speak, are the "days of the Messiah;" and Christian commentators unanimously apply these expressions to the period of that glorious dispensation which was introduced by our Lord and Saviour Jesus Christ. Accordingly, the actual predictions of his coming are elsewhere accompanied with similar descriptions. In Isaiah ix, 6, the Messiah is expressly called " The Prince of Peace." In Isaiah xi, the reign of Christ is painted in glowing colours, as accompanied by the universal harmony of God's creation. Lastly, in Zech. ix, 9, 10, we read as follows: " Rejoice greatly, O daughter of Zion; shout, O daughter of Jerusalem; behold, thy King cometh unto thee: he is just, and having salvation; lowly, and

[5] Ver. 2—4.   [6] Micah iv, 1—4.

riding upon an ass, and upon a colt the foal of an ass. *And I will cut off the chariot from Ephraim, and the horse from Jerusalem, and the battle-bow shall be cut off: and he shall speak peace unto the heathen: and his dominion shall be from sea even to sea, and from the river even to the ends of the earth.*[7]

It is undeniable that, in these passages a total cessation from the practice of war is described as one of the most conspicuous marks of Christianity. Such a consequence is represented by Isaiah as arising from the conversion of the heathen nations—as resulting from their being led into the ways, instructed in the law, and enlightened by the word of the Lord. Whoever, indeed, were to be the members of the true church of God, she was no longer to participate in the warfare of the world. The chariot was to be cut off from Ephraim, and the war-horse from Jerusalem. It is true that, for the full accomplishment of these glorious prophecies, we must look forward to a period yet to come. But let us not deceive ourselves. The inspired writers describe this complete and uninterrupted peaceableness, as a distinguishing feature of the dispensation under which Christians are living— as the result of obedience to that law which they are at all times bound to follow; and we may therefore infer, that if the true nature of the Christian dispensation were fully understood, and if the law by which it is regulated were exactly obeyed, a conversion to our holy religion, or the cordial and serious holding of it, would be uniformly accompanied with an entire abstinence from warfare. Thus the prevalence of the

[7] *Comp.* Psalm xlvi, 9.

law of peace would be found commensurate, in every age of the church, with the *actual* extent of the Messiah's kingdom over men.

As the language of the prophecy clearly suggests this doctrine, so it will be found that, on the introduction of Christianity, there were promulgated certain moral rules, which when fully and faithfully obeyed, infallibly lead to this particular result. Here I am by no means alluding exclusively to those divine laws which condemn aggressive warfare and every species of unjust and unprovoked injury; for these laws (however it may be the intention of Christians to obey them) are far from being powerful enough to produce the effect in question. They were, indeed, commonly admitted in the world, long before the commencement of the Christian dispensation; and neither before nor after that era, have they ever been found sufficient to convert the sword into the ploughshare, and the spear into the pruninghook. In point of fact, the distinction which men are accustomed to draw between just and unjust warfare is, in almost all instances entirely nugatory; for there are few wars, however atrocious, which are not defended, and not many, perhaps, which the persons waging them do not *believe* to be justified, by some plea or other connected with self-preservation or honourable retribution. In addition, therefore, to the laws which forbid *spontaneous* injury, some stronger and more comprehensive principles were obviously needed, in order to the accomplishment of this great end; and these principles are unfolded in that pure and exalted code of morality which was revealed, in connexion with the gospel. They are, *the non-resistance of injuries, the return of good for evil, and the love of our enemies.*

It was the Lord Jesus himself who promulgated these principles, as distinguishing his own dispensation. "Ye have heard that it hath been said, An eye for an eye, and a tooth for a tooth: but I say unto you, *That ye resist not evil:* but whosoever shall smite thee on thy right cheek, turn to him the other also. And if any man will sue thee at the law, and take away thy coat, let him have thy cloak also. And whosoever shall compel thee to go a mile, go with him twain," &c. "Ye have heard that it hath been said, Thou shalt love thy neighbour, and hate thine enemy. But I say unto you, *Love your enemies, bless them that curse you, do good to them that hate you, and pray for them that despitefully use you and persecute you;* that ye may be the children of your Father which is in heaven: for he maketh his sun to rise on the evil and on the good, and sendeth rain on the just and on the unjust. For if ye love them which love you, what reward have ye? do not even the publicans the same? And if ye salute your brethren only, what do ye more than others? do not even the publicans so? *Be ye therefore perfect, even as your Father which is in heaven is perfect.*" [8] So, also, the apostle Peter commands the believers not to render "evil for evil, or railing for railing, but contrariwise, blessing:" [9] and Paul, in the following lively exhortation, holds up the very same standard of Christian practice: "Dearly beloved, avenge not yourselves, but rather *give place*

[8] Matt. v, 38—48: *comp.* Luke vi, 27—29.
[9] 1 Peter iii, 9.

unto wrath: for it is written, Vengence is mine; I will repay, saith the Lord. Therefore, if thine enemy hunger, feed him; if he thirst give him drink: for in so doing thou shalt heap coals of fire on his head. Be not overcome of evil, *but overcome evil with good.*"[1]

In the delivery of that holy law, by obedience to which Christians may be brought, in their small measure, (*and yet with completeness according to that measure,*) to a conformity with the moral attributes of their heavenly Father, *our Lord has laid his axe to the root.* He has established certain principles which, as they are honestly observed in conduct, must put an end to every evil practice; and thus is the tree which bears the fruit of corruption cut down and destroyed. Precisely of this nature are the principles which we are now considering, and which, when followed up with consistency, cannot fail to abolish warfare, whether offensive or defensive, whether aggressive or retributive, whether unjust or just. The great law of Christ, which his disciples are ever bound to obey, is the *law of love*—love complete, uninterrupted, universal, fixed upon God in the first place, and afterwards embracing the whole family of man. And, since war (of whatsoever species or description it may be) can never consist with this love, it is indisputable that, where the latter prevails as it ought to do, the former must entirely cease.

It is observed that our Lord's precepts, which have now been cited, are addressed to *individuals.* Since this is unquestionably true, it is the clear duty of individual Christians to obey them; and to obey them

[1] Rom. xii, 19—21.

uniformly and on every occasion. If, during the common course of their life, they are attacked, insulted, injured, and persecuted, they ought to suffer wrong, to revenge no injury, to return good for evil, and to love their enemies. So, also, should it happen that they are exposed to the more extraordinary calamities of war, their duty remains unaltered; their conduct must continue to be guided by the same principles. If the sword of the invader is lifted up against them, the precept is still at hand, that they resist not evil. If the insults and injuries of the carnal warrior are heaped upon them, they are still forbidden to avenge themselves, and still commanded to pray for their persecutors. If they are surrounded by a host of enemies, however violent and malicious those enemies may be, Christian love must still be unbroken, still universal. According then to the law of Christ, it is the duty of *individuals* to abstain from all warfare; nor can they avoid such a course if they follow his law. We are informed by Sulpitius Severus, that, when the Roman emperor Julian was engaged in bestowing upon his troops a largess, with a view to some approaching battle, his bounty was refused by Martin, a soldier in his army, who had been previously converted to Christianity. "Hitherto," said he to Cæsar, "I have fought for thee: permit me now to fight for my God. Let those who are about to engage in war accept thy donative; I am the soldier of Christ; *for me* the combat is unlawful."[2] Where is the solid, the sufficient reason why such, under similar circumstances, should not be the expressions of every true Christian?

[2] *De Vita B. Mart.* Ed. Amst. A. D. 1665, p. 445.

The man who engages in warfare retains his private responsibility; and, whatever may be the proceedings of his countrymen, whatever the commands of his superiors, he can never dispossess himself of his individual obligation to render to the law of his God a consistent and uniform obedience. But secondly, the unlawfulness of war, under any of its forms, is equally evident when it is regarded as the affair of nations. Doubtless there may be found in the Scriptures, a variety of injunctions relating to the particulars of human conduct, and applicable to men and women only as individuals; but it is one of the excellencies of the moral law of God, that its *principles* are of universal application to mankind, whatever may be the circumstances under which they are placed; whether they act singly as individuals, or collectively as nations. No one, surely, who has any just views of morality, will pretend for a moment, that those fundamental rules of conduct, which are given to guide every man in his own walk through life, may be deserted as soon as he unites with others, and acts in a corporate capacity. The absurd consequences of such a system would be manifestly this—that national crimes of every description might be committed without entailing any national guilt, and without any real infraction of the revealed will of God.

Now, among these fundamental rules—these eternal, unchangeable, principles—is that of *universal love*. The law of God, which is addressed without reservation or exception, to all men, plainly says to them, Resist not evil; revenge not injuries: *love your enemies*. Individuals, nations consisting of individuals, and governments acting on behalf of nations, are all unquestionably bound to obey this law; and whether it is the act of an individual, of a nation, or of a government, *the transgression of the law is sin.*[3] Nations or governments trangress the Christian law of love, and commit sin, when they declare or carry on war, precisely as the private duellist transgresses that law, and commits sin, when he sends or accepts a challenge, and deliberately endeavours to destroy his neighbour. It ought also to be observed that, through the medium of the nation, the case is again brought home to the conscience and responsibility of the individual. The man who takes a part, either himself or by substitute, in the national warfare, takes a part also in the national sin. He aids and abets his nation in breaking the law of Christ. So far, then, is the example of his countrymen—the authority of his legislature—the command of his monarch—from being sufficient to justify his engagement in warfare, that he cannot follow that example, avail himself of that authority, or obey that command, *without adding, to his private transgression, the further criminality of actively promoting the transgression of the state.*

For the reason now stated, I consider it evident that a total abstinence from warfare, on the part both of individuals and of nations, would be the necessary result of a strict adherence to the principles of the law of Christ, but it will not be difficult to carry the argument a step further, and to shew that one of the precepts, now cited from the sermon on the mount, appears to bear a specific and peculiar allusion to the

[3] 1 John iii, 4.

subject of war. "*Ye have heard that it hath been said, Thou shalt love thy neighbour and hate thine enemy; but I say unto you, Love your enemies.*" In the preceding chapter, I have found occasion to remark that our Lord, in the first part of his discourse, has instituted a comparison between the system of morality which, under the sanction and influence of the Mosaic institution, prevailed among the Israelites, and that purer and more comprehensive law of action of which he was himself both the author and the minister. In calling the attention of his hearers to the sayings uttered "by them of old time" on the several moral points of his discourse, such as killing, adultery, divorcement, perjury, and retaliation—he has uniformly quoted from the law of Moses itself. It was with the principles of that law, *as they were understood and received by the Jews*, that he compared his own holier system; and he improved, enlarged, or superseded, this introductory code of morals (as was in each particular required) in order to make way for one which is capable of no improvement, and must endure for ever. Now the precepts of ancient times to which he last refers—the precepts respecting love and hatred—formed, in all probability, like the whole preceding series, a part of those divine edicts which were delivered to the Israelites by Moses. That which related to the love of their neighbour is recognised at once, and is as follows; "Thou shalt not avenge nor bear any grudge against the *children of thy people*, but thou shalt love thy neighbour as thyself."[4] The reader will observe that the love here enjoined was to be

[4] Lev. xix, 18.

directed to the *children of the people of Israel*. The neighbour to be loved was the fellow-countryman; or if a stranger, the proselyte; and the precept, in fact, commanded no more than that the Israelites—the members of the Lord's selected family—should *love one another*. So also the injunction of old, that the Israelites should hate their enemies, was exclusively *national*. They were not permitted to hate their private enemies, who belonged to the same favoured community. On the contrary, they were enjoined to do good to such enemies as these: " If thou meet thine enemy's ox or his ass going astray," said the law, " thou shalt surely bring it back to him again."[5] But they were to hate[6] their national enemies—they were to make no covenant with the foreign and idolatrous tribes who formerly possessed the land of Canaan. " When the Lord thy God shall bring thee into the land whither thou goest to possess it," said Moses to the assembly of his people, " and hath cast out many nations before thee, the Hittites, and the Girgashites, and the Amorites, and the Canaanites, and the Perizzites, and the Hivites, and the Jebusites, seven nations greater and mightier than thou; and when the Lord thy God shall deliver them before thee, thou shalt smite them, and utterly destroy them; thou shalt make no covenant with them, nor show mercy unto them."[7] On another

---

[5] Exod. xxiii, 4.

[6] The verb " to hate," as used in the Holy Scriptures (Heb. שנא Gr. μισέω,) does not imply *malignity of mind* so much as *opposition and enmity in action;* as the reader may be fully convinced on a reference to the concordances: see *Schleusner, Lex. voc.* μισέω, No. 1.

[7] Deut. vii, 1, 2 ; *comp.* Exod. xxxiv, 11—13.

occasion, a similar injunction was delivered respecting the Amalekites: " Therefore it shall be, when the Lord thy God hath given thee rest from all thine enemies round about, in the land which the Lord thy God giveth thee for an inheritance to possess it, that thou shalt blot out the *remembrance of Amalek from under heaven; thou shalt not forget it.*"[8]

Such was the hatred of enemies enjoined upon ancient Israel, and such was the manner in which it was to be applied—in the persevering, exterminating, use of the national sword.[9] Now, it is to these edicts, delivered in times of old, and under the peculiar circumstances of the dispensation then existing, that the law of Christ is placed in opposition: " Ye have heard that it hath been said, Thou shalt love thy neighbour and hate thy enemy; but *I* say unto you, *Love your enemies.*" How much soever, then, we may be justified by the undoubted universality of this law, in applying it to the circumstances of private life, we can scarcely fail to perceive that it was principally intended to discountenance these *national* enmities; and that the love here enjoined was peculiarly such as would

[8] Deut. xxv, 19.

[9] Grotius, in his work, *De Jure Belli ac Pacis*, has himself insisted on this interpretation of the saying of old times respecting hatred, *Odio habebis inimicum tuum*, puta septem populos, quibuscum amicitiam colere, quorumque misereri, vetantur:" Exod. xxxiv, 11 ; Deut. vii, 1. " His addendi Amalecitæ, in quos Hebræi jubentur bellum habere implacabile:" Deut. xxv, 19, lib. 1, cap. 2. The correctness of the observation thus made by this learned defender of war is, I think, indisputable ; but it is surprising that he did not notice the argument which it so obviously affords, in favour of the doctrine, *that, under the Christian dispensation, war is unlawful.*

prevent the practice of war. The Israelites were commanded to combat and destroy with the sword the nations who were their own enemies, and the enemies of God. But Christians are introduced to a purer and lovelier system of morals; and the law which they are called upon to obey, is that which proclaims peace upon earth and good will to men: they are commanded to be the friends of all mankind. If they are sent forth among idolatrous nations, it is as the ministers of their restoration, and not as the instruments of their punishment; and as they may not contend with the sword against the enemies of their God, much less may they wield it for any purpose of their own, whether it be in aggression, retribution, or defence. Armed with submission, forbearance, and long-suffering, they must secede from the warfare of a wrathful and corrupt world: and, whatever may be the provocations to which they are exposed, must evince themselves, under the softening influence of universal love, to be the meek, the harmless, the benevolent followers of the PRINCE OF PEACE.

I know of nothing in the New Testament which has any appearance of contravening the force of these divine precepts, or of the deductions now made from them, but a single passage in the Gospel of Luke. We are informed, by the sacred historian, that after our Lord's paschal supper, and immediately before he was betrayed into the hands of his enemies, Jesus thus addressed his disciples: "When I sent you without purse, and scrip, and shoes, lacked ye any thing? And they said, Nothing. Then said he unto them, But now he that hath a purse, let him take it, and likewise his scrip: *and he that hath no sword, let him sell his garment and buy one.* For I say unto you, that this that is written must yet be accomplished in me, And he was reckoned among the transgressors: for the things concerning me have an end."[1] The words employed by the Lord Jesus on this occasion when superficially considered, may be deemed to inculcate the notion, that his followers were permitted and enjoined to defend themselves and their religion with the sword: but the context, and the circumstances which followed after these words were uttered, evidently decide otherwise. The disciples appear, after their usual manner, to have understood their Lord literally; and they answered, " Here are two swords;" and Jesus replied, " *It is enough.*" Now, in declaring that two swords were *enough*, although they were then exposed to extreme danger, he offered them an intelligible hint that he had been misunderstood—that the use of the sword, in defence of their little company, was neither consistent with his views, nor really implied in his injunction. But the opportunity was at hand, on which the disciples were to be completely undeceived. The enemies of Jesus approached, with torches and weapons, as if they were in pursuit of some violent robbers. When the disciples saw what would follow, they said unto Jesus, " Lord, shall we smite with the sword?" And Peter, the most zealous of their number, without waiting for his Master's reply, rushed forward and smote the servant of the high priest, and cut off his ear. Then were he and his brethren clearly instructed by their Lord, that it was their duty, not to fight, but

[1] Luke xxii, 35—37.

to suffer wrong. " Suffer ye thus far," said he to Peter; and immediately afterwards he confirmed his doctrine by action: he touched the wounded man, and healed him. Afterwards, in words of peculiar force, he thus addressed Peter: " Put up thy sword into the sheath: the cup which my Father hath given me, shall I not drink it?"[2] And as a universal caution against so antichristian a practice as that of using destructive weapons in self-defence, he added, " *All they that take the sword shall perish with the sword.*"[3] Lastly, when, soon afterwards, he was carried before Pilate the Roman governor, he plainly declared that his kingdom was of such a nature, that it neither required nor allowed the defence of carnal weapons. " My kingdom," said he, " is not of this world. If my kingdom were of this world, *then would my servants fight, that I should not be delivered to the Jews; but now is my kingdom not from hence.*"[4]

It is sufficiently evident, therefore, that, when our Lord exhorted his disciple to sell their garments and buy swords, his precept was not to be understood *literally.* Such indeed, is the explicit judgment of the generality of commentators. We may, therefore either conclude, with Erasmus, that the sword of which our Lord here spake was the sword of the Spirit—the word of God,[5] or we may accede to the more prevalent opinion of critics, that the words of Jesus imported nothing more than a general warning to the disciples, that their situation was about to be greatly changed—that they were soon to be deprived

[2] See John xviii, 11.
[3] Matt xxvi, 52.   [4] John xviii, 36.   [5] See *Com. in loc.*

of the personal presence of their divine Master—that they would be exposed to every species of difficulty, and become the objects of hatred and persecution—and would, therefore, be driven to a variety of expedients, in order to provide for their own safety.[6]

In order to complete the present branch of the argument, I have, in the last place, to remark, that the doctrine of the Society of Friends, respecting the absolute inconsistency of warfare with the moral code of the Christian dispensation, was one which prevailed, to a very considerable extent, during the early ages of the Christian church. Justin Martyr, (A. D. 140,) in his First Apology, quotes the prophecy of Isaiah (already cited in the present chapter) respecting the going forth of the law and of the word of God from Jerusalem, and the consequent prevalence of a state of peace. " That these things have come to pass," he proceeds, " you may be readily convinced: for twelve men, destitute both of instruction and of eloquence, went forth from Jerusalem into the world, and by the power of God gave evidence, to every description of persons, that they were sent by Christ to teach all men the divine word: *and we who were once slayers of one another* (that is to say, commonly engaged in warfare) *do not fight against our enemies.*"[7] Irenæus, bishop of Lyons, (A. D. 167,) discusses the same prophecy, and proves its relation to our Saviour, by the fact, that the followers of Jesus had disused the weapons of war, and no longer knew how to

---

[6] See *Estius, Vatablus, and others, in Poli Syn. Gill, &c.*
[7] οὐ πολεμοῦμεν τοὺς ἐχθροὺς. *Apol.* i, cap. 39, p. 67, Ed. Ben.

fight.[8] Tertullian, (A. D. 200,) in one part of his works, alludes to Christians who were engaged, together with their heathen countrymen, in military pursuits;[9] but, on another occasion, he informs us that many soldiers, who had been converted to Christianity, quitted those pursuits, in consequence of their conversion;[1] and he repeatedly expresses his own opinion, that any participation in war was unlawful for believers in Jesus — not only because of the idolatrous practices enjoined on the soldiers of the Roman armies, but because Christ has forbidden the use of the sword and the revenge of injuries.[2] Origen, (A. D. 230,)

[8] "Si autem libertatis lex, id est, verbum Dei ab apostolis, qui ab Hierusalem exierunt, annuntiatum in universam terram, in tantum transmutationem fecit, ut gladios et lanceas bellatorias in aratra fabricaverit ipse, et in falces quæ donavit, ad metendum frumentum demutaverit, et *jam nesciunt pugnare, sed percussi et alteram præbent maxillam;* non de aliquo alio Prophetæ dixerunt hæc, sed de eo qui fecit ea." *Adv. Hær.* lib. iv, cap. 34, Ed. Ben. p. 275.

[9] *Apol.* cap. 42, Ed. Semler. v. 102. "Navigamus et nos vobiscum et militamus."

[1] "Plane si quos militia præventos fides posterior invenit, alia conditio est, ut illorum quos Ioannes admittebat ad lavacrum; et centurionum fidelissimorum, quem Christus probat, et quem Petrus catechizat: dum tamen suscepta fide atque signata, aut deserendum statim sit *ut a multis actum;* aut omnibus modis cavendum, ne quidquid adversus Deum committatur." *De Cor. Mil.* cap. ii.

[2] "Quomodo autem bellabit, imo quomodo etiam in pace militabit, sine gladio, quem Dominus abstulit? Nam etsi adierant milites ad Ioannem et formam observationis acceperant: si etiam centurio crediderat: *omnem postea militem Dominus in Petro exarmando discinxit:*" .... "Licebit in gladio conversari, Domino pronunciante gladio periturum, qui gladio fuerit usus? Et prælio operabitur filius pacis, cui nec litigare conveniet? Et vincula et carcerem et tormenta et supplicia administrabit, nec suarum ultor injuriarum?" *De Idol.* 19; Ed. Semler. iv. 176; *De Coron. Mil.* 12. iv. 355.

in his work against Celsus, says of himself and his brethren, " We no longer take up the sword against any nation, nor do we learn any more to make war. We have become, for the sake of Jesus, *the children of peace.*"[3] In another passage of the same work, he maintains that Christians are the most useful of subjects, because they pray for their monarch. " By such means," says he, " we fight for our king abundantly: *but we take no part in his wars, even though he urge us.*"[4] Here we have, not only this ancient father's declaration of his own sentiment that war is inconsistent with the religion of Christ, but a plain testimony (corresponding with that of Justin and Irenæus) that the Christians of those early times were *accustomed* to abstain from it. Traces of the same doctrine and practice are very clearly marked in the subsequent history of the church. Under the reign of Dioclesian (A. D. 300,) more espécially, a large number of Christians refused to serve in the army, and, in consequence of their refusal, many of them suffered martyrdom.[5] Now, although the conduct of these Christians might partly arise, as Grotius suggests, from their religious objections to the idolatrous rites at that time mixed up with the military system, it is evident that the unlawfulness of war itself, for the followers of Christ, was also a principle on which they acted. Thus Lactantius, who wrote during the reign of this very emperor, expressly asserts, that " *to engage in war can-*

[3] Lib. v, 33, Ed. Ben. i, 602.

[4] οὐ συστρατευόμεθα μὲν αὐτῷ, κἂν ἐπείγῃ. Lib. viii, 73, Ed. Ben. i, 797.

[5] Vide *Grot. de Jure Bell.* lib. vi, cap. ii, § 8 ; *Ruinart. Acta Martyrum ; de S. Maximiliano,* Ed. Amst. p. 300.

not be lawful for the righteous man, whose warfare is that of righteousness itself."6 And again, in the twelfth canon of the council of Nice, held under the reign of Constantine, (A. D. 325,) a long period of excommunication is attached, as a penalty, to the conduct of those persons who, having once, in the ardour of their early faith, renounced the military calling, were persuaded by the force of bribes to return to it—" like dogs to their own vomit."7 The circumstances particularly alluded to in this canon might, indeed, have taken place during the tyranny of the idolatrous Licinius, whom Constantine had so lately subdued; but the canon itself was, I presume, intended for the future regulation of the church; and such a law would scarcely have been promulgated under the reign of the converted Constantine, had not an opinion been entertained in the council, that *war itself*, however prevalent and generally allowed, was inconsistent with the highest standard of Christian morality. We have already noticed the declartion of Martin, addressed to the emperor Julian, (A. D. 363,) that it was unlawful for him to fight, because he was a Christian; and even so late as the middle of the fifth century, Leo the pope declared it to be " contrary to the rules of the church that persons, after the action of penance, (persons then considered to be pre-eminently bound to obey the law of Christ,) *should revert to the warfare of the world.*"8

6 " Ita neque militare justo licebit, cujus militia est ipsa justitia." *De Vero Cultu*, lib. vi, cap. 20.
7 Vide *Mansii Coll. Concil.* tom. ii, p. 674.
8 Epist. ii. " Contrarium esse ecclesiasticis regulis, post pœni-

It appears then that all participation in this warfare of the world was deemed, by the early Christians, as it now is by ourselves, to be forbidden by the law of Christ, and especially by that provision of it which enjoins the *love of our enemies.* In order, however, to do full justice to the present important subject, I must advert to another principle, which appears to me *equally* to evince the total inconsistency of the practice of war with the true character of the Christian religion—the principle, *that human life is sacred, and that death is followed by infinite consequences.* Under the Mosaic dispensation, the Israelites were, on various occasions, enjoined to inflict death; both in the capital punishment of their own delinquents. and in those wars which had for their object the extermination of idolatrous nations. When the destruction of the life of men was thus expressly commanded by the Creator, it is clear that the life of men was rightly destroyed: but the searcher of the Scriptures will not fail to remark, that the sanction thus given to killing was accompanied by a comparatively small degree of light respecting the true nature of life and death— respecting immortality and future retribution. Bishop Warburton, in his work on the divine legation of Moses, has endeavoured to prove the truth of the miraculous history of the Pentateuch, on the ground that the Israelites, who were destitute of all knowledge on the subject in question, could be governed, as they were governed, *only* through the medium of miracles. Now, although the Bishop may have overstrained

tentiæ actionem redire ad militiam secularem." *Quoted by Grotius, De Jure Bell.* lib. i, cap. ii. § 9.

CHAP. 11.]   *On War.*   367

his argument, and although there are passages in the Old Testament which allude to a life after death, and to a future judgment, it is sufficiently evident that the *full* revelation of these important truths was reserved for the dispensation of the gospel of Christ. Those who are accustomed to read the declarations of Jesus and his apostles, can no longer conceal from themselves that man is born for eternity; that after death cometh judgment; and that, in the world to come, we shall all reap the never-ending consequences of our belief or our unbelief, of our virtue or our vice. Christians, thus instructed and enlightened, are constrained to acknowledge that the *future* welfare of an individual man, is of greater importance than the merely temporal prosperity of a whole nation. If they are consistent with themselves they cannot refuse to confess, that unless in such an action they are sanctioned by the express authority of their divine Master, they take upon themselves a most unwarrantable responsibility, when they cut short the days of their neighbour, and transmit him, prepared or unprepared, to the awful realities of an everlasting state. Since, then, no such express authority can be found in the New Testament; since, on the contrary, it is clearly declared, in that sacred volume, that the kingdom of Christ is not of this world, and that his followers war not after the flesh—I cannot but conclude that for one man to kill another, (under whatever circumstances of expediency or provocation the deed may be committed,) is utterly unlawful under the Christian dispensation.

The *visible* effects of the far-famed battle of Waterloo

were sufficiently appalling—multitudes of the wounded, the dying, and the dead, spread in wild confusion over the bloody plain! But did Christians fully know the *invisible* consequences of such a contest—could they trace the flight of thousands of immortal souls (many of them disembodied, perhaps, while under the immediate influence of diabolical passions) into the world of eternal retribution— they would indeed shrink with horror from such a scene of destruction, and adopt, without further hesitation, the firm and unalterable conclusion, that war and Christianity are utterly at variance.[2]

Such, then, are the grounds on which Friends consider it to be their duty entirely to abstain from the practice of war. On a review of the whole argument, the reader will recollect, that the wars of the Israelites

---

[2] It is evident that the principle now stated applies to the punishment of death as well as to war. The use of such a punishment was, indeed, consistent with that inferior degree of moral and religious light which was enjoyed by the people of God before the coming of the Messiah; but on the ground now mentioned, it appears to be at total variance with the principles of the Christian revelation. Such was the opinion of some of the early fathers of the church, as well as of more modern philanthropists. Tertullian classes a participation in capital condemnations with the aiding and abetting of idolatry itself: for, in one of the passages already cited from his works, we find him reasoning on the possible innocence of a war, *cui non sit necessitas immolationum* (of sacrifices to idols) *vel capitalium judiciorum. De Idol.* 19. So also Lactantius : " It is unlawful for a righteous man to prosecute any person capitally ; for it matters not whether we kill by the sword or by the word—*since all killing is prohibited.* This divine law allows of no exception. It must ever be a forbidden wickedness *to put man to death :* for God has created him a *sacred* animal." *De Vero Cultu,* lib. vi. cap. 20.

bore, in various respects, so peculiar a character as to afford no real sanction to those of other nations—also that the precept of John the Baptist to soldiers appears, in reference to the present question, to be negative— but that the opinion of Friends on the question rests principally on the moral law, *as revealed under the Christian dispensation*—that abstinence from warfare among the followers of the Messiah was predicted, by the prophets, as one of the leading features of that dispensation—that, in the code of Christian morality, are unfolded the principles which are alone sufficiently strong to produce this effect; namely, those of suffering wrong, returning good for evil, and loving our enemies—that, since these principles were so clearly promulgated by Jesus and his apostles, the *individual* who engages in warfare, and destroys his enemy, whether it is in aggression or defence, plainly infringes the divine law—that nations when they carry on war, do also infringe that law—and that the Christian who fights by the command of his prince, and in behalf of his country, not only commits sin in his own person, but aids and abets the national transgression—that, on a view of the Jewish precepts, with which is compared the precept of Christ to his followers respecting the love of their enemies, it appears that this precept was specifically directed against national wars—that, when our Lord exhorted his disciples to sell their garments and buy swords, it is evident, from the circumstances which followed, that his expressions were to be understood figuratively — that the sentiments and practices of Friends, in reference to the present subject, are so far from being new and extraordinary, that they form a striking and prevalent feature in the early history of the Christian church—lastly, that the practice of warfare is directly at variance with the full light imparted by the gospel, respecting life, death, and eternity.

Notwithstanding the clearness and importance of those principles which evince the utter inconsistency of the practice of war with the Christian dispensation, it is continually pleaded that wars are often expedient, and sometimes absolutely necessary for the preservation of states. To such a plea it might be sufficient to answer, that nothing is so expedient, nothing so *necessary*, either for individuals or for nations, as a conformity, in point of conduct, with the revealed will of the Supreme Governor of the universe. I may, however, in conclusion, venture to offer a few additional remarks on this part of our subject.

Let reflecting Christians, in the first place, take a deliberate survey of the history of Europe during the last eighteen centuries; and let them impartially examine how many of the wars waged among Christian nations have been, on their own principles, really expedient or *necessary*, on either side, for the preservation of states. I apprehend that the result of such an examination would be a satisfactory conviction, that by far the greater part of those wars are so far from having truly borne this character, that notwithstanding the common excuse of self-defence, by which, in so many cases, they have been supposed to be justified, they have, in point of fact, even in a political point of view, been much more hurtful than useful to all the parties engaged in them. Where, for instance, has England found an equivalent for the boundless profusion of blood and treasure which she has wasted on her many wars? Must not the impartial page of history decide that *almost the whole* of her wars, although often justified in the view of the world by the pleas of defence and retaliation, have, in fact, been waged against imaginary dangers, might have been avoided by a few harmless concessions, and have turned out to be extensively injurious to her in many of their results? If Christians would abstain from all wars which have no better foundation than the false system of worldly honour—from all which are not, on political grounds, absolutely inevitable—from all which are plainly hurtful to their country—they would take a very important step towards the adoption of that entirely peaceable conduct which is upheld and defended by the Society of Friends.

After such a step had been taken, it must, indeed, be admitted, that certain occasions might remain, on which warfare would appear to be expedient; and, according to the estimate of most persons, *actually necessary*, for the *mere* purposes of defence and self-preservation. On such occasions, I am well aware that, if we are to abide by the decisions of that lax morality which so generally prevails among the professors of the Christian name, we must confess that war *is right, and cannot be avoided.* But for true believers, for those who are brought under the influence of vital religion, for those who would "follow the Lamb *whithersoever* he goeth," war is *never* right. It is *always* their duty to obey his high and holy law—to suffer wrong—to return good for evil—to love their enemies. If, in consequence of their obedience to this law, they apprehend themselves to be surrounded with many dangers—if tumult and terror assail them—let them still remember that " cursed" is " the man that trusteth in man, and maketh flesh his arm;" let them still place an undivided reliance upon the power and benevolence of their God and Saviour. It may be his good pleasure that they be delivered from the outward peril by which they are visited; or he may decree that they fall a sacrifice to that peril. But, whatever be the result, as long as they are preserved in obedience to his law, so long are they safe in his hands. They " *know* that ALL THINGS work together for good to them that love God."[3]

Godliness, however, has the promise of this life, as well as of that which is to come: we may, therefore, entertain a reasonable confidence that our temporal happiness and safety, as well as our growth in grace, will, in general, be promoted by obedience to our heavenly Father. It is not in vain, even in an outward point of view, that God has invited his unworthy children to cast their cares upon him, and to trust him for their support and protection; for, though he may work no miracles in their favour, the very law which he gives them to obey is adapted, in a wonderful manner, to convert their otherwise rugged path through life, into one of comparative pleasantness, security, and peace. These observations are applicable, with a peculiar degree of force, to those particulars in the divine law, which, as they are closely followed, preclude all warfare. No weapons of self-defence will be found so effectual as Christian meekness, kindness, and forbear-

[3] Romans viii, 28.

ance; the suffering of injuries; the absence of revenge; the return of good for evil; and the ever-operating love of God and man. Those who regulate their life and conversation with true circumspection, according to these principles, have, for the most part, little reason to fear the violent hand of the enemy and the oppressor. Whilst clothed in the breastplate of righteousness, and firmly grasping the shield of faith, they are quiet in the centre of storms, safe in the heart of danger, and victorious amidst a host of enemies.

Such, in a multitude of instances, has been the lot of Christian individuals, and such might also be the experience of Christian nations. When we consider the still degraded condition of mankind, we can hardly, at present, look forward to the trial of the experiment; but, was there a people who would renounce the dangerous guidance of worldly honour, and boldly conform their national conduct to the eternal rules of the law of Christ—was there a people who would lay aside the weapons of a carnal warfare, and proclaim the principles of universal peace; suffer wrong with condescension; abstain from all retaliation; return good for evil, and diligently promote *the welfare of all men*— I am fully persuaded that such a people would not only dwell in absolute safety, but would be blessed with eminent prosperity, enriched with unrestricted commerce, loaded with reciprocal benefits, and endowed for every good, and wise, and worthy purpose, with irresistible influence over surrounding nations.

ADDENDUM TO CHAPTER XI.

A.D. 1834.

Although the number of individuals who have of late years joined our society has not been large, several of our distinguishing views are spreading with considerable rapidity. On the subject of war, more especially, an extensive change of sentiment has manifested itself among serious Christians during the last ten years; and a gradual approximation appears to be taking place to the standard maintained by the primitive believers, and by some of the early fathers of the church. A large number of persons, not of our religious body, have joined the Peace Society, which is formed on the very principles advocated in the foregoing chapter. By these persons it is fully allowed, that to take away the life of any man, for the purpose of self-defence, is an *action unlawful to the Christian;* and many others, who have not fully subscribed to this doctrine, seem *almost ready* to admit, that defensive as well as offensive warfare, is opposed to the precepts of Jesus Christ. As these precepts become more influential, and as a sense of the awful importance of death and eternity spreads among men, there can be no doubt that the cause of *permanent and universal peace* will prevail over all opposition.

The diffusion of truly Christian sentiment on the subject, is the only radical remedy for that tremendous evil, *war*. In the mean time, however, the nations of Europe appear to be increasingly convinced, that to waste their blood and treasure in afflicting and destroying each other, is the greatest of political follies. May the peace which has so long subsisted among them, soon rest upon a more stable basis, than that of a mere system of *balancing* and *check* ; may it gradually ripen into a kindly Christian union, which shall never again be broken![1]

[1] It is a circumstance much calculated to enhance our hopes on this subject, that civilized nations are evidently disposed to adopt the salutary practice of settling their disputes by arbitration. A third power is often chosen by two governments in dispute, to fill the office of a friendly judge between them ; and such a mode of proceeding has in various instances produced the desired effect. May we not hope to see the day when a solemn court of national arbitration and adjustment shall be formed by the united powers of Europe and America, in which all differences among any of the contracting parties, may be finally settled, not merely by way of recommendation, but by a plenary authority, grounded on the joint compact of the whole of Christendom ?—1842.

CHAPTER XII.

ON THE MORAL VIEWS OF FRIENDS. PLAINNESS OF SPEECH, BEHAVIOUR, AND APPAREL.

From the statements contained in the two preceding chapters, it will have been observed, that, on two practical points of great importance, Friends have been led to adopt a higher and purer standard of action, and one which appears to be more exactly conformed to the requisitions of the divine law, than that which generally prevails among their fellow Christians.

In point of fact, the adoption of an exalted standard of action is the proper result of their main and fundamental principle, that, in matters of conduct, man is bound to follow the guidance of a perfectly wise and holy Monitor—even the word of the most high God, revealed in the heart: a guide which will never fail to distinguish the good from the evil, the precious from the vile. According to the doctrine of the inspired author of the epistle to the Hebrews, this " word of God is quick, and powerful, and sharper than any two-edged sword, piercing even to the dividing asunder of soul and spirit, and of the joints and marrow, and is a discerner of the thoughts and intents of the heart. Neither is there any creature,"

CHAP. 12.]   *Moral Views of Friends.*   377

adds the apostle, "that is not manifest in his sight; but all things are naked and opened unto the eyes of him with whom we have to do."[1]

True Christians of every name and nation, will ever be found producing the fruits of the Spirit: it is by those fruits alone that they are known and distinguished; nor can any one who does not bear them, however right his opinions, or orthodox his profession, justly claim a membership in the body of Christ. Being thoroughly convinced of these truths, I am little disposed to forget either the virtues of those real Christians who do not agree with us in our peculiar views, or the moral defects and delinquencies which, when we forsake the Fountain of living waters, quickly make their appearance among ourselves. Nevertheless, the impartial observer will, probably, allow that the force and clearness with which Friends maintain that great principle of religion to which I have now adverted, is accompanied, in the serious part of the Society, with a corresponding *completeness* of view respecting good and evil. "Wherewith shall I come before the Lord, and bow myself before the high God? Shall I come before him with burnt-offerings, and calves of a year old? Will the Lord be pleased with thousands of rams, or with ten

[1] Heb. iv, 12, 13. When we view this passage *as a whole*, we can scarcely fail to perceive that the apostle is speaking of the essential Word of God: that divine Person "*with whom we have to do*," and who, in the subsequent verse, is plainly described as "a great High Priest—Jesus the Son of God:" see ver. 14. Such is the express judgment of a variety of able commentators: see *Poli Synopsis.* On the supposition that the passage describes the Son of God, it appears very plainly to relate to *the secret operations of his Spirit in the hearts of men.*

thousands of rivers of oil? Shall I give my first-born for my transgression, the fruit of my body for the sin of my soul? He hath showed thee, O man, what is good; and what doth the Lord require of thee, but *to do justly, and to love mercy, and to walk humbly with thy God?*"[2] As Friends have been much impressed with the inefficacy of sacrificial rites and other formal ordinances, so have they been led to direct a very particular attention to the several branches of *moral duty* which are enjoined in this passage of Scripture, and which, under the gospel dispensation, are unfolded and required in their true perfection. A few examples will elucidate and justify this assertion—it being always understood that my appeal is not to the practice of the unsound professor or mere formalist amongst us, but to the principles of the Society, as they are set forth and enforced in its public acts,[3] and as they are, in some small measure, I trust, manifested in the known conduct and deportment of its more consistent members.

With regard, then, in the first place, to the great Christian law of *truth and integrity*, the reader may already have remarked that the testimony of Friends, against the use of the *oath* in confirmation of the

[2] Micah vi, 6—8.

[3] The disciplinary regulations of the Society, as well as the moral and religious principles by which it is distinguished, will be found recorded under various heads, (as many of my readers are probably well aware,) in a highly valuable volume, entitled the "Book of Extracts"—a book consisting of selections, made by the authority of our yearly meeting, from the public acts and advices of that body.

The last edition of this work, published in 1834, is entitled Rules of Discipline and Advices.—1842.

assertion, is partly founded on a just though exalted sense of this law. A similar high standard, with respect to the same law, may be observed in the peculiar care exercised (by means of our meetings for discipline) throughout the Society in this realm, that the king may not be defrauded, by any of our members, of his customs, duties, or excise; and that there be no using of goods or dealing in them, if they be even *suspected* to be contraband.[4] The view of Friends, with respect to the nice honesty which ought ever to be observed in trade, are also conspicuously strict. Thus, for example, it is universally understood amongst us, that, although a tradesman, who has entered into a composition with his creditors, or has been made a bankrupt, may have become legally clear of all pecuniary demands against him, he is, nevertheless, bound, *whenever the means are in his power*, to carry on and complete the liquidation of his debts. The Quaker who, under the circumstances alluded to, omits the performance of such a duty, is considered by his brethren as a delinquent and a dishonest man:[5] nor is it customary with Friends, even for the support or education of their poor, to receive contributions from

[4] The following query is addressed to the preparative and monthly meetings of Friends, throughout Great Britain and Ireland, and answered by them respectively to their superior meetings, *once every year*. "*Are friends clear of defrauding the king of his customs, duties, and excise, and of using or dealing in goods suspected to be run?*"

[5] And it is the sense and judgment of this meeting, if any fall short of paying their just debts, and a composition is made with their creditors to accept a part instead of the whole, that, notwithstanding the parties may look upon themselves legally discharged of any obligation to pay the remainder, yet the principle we profess

any persons who have failed in business, until such a liquidation has been effected.

With reference, secondly, to the Christian law of mercy, charity, and love, the same high standard will be found to prevail in the professed sentiments, and to a great extent in the known history of the Society of Friends. On this ground rests, as has been already stated, their total abstinence from military operations — the care which has prevailed among them, from their first origin to the present day, to afford no support or encouragement to the warfare of the world. A similar quickness and nicety of view, and general clearness of conduct, has been the result of their religious principles, with regard to *capital punishments, the slave trade, and slavery.*

It has long been the usual practice of Friends, at whatever cost to their own convenience, to abstain from prosecution in such criminal cases as might probably terminate in the death of the persons prosecuted George Fox, so early as the middle of the seventeenth century, publicly remonstrated with the rulers in his day, respecting the cruelty, antichristian tendency, and radical injustice of the punishment of death, as it was then enacted by British law, and applied to so many offences of a secondary nature. Since that period, Friends have often declared their sentiments, and sometimes have addressed the authorities of the

---

enjoins full satisfaction to be made, if ever the debtors are of ability. And in order that such may the better retrieve their circumstances, we exhort them to submit to a manner of living in every respect the most conducive to this purpose. 1759. P. E. See *Book of Extracts,* "*Trade,*" p. 196, § 5.

state, on this subject; and, in so doing, they have abstained from all political views of it, and have grounded their testimony against the bloody provisions of our criminal code, on the principles of the gospel of Christ.

The line of conduct which they have followed, in reference to the slave trade and slavery, is very generally known. Suffice it now to say, that long before those interesting topics successively claimed the attention of the Christian world in general, the sentiments of the Society had been both established and declared, that the nefarious and abominable traffic in men, and also the holding of them in cruel, degrading bondage, are utterly inconsistent with the unalienable rights of the human race, and still more obviously so with the dictates of Christian love.[6]*

It is unnecessary to advert particularly to the various efforts which Friends, in unison with other Christians, have found it their duty to make, with a view to the relief of the distressed, and in promotion of philanthropic objects; and I may conclude this branch of my remarks on the moral views of the Society, by simply calling the attention of the reader, to the care which has always been exercised by Friends in the support and education of their poor, and in the main-

[6] See *Book of Extracts, Slave Trade and Slavery*, p. 177.

* 1842. The vast progress which has been made in this country, since the time when this work was written, in the amelioration of the criminal code, and that blessed event, the abolition of British Colonial slavery, afford a palpable evidence that the steady adherence of Friends to their *testimony* on these subjects has not been in vain. Truth has triumphed. Public opinion has been enlightened, and has prevailed.

tenance of love and harmony among all the members of their own body. If any Friends fall into poverty, and are found to be unable to provide for their own wants, and those of their families, they are not accustomed to avail themselves of that parochial aid to which the poor of this country so frequently have recourse; for it is the uniform practice of the religious society to which they belong, to supply them with such things as are needful for their sustenance and comfort. A similar care is maintained with respect to the education of their children; who, under such circumstances, are usually sent to our public schools, where they are clothed and fed, and instructed both in the elements of useful learning, and in the principles of religion. With regard to love and harmony among all the members of the body, this is a subject which occupies much of private care throughout the Society, and on which we are almost annually advised by our yearly meeting; and in order, moreover, that it may never be neglected amongst us, our subordinate meetings are called upon, three times in every year, to render an explicit answer to the following inquiry: "Are Friends preserved in love towards each other; if differences arise, is due care taken speedily to end them; and are Friends careful to avoid and discourage talebearing and detraction.

Lastly, with respect to a *humble walk with God*. This essential characteristic of true religion is evinced more clearly by nothing than by a transformation from the spirit of the world, and by the watchful avoidance of the lusts, follies, vices, and vanities, so prevalent among unregenerate men. "Know ye not," says the

CHAP. 12.]   *Moral Views of Friends.*   383

apostle James, " that the friendship of the world is enmity with God? Whosoever, therefore, will be a friend of the world, is the enemy of God."[7] Such a circumspect and harmless walk in life is the sure consequence of that change of heart--that new and heavenly birth—without which no man can be a true Christian, and will indeed be ever found to distinguish the sincere and devoted followers of Jesus, of every name and profession. On the present occasion I would only remark, that no one sect of Christians, of whom I have ever heard, have been led to uphold a higher standard than that maintained among Friends, respecting the importance of an entire abstinence from those customs, prevalent in the world, which are fraught with moral evil; for example, from profuse and extravagant entertainments—from the unnecessary frequenting of taverns and public houses—from excess in eating and drinking—from public diversions—from the reading of useless, frivolous, and pernicious books— from gaming of every description, and from vain and injurious sports[8]—from unnecessary display in funerals, furniture, and style of living—from seductive and dan-

[7] James iv, 4.

[8] The following extract, from one of the printed epistles of our Yearly Meeting, is well worthy the attention, not only of Friends, but of Christians of every name: " We clearly rank the practice of hunting and shooting, *for diversion*, with vain sports; and we believe the awakened mind may see that even the leisure of those whom Providence hath permitted to have a competence of worldly goods, is but ill filled up with these amusements. Therefore, being not only accountable for our substance, but also for our time, let our leisure be employed in serving our neighbour, and not in distressing the creatures of God for our amusement." *Book of Extracts,* " *Conduct and Conversation,*" p. 25.

gerous amusements—and, generally, from all such occupations of time and mind as plainly tend to levity and forgetfulness of our God and Saviour.[9]

[9] There is much reason to fear that some individuals among Friends, who take a strong view of the inconsistency of worldly vanities with the pure and devotional religion of Christ, have not been equally alive to the necessity of avoiding that "*covetousness* which is idolatry.*" Excluded as we are, by our principles, from some of " the professions," and belonging so generally to the middle class of the people, it is very usually our lot to be engaged in trade; and such being the case, peculiar watchfulness is undoubtedly required of us—even watchfulness unto prayer—that we may not be numbered among those whose delight and trust are in riches; for truly it remains to be impossible to " serve God and Mammon." However blameable may be the disposition and conduct of some of us, in this important respect, the Society to which we belong has not failed, in its public advices, to hold out for our instruction a pure standard on the subject; as will be amply evinced by the following passages selected from the Book of Extracts: see head " *Trade*," p. 195, *et seq.*

1. " Advised that none launch into trading and worldly business, beyond what they can manage honourably and with reputation; so that they may keep their words with all men, that their yea may prove yea indeed, and their nay, nay: and that they use few words in their dealings, lest they bring dishonour to the truth." 1688. P. E.—1675.

3. " It is earnestly desired that Friends be very careful to avoid all pursuit after the things of this world, by such ways and means as depend too much on hazardous enterprizes; but rather labour to content themselves with such a plain way and manner of living as is most agreeable to the self-denying principle of truth which we profess; and which is most conducive to that tranquillity of mind which is requisite to a religious conduct through this troublesome world." 1724. P. E.—1801.

7. " Dear Friends, the continuance of covetousness and of earthly-mindedness, in many, calls upon us to endeavour to awaken such as are infected by it, to a sense of what they are pursuing and at what price. The great Master hath shown the unprofitableness of the whole world, compared with one immortal soul; and yet many are pursuing a delusive portion of it, at the

Before we proceed further, I must request the candid reader explicitly to understand, that, in making the observations which have now been offered, on the moral system maintained among Friends, I have been very far from any intention to *panegyrize* the members of that Society. On the contrary, when we consider the high degree of religious light which has been so mercifully bestowed upon us, and the clear views into which we have been led of the spirituality of the gospel dispensation, we may readily confess that, in the inadequacy and shortness of our good works, we have peculiar cause for sorrow and humiliation. Nevertheless, the known views of the Society, and the general conduct of many of its members, may be sufficient to evince that our religious principles have an edifying *tendency*. It is, then, to the practical efficacy of *those principles* that I am desirous of inviting a more general and closer attention; and, especially, to the unspeakable value and power of that word of God in the heart—that law of the Lord inwardly revealed—which it is so much our profession to follow, and

expense of their soul's interests. But, were all thus awakened, what place would be found for extensive schemes in trade, and fictitious credit to support them? To mix with the spirit of the world in the pursuit of gain, would then be a subject of dread; and contentment under the allotment of Providence, a sure means of preservation." 1788 P. E.

8 " Circumscribed even as we are more than many, it is not unusual, in our pursuit of the things of this life, for our gain and our convenience to clash with our testimony. O then may we be willing to pause and give time for those passions to subside, which would hurry us to the accomplishment of the desired purpose, ere the still voice of wisdom be distinctly heard, to guide us in the way in which we should go!" 1795. P. E.

which, *as it is followed*, will never fail to detect for us all that is vain and evil in the customs of men, and to lead us into the pure and solid excellence of the Christian character.

Having again insisted upon this point, I may now proceed to discuss a subject, to which it will be desirable to allot the remainder of the present chapter; viz. *plainness of speech, behaviour, and apparel.* This *plainness* is one of the most obvious of our characteristics. Wherever we bend our steps, and in whatever business we are engaged, it continually meets the eye or the ear of those among whom we dwell, and manifests itself in a variety of particulars, which, though little, are striking. But obvious and constantly perceptible as are these minor features of our conduct and conversation, there is reason to believe that the grounds on which we have adopted them are by no means generally understood; and indeed, the laxity apparent in so many individuals of our own body, with respect to these peculiarities, affords a strong presumption that the principles from which they spring have not been sufficiently considered even amongst ourselves. It is a prevalent notion in the world, and one which many young persons in the Society have, probably, been led to entertain, that the peculiarities in question are employed only because of their expediency; and that they are to be regarded in no other light than that of a sectarian badge, intended for the purpose of distinguishing and separating us from the rest of mankind. In treating, then, on the peculiar plainness of Friends—a subject which, according to my view, is fraught with no little interest—I shall endeavour to show that our practice, in this respect, is by no means adopted merely because it is considered expedient; but that, on the contrary, it is truly grounded on the law of God;—that, in point of fact, it is one result (perfectly consistent with others already mentioned) of a complete view of Christian morality.

I. PLAINNESS OF SPEECH.

The phraseology which prevails in the modern world, and, with the exception of Friends, among Christians of all denominations, is replete with a variety of expressions, used either in addressing or describing persons, which are of a nature simply complimentary, and have no foundation in truth. The terms to which I allude are familiar to every one, but, for the sake of clearness, the principal of them may now be specified.

The word *Sir*, or *Madam*, is very generally employed, both in speech and writing, as a form of address; and of written addresses, to any individual, one of these words mostly forms the commencement. He who makes use of such terms, professes that the person to whom he is speaking or writing is his lord or his lady. Such I conceive to be the generally acknowledged meaning of the expressions in question; for the word *Sir* is obviously a contraction of the French term *Seigneur, Lord;*[1] and *Madam*, also derived

[1] Johnson derives *Sir* from the French *Sire*, an expression denoting the rank and authority of a *father;* but, when we consider the use of the French word *Monsieur*, and the easy transition from *Seigneur* to *Sieur*, and from *Sieur* to *Sir*, little doubt can remain that the latter is the true origin of the English term.

from the French, plainly signifies *My lady*. This verbal profession of subjection to the individual addressed is frequently completed by a declaration, very usual at the conclusion of letters, that the writer is the *humble* or *obedient servant,* or *most humble* or *most obedient servant,* of the person to whom he writes; and among foreigners, more particularly, expressions to the same effect are accumulated with a profuseness which renders the art of complimenting conspicuously ridiculous.

Precisely on a similar principle the man is called *Mister*, the boy, *Master*, the married woman, *Mistress*, and the unmarried woman *Miss*—being the same term contracted. These expressions severally denote that the persons to whom they are applied are placed in a situation of authority or mastery over others, and, if I mistake not, more particularly over the individual by whom the terms in question are employed. They, therefore, represent that which is, by way of compliment, supposed, but which, generally speaking, is nevertheless untrue.

Again, by a similar abuse of language, epithets expressive of a high degree of personal excellence are applied *pro forma*, and worthily or unworthily, (as it may happen,) to a number of individuals who hold certain offices, or enjoy particular stations, in religious or civil society. Thus, whatever be their real character—whatever their conduct or conversation, either in public or in private life—a king is *his most gracious Majesty*—a duke, *his Grace*—a peer of another rank, and a member of the privy council, *Right Honourable*—a son of a peer and a judge, *Honourable*—an archbishop, *Most Reverend*—a bishop, *Right Reverend*—

a dean, *Very Reverend*—an archdeacon, *Venerable*—a priest or deacon, *Reverend*. Similar terms are often applied in the loose extravagance of compliment, to other individuals who are destitute both of office and of high station. Those who are acquainted with the language and manners of the Italians, must be well aware, for example, how frequently and indiscriminately they employ their *illustrissimo* and *eccellenza*. In the common parlance of Spain, every gentlemen is addressed as *Your Worship:* and in this country, persons of no peculiar virtue or eminence are often represented, at the conclusion of letters which they receive, as being *so* honourable, *that it is an honour to be their most humble servants*. Again, among modern Latin critics, a member of their own fraternity, however obscure, is seldom, if ever, mentioned without the passing declaration, that he is *most celebrated*. So common is become the *celeberrimus*, on such occasions, that it is now reduced into the particle *cel.*, and is in this shape prefixed to the name of every writer of the description now mentioned, almost as regularly as is the English contraction, *Mr.*, to those of other men. Not unfrequently, indeed, do these authors attach to the name of any brother critic whom they may happen to cite, a Greek term, which may be considered the highest point of complimentary phraseology; for it denotes nothing less than that the writer cited is *entirely* excellent, or that he comprehends in his own person *the universality of learning and talent*.[2]

In Great Britain, as in other civilized states, there are a variety of legal dignities, corresponding with

[2] ὁ πάνυ.

certain situations in the body politic, and constituting what is usually called *rank*. The lowest of these dignities is that of an *Esquire*, which legally appertains to many individuals, and especially to all those persons who hold any office or commission under the king. Now, the world appears to imagine that the possession of some title or other is indispensable to the character of a gentleman; and, therefore, by a falsification of speech, perfectly similar, in principle, to those already noticed, every person of gentlemanlike station in life, who is destitute of all legal dignity, is *denominated* an *Esquire*. The gentleman, to whom a letter is directed without the addition of that title, is considered, in the world, to be almost affronted by the omission.

But, among the various modes of expression, upon which it is my present object to treat, the most common, and at the same time most absurd, is the application to *individuals* of pronouns and verbs in the *plural* number. The use of the plural form of the first personal pronoun, instead of the singular, is commonly adopted, in their public rescripts and other documents, by monarchs, and, sometimes, by other persons placed in a situation of high authority. The common style of a royal mandate or declaration is as follows: " We George," or " We Frederick," or " We William, command or declare," &c.; and the fiction which such a form of speech represents appears to be precisely this—that the monarch is not to be regarded as an individual, but as may persons combined—that in that single man are centred the authority, wisdom, dignity, and power of many. Since this rhetorical fiction is thus employed by powerful and exalted personages, as a mark of their superior dignity and authority, it easily became a matter of compliment among men in general, to apply it in their addresses one to another. Such a custom, in its early commencement, was probably adopted only as a mark of respect to *superiors;* and unquestionably, for a long period of time, it found no place in addresses made to *inferiors.* But even this distinction is gradually wearing away; a form of speech, which was at one time a mark of distinction, is become universally familiar: the Thou and Thee, in the daily communications between man and man, are disused; and every individual, as if supposed to consist of several persons combined, is addressed with plural pronouns and plural verbs.[3]

Now, we apprehend that our heavenly Guide, whose Spirit is expressly called " the Spirit of Truth," and whose will is directly opposed to all unrighteous vanities, of whatsoever magnitude and description they may be, has taught us, in our communications one with another, and with our fellow-men, to abstain from the use of these various complimentary fictions. The substitution of a plain mode of expression, in the place of one so nearly universal, has, indeed, the effect of rendering us singular; and the singularity

[3] In Germany, the art of complimentary phraseology is carried to a very high point. The German, in addressing his superiors or his equals, is not content with the commonly-received use of the plural pronouns and verbs, but, for the sake of manifesting a yet more profound deference and respect, recites them *in the third person.* Thus, instead of " Will thou eat or drink ?" he would say to his honoured guest, " Will *they* eat or drink ?"

which is thus occasioned, and which sometimes entails upon us ridicule and contempt, is often in no slight degree mortifying to the natural inclinations, especially to those of the young and tender mind. Nevertheless, we are persuaded that this is one of the particulars of conduct, in which, however trifling the subject may appear to some persons, a duty is laid upon us to deny ourselves, patiently to endure the cross, and faithfully to bear our testimony against the customs prevalent in the world at large. It is plain, according to our view of the subject, that the common mode of speech, from which we have thus been led to abstain, is at variance with certain acknowledged principles in the divine law. Such a phraseology may very fairly be deemed objectionable; *first*, because it is intended to flatter the pride of man; and *secondly*, because it is inconsistent with truth.

I. It was one of the charges which our Saviour adduced against the unbelieving Jews, that they received honour " one of another," and sought not " *the honour that cometh from God only;*"[4] and truly, a similar character is still very generally prevalent among men. While they neglect to strive after that true " glory" which is the end of a " patient continuance in well doing;"[5] there is nothing on the pursuit of which they are more generally intent than the honour of the world—the honour which is bestowed by man. To be exalted among our fellow creatures, to receive the tribute of their homage and the incense of their flattery, to be the objects of their eulogy and polite submission—are circumstances perfectly adapted to

[4] John v, 44.   [5] Rom. 11, 7.

Chap. 12.] *Plainness of Speech.* 393

the pride of our own hearts, and grateful, beyond almost any other worldly advantages, to the natural disposition of the human mind. Here it may be observed, that the eager desire to be thus exalted, admired, and commended, is closely and almost inseparably connected (though perhaps, in a somewhat hidden manner) with a spirit of undue fear and subserviency towards our fellow men. And this, probably, is the reason why those persons who are themselves the most desirous of receiving adulation, are often the most ready to bestow it. There appears to exist, among the children of this evil world, a sort of understood convention, that they shall praise and be praised, shall flatter and be flattered.

Among the various means which mankind have invented in order to effect this object, and to gratify their own antichristian disposition to adulation on the one hand, and pride on the other, is evidently to be numbered the complimentary mode of speech to which we have now been adverting. We read that the worldly-minded Pharisees, who loved the uppermost rooms at feasts, and the chief seats in the synagogues, loved also the "*greetings in the markets, and to be called of men, Rabbi, Rabbi.*"[6] Since, therefore, the use of the expressions in question proceeds from a corrupt source, and is plainly intended to foster the vain desires of the carnal mind, it may reasonably be concluded, that a total abstinence from them is not only commendable and desirable, but necessary to a *complete* conformity with the divine law.

It is needless, on the present occasion, to cite the

[6] Matt. xxiii, 6, 7.

numerous passages of Scripture, and more especially of the New Testament, which forbid the exaltation of the creature, and enjoin humility and self-abasement. One passage alone will suffice, in which our Lord insists on this branch of the divine law in immediate connexion, as it appears, with the subject of the present section. When charging the Pharisees with pride, and with their love of being called of men, Rabbi, Rabbi, he adds the following emphatic injunction, addressed to his own followers: " But be not ye called Rabbi; for one is your Master, even Christ, and all ye are brethren. And call no man your father upon the earth (namely, as a complimentary title;) for one is your Father, which is in heaven. Neither be ye called masters; for one is your Master, even Christ. But he that is greatest among you, shall be your servant. And whosoever shall exalt himself, shall be abased; and he that shall humble himself, shall be exalted."[7] This instructive passage of Scripture may be regarded in two points of view. We may allow, in the first place, that it indirectly inculcates the general doctrine, that, in matters of religion, Christians are not to depend upon the teaching and authority of their fellow men, but rather upon those of the Father and of Christ. They must, in this respect, be careful to set up neither themselves nor others. They must ever remember that they have all cause for deep humiliation; that they are all brethren; that one is their Father, even God; that one is their Master, even Christ. And, secondly, the use of merely formal and complimentary titles, as one of the

[7] Matt. xxiii, 81—2.

CHAP. 12.]   *Plainness of Speech.*   395

means by which men are accustomed to exalt themselves and others—a means which had been so eagerly adopted by the scribes and Pharisees—is, in this passage, forbidden to the followers of Christ. The complimentary titles here mentioned by our Saviour. viz. *Rabbi*, *Father*, and *Master*, were, at that period, of very recent origin.[8] In the better times of Israelitish history, as some of the Jews themselves confess, no such corruption of speech was known; for the patriarchs, the prophets, and even the earliest doctors of the Rabbinical schools, were called and addressed by their simple names. But, as the Jews gradually departed from their ancient simplicity, and shortly before the coming of our Saviour, their leading men of learning and authority claimed the distinction of these appellations; and if, perchance, any of their disciples addressed them according to that simple method which was usual in better times, it was even pretended that such persons *offended against the majesty of heaven*. In the discourse of which the passage before us forms a part, our Lord sharply reproves the scribes and Pharisees on account of their attach-

---

[8] The Greek words ῥαββί or διδάσκαλος, πατήρ, and καθηγητής, as Lightfoot has observed, represent respectively the Hebrew terms, רבי (honourable person), אבי (father), and מרי (master); expressions which appear to have been used, at the Christian era, in the same formal and complimentary manner, as are the terms, Sir, my Lord, your Grace, &c. in the present day. In order to recommend those titles, one of the Talmudic authors pretends that king Jehosaphat made much point of employing them in addressing any scribe. "Whenever Jehosaphat," says this author, "saw a disciple of the wise men, he rose from his throne, embraced him, kissed him, and thus addressed him, Father, Father; Rabbi, Rabbi; Master, Master." *Babyl. Maccoth.* fol. xxiv, 1; *Lightfoot.*

ment to so absurd and ungodly a practice—an attachment which he mentions as one among many fruits of their vanity, pride, and presumption; and then, turning round to his own disciples, he distinctly forbids them to assume for themselves, or to apply to others, the complimentary titles in question: showing that the formal use of such expressions is at variance with the true condition of those persons who are children and disciples of one Lord, and whose duty and privilege it is to humble themselves before God, and to serve one another for his sake.[9] It may, indeed, be observed, that the scribes and Pharisees probably claimed these verbal distinctions, as marks of their *religious* superiority; and that the expressions of the same nature, which are now so common, have a more general application. But whether such expressions are addressed to clergy or to laity, whether they are intended as compliments to the ministers of the church, or to the members of society at large, they are still objectionable, on our Lord's principle of Christian simplicity and humility. They are still derived from the pride of man; and still do they foster the passion from which they spring.

Our Lord's precept, on this subject, was remarkably exemplified, both in his own conversation, and in the verbal or written communications of his inspired disciples. The mode of address which he employed, and which the evangelists and apostles also adopted, though, in many instances, distinguished for its kindness and true courtesy, was not less remarkable for its plainness, and for the absence of all complimentary

[9] See *Lightfoot, Hor. Heb. in loc. Poli Syn.*

CHAP. 12.] *Plainness of Speech.* 397

phraseology. I know of nothing in the New Testament which has a contrary appearance, unless it be the epithets *Most excellent and Most noble;* the former applied by Luke to Theophilus;[1] the latter by Paul to Festus;[2] and also the title *Sirs,* by which that apostle is represented as addressing the inhabitants of Lystra, and the companions of his voyage to Rome.[3] But, in all these instances, our common English version is in fault; and there is no reason to suppose that the expressions, as used in the original Greek, were in any degree, misapplied. The Greek adjective,[4] which, in Luke i, 3, is rendered *most excellent,* and in Acts xxvi, 25, *most noble,* properly denotes neither excellence nor nobility, but an eminent degree of *power.* The epithet was, probably, not inapplicable to Theophilus, of whom we know almost nothing, but, who, from the use of this very word, is supposed by commentators to have been the governor of some province: and, certainly, it was properly descriptive of Festus, who, as proconsul of Judea, was, in that country, possessed of the supreme authority.[5] With respect to the appellation rendered *Sirs,* in Acts xiv, 15; xxvii, 10, 21, 25, it signifies, not *lords or masters,* but simply *men.*[6] The term used in the passages is not, indeed, the generic name of man. It is applicable only to the male sex; and, inasmuch as it represented the strength and manliness of that sex, it was probably considered as a term of respect. Nevertheless, it described literal truth, and was, therefore, no complimentary expression.

[1] Luke i, 3.   [2] Acts xxvi, 25.
[3] Acts xiv, 15; xxvii, 10, 21, 25; *comp.* vii, 26.
[4] κράτιστος.   [5] See *Schleusneri Lex in voc.*   [6] ἄνδρες.

I have often thought that the speeches of Paul to Felix and Agrippa afford an excellent specimen of the true Christian method of addressing our superiors; for they are distinguished by respectful courtesy, united to entire plainness. "Forasmuch as I know," said he to Felix, "that thou hast of many years been a judge unto this nation, I do the more cheerfully answer for myself:" again, "I think myself happy, king Agrippa, because I shall answer for myself this day before thee, touching all the things whereof I am accused of the Jews; especially because I know thee to be expert in all customs and questions which are among the Jews: wherefore I beseech thee to hear me patiently:" again, "King Agrippa, believest thou the prophets? I know that thou believest," &c. To these speeches we may find an excellent parallel, in point both of propriety and of plainness, in the public addresses which have, at various times. been made by Friends to high and royal personages; and more particularly in Robert Barclay's celebrated dedication of his "Apology" to King Charles II.

II. It has been already remarked, that, in this, as in most other civilized states, there are various titles legally attached to persons who occupy particular offices or stations in the body politic. To the use of these titles there does not appear to be any moral objection. There is no good reason, as is generally allowed by Friends, why kings, earls, barons, baronets, esquires, &c. should not, in the conversation or letters of Christians, be so denominated, since these are not names of mere courtesy, but are given in conformity with the constitution of the country, and properly represent the office or condition of the persons who bear them. Nor ought the servant to feel the least reserve or hesitation, in calling his master, *Master*, and his mistress, *Mistress*. So far, indeed, is it from being inconsistent with Christian principle, to describe our fellow creatures by the titles which properly belong to them, and which correctly represent their *actual situation*, that such a practice may rather be deemed to be enjoined by the apostolic precept—"Render to all their dues."[7] But, to those various complimentary expressions, from the use of which Friends consider it to be their duty to abstain, there is, on the other hand, this radical objection, that, according to their general usage, and in a great plurality of instances, they represent falsehood. To call a man *Sir*, or *Master*, who has no authority over us—to declare ourselves to be his obedient servants, when we know that we are no such thing—to style him, as a matter of course, honourable or reverend, when he is neither the one nor the other, and to describe him as most celebrated, though he is destitute of all celebrity—is, in our apprehension, to depart from that plain law of truth, by which the words of Christians ought ever to be strictly regulated. That truth of speech, which in the Holy Scriptures is opposed to the lying tongue, and which is so clearly and so earnestly enjoined, obviously consists in the honest and complete conformity of our words (according to their acknowledged signification) to facts and realities. Since, then, these complimentary expressions are not truly conformed to facts

[7] Romans xiii, 7.

and realities; since, according to their commonly-received meaning, they denote feelings, dispositions, or relations, in those who use them, which have no existence; they may justly be considered inconsistent with simple and unbending veracity.

Persons are sometimes heard to remark that the expressions in question are not to be understood literally—that those which appear to express subjection, are to be interpreted as indicative only of civility—that their signification is either lessened or lost—that they may even be considered as meaning *nothing*—and hence, it is easily concluded, that the formal use of such terms involves no sacrifice of truth. But the reflecting reader will scarcely fail to detect the fallacy of these observations. There are none of the expressions in question, which can fairly be interpreted in a subordinate sense. Used as they are, in a familiar manner, as current tokens of respect, it is evident, that they serve such a purpose, only because of their intrinsic meaning; and that meaning is undisputed and unaltered. So far, indeed, are some of these terms from being of uncertain application, or destitute of signification, that there are scarcely any words in our language, of which the sense is more obvious, or more clearly fixed. Who does not know, for example, that *a humble and obedient servant* is a person of lowly mind and servile condition, who obeys his master—that an *honourable* or *reverend* individual is an individual truly worthy of honour or reverence—that a *most celebrated* or *most illustrious* author is an author who has attained to a very high degree of literary fame—and that the plural personal pronouns denote a plurality of

CHAP. 12.] *Plainness of Speech.* 401

persons? The meaning of such terms is plain, and cannot be disputed; and all that can be urged on the other side of the question, will, probably, be found to resolve itself into a single position; viz. *that the falsehoods which these expressions represent are so customary, that they are become inefficacious—that they no longer deceive.* That this effect has, in a very considerable degree, taken place, may readily be admitted; but this result affords no sufficient excuse for the adoption of such a mode of speech. It may justly be contended, that the use of words which, according to their *known signification,* represent things untrue, constitutes a falsehood—that, however absurd or unavailing that falsehood may be, it is nevertheless real—that such a practise arises out of an evil origin—that it is, in its nature, evil—and that, although it may defeat its own ends, and lose its effect in proportion to its prevalence, it can never change its character, or cease to be inconsistent with an *exact* obedience to the law of Christ.

To the sincere-hearted Christian, who has, hitherto, perceived no evil in the use of a complimentary phraseology, may be addressed the remark, that there are various degrees of insincerity, and that the passage from the lesser to the greater measures of it is exceedingly easy. He who has no scruple, for example, to declare himself (without any foundation in literal truth) to be the humble, obedient, or devoted servant of the person whom he addresses, is in danger, as it appears to me, of advancing a step further, and of making other less formal professions of civility or service, which he is equally without the intention of

2 D

fulfilling. Thus his sense of truth is gradually weakened; his feelings and intentions, and the words by which he expresses them, become more and more dissonant; and, at length, his communications assume the character of insincerity in so great a degree, that our dependence upon them for practical purposes is materially shaken. Scarcely any one, who is conversant with the business of the world, can fail to have remarked how easily these consequences result from the sacrifice, however formal, of literal truth. It may, indeed, be admitted, that this remark will not apply, in any great degree, to the more common and less conspicuous terms of compliment; but all these expressions are of the *same nature*, they appertain to the *same principle*, and they naturally lead one to another. On the whole, therefore, it may fairly be concluded, that the line of true safety, in reference to the present subject, must be drawn at the bottom of the whole system, and must preclude the use, in conversation and addresses, of *any* expressions which are merely complimentary, and which, according to their plain and acknowledged meaning, represent any falsity.

There is another particular, connected with the plainness of speech peculiar to Friends, of which a very brief notice will be sufficient. It is their practice, as my reader is probably aware, to avoid the commonly-adopted names of months and days, and to indicate those periods by numbers, according to the order of their succession: as, the *first, second*, or *third month;* the *first, second*, or *third day, &c.* Their reason for making this alteration is simple and forcible.

All the days of the week, and many of the months of the year, have received the names, by which they are usually described, in honour of *false gods*. Thus, January is the month of Janus, Thursday the day of Thor, &c. This relic of heathenism is not only needless and indecorous, but, according to our sentiments, is opposed to the tenor and spirit, as well as to the letter, of those divine commandments addressed to the Israelites, which forbade the use of the names of false gods, and every other the slightest approach to idolatrous practices.[8] Idolatry was, indeed, a sin which easily beset that ancient people, and to which, in the present enlightened state of society, *Christians* are but little tempted. But, it will scarcely be denied, that the various precepts contained in the Old Testament on the subject, form a part of that law which changes not; and that the standard of truth, in this particular, was elevated rather than lowered by the introduction of the gospel dispensation. Although, therefore, we may now be in no danger of falling away into the worship of false gods, it appears that the maintenance of a custom which had its origin in such a worship, and by which a *verbal* honour is still given to ideal deities, or to devils, is inconsistent with the *pure* piety and *unmixed* devotion of the simple Christian.[9]

[8] See Exodus xxiii, 13; Joshua xxiii, 7: *comp.* Deut. xii, 3; Psalms xvi, 4, &c.

[9] May it not be considered, in some degree, discreditable to the religious profession of our country, that the votes of the British parliament, passed, as they are, after the daily recitation of prayers addressed to the ever blessed Jehovah, in the name of Christ,

II. PLAINNESS OF BEHAVIOUR.

The more consistent part of the Society of Friends consider it to be their duty to uphold the standard of plainness, not only in speech, but in manners, or behaviour. Their *general* views, on this branch of our subject, are in full accordance with those of all the humble followers of a crucified Redeemer. Where is the seriously-minded Christian, who will not allow, that servility, vanity, and affectation in manners, afford a sure indication of a worldly spirit, and of a heart not yet converted from darkness to light; and, on the other hand, that a true simplicity in our carriage towards other men, whether they are our inferiors, our equals, or our superiors, is one of the most genuine ornaments of the Christian character.

There is also another part of plainness in behaviour, respecting which Friends are on common ground with other Christians; I mean the absence of levity—*religious seriousness*. An innocent and wholesome cheerfulness is far, indeed, from being precluded by the law of Christ: for what persons have so true an acquaintance with *pure pleasure*, as those upon whom are shining the beams of the Sun of Righteousness; or, who are so much at ease and at liberty to enjoy

should, when printed, uniformly bear about them the stamp of classical heathenism? These documents are dated in Latin; "*Die Veneris, Quarto Martis; Die Mercurii, Secundo Julii,*" &c.

themselves, as they who have obeyed the calls of duty, and have trodden the path of the cross? While this allowance may be made without reserve, it is, perhaps, no less evident that a lightness and wantonness of manners, and an ill-regulated, extravagant mirth, are totally at variance with the great features of the Christian life. No one, surely, will be found to indulge in them, who entertains any adequate notions of the importance of his moral condition, of the great purposes for which he is called into being, of the immortality of his soul, and of the terrors and hopes respectively set before him in the Christian revelation.

Having made these remarks on that simple and serious deportment which all real Christians endeavour to maintain, I may proceed to remark, that there are certain particulars of conduct and manners, in which Friends observe a plainness of behaviour, in a great degree peculiar to themselves. We conceive it to be our duty to abstain from the use of those *obeisances*, upon which, in the world, and more especially in the upper classes of society, a scrupulous attention is very generally bestowed. In presenting ourselves before our fellow creatures, we believe it right to avoid the *submissive* inflection of the body and the taking-off of the hat, as a token of personal homage.

The principles on which is founded our objection to these practices are, in part, the same as those which have been stated under the last head. The bowing-down of the body and the pulling-off of the hat, in honour of man, are actions perfectly coincident with a servile and complimentary phraseology. Words in the one case, and actions in the other, are obviously intended to denote the same thing; namely, that the person addressing *submits himself* to the superior dignity and authority of the person addressed. Whether, then, it be by our expressions or by our carriage that we cherish and foment the vanity one of another—whether the complimentary *falsehood* be spoken or acted—we cannot but entertain the sentiment, that, in adopting, in either way, the customs prevalent in the world, we should be departing from that simplicity and godly sincerity by which our conversation among men ought ever to be regulated.

There is, however, another reason, of a very substantial nature, why Friends conceive it to be their duty to avoid some of these obeisances; namely, that they are the very signs by which Christians are accustomed to denote their submission *to the Almighty himself.* This is generally understood to be the case, more particularly with the taking-off of the hat, as a mark of homage—a practice usual among Friends, as well as among other Christians, on certain occasions of a religious nature. When we approach God in prayer, or address others in his name, we uniformly take off the hat, and kneel or stand *uncovered* before him. It is probable that, in every age of the world, there have been certain customary external marks of the worship of Jehovah; and this, undoubtedly, is one of those marks, in the present day. The action, in itself, is absolutely indifferent; but, through the force of custom, it has become significant of religious homage offered to the Supreme Being. Now, we consider it to be inconsistent with that reverence which is exclusively due to the Deity, and hold that it involves a very dangerous confusion, to address to our fellow creatures, however exalted they may be, those very acts which, on other occasions, denote nothing less than the worship of *Him* who " bringeth the princes to nothing, and maketh the judges of the earth as vanity."

Such are the principles which have given rise to one of the most conspicuous peculiarities in the deportment of the plain Quaker. It is generally known, that when a person of this description approaches even the earthly *monarch* to whom he both owes and feels a real allegiance, he dares not either to bend the knee, or to uncover the head, in token of that allegiance; and for this plain, and as it appears to me, fully sufficient reason; that these are the very outward signs by which he is accustomed to designate his submissive approaches to the Lord of lords and King of kings—the God and Father of us all.

In bearing this testimony against the semi-idolatrous practices of the world, I cannot but consider it plain that Friends are acting in conformity with the divine law, which, while it forbids us either to flatter or deceive our neighbours, is, if possible, still more imperative as to the restriction of the acknowledged acts of worship to their only proper object—Jehovah. " All these things will I give thee," said the tempter to Jesus, " if thou wilt *fall down and worship me*.[1] Then saith Jesus unto him, Get thee hence, Satan: for it is written, Thou shalt worship [2] the Lord thy God, and him *only* shalt thou serve."[3]

[1] προσκυνήσῃς.   [2] προσκυνήσεις.   [3] Matt. iv, 9, 10.

The prostration of the body on the ground (like the taking-off of the hat, or kneeling, among modern Europeans) was one of those tokens by which the ancient inhabitants of the East were accustomed to designate *worship*, whether that worship was addressed as homage to their superiors among men, or as religious adoration to the Deity himself; and the Greek verb, signifying to worship, literally imports such a prostration. Had that divine mandate, which our Saviour quoted in answer to the tempter, been fully observed by the Israelites of old, they would surely have confined these obeisances to the Lord himself; and their not having done so appears to afford one proof, among many, that even the more enlightened of their number fell short of a just apprehension of the extent and perfection of the law of God. But the history of the New Testament affords satisfactory evidence that, under the purer light of the gospel dispensation, so dangerous a confusion in the application of these obeisances is strictly precluded. We find, from the records of that sacred volume, that the prostration of the body on the ground was an act frequently employed by Christians in the worship of the Father,[4] and also in that of the Lord Jesus Christ, who is the Son of God, partaking in the Father's nature, and *one* with him.[5] It was, I think, plainly for this reason, that Jesus never refused to receive such a homage: but no sooner was it addressed to the *creature*, than it called forth the just and earnest reprehension of the Lord's servants. Two in-

---

[4] 1 Cor. xiv, 25; Rev. vii, 11, &c.   [5] Matt. xiv, 33; John ix, 38.

CHAP. 12.]   *Plainness of Behaviour.*   409

stances of this kind are recorded in the New Testament. When the apostle Peter was coming into the house of Cornelius, the latter "met him, and fell down at his feet, and worshipped him (or prostrated himself before him): but Peter took him up, saying, Stand up, *I myself also am a man.*"[6] So again, in the book of Revelation, we read that the apostle John, struck, as we may presume, with the glory of the angel who showed him the vision, fell down at his feet "to worship him," or to *prostrate himself before him.* Yet the angel earnestly forbad his doing so;—"*See thou do it not,*" said he; "I am thy fellow servant, and of thy brethren that have the testimony of Jesus: *worship God.*"[7]

It cannot, with any reason, be supposed, that the act of reverence addressed by Cornelius to Peter, and by John to the ministering angel, was, in either case, intended as a sign of spiritual worship. Cornelius, who was a devout man, redeemed from the errors of idolatry, and taught to live in the fear of the Lord, could never, for a moment, have entertained the notion that Peter was to be adored as a god; nor is there any probability in the supposition, that the apostle John, after having been favoured with so repeated a vision of the glory both of the Father and of the Son, should mistake for either of them that messenger of Christ, who was appointed *to show him these things.*[8] We may conclude, therefore, that this act of reverence, as employed by Cornelius and the apostle, was,

[6] Acts x, 25, 26.
[7] Rev. xix, 10.   [8] Rev. xxii, 8.

like the obeisances of the present day, directed *solely* to the purpose of evincing respect and subjection in the presence of a superior. Nevertheless, since it was otherwise used as a sign of religious adoration, it was on both these occasions strenuously forbidden, on that main and simple principle of religion, that *God alone is the object of worship*. Now, this principle appears to be applied, with equal propriety, in prohibition of the modern and similar practices of kneeling and uncovering the head, as tokens of our submission to *men*.

In the observations which have now been offered on plainness of speech and behaviour, I have been very far from any intention to disparage so useful and amiable a quality as *courtesy*. On the contrary, experience has thoroughly convinced me of the great practical importance of that quality, as a means of smoothing down the little asperities of society, and of rendering the communications between man and man profitable, easy, and agreeable. Under these impressions, I cannot rightly do otherwise than express my earnest desire, that the younger members of our Society may more and more estimate the advantage of polite manners, and study a true civility towards all around them. May they never so mistake our religious principles as to imagine that there is any thing to be found in them, which justifies a want of refinement, gentleness, and delicate attention, or which can lead us to withhold from our superiors that respectful demeanour, and that willing service, so evidently their due.[9]

[9] I venture to take the present opportunity of suggesting to the consideration of my young friends, whether it is not proper for

True courtesy of manners is one of the natural fruits of the love of God "shed abroad" in the heart. It is Christian benevolence carried into detail, and operating upon all the circumstances of life. "Be kindly affectioned one to another," says the apostle Paul, "with brotherly love; *in honour preferring one another.*"[1] "Be ye all of one mind," exclaims Peter, in the same spirit, "having compassion one of another; love as brethren; be pitiful, be *courteous.*"[2] It is surely undeniable that a true politeness—a Christian courtesy—may be exercised without the aid of complimentary phraseology, or of bodily obeisances. It is, indeed, very evident that these practices, especially when applied in excess, are nothing more than a formal and fictitious representative of the genuine quality; and that, in the society of the world, they are very frequently employed as a mere cover for the want of it. Those persons who are brought to abstain from them, on Christian principles, from the humble desire to walk circumspectly before God, and from a genuine love of the law of their Redeemer, will be preserved in *meekness and tenderness of mind* towards their fellow creatures. Obedience to the "still, small voice" of the Spirit of Christ is, in an eminent degree, calculated to promote these disposi-

us, when we speak to a person much older than ourselves, or otherwise our superior, to use the family name, in addition to the first name of the person addressed. This simple and unexceptionable mark of deference prevents the appearance of undue familiarity; and let it be remembered that undue familiarity not only involves a breach of good manners, but is often productive of moral injury.

[1] Rom. xii, 10.   [2] 1 Peter iii, 8.

tions; and the very cross which this obedience entails upon us, will be found efficacious in promoting the same end. Now, this meekness and tenderness of mind is the best of antidotes against unkindness of conduct, or rudeness and incivility in manners. United with Christian benevolence, they will generally be effectual in polishing the roughest materials, and in converting even the homely tradesman, or the humble mechanic, into the *real* gentleman.

III. PLAINNESS OF APPAREL.

It is much to be regretted, as the more reflecting observers of the Christian church will probably allow, that so many persons, who are blessed with a serious view of religion, and who profess to be the dedicated followers of a crucified Lord, appear to entertain scarcely any objection to the decking of their frail bodies; bodies destined so soon to moulder into dust, and to become a prey for worms! Such a conduct, although general in the world, and although slightly observed, because of its being general, is far more worthy of the untutored Indian, who fondly delights in the bauble and the bead, than of the Christian who serves a spiritual Master, and who lives with eternity in view.

No one can move in what is called the *religious world*, without meeting with instances which justify these reflections; and although we find exceptions to this remark, (especially, I believe, among the Wesleyan Methodists,) yet entire plainness of apparel may not unfairly be regarded as one of the distinguishing marks of the Society of Friends.

CHAP. 12.] *Plainness of Apparel.* 413

The principles which we entertain on this subject are very simple; and they appear to have an immediate connexion with the divine law. Among those numerous modifications of self-love which are displayed in the character of unregenerate man, is to be numbered *personal vanity*. Absurd as is this petty propensity of the human mind, it may reasonably be questioned whether there is any passion more general. While the prevalence of such a disposition affords a lamentable proof (among many others) that the heart of man is "*deceitful* above all things," it must surely be allowed that this is one of those affections which the law of Christ forbids us to indulge, and commands us to mortify. Since, then, the custom of ornamenting the body plainly originates in personal vanity, and is as plainly calculated to encourage the passion from which it springs; it follows, that such a custom must be at variance with the law of Christ.

We ought to distinguish between *clothing* and *ornament*. Clothing is intended to cover and protect the person; ornament to beautify it. The former is necessary, both for the maintenance of decency and for the preservation of health; and the provision which is made for it, in nature, calls aloud for the tribute of thankfulness to the Author of all our mercies. The latter is altogether needless for the body, and evidently hurtful to the mind. The world has mixed clothing and ornament together. Some parts of dress are made to serve the purpose of clothing, and others that of ornament. Now, it is the principle of Friends to retain those parts of dress by which the body is *protected*, and to disuse those by which it is only *adorned*.

It may, indeed, be observed, that those parts of dress which are necessary for protection may be more or less ornamental. There are the coarser and finer materials, the more sober and the brighter colours. On this point I would remark, that, excluding splendid and costly apparel, the materials of our clothing may fairly be regulated, to a great degree, by our circumstances in life; and that, with respect to colours, those which are the least showy and glaring appear to be the most in *harmony* with the sobriety of the Christian character.

That there can be no virtue in any particular form of dress, is obvious; and the reflecting reader will, probably, agree with me in the sentiment, that to insist upon any such form, as if the wearing of it were a religious obligation, is to interfere with genuine Christian simplicity, and to substitute superstition for piety. It is not an uncommon error to suppose, that Friends make it a matter of religious principle to insist upon a certain form of dress. As far as I am acquainted with their sentiments, the main principle which they entertain, with respect to the subject, is that to which I have already adverted—namely, that personal vanity is a passion which Christians ought not to indulge, and, therefore, that nothing is to be introduced into our clothing, or added to it, *for the sake of ornament*. The appearance of form, I might rather say, "uniform," in the dress of Friends, may be considered as arising, in a great degree, from two causes: *first*, that the disuse of all the ornamental parts of dress has, in itself, the inevitable effect of making them in their attire *differ* from other people, and *resemble* one another; secondly, that Friends have not allowed themselves to change their mode of dress, from time to time, in pursuance of the ever-varying *fashions* of the world. Those who refuse to comply with such changes in fashion, except when they really promote convenience, will presently discover that their personal appearance is singular. And yet, such a refusal to follow a series of changes, so generally grounded on the merest folly and vanity, is surely no more than consistent with Christian simplicity and gravity.

The precepts in Scripture, respecting plainness of apparel, are addressed to the female sex. In considering those precepts, however, it becomes us to remember, that the principles on which they are founded are equally imperative upon both sexes; nor will it be disputed that, if the adorning of the person is blameable in women, it must be much more so in men, whose circumstances place them under much less temptation to any practice of the kind.

From certain descriptions in the Old Testament, it may be inferred, that, under the legal dispensation, the standard maintained of plainness in dress, like that of several other particulars of conduct and conversation, was by no means uniformly of the highest or strictest order. Thus, among the gifts which Abraham sent to Rebekah, were earrings and bracelets, with jewels of gold and silver;[3] and the virtuous wife who is so much commended by king Lemuel, is described as making for herself " coverings of tapes-

[3] Gen. xxiv, 53.

try," and as being clothed in "purple."[4] Nevertheless, we may learn, from the apostle Peter, that many of the holy women of old were exemplary in this respect;[5] and we know that the profusion of ornament, by which the Jewish women, of a worldly character, displayed their personal vanity, called forth the righteous indignation of the Supreme Being. "Moreover, the Lord saith, Because the daughters of Zion are haughty, and walk with stretched forth necks, and wanton eyes, walking and mincing as they go, and making a tinkling with their feet; therefore the Lord will smite with a scab the crown of the head of the daughters of Zion. In that day, the Lord will take away the bravery of their tinkling ornaments about their feet, and their cauls, and their round tires like the moon, the chains, and the bracelets, and the mufflers, the bonnets, and the ornaments of the legs, and the headbands, and the tablets, and the earrings, the rings, and the nose jewels, the changeable suits of apparel, and the mantles, and the wimples, and the crisping pins, the glasses, and the fine linen, and the hoods, and the veils," &c.[6]

I have endeavoured to show that the sentiments which Friends entertain, on the subject of plainness of apparel, arise out of the principles of that branch of the divine law, which enjoins the mortification of the carnal affections and vanities of the human heart—of the "lust of the flesh, the lust of the eye, and the pride of life." Now, it will, probably, be allowed, that the extent of the demands of the law of God, in

---

[4] Prov. xxxi, 22.   [5] 1 Pet. iii, 5.   [6] Isa. iii, 16—24.

CHAP. 12.]   *Plainness of Apparel.*   417

these respects, was made *fully* apparent only under the more spiritual dispensation of Christianity; and, accordingly, it is in the New Testament alone that ornament or finery in attire is expressly forbidden. There are, in the apostolic epistles, two passages to this effect. "I will, therefore," says Paul to Timothy, "...... that women adorn (or dress) themselves in modest (or neat) apparel, with shamefacedness and sobriety; *not with broidered (or curled and braided*[7]*) hair, or gold, or pearls, or costly array;* but (which becometh women professing godliness) with good works."[8] The apostle Peter gives very similar directions. "Likewise, ye wives," says he, "be in subjection to your own husbands, &c. .... whose adorning, *let it not be that outward adorning, of plaiting the hair, and of wearing of gold, or of putting on of apparel;*[9] but let it be the hidden man of the heart, in that which is not corruptible; even the ornament of a meek and quiet spirit, which is in the sight of God of great price."[1]

It has been sometimes remarked, that in the two passages now cited, the female Christian is not absolutely required to disuse ornament in dress, but only

[7] πλέγμασι· "πλέγματα notat cincinnos, crines intortos, capillos artificiose flexos et inter se nexos." *Schleusner in voc.*

[8] 1 Tim. ii, 8—10.

[9] It plainly appears from the context, that, by "the putting on of apparel," the apostle means, the putting on of costly or splendid apparel. The Syriac and Ethiopic translators have added epithets to that effect. "The Apostle," says Gill, "means such apparel as is unbecoming and unsuitable; for he cannot be thought to forbid the putting on of any apparel." *Com. in loc.*

[1] 1 Pet. iii, 1—4.

2 E

to make the graces and fruits of the Spirit (which by these apostles are described as ornaments) the *principal* object of her attention and pursuit. But I would submit, that the impartial examiner of the words of Paul and Peter will by no means accede to such an observation. Each of these passages contains both a positive and a negative injunction: each of them teaches us how Christian women *ought*, and how they *ought not*, to adorn themselves—what things *are*, and what things *are not*, to be their ornaments. Peter assigns to them, for an ornament, "a meek and quiet spirit, which is, in the sight of God, of great price;" and Paul, a modest dress, with good works. On the other hand, Peter declares that their adorning ought *not* to be " that outward adorning of plaiting the hair, and of wearing of gold, and of putting on of (splendid) apparel;" and Paul plainly commands them *not* to adorn themselves with " curled or braided hair, or gold, or pearls, or costly array." Between the positive and the negative injunction, respectively given by the two apostles, there is evidently preserved a complete parallel. Both are to be taken according to their obvious meaning, and both must, in all fairness, be considered as binding on the followers of Christ. Since, therefore, a decent and modest dress, good works, and a meek and quiet spirit, are here plainly *enjoined*, it must surely be allowed, that the wearing of splendid apparel, the curling and braiding of the hair, and the use of other personal ornaments, are *forbidden*.

It was the remark of a noted infidel writer, in reference to that plainness of dress so customary in the

CHAP. 12.]   *Plainness of Apparel.*   419

Society of Friends, that there is no *quakerism in the works of nature ;* and nothing, perhaps, is more usually urged, in justification of splendid and ornamental apparel, than the brightness of the flowers, and the gay plumage of the feathered tribes. True, indeed, it is, that the great Creator, who has made so many gracious provisions for the gladdening of our hearts, and for the gratification of our eyes, has scattered his ornaments in rich profusion over the face of nature; nor is there any thing, save redeeming mercy, more calculated to excite, in the Christian, the feeling of humble adoration, than the harmony and beauty of created things. Were, then, our objection against finery in dress grounded on the absurd principle that *nothing beautiful or splendid can be good*, such an objection must, undoubtedly, vanish before the plumage of the peacock, the beauty of the rose, the gaiety of the butterfly, and the variegated radiance of the setting sun. But we are not so foolish as to object to beauty, under any of its forms, merely because it is beauty; we disapprove only of *such a misapplication of things supposed to be beautiful, as is attended with an evil effect on the human mind.* In a happy sense and grateful admiration of the ornaments of nature, there is nothing inconsistent with a religious objection to *those* ornaments which deck the persons of the children of fashion. The former appertain to the excellent order of God's creation, and are so far from producing any undesirable moral effect, that they tend to exalt his praises, and teach his intelligent creatures to adore his power, his wisdom, and his goodness. But the latter are ornaments misplaced and perverted: they serve only to amuse the thoughtlessness, and to gratify the vanity, of fallen man.

Besides the objections entertained by Friends to the indulgence of so antichristian a passion as personal vanity, there is a further reason why they regard a plain dress as peculiarly adapted to the profession and views of the Christian; namely, *that it demands very little thought, and occupies very little time.* Every one, on the other hand, who has followed the footsteps of the fashionable world, must be aware that there are few things which engage more attention, or consume a greater number of precious hours, than a gay, fanciful, and studied attire. The advantage, in this respect, of plain apparel, over that of an ornamental character, will be most properly appreciated by those persons who desire to devote their time and talents to their Redeemer, and who are looking forward to the day when they must render, to the Judge of all flesh, *an account of their stewardship.*[2]

[2] The general principles on which Friends consider it their duty to maintain plainness in their apparel, are applicable, in a great extent, to *furniture.* A due moderation in this respect is particularly recommended to us in those general advices of the Yearly Meeting which are ordered to be read once in the year in our Quarterly, Monthly, and Preparative Meetings. See *Book of Extracts.* The following caution, on the subject of furniture, contained in the printed epistle from the Yearly Meeting of 1809, is well worthy of our continued attention : " A fear has prevailed among us, at this time, that not a few elder Friends, and even some who take part in our discipline, have not been sufficiently exemplary with regard to plainness ; particularly in the *furniture of their houses.* It seems, therefore, right to caution all against giving way, in this respect, to the varying and often costly fashions

On reverting to the principal heads of this essay, the reader will recollect that the subject has been treated in reference respectively to speech, manners, and dress. The *plainness of speech*, which distinguishes Friends, consists in the disuse of a complimentary mode of speech, to which they object, *first*, because it is intended to flatter the pride of man, and *secondly*, because it is made up of falsehoods. To the *plainness of behaviour*, observed by all true Christians, Friends have added the peculiarity of avoiding bodily obeisances; *first*, because, like the phraseology already adverted to, they are merely complimentary; and, *secondly*, because some of these obeisances are the known outward signs of the worship of God himself. *Plainness of apparel* has been adopted by the Society partly to prevent the undue engagement of time, but chiefly, because ornament in dress is employed to gratify that personal vanity which, with every other modification of the pride of the human heart, Christians are forbidden to indulge, and enjoined to subdue. It will, moreover, be recollected that these peculiarities in our conversation, carriage, and appearance, grounded as they thus are on certain plain principles of the divine law, are severally supported by explicit injunctions contained in the New Testament.

of the age. Though it is a weakness which does not seem to savour so much of personal pride as does vain attire; yet it bespeaks a mind engaged with trifles, and a fondness for show which is inconsistent with the Christian character; and it disqualifies for duly advising such as may rush into further degrees of extravagance."

This branch of our subject suggests, in conclusion, a few general remarks.

I. We are much accustomed to denominate our scruples respecting speech, behaviour, and apparel, "*minor* scruples;" and since it is evident that supporting a paid ministry, the awful practice of swearing, and engaging in warfare and bloodshed, would constitute a more serious infraction of what we deem to be our religious duty, than a failure of strictness with respect to plainness, it may be allowed, that the word *minor*, as thus used, is not improperly applied. But let it be remembered, that, while the particulars of conduct into which these scruples lead, are comparatively *little*, the principles on which they are founded are *great*. Nothing is insignificant which really appertains to the divine law; nor are there any parts of that law more important than those with which our sentiments respecting plainness are connected, and which enjoin upon the followers of Christ a godly sincerity, a true simplicity, and a consistent humility. The present life is, in great measure, filled up with comparatively trifling circumstances: and, although the Christian is sometimes called upon to act on occasions of moment, his conduct, if narrowly examined, will be found to consist, generally and chiefly, in the constant succession of the *little* fruits of *great* principles. If plainness of speech, behaviour, and apparel, is reckoned, as I think it clearly ought to be, among the *little fruits of great Christian principles*, let it not be disregarded or despised: for its importance is to be estimated not so much by the minuteness of the particulars in which it is manifested, as by the magnitude of the fundamental rules out of which it arises.

II. Plainness of speech, behaviour, and apparel, being thus grounded on great and important principles, and being required, as we apprehend, to complete the circumspect walk of the Christian, is attended with certain practical consequences very influential in promoting our religious welfare. Such a plainness produces a striking distinction, which is, in itself, of real value. Who does not perceive that the young Friend, who submits to such restraints upon his language and personal appearance, is armed with an important defence against the temptations of the world? While he adheres to that simplicity of diction which marks the profession of a strict and spiritual religion, he cannot easily join in the loose ribaldry and obscene conversation of the idle and the dissolute; and, while he maintains in his apparel an entire plainness of appearance, his access will be very difficult to the haunts of folly, fashion, and dissipation. The language and dress which distinguish him will not only have the effect of discouraging others from any attempt to entice him into the vices of the world, but, by reminding him, from hour to hour, of the high profession which he is making, will be found to operate as a constant check upon himself, and thus will not fail to prove a useful barrier against those multiplied vanities and vices which abound among men.

III. Such being the practical effect of the peculiar plainness of Friends, I may now remark that, although it is not adopted by them on any principle of mere expediency, it is nevertheless useful and *expedient*.

Nor is this utility confined to the experience of individuals; it extends to the Society at large. Our plain language, manners, and dress, may be regarded as forming an external bulwark, by which Friends, considered as a religious community, are separated from the world, and, in some degree, defended from its influence. Did we differ from other Christians only in the maintenance of certain speculative views, such a bulwark would, perhaps, be little needed. But this is not the true state of the case. The whole religious peculiarity of Friends consists *in a series of testimonies, which they believe it to be their duty to bear, in their own conduct, against a variety of particular practices, affecting partly the worship of God, and partly his moral law, which are still prevalent not only among unregenerate men, but among sincere Christians.* In thus running counter to many of the common customs, both of mankind at large, and of other Christian societies, and in upholding what we deem to be a higher and purer standard of action, it is plain that we have to tread a path of some difficulty; and in order to a consistent walk in such a course, while our dependence must ever be chiefly placed on the power of the Lord's Spirit, we, nevertheless, need every outward assistance and defence which can be lawfully derived from our own principles. Such an assistance and such a defence are, undoubtedly, found in our peculiar plainness.

We well know, from experience, that, when any persons amongst us allow themselves to disuse the customary language, deportment, and dress of Friends, the effect very often produced is this—that they become negligent of our other Christian testimonies, gradually depart from religious communion with us, and finally, perhaps, connect themselves with societies of less strictness, or merge in the irreligious world. Instances of this description must be familiar to every one who has any intimate acquaintance with the circumstances and history of Friends. Now, there is much reason to believe that the causes which thus operate on individuals would, in the same manner, affect the Society at large; and that, were we to sacrifice these protecting peculiarities, we should not long continue to maintain, in other respects, our true and appropriate place in the church of Christ. Not only would such a sacrifice of our minor scruples naturally introduce a relaxation respecting those major ones which arise out of the same root, but the line of demarcation, by which we are now so providentially surrounded, being removed, there would be little to prevent our becoming *completely mixed up with general society.* Thus should we be gradually subjected to an influence directly opposed to all our peculiar views; and, with our distinctness and singularity, as a religious body, might probably be lost the high and conspicuous standard which it is now our privilege to uphold, respecting the Christian law of peace, and respecting the complete spirituality of the gospel dispensation.

If then, our young men and women are aware of the importance and excellency of that standard—if they have good reason to believe that our religious Society is raised up for the purpose of *showing forth* certain practical truths, not yet fully embraced by

Christians in general—let them not venture to break down that "hedge round about us," which not only affords a useful protection to themselves, but appears to be graciously provided by our heavenly Father, for the purpose of preserving us in our right place, and of facilitating the performance of our own duties, in his church universal. Nor will those distinguishing habits, which are thus useful in promoting our peculiar views, produce the slightest interruption in our harmony and unity with the serious members of other Christian communities. Experience amply proves the contrary to be the fact. The religious and consistent Friend is at peace with all the world, and is capable of a free communion of spirit with many who have little or no part in some of his sentiments. The more faithful we are in filling up that place in the body, which has been assigned to us by the Great Head of the church, the greater will be our capacity for a true brotherhood with all those persons who are building on the same foundation—with all who love, serve, and follow, the Lord Jesus Christ.

ADDENDUM TO CHAPTER XII.

A. D. 1834.

ON PLAINNESS.

During the ten years which have elapsed since the foregoing chapter was written, I have been furnished with abundant evidence, that the subject to which it relates, is truly fraught with practical importance.

Many young people, whose situations expose them to a variety of dangers, have frankly confessed to me, that they find their plain dress and language a salutary defence against many temptations. Being known by their attire to be Quakers, and being accustomed to the faithful use of the plain language to all men, they find a bar between themselves and the vanities and vices of the world, over which they cannot easily pass; and they are wise enough not to disdain so useful an ally to virtue. On the contrary, the surrender of these peculiarities opens an easy access to unprofitable associations, to marriages out of the Society, and to other compromises of our religious testimonies. Too often, indeed, has it been found a first step to grievous departures from the paths of rectitude and purity.

Knowing, as I do, the truth of these facts, I cannot do otherwise than mourn, when I observe our younger brethren and sisters, who have been educated in the habits of Friends, throwing off the restraints of their childhood, and adopting, by degrees, the common dress and language of the world. Although such persons may endeavour to pacify their consciences under the notion that our peculiar plainness is of small importance, I would affectionately inquire of them, whether this easy change works well in practice? Does it bring them nearer to their God and Saviour? Does it tend to separate them from an evil world? Is it accompanied with increased diligence in the attendance of their religious meetings, or with greater fervency in private prayer? Has it brought their souls into that peace which is ever found to be the reward of a patient bearing of the cross of Christ? If they know that the precise contrary of these things is true, have they not great reason to pause in their course, to humble themselves before God, and to seek for a more entire conformity to his blessed will?

I would encourage such of my young friends as are tempted to make this change for the worse—as I am constrained to consider it—to scrutinize their motives. If the motive be an impatience of restraint, and a love of the world, there is too much reason to fear that the change itself will be to them, an *entrance* at the "wide gate." May no plausible pretences of our great adversary ever induce us to forget, that "wide is the gate, and broad is the way, that leadeth to destruction!"

It is a painful circumstance, when members of our Society, who strictly adhere to plainness, are found to be negligent of the weightier matters of the law, "justice, mercy, and faith." And equally lamentable is it, when persons under our profession assume one character at one time, and another at another; plain Quakers at their meetings, and soon afterwards, perhaps, without a vestige of Quakerism—the gay companions of the gay—at some place of public amusement. But who can seriously entertain the opinion, that these instances of weakness and hypocrisy—these mere mockeries of truth—afford a valid pretext for our sacrificing one iota of our duty, as Christians and as Friends?

In the education of children, it is of great importance that we should pursue a wise and enlightened course with regard to plainness. If there be an uncompromising strictness on this subject, without sound Christian instruction, and without the softening influence of piety on the part of parents, one extreme may easily produce another; and what is felt to be a yoke of bondage may often end in unrestrained liberty. But if, on the contrary, we humbly endeavour, both by word and example, to acquaint our children with the love of Christ, and with its constraining influence on the heart; and if we train them up in plainness as part of their duty towards *him*, we need not greatly fear their afterwards departing from this narrow course.

There may possibly have been periods in the annals of our Society, when the laying of an injudicious stress on these peculiarities was no uncommon error. But the calm observer of facts may easily perceive, that, in the present day, our prevalent danger lies on the opposite side. Would that many parents amongst us, who earnestly desire the religious welfare of their children, but have adopted a lax standard in reference to these particulars, might be induced, with fervency of spirit, to seek of God, both counsel and strength, with regard to this branch of their duty. Were this their practice, I believe they would avoid the opening of a door for their families, which may prove an inlet to many dangers.

Here, however, I would address a few sentences to some of my young friends, who have not been brought up in plainness, but who are, nevertheless, sincerely attached to our principles, and are, as I believe, often visited with the day-spring from on high. If in moments of solemnity and divine favour, the inward Teacher whispers in their souls, that plainness of speech and apparel is a sacrifice required of them, I would beseech them not to reason against the Shepherd's voice. Rather let them follow that voice *in faith*, and they will not lose their reward. Timely obedience in a matter which, though called trifling, is of a very humbling nature, may introduce them to a degree of peace which they have not hitherto known, and will probably open their way to enlarged usefulness, as well as happiness, in the church of Christ. It is dangerous for any of us to despise " the day of small things." A chain graciously constructed by Divine Providence, for important and desirable purposes, may be severed by the lapse of its smallest, as well as by that of its largest link.

It is worthy of remark, that although an alteration in dress, and the substitution of " thee and thou" for the plural pronoun, when addressed to an individual, appear to be sacrifices of little cost, there are few things which, in many tender minds, occasion a greater struggle. As is the smallness of the required sacrifice, so appears to be the greatness of their fear to offer it. But is it not Satan, the father of lies, who makes the path of duty, even in very little things, appear distressing and difficult ? And would not the constraining love of Christ render every cross to our own wills, which we might undergo *for his sake*, both easy and pleasant ?

Opportunities have been afforded me, during the last few years, of conversing, on the present subject, with *many* persons in different parts of the kingdom, who have not been educated in our Society, but have become convinced of the truth of our Christian principles. With very little exception, I have observed that they are made sensible of the duty of plainness—especially of using the plain language; and in some instances, this has happened before there was any acquaintance with Friends, or with their writings.

In the course of their religious experience, and mostly in an early stage of it, these persons are brought to a pass on their journey, which may well be compared to a narrow bridge over a deep river. If they have faith to take up their cross, and to walk over it, they are generally enabled to go on and prosper; but if they give way to reasoning, and conclude that this passage is either useless or impracticable, the consequences are often lamentable. After looking at it for a long season, until they are weary of the sight, they turn back, and fall by degrees into a state of religious dwarfishness. Not daring to be Christians according to that particular line of duty which the Lord had cast up for them, they appear almost to cease from being Christians at all.

That this statement is neither untrue nor exaggerated, many can testify, from what they have known in themselves, and seen in others. Now, for such a uniformity of experience, in connexion with our views of the spirituality of the gospel, I cannot conceive that any thing can account, but *truth*. It appears to afford a substantial evidence, that these little sacrifices of self are consistent with the will of our Heavenly Father; and that they are required of us, in the order of his grace and providence, *for some wise and sufficient purpose.* Whatsoever is the duty assigned to us of the Lord, " rebellion is as the sin of witchcraft ;" and it is only in " the obedience of faith" that we shall find *peace.*

CONCLUSION.

Our discussion of the distinguishing religious sentiments and practices of the Society of Friends being now brought to its conclusion, the reader is invited to take a short and general review of that train of reflection which has been pursued in the present volume. For this purpose, his recollection will be assisted by the following summary.

However the members of any particular religious community may rejoice in those privileges which, in consequence of the adoption of certain principles, attach in a pre-eminent manner to themselves, they ought never to lay aside a just and candid view of the spiritual blessings which are offered to all mankind; and of those, more particularly, which appertain to all the living members of the church of Christ. All men are the children of God by creation, and over all he extends his loving-kindness and tender mercy. Christ died for all men; and upon all, as we may conclude from certain passages of Scripture, is bestowed a measure of the light and influence of the Spirit of truth. With respect to the true members of the visible church of Christ, these, to whatever name, sect, or country they may belong, are the common partakers of the *especial* favours of their Lord. It is their happiness to love and serve an incarnate, crucified, risen, and glorified Redeemer. They enjoy an abundant light; an exceeding grace; a revealed and established hope; and a pre-eminent degree of the influence of the Holy Spirit.

United, as all real Christians are, on the basis of fundamental truth, they are found to differ one from another in their view and estimate of various particulars in religion. Thus (for the present) do those principles which are essential to the salvation of souls pass to the various classes of true Christians, through as various mediums; and although some of these mediums are, evidently, purer and more spiritual than others, it may be acknowledged, (with gratitude to that Being whose mercies are manifold and whose resources are infinite,) that this variety of administration is, in some respects, overruled for good. At any rate, it affords a scope for the exercise of mutual forbearance and charity.

Christians, however, while they abstain from judging one another on such matters, and rejoice in their great and common salvation, ought, nevertheless, to endeavour after a *full persuasion* respecting their peculiar religious views;—to examine the foundation on which they rest; to let go their hold of them, and suffer them to pass away, if their foundation is a bad one; but if they are grounded, according to the decision of their deliberate judgment, on the unchangeable truth of God, to cleave to them with integrity, patience, and perseverance. Let us, who belong to the

Society of Friends, apply these remarks to our own religious peculiarities. They are, evidently, of a striking character, and of considerable importance in their practical results, and even, at first sight, they appear calculated to promote the tranquillity of the world, and the spiritual prosperity of the church of Christ. What, then, is the nature, what the authority, of those principles out of which they spring?

In reply to this inquiry, it may be observed, in the first place, that the great doctrine which lies at the root of them—a doctrine declared in Scripture, and admitted to be true by the generality of pious Christians—is that of the immediate and perceptible guidance of the Holy Spirit. Whatever may be the experience of other persons, it is certainly *our* experience, that the very same guiding and governing Spirit which leads the right-minded amongst us into the practice of universally acknowledged Christian virtues, *also* leads into these peculiarities; and hence we derive a satisfactory conviction that they are truly consistent with the law of God, and arise out of its principles.

In order to the confirmation of this general argument, we cannot do better than bring our several peculiarities, respectively, to the test of that clear revelation of the divine will which is contained in the Holy Scriptures, and which more particularly distinguishes the New Testament. Such has been the work attempted in the present volume. The points first considered, in pursuance of this plan, have been those which have a more immediate connexion with our religious duties towards God himself. Again to recapitulate the arguments adduced on the several particular subjects alluded to, would be at once tedious and unnecessary; but the reader will recollect that our disuse of typical ordinances—our refusal to admit any ministry in our congregations but such as flows from the immediate influences of the Holy Spirit— our views respecting the selection, preparation, and ordination, of the ministers of the gospel—our declining to unite in the prevalent system of hiring preachers, or of otherwise making pecuniary returns for the ministry—our allowance of the public praying and preaching of females—and our practice of waiting together upon the Lord *in silence*—are all grounded on the great Christian law, that they who worship God, who is a Spirit, "*must worship him in spirit and in truth.*" We conceive it to be in precise accordance with the principle of this law—a law which, in some respects, distinguished the dispensation of Christianity from that of Judaism—that we abandon all ceremonial and typical ordinances, all forms of public prayer, all written and prepared ministry, all human interference in the steps preceding the exercise of the sacred office, and all purchase or hire of its administrations; that we attempt not the use of words when words are not required of us; and that, while we endeavour to place an exclusive reliance on the Great High Priest of our profession, we do not hesitate to make way for the liberty of his Spirit, and to suffer the wind to blow *where it listeth.*

The views thus entertained by the Society of Friends, on the subject of worship, are in strict accordance, as we believe, with the spiritual nature of the

Christian dispensation. We conceive, however, that the divine Author and Minister of that dispensation not only brought to light and instituted, among his followers, the highest standard of divine worship, but promulgated also a perfect code of practical morality. It is the deliberate opinion of Friends—an opinion which they have often found it their duty to declare, —that this moral code ought to be maintained, by the followers of Jesus, in *all its original purity;* that no compromise ought to be made between the law of the world and the law of God; that the latter can never rightly yield, either to the dictates of human wisdom, or to the demands of apparent expediency. In consequence of the impression made on our minds by this general sentiment, (a sentiment which, however far it may be from being confined to ourselves, is, probably, maintained in our Society with a more than common degree of completeness,) we have been led to avoid various practices which are still usual, not only among worldly-minded persons, but among many sincere and even pious Christians. We conceive it to be in true consistency with the divine law, when rightly understood, that we abstain from lowering the standard of *truth*, and from a conditional cursing of self, by the utterance of oaths; from infringing the law of *love*, by taking any part either in offensive or defensive warfare; from fomenting the pride of man, by the use of flattering titles, and other complimentary expressions; from addressing to mortals those acts of reverence which are, on other occasions, employed to mark our allegiance to the Deity himself; from gratifying our vanity, by the useless ornamenting of the person or the apparel; and from a conformity with some other common customs which we consider to have an evil tendency.

Now, the reader will recollect that these several peculiarities — appertaining partly to worship, and partly to the conduct of common life—are not only, according to our apprehension, the natural and lawful results of important Christian principles, but are found to derive no slight confirmation from particular passages of the sacred writings, and especially of the New Testament, which appear to bear to them, respectively, a precise and specific relation.

Such is a short and general summary of the contents of the preceding essays. It may now be remarked, that another general argument, in favour of the Christian origin of our religious peculiarities, is suggested by the consideration of them *as parts of a whole*. The religion of Friends, when regarded as *a system* of doctrine and practice, may be described as consisting of many points, on which their views are coincident with those of their fellow Christians; and of others, the holding of which is, more or less, confined to themselves. Now, among the various parts which constitute this whole, there exists an uninterrupted and very striking harmony. Whilst our distinguishing views and practices are in no degree inconsistent with those fundamentals in religion, which are common to all true Christians, they will be found, in a remarkable manner, *adapted to each other*. Our high view respecting the unprofitableness of religious ceremonies, and the abolition of types, is completely in accordance with views equally high, in relation to the

Conclusion. 439

true nature and right exercise, the divine origin and absolute freedom, of the Christian ministry. And with our sentiments in regard to the ministry, nothing can more properly coincide than our doctrine respecting the value and usefulness of silent worship. Nor is it less evident, that the estimate which we have been led to form of Christian morality, as evinced in a practical testimony, borne against all swearing and fighting, and in favour of plainness and simplicity in conduct and conversation, is *on a level* with such of our principles as appertain to the subject of worship, and constitutes a necessary part of one complete and harmonious view of the purity, spirituality, and true perfection of the gospel dispensation. We know that in systems of religion which are of merely human invention—which have no better authority than the wisdom of the creature—there are ever found some inconsistent and discordant particulars, which betray the secret that the work is of man. In the absence of such inconsistency, therefore, in the nice adjustment of part with part, of sentiment with sentiment, of practice with practice, in the unbroken harmony which pervades the great whole—I cannot but perceive a strong confirming evidence, that the religious system of Friends results from the operations of the Divine Spirit, and is based on the unvarying principles of the law of God.

Since, then, the views and practices which have been considered in the present work are maintained, *as a whole*, by no Christian society except that of

Friends, and since they appear to be rightly grounded on certain essential principles in the divine law, and to be adapted, with singular exactness, to the purity and spirituality of the gospel dispensations, I may venture, with humility, to express my own sentiment, that Friends, viewed as a distinct fraternity in the church universal, have been brought to a greater degree of religious light, and to juster views of the true standard of worship and conduct, than any other class of Christians with whom I have the privilege of being acquainted. While, therefore, I well know the value of that fellowship in the gospel which subsists among all true believers in the Lord Jesus, and while I hope never to forget the vastly *paramount* importance of those great and fundamental principles which are common to them all, I find myself, in an especial manner, attached to that particular Society; and the conviction which I have now expresed is the ground of this attachment. While I would by no means underrate the usefulness of any of the existing classes of serious Christians, and while I believe that they are severally permitted to occupy appropriate departments in the fold of the Great Shepherd, I nevertheless entertain the sentiment, (in unison, it may be hoped, with the views of many of my readers,) that a peculiar importance attaches to the station maintained, in the church of Christ, by the pious among Friends; and for this reason—that they appear to be the appointed depositaries of certain plain, practical, Christian truths, which are, at present, far from being generally received, but which, originating in the will of God, as it is both inwardly and outwardly revealed, may be expected, as the church on earth advances to a condition of greater spirituality, to become more widely diffused, and more fully allowed.

Small as are the numbers who properly belong to our Society, and who are connected by the wholesome rules of its discipline, it will, perhaps, be admitted, that this result has already taken place, in a considerable degree. The inefficacy of all merely human forms and contrivances in the work of religion, —the inconsistency of typical rites with the spirituality of the Christian law of worship—the propriety of waiting upon God, from time to time, in reverent silence—the excellence and advantage of a ministry of the gospel, neither appointed nor paid by man, but freely exercised under the direct influence of the Spirit of Christ—the danger and sinfulness of all swearing—the value of an *undeviating* principle of Christian love, forbearance and peace—and the beauty of a complete simplicity in word, appearance, and behaviour—are points, as we may humbly hope, gently, yet plainly, opening to the view of many serious Christians, of different names, and in various parts of the world. Nor can I conceal from myself that any such approach towards the religious sentiments entertained by our Society must be of real and important advantage to the church at large. Although the name of Quakerism may be disregarded, and ultimately perhaps forgotten, the more general adoption of those principles by which Friends are at present distinguished, must, according to my apprehension, have a decided and very powerful tendency to the introduction of a *better day*—a day, when all men shall cease to place an undue dependence upon the teaching of their neighbour, and shall know the Lord for themselves; when the government of his own church shall rest more exclusively upon him who is called Wonderful, Counsellor, the Prince of Peace; when the sword shall be beaten into the ploughshare, and the spear into the pruninghook; when the wolf shall dwell with the lamb, and the lion lie down with the kid; when the glory of the Lord shall be more immediately and abundantly revealed, and when "all flesh shall see it together."

The reader can scarcely fail to understand that, in thus expressing my attachment to the Society of Friends, in preference to other Christian bodies, my attention is still directed, exclusively, to the religious principles which Friends profess, and by which many of them sincerely endeavour to order their walk in life. I am very far from forgetting our deficiencies and imperfections, as a community, or how very apt we are to fall short, in our individual conduct, of that high spiritual and moral standard which so preeminently attaches to our profession. One great reason why the religious principles of Friends are not found to take a more rapid and extended course in the church and in the world, is probably this—that so many of us fail, in various respects, from properly regulating our practice according to those principles. I desire to apply this observation, in the first place, to myself; and, secondly, I cannot be satisfied to conclude these essays without urging on my young friends, and on all my brethren and sisters in religious profession, the importance, to ourselves, to the Society of which we are members, and to the church universal, *of our walking worthily of the vocation wherewith we are called.*

This subject may be considered, in the first place, as it relates to those Christian testimonies which distinguish our own body in the church, and which have been considered, at large, in the present volume. Since we have so much reason to be convinced that these religious peculiarities have originated, not in the imagination of man, but in the will of God—that we have been led into the practice of them by the Spirit of truth—that they accord with the dictates of the divine law, as it is recorded in the Scriptures—that they are of an edifying tendency, and are calculated to promote the spiritual welfare both of our own Society, and of the church at large—and, finally, that they are, in a particular manner, deposited in our keeping—it unquestionably becomes us to maintain them, during our walk through life, with simplicity, sincerity, firmness, and diligence.

That it is our true interest, as well as duty, to be faithful in the observance of such a course, is sufficiently evident from this single consideration—that, in the sight of Him who is the Judge of all men, and the Author of every blessing, "*to obey is better than sacrifice, and to hearken, than the fat of rams.*"[1] But the same inference may be deduced from another position, equally incontrovertible; namely, that the Christian's religious prosperity and advancement in grace will ever be found to depend, in a great degree, upon his keeping his own *right place* in the body of Christ.

[1] Sam. xv, 22.

It is by no means difficult to figure to ourselves the case of a loose and *latitudinarian* Quaker, and to mark the dangers by which he is surrounded. Placed, by the good hand of Divine Providence, under that pure administration of Christianity, which I have now been endeavouring to describe, and plainly called upon to glorify God by the steady maintenance of our religious testimonies, he flies from the mortifications which they involve, and pacifies his conscience with the persuasion that nothing more is necessary for him than an adherence to those fundamental truths, the profession of which is common to Christians in general. The impartial observer will, probably, allow that such an individual greatly deceives himself, and falls into a dangerous snare. He stifles the secret convictions of his own mind, quenches the gentle and salutary influences of the Lord's Spirit, leans to his own understanding, indulges himself in plausible and misapplied reasoning, and departs from that *practical* confidence in God, which is the life and substance of true religion. Although he may cherish the notion, that he is still maintaining the general principles of Christianity, he neglects to carry those principles into detail, omits his *own* duty, and fails to occupy that station in the church which has been assigned to him by the Shepherd and Bishop of souls. The lamentable consequences of such a failure—of such a frustration of the gracious purposes of his Divine Master—are but too evident. So far is he from growing in grace, and from prospering in that course which is trodden by all the followers of Christ, that he too often dwindles into a carnal, lifeless, and worldly spirit, and gradually loses his footing on the Rock of Ages.

It has occasionally happened, that some of our members, who have never thoroughly understood or embraced the sentiments of Friends, and who have been thrown into much intimate association with other Christians, have quitted the ranks of the Society, and have been permitted, under some other administration of religion, to pursue their course with religious zeal and fidelity. Although I am persuaded that such persons would never have forsaken so pure and practical a form of Christianity, had they been more fully aware of the Christian grounds and real value of our principles, it is not *to them* that the observations now offered are intended to be applied, but to another class of persons, somewhat more numerous than they—persons, whose notions of religion are derived, almost exclusively, through the medium of Friends, and who are secretly convinced of the truth of our principles; but who, nevertheless, are unfaithful to the light bestowed upon them, and pusillanimously forsake the peculiar testimonies of the Society, as soon as they are exposed by them to the necessity of denying their own wills, and of bearing the cross of Christ. Such persons have both known and slighted the visitations of divine love in their hearts; and now, perhaps, they are left in a state of dwarfishnesss and sterility, destitute at once both of the form and substance of religion. Our gracious Redeemer appears to have marked out for us, within his varied and extended fold, a little space, where we may dwell in safety, and find abundant opportunity to promote "the glory of God in the highest, and on earth peace, and good will to man." But no sooner do we transgress the limits by which we are encircled, forsake our own station, and neglect the performance of those particular duties in the church which are committed to our charge, than we lose our religious strength, and are in great danger of falling back into the spirit of a vain and irreligious world. Finally, when this lamentable effect is produced, "the salt has lost its savour," and is "thenceforth good for nothing but to be cast out, and to be trodden under foot of men."[2]

Let us, then, be circumspect, steady, and bold, in the observance of our distinguishing religious testimonies. Believing, as I trust we do, that they are given us in charge by Him who "hath all power in heaven and in earth," let us pray for his grace, that we may be preserved from the snares of the enemy, and may be enabled, in an awful day to come, to give a good account of our stewardship. We know that, in exact proportion with the measure of light bestowed upon us, is the weight, the extent, the awfulness of our responsibility.

Here it may not be improper to remark, that the true efficacy of our religious peculiarities will greatly depend on the degree of *completeness* with which we maintain them. The double-minded man is declared to be "unstable in all his ways;" and nothing, surely, is more calculated to diminish our usefulness in the church, than a want of true consistency. The gar-

[2] Matt. v, 13.

ment "mingled of linen and woollen" was forbidden under the law; and such a garment (to employ the expression in a metaphorical sense) is worn by those persons, who, in some of their actions, adopt the highest standard of Christian conduct, and on other occasions are content with one of a much lower character. Is not such a description, in some degree, applicable to the member of the Society of Friends, who refuses to take an oath, but consents to the payment of ecclesiastical demands? or to him who bears a clear testimony in respect to tithes, but indirectly assists in military operations, or carries arms in self-defence? or to him who is faithful in all these particulars, but conforms to the fashions of the world in his language, manners, and appearance? or to him who wears a plain dress, but scruples not the use of flattering titles? I have already found occasion to remark, that throughout the religious system adopted by Friends, there exists an unbroken harmony—a real fitness of practice to practice, and of part to part; and no sooner is any one of our testimonies forsaken, than this harmony is interrupted, and the work is, in some degree, (whether greater or less,) marred upon the wheel. It cannot, indeed, be expected that those persons, whether members of the Society or otherwise, who are under the influence of *convincement*, should be brought to see the whole of their duty at once. It is more probable that the several points of prospect should open upon them in succession. But, as they are preserved in watchfulness unto prayer, and enabled to "*follow on* to know the Lord," I believe they will find that our several religious views and practices are the result of perfectly accordant principles, and flow from the same Spirit; and that, in order to glorify God in the way which he has thus cast up for us, it is needful that we maintain them *all*, in a simple, undeviating, and consistent manner.

Many of my readers must, indeed, be well aware, that the performance of our duty, in these respects, is no light, easy, or familiar matter. In abstaining from so great a variety of practices which we deem to be inconsistent with the spirituality and purity of the gospel, and in thus opposing the opinions and habits of the generality of our fellow Christians, it is our lot, as I have already observed, to tread a very narrow path, and to be exposed to many circumstances of a mortifying nature. Let us, then, seek to be preserved in *deep humility;* for this is a condition of mind which, above all others, will be found to soften the asperities, and to diminish the difficulty, of our course. The more our own pride and vanity are laid low, the more we are redeemed from the pursuit of that false honour which is given and received by man--the better shall we be prepared for the service of Christ, and the less will be the pain of our conflict, in *becoming fools in the sight of the world, for his sake.* And, truly, we need not fear to take up the cross, which we are thus called upon to bear; for if we be but faithful in following the monitions of our heavenly Guide, we shall find that his grace is sufficient for us, and that true wisdom is still "justified of her children." It will be amply proved in our experience, as it is in that of every humble and devoted Christian, that the "foolishness of God is wiser than men, and the weakness of God stronger than men." Nor shall we dare to repine, when we reflect on the known character of the Christian calling: "For ye see your calling, brethren," said the apostle, "how that not many wise men after the flesh, not many mighty, not many noble are called; but God hath chosen the foolish things of the world to confound the wise; and God hath chosen the weak things of the world to confound the things which are mighty; and base things of the world, and *things which are despised*, hath God chosen, yea, and things which are not, to bring to nought things that are; that no flesh should glory in his presence."[3]

Having thus considered the dangers and evils which attach to the latitudinarian professor of the truth, as we hold it, we ought by no means to forget those which are equally inseparable from the condition of the *formalist*. Such is the weakness, such the deceitfulness, of our hearts, that our very abstinence from forms may sometimes become formal, and our several religious peculiarities may be maintained in the spirit of the Scribes and Pharisees, who paid "tithe of mint, and anise, and cummin," and omitted "the weightier matters of the law—judgment, mercy, and faith."[4] It is an awful thing to be liable, in any respect, to the charge of hypocrisy; for this is a sin which, as it finds a place in us, must not only render us very

---

[3] 1 Cor. i, 26—29.   [4] Matt. xxiii, 23.

offensive in the sight of God, but can never fail to retard the progress of that cause, which we profess to love and to promote. When those who object to war in all its forms, as inconsistent with the Christian principle of love, forget, in their private life, the law of meekness and long-suffering, and yield themselves a prey to wrath, malice, envy, and bitterness; when those who speak of worshipping the Father in a pre-eminently spiritual manner, are really living in the neglect of devotional duty; when those who sedulously shun the idle vanities of general society, are seduced into that covetousness which is idolatry, or are found indulging their gross and sinful appetites; when those who, in professed adherence to the law of truth, refuse to substitute even the You for the Thou, are found defective in common sincerity of language, or integrity of conduct;—then, indeed, the cause of truth is fearfully laid waste, and all that is distinguishing in our religious system is thrown, to the eyes of an inquiring world, into a deep and almost impenetrable shade.

Although we may reasonably entertain the hope, that the character of but few of our members will correspond, in any great degree, to the description now given, that description may, neverthless, be partially and slightly applicable to many; and all of us, indeed, who are attached by the force of long-continued habit to the practices of Friends, have great need of watchfulness, lest we fall into this snare of our enemy;—lest, while he leaves us in quiet possession of the *figure* or *shell*, he rob us of the *substance* and *kernel* of our religion.

In conclusion, I would remark, that the true preservative from any such dereliction of the virtue, honour, and love, which become our religious profession, as well as from the neglect of those duties, which are, in some degree, confined to ourselves, will ever be found in the fear of God, and in a steady, abiding reliance upon our Lord and Saviour Jesus Christ. If Christ be made unto us, of the Father, " wisdom, righteousness, sanctification, and redemption," we shall not fail to live as " obedient children." Reconciled unto God through faith in our Redeemer, and subjected to the government of the Holy Spirit, we shall order our steps aright, imitate the goodness of our heavenly Pattern, grow in grace and holiness, and experience a happy deliverance from the power and dominion of the prince of darkness.

Let us ever remember that there is no use or security in the superstructure, except it be erected upon a sure foundation: and that, in religious matters, " *other foundation can no man lay than that is laid, which is Christ Jesus.*" Solicitous as I am that our peculiar testimonies should be maintained by us with all that faithfulness and vigour which their practical importance demands, I am perfectly aware that they are no sooner separated from *vital Christianity* than they become vain and unprofitable—deprived at once of all their efficacy and of all their stability. May it, then, be our humble and diligent endeavour to draw nigh unto the Father of mercies, through " *the blood of the everlasting covenant,*" and to live " *by faith in the Son of God.*" Thus, and thus only, shall we be enabled to bear with acceptance the goodly fruits of righteousness, to glorify the name of our God, and to fulfil the particular purposes for which he has seen meet to raise us up from among the children of men, to be, during his own good pleasure, a distinct and separate religious people.

ESSAY

ON THE

DISCIPLINE OF THE PRIMITIVE CHRISTIANS,

AND ON THAT OF THE

SOCIETY OF FRIENDS.

ESSAY.

THE supremacy of Jesus, over the little band of his followers, was never for a moment disputed. They were not permitted to call any man master, or to exalt each other with the title of Rabbi, Rabbi;—One was their Master—even Christ. Nor was this view of the subject obscured or weakened, after he had withdrawn his personal presence. Although he had "ascended up on high, far above all heavens," he was still with them, by his Spirit; and they knew that he ruled supreme, not only over the church, which he had purchased with his blood, but over the universe itself, for the church's sake.[1] They confessed that he was their High Priest for ever after the order of Melchizedek—the king of righteousness—the king of peace; and they lived in filial reliance upon his love.

While they thus looked upon Christ as the Head of his *whole* church, the believers were soon planted in distinct communities; and in each of these, it was their privilege to depend on the immediate government of their Lord. Wherever they were raised up and gathered together, whether few or many in num-

[1] Eph. i, 20—23.

ber, there they found their ever-present helper, friend, and teacher. They sat " under his shadow with great delight, and his fruit was sweet to their taste."

But the dependence of the primitive Christians on their holy High Priest and King, afforded them no pretext for a neglect of their duties as members of his body. The religion to which they had been introduced was found to be of a social character; its main practical feature was love: " By this shall all men know that ye are my disciples, if ye have love one to another."[2] For the sake of that God and Saviour who was now the supreme object of their affections, they were willing to labour for the benefit of each other, and of the church; and this they did, according to their respective callings, under the government and influence of the Holy Ghost.

One obvious duty which devolved upon them, was to provide for the poor. They were prepared, in this respect as well as in others, to "do good unto all men, especially to them that were of the household of faith." Thus we find that the deacons were appointed in the very infancy of the church, to provide both the Greek and the Hebrew widows with their daily food—a service of benevolence, for which seven men were chosen, of " honest report, full of the Holy Ghost and wisdom." Liberal collections were afterwards made, in the churches of Greece and Macedonia, for the poor saints at Jerusalem.

But we cannot doubt that the *spiritual welfare* of their fellow believers was still nearer to their hearts;

---

[2] John xiii, 35.

they were taught by the apostles to "consider one another to provoke unto love and to good works."[3] "Brethren," said Paul to the Galatians, "if a man be overtaken in a fault, ye which are spiritual restore such an one in the spirit of meekness; considering thyself, lest thou also be tempted. Bear ye one another's burdens, and so fulfil the law of Christ."[4] In order to effect the object here set forth, the most important means must have been private, brotherly expostulation and advice. When one Christian, in tender love, reproved another for his fault, and thus endeavoured to restore him to the fold of Christ, this was no improper interference with individual liberty—it was but one needful fruit of the law of love. "Thou shalt in any wise rebuke thy neighbour, and not *suffer sin upon him.*"[5]

By our Saviour himself, they were left in possession of a rule, which lay at the very foundation of Christian discipline; "Moreover, if thy brother shall trespass against thee, go and tell him his fault between thee and him alone: if he shall hear thee, thou hast gained thy brother. But if he shall not hear thee, then take with thee one or two more, that in the mouth of two or three witnesses, every word may be established. And if he shall neglect to hear them, tell it unto the church."[6]

Although the duty of private admonition rested on all true believers, as occasion might require it, yet it especially devolved on the most experienced members

---

[3] Heb. x, 24.   [4] Gal. vi, 1, 2.   [5] Lev. xix, 17.
[6] Matt. xviii, 15—17.

of the church. While the communities of Christians, in that day, were taught in the first place to submit to the government of Christ, and in the second, to exercise a mutual care among themselves, they were not left without rulers. " Obey them that have the rule over you," said the apostle to the Hebrews, " for they watch for your souls, as they that must give account."[7]

These persons were called indifferently *elders* or *overseers*,[8] and although it sometimes happened that they possessed a gift for the ministry of the word, they were in their official capacity (as has been already remarked)[9] distinct from the prophets or preachers. It was their duty to guard and nourish the people of God, " taking the *oversight* thereof, not by constraint, but willingly; not for filthy lucre, but of a ready mind; neither as being *lords* over God's heritage, but being ensamples to the flock."[1] In these labours of love they acted in behalf of the " Chief Shepherd," at whose hands alone they were to receive their crown of glory; and although they were often ordained by the apostles, and other inspired persons, it was the Holy Ghost who *made* them overseers—it was the Chief Shepherd himself who called them into their office.

It was, indeed, a primary principle in the early Christian church, that whatsoever office any man occupied for the *spiritual edification* of his brethren,

[7] Heb. xiii, 17.
[8] The word ἐπίσκοπος, rendered in our version " bishop," signifies only an " overseer."
[9] See chap. vi, p. 223—226.   [1] Peter v, 1—3.

nothing short of divine authority and power could truly bestow the commission, or qualify for the work. Sometimes the gifts of Christians are ascribed to God the Father—" God hath set some in the church, first, apostles, secondarily, prophets, thirdly, teachers, &c."[2] Sometimes, to Christ—" He (Christ) gave some apostles, and some prophets, and some evangelists, and some pastors and teachers."[3] Sometimes, to the Spirit—" All these worketh that one and the selfsame Spirit, dividing to every man severally as he will."[4]

But although the " elders and overseers," or " pastors and teachers," were the leading persons in the church, and had an important sway in the government of the body, they exercised no exclusive power in the regulation of the churches; much less did any such power devolve on the prophets or preachers. On all subjects connected with the interests of religion, and with the welfare and good order of the body, the ultimate authority, under Christ, rested on the *community of believers*.

Many instances are on record of meetings of the churches, for the consideration of such matters; and on these occasions, even the apostles were accustomed to act in unison with their less gifted brethren, and as members of an undivided body. When a new apostle was to be appointed in the place of Judas, the whole company of believers united in the nomination of Joseph and Matthias, and in that giving forth of

[2] 1 Cor. xii, 28.   [3] Eph. iv, 11.
[4] 1 Cor. xii, 11.

the lots, which resulted in the choice of the latter.[5] When deacons were to be set apart, who should undertake the care of the poor, it was upon *all the brethren* that the duty of selection devolved.[6] And on the same principle of discipline, the persons who were to accompany Paul in conveying the contributions of the European Christians to the poor saints at Jerusalem, were elected " by *the churches.*"[7]

It was to the apostles and *brethren* at Jerusalem that Peter apologized, when he had been preaching the gospel to Cornelius and his family. It was to the *church* at Antioch that Paul and Barnabas, on returning from their mission, gave a report of their proceedings in the work of the gospel.[8] And it was the same body of persons which brought them on their way, when they were again leaving that city, for their journey through Phenice and Samaria.[9]

That important discussion which resulted in the declaration of Gentile liberty from the yoke of the Jewish law, took place in a general assembly of the Christians at Jerusalem. Paul and Barnabas then stated their case to the " multitude" of believers; and the " whole church" united with the apostles in sending messengers to declare their will on the subject. The letters respecting it, addressed to the church of Antioch, were inscribed as coming from the apostles, and elders, and *brethren.*[1]

On this occasion a rule, intended to be binding on all Gentile believers, was settled in a meeting of the

[5] Acts i, 15—26.   [6] Acts vi, 3.
[7] 2 Cor. viii, 19.   [8] Acts xiv, 27.   [9] Acts xv, 3.
[1] Acts xv, 23.

Lord's people. But although the fixing of a general rule is a highly important act of discipline, it does not so nearly affect an individual, as the suspension of his own membership in the body. It is, therefore, satisfactory to find, that when an unfaithful professor was to be separated from communion with his brethren, this also was to be an act, not of the elders and overseers alone, but of the *church.* The directions of Paul to the Corinthians respecting an offender of this description, are entirely to the point. " For I verily, as absent in body, but present in spirit, have judged already as though I were present, concerning him that hath so done this deed. In the name of our Lord Jesus Christ, *when ye are gathered together*, and my spirit, with the power of our Lord Jesus Christ, to deliver such an one unto Satan for the destruction of the flesh, that the spirit may be saved in the day of the Lord Jesus."[2] It is probable that some painful disease was the punishment about to be inflicted through the Lord's power, on this transgressor; but there was also to be an act of excommunication —" Purge out therefore the old leaven, that ye may be a new lump, as ye are unleavened."[3] The whole passage contains an authority for the separation of an unfaithful member, *as an act of the body itself*—and it was by the same body, as we afterwards find, that the offender, when penitent, was to be restored to his membership.[4]

Since *women* were not permitted to speak in the churches, except under the immediate influence of the

[2] 1 Cor. v, 3—5.
[3] Verse 7.
[4] 2 Cor. ii, 6, 7.

Spirit, and since they were forbidden to "usurp authority over the man," I conclude that no active part was assigned to them in public assemblies for the settlement of the affairs of the church. No such restriction, however, could be laid upon them, in case of their meeting together at any time, without their brethren, and it is certain that the elderly among them were intrusted with the instruction of their younger sisters. "The aged women likewise, that they be in behaviour as becometh holiness ..... that they may teach the young women to be sober, to love their husbands, to love their children; to be discreet, chaste, keepers at home, obedient to their own husbands, that the word of God be not blasphemed."[5]

On a similar principle, there could be no reason why the elders and overseers, and other gifted members of the church, should not hold select conferences on subjects which concerned their own station in the body; or even on points affecting the body at large, so long as they assumed no authority which interfered with the functions of the church itself. Examples of such conferences are afforded us in the history of the apostle Paul. When he went up by revelation to Jerusalem, he conversed on the subject of his own calling, with the apostles and others who were "of reputation" in the church. On another occasion, the *elders* of the church at Ephesus met him at Miletus, when he unfolded to them the principles on which he acted as a preacher of the gospel, and exhorted them to the faithful discharge of their peculiar duties.[6]

[5] Titus ii, 3—5.   [6] Acts xx, 17.

Again, it appears to have been by a select company of the same character, that he and Barnabas were separated from their brethren for their mission to lesser Asia.[7]

Now, whatsoever was the subject on which the primitive believers were called upon to deliberate, they depended for counsel and direction on the Divine Head of the church, and acted *under the immediate guidance of the Holy Spirit.* Their democracy was safe, because it was also a theocracy. The church was enabled to conduct its own affairs, only because Christ was its ruler.

After giving directions to his disciples respecting the treatment of a delinquent brother—showing that, when private endeavours had failed, the offence was to be laid before the *church*—our Lord expressed himself as follows: " Verily I say unto you, Whatsoever ye shall bind on earth, shall be bound in heaven, and whatsoever ye shall loose on earth, shall be loosed in heaven." These expressions are best understood as relating to discipline, which was to be administered on earth, and to be confirmed " in heaven." The divine sanction was to accompany the decision of the body, as in the case of the Corinthian

---

[7] "Now there were in the church that was in Antioch, certain prophets and teachers, as Barnabas and Simeon that was called Niger, and Lucius of Cyrene, and Manaen, which had been brought up with Herod the Tetrarch, and Saul. As they ministered to the Lord and fasted, the Holy Ghost said, Separate me Barnabas and Saul, for the work whereunto I have called them. *And when they had fasted and prayed, and laid their hands on them, they sent them away:*" Acts xiii, 1—3.

transgressor, whom the church condemned, and whom (as we may infer from the passage) *the Lord* afflicted. A peculiar authority in these respects was, no doubt, bestowed on the apostles, but the same principle applied, in its measure, to the believers in general.

Now it is quite obvious, that whether the degree of this authority for binding and loosening was greater or less, the act of discipline could be confirmed in heaven only on one ground; namely, that in applying it, the Lord's servants followed the counsels of their divine Master, and formed their conclusions under the influence of his Holy Spirit. Accordingly our Lord concludes his discourse on the subject by an express promise of a most cheering nature—" When two or three are gathered together in my name, there am I in the midst of them."[8]

Certain it is, that the early believers were accustomed to realize this promise, not only when they met for the sole purpose of worship, but when their attention was directed to discipline—to affairs of whatsoever description, connected with the order and welfare of the body. Thus, in their first meeting after the ascension of Jesus, when the important duty devolved on them of setting apart an apostle, the Lord himself was present to listen to their prayers and to direct the lot; nor can we doubt, that when the seven deacons were chosen, the choice was guided by wisdom from above. The general rule already alluded to respecting the Gentile converts, was formed under a direct divine influence; for the written declaration of the church on the subject is thus prefaced—" It seemed

[8] Matt. xviii, 20.

good to *the Holy Ghost, and to us,* to lay upon you no greater burden than these necessary things."⁹

When the company of the prophets and teachers at Antioch were met in one place, and while " they ministered to the Lord and fasted," it was the *Holy Ghost* who said unto them, " Separate me Barnabas and Saul for the work whereunto I have called them."¹ Again, when the Corinthian transgressor was to be excommunicated, and delivered up, for a season, to Satan for the destruction of his flesh, it was " in the name of the Lord Jesus" that the church was to assemble for the purpose, and in dependence on his power alone, was the chastisement to be inflicted." ²

Thus it appears, that, in primitive times, the discipline of the church of Christ was carefully maintained, and at the same time was conducted with remarkable simplicity. Certain great principles, not formally determined upon, but arising out of the nature of Christianity itself, pervaded the whole system. The *first* was, that Christ is the Supreme and only Head of his own church, who rules over her, and ministers to all her need ; the *second,* that Christians are to care for the temporal and spiritual benefit one of another, in privacy and love. *Thirdly*, it was provided that the most experienced persons in the church, in the character of elders and overseers, should be the guardians of the flock, watching over them and ruling them in the Lord—their gifts for these purposes being distinct from that of inspired preaching. *Fourthly*, it was universally understood, that these

⁹ Acts xv, 28.   ¹ Acts xiii, 2.   ² 1 Cor. v, 4.

individuals were not to be lords over God's heritage, but that the final authority, on all questions of church government, rested on the Lord's people, in their collective capacity. *Lastly*, this authority could be duly exercised, and the discipline rightly conducted, only under the immediate control and guidance of the Holy Spirit. Through a stedfast adherence to these principles, the primitive Christians were established in the truth, and prospered. They grew " up into him in all things, which is the head, even Christ : from whom the whole body fitly joined together and compacted by that which every joint supplieth, according to the effectual working in the measure of every part, maketh increase of the body unto the edifying of itself in love."[3] The power, the work, was the Lord's, and his alone was the praise!

Christianity was established in the world under the most extraordinary outpouring of the Holy Spirit ever witnessed among men. During all preceding ages of man's history, indeed, the Lord had reserved for himself a church of believers, to whom were committed the oracles of God; but now the Sun of righteousness had arisen, in all his splendour, upon a corrupt and slumbering world. After the resurrection and ascension of our Lord Jesus Christ, his religion was spread among many nations, through the wondrous working of his own power. The miracles which the apostles and their companions wrought in his name, were precisely suited to the nature of their calling, as the promulgators of truths

[3] Eph. iv, 15, 16.

hitherto unknown; and under a divine influence, adequate to the occasion, they were enabled to write the books of the New Testament, which were to form the standard of Christian doctrine and practice in all succeeding ages.

Yet it is certain, that the truth, which was thus revealed with power, could maintain a permanent footing on the earth, only through the operation of the same Spirit; nor can we doubt that in every age of the church, and even amidst its deepest corruptions, a people, through divine grace, was still preserved for the Lord. Hidden and scattered as the true church of Christ may often have been, and more or less weakened through the superstitions of men, still we have every reason to believe that a remnant of true believers has never failed from the earth; like the seven thousand men, in the days of Elijah the prophet, who had not bowed the knee to Baal. And not only has there existed among Christians this continued work of grace, but fresh outpourings of the Holy Spirit have, on various occasions, taken place, which have led to important consequences in the history of the church. When such men as Ignatius, Polycarp, Irenæus, Cyprian, Ambrose, Augustine, and Bernard, were raised up to bear a noble testimony to the truth, even though that testimony was shaded with some portions of error—when Claudius of Turin fought single-handed against the corruptions of the day—when the Paulicians of Asia, in the ninth century, and the Cathari of Germany, in the eleventh, maintained a far purer system of doctrine and practice than was customary in the professing church—when, in the thirteenth century, Peter Waldo boldly proclaimed the doctrine of the cross, and the Lord's people, who had so long been dwelling in the Alpine valleys, openly declared, amidst innumerable sufferings, their adherence to simple Christianity—when in the fourteenth and fifteenth centuries Wickliffe and the Lollards in England, and Huss and his followers in Hungary and Bohemia, stemmed the tide of ecclesiastical corruption—and when, at last, in the sixteenth century, the reformation, under the banners of Luther, Melancthon, and other soldiers of Christ, burst forth with irresistible force in almost every part of Europe—it is impossible to deny that God was at work in the bosom of his church, and was carrying on his own gracious designs, by means of the especial effusions of his Holy Spirit.

On none of these occasions was there any revelation of new truth—any addition to original Christianity. There was only the renewed publication, again and again, of the gospel of our Lord Jesus Christ, under different degrees of divine light, and with more or less of the darkening mixture of human wisdom, according to the features of each particular case.

The reformation, which took place in the sixteenth century, from the corruptions of the papal system, went far towards restoring the profession of Christianity to its native purity. But who can wonder that it did not go the *whole way* in this blessed and necessary work? And who is not aware that much was left among the protestant churches, which still required the reforming hand of divine wisdom and power?

In our own country the founders of that system of doctrine and discipline, which now distinguishes the established church of England, were generally men of enlightened minds and profound piety; and many of them gave, at the stake, the *highest proof* of fidelity, to the Lord Jesus. Yet they left a scope to the puritans and other nonconformist divines, for further efforts in the work of purification; and these again, still retained many views and practices, which by no means precisely accorded with the spirituality of the gospel.

Now I conceive, that it was under another and very powerful effusion of the one blessed Spirit, and for the purpose of carrying on the work of reformation, in the Christian church, to a greater extent than had been before experienced, that Friends were so remarkably raised up in the course of the following century. The Lord's call was sent to a very young person, in a situation of comparative obscurity; and it was after the patient endurance, for several years, of the deep baptism of mental conflict—after a long preparation of prayers and tears, with searching of heart and searching of the Scriptures—that George Fox went forth, to proclaim amongst men the spirituality of true religion. No one can impartially peruse his history without perceiving that a remarkable power attended his ministry; many fellow labourers under the same anointing were raised up, chiefly through his instrumentality; and multitudes of persons were weaned from a dependence on human systems in religion, to sit down under the teaching of Christ himself. Thus the first meetings of the people called Quakers were gathered and settled in almost every part of Great Britain and Ireland ; and, before very long, in several places on the continent of Europe, in the West Indies, and in North America.

The era when Friends arose in this country was one of great excitement, and it ought to be freely allowed, that some of them were at times carried off their centre by a warm imagination. In taking a calm review of their history, I am by no means prepared to justify all that they did, or all that they said. They were liable to error and infirmity like other men ; they had their treasure in earthen vessels. We need not, therefore, be at all surprised, if we find them occasionally giving way to that enthusiasm in practice, and to that heat in argument, which were leading temptations of the day. But, while I willingly make these admissions, I am deliberately of opinion, that George Fox and his brethren were enabled to uphold a high standard of truth, and to make a very near approach to the incorruptness of primitive Christianity. While they were deeply read in the Scriptures, they gave themselves up to the guidance and government of the Holy Spirit. They discarded *expediency*, when it interfered with *principle ;* and they were calmly resolved to " follow the Lamb " whithersoever he might lead them. The consequence was, that they renounced all merely ceremonial observances; all secular views in the pursuit and maintenance of religion ; and all dependence on the systems of men, in the things of God.

From time to time they were gathered together in silence before the Lord ; and such was their contrite state, that the floors of their meeting-houses were often wetted with their tears. Nor did they dare to omit their public worship, which they regarded as an essential mark of their allegiance to the King of kings. In the midst of the fire of persecution, and when the dissenters of the day met only in private places, that they might avoid the terrors of the law, the despised Quakers persisted in the assembling of themselves together, and worshipped God in public, in the face of their enemies.

The same unbending principle they manifested in their uniform refusal to pay tithes—to join in the warfare of the world—to swear even in courts of justice—to give that honour to men, which is due to God alone—or to use those forms of homage and compliment, which had no better origin than vanity and falsehood. In consequence of their firm Christian conduct in these matters, they underwent an amount and variety of suffering, which have not many parallels in the history of the church of Christ. Their goods were spoiled, and their families reduced to poverty; multitudes of them were thrown into filthy dungeons among the worst of felons; considerable numbers lost their lives in consequence of these hardships, and a few (in New England) suffered death by the hand of the executioner.

During this time of severe trial, they were enabled to exhibit the peaceful triumphs of Christian principle. So ardent was their love for each other, that they frequently offered to lie in prison for their brethren, body for body;[4] and so undoubted was their

[4] See "*Besse's Sufferings of the Quakers.*"

integrity, that even by their persecutors their word was acknowledged to be as valid as an oath. Thus the name of Jeshurun, the "upright people," was truly applicable to them; and as was their integrity, so was their patience. Nothing daunted their fortitude or shook their perseverance. They quietly endured their sufferings, in submission to the will of God; and God did not forsake them. In the depth of the noisome prison-house, they were often permitted to feel the sweetness of his presence, and their mouths were filled with his praise.

Making a due allowance for the difference between heathen and Christian countries, we may perceive a remarkable similarity between the first settlement of the meetings of Friends in Great Britain and Ireland, and the planting of the primitive Christian churches. In both cases, societies were raised up in various distinct places, consisting of persons who differed in a *striking* manner from the surrounding community, and who were associated in the bond of common principles. At once distinguished from their fellow countrymen, and agreeing among themselves, the early Friends were well compacted together, and were baptised by one Spirit into one body.

Now I conceive that their system of discipline, like that of the primitive Christians, originated in the very nature of their social and religious union. Gathered together by a divine hand, they were taught to love as brethren, and to watch over each other for good; nor can it be doubted, that from the first rise of the Society, the most pious and experienced of their number were led, in an especial manner, to superintend the flock, and to supply, as far as possible, both their temporal and spiritual need. " As the church of God in those days increased," said one of our worthy elders about the year 1655, in reference to the meeting of Friends at Colchester, " my care daily increased, and the weight of things relating both to the outward and inward condition of poor Friends, came upon me . . . . the more I came to feel and perceive the love of God and his goodness to me, the more was I humbled and bowed in my mind to serve him, and to serve the least of his people amongst whom I walked; and as the word of wisdom began to spring in me, and the word of God grew, so I became a counsellor of those who were tempted in like manner as I had been."[5]

In the year 1656, a general meeting of Friends was held at Balby, near Doncaster, which issued many important precepts on subjects connected with the good order and welfare of the body—such as the method of proceeding with delinquents, and the duties of husbands, wives, parents, children, servants, and masters, justice in trade, and faithfulness in the performance of civil duties. A similar meeting was held at Skipton, A. D. 1660, " for the affairs of the church, both in this nation, and beyond the seas." This, indeed, was only one session of a meeting established by the advice of George Fox, for the purpose of caring for the Society, and of providing for its poor members, under the pressure of persecution.

[5] *Stephen Crisp, Introd. to Book of Extracts*, p. xix.

In the mean time, there were established, by degrees, quarterly meetings, which exercised a general superintendence over the Friends *in each county ;* and, for a time, the discipline of the Society mainly rested on these bodies.

But in the year 1666, the form of our church government became more detailed and settled. George Fox says in his journal under that date, " Then was I moved of the Lord to recommend the setting up of five monthly meetings of *men and women Friends* in the city (London) besides the women's meetings and the quarterly meetings, to take care of God's glory, and to admonish and exhort such as walked disorderly or carelessly, and not according to truth. For, whereas Friends had had only quarterly meetings, now truth was spread, and Friends were grown more numerous, I was moved to recommend the setting up of monthly meetings throughout the nation." In 1688, he writes thus—" The men's meetings were settled throughout the nation. The quarterly meetings were generally settled before. I wrote also into Ireland, Scotland, Holland, Barbadoes, and several parts of America, advising Friends to settle their monthly meetings in those countries, for they had their quarterly meetings before."

The quarterly meetings now received reports of the state of the Society from the monthly meetings of which they were severally composed, and gave such directions to them as they thought right. Finally, in the year 1678, a general meeting of representatives from the quarterly meetings was convened in London ; which received reports from those bodies, deliberated on the state of the Society, issued advices in the form of an epistle, and finally agreed to meet again, the following year, in like manner. This representative assembly has since continued to meet every year in London, at or near "the time called Whitsuntide," with unbroken regularity, to the present date; and in it centres the authority of discipline for the whole Society in Great Britain.

The reader will have observed that George Fox was led to recommend the setting up of *women's meetings* both in London and in country places. These meetings, before very long, became as regular as those of the brethren; being held at the same time with them, and being constituted on the same orderly system. While it belonged to the brethren only to form rules for the government of the Society, and ultimately to carry them into effect, the women's meetings were established for the purpose of exercising a wholesome care over their own sex. To this object their attention was, from the beginning, exclusively directed, as is the case in the present day.

We do not, however, forget that the gifts of the Spirit, and amongst others that of spiritual discernment, are freely bestowed upon Christians of both sexes. When therefore our ministers apply to their monthly meetings for leave to travel in the work of the ministry, the women unite with the men in the consideration of the subject. For the same reason they, as well as the brethren, are often appointed to the station of *elder*, in which capacity it is their duty to watch over the ministry both of men and women.

The free scope allowed to women in the exercise of

the gifts of the Spirit, and the share assigned to them in the discipline of the church, are circumstances of a distinguishing character, which have produced very beneficial results to the Society of Friends. Not only have the Christian care and counsel, as well as the gospel ministry of women, been greatly blessed to the body at large; but under the grace of God, a more than common stability has been imparted to the female character—this has wrought well for our domestic comfort, for our temporal safety, and for our religious edification.

Previously to the regular institution of our annual assembly, meetings had been occasionally held in London consisting only of the ministers of the Society, who were convened from various parts of the country, in order to confer on subjects connected with their common cause. These conferences continued to be held in connexion with the yearly meeting; and were soon joined by the elders, on whom it devolved to cherish and guard the ministry. In process of time similar meetings were formed, in connexion with the quarterly and monthly meetings, in every part of the country, and they are still regularly maintained. Their specific object is to exercise a watchful care over their own part of the body; and they have been found of great use in assisting to secure the right religious standing, and harmonious operations, of those amongst us who are called to labour in the gospel, or to watch over the flock of Christ. But the meetings of ministers and elders have no concern with the conduct of the discipline; they are entirely destitute of legislative authority.

That authority has uniformly rested with the yearly meeting—that is, with the body at large;[6] and the monthly meetings were set up for the express purpose of carrying the discipline into effect. They are the hands of the body, the executors of the law, intrusted with a parental authority over their individual members. In point of fact, it is by means of these subordinate assemblies, that the church, in its separate and local associations, regulates its own affairs, and governs itself.

It cannot be necessary, on the present occasion, to enter at large into a view of the business which devolves on our *monthly meetings*. No sooner were they regularly established, than a variety of objects came under their attention; the care of the poor, the protection and assistance of the afflicted and imprisoned, the Christian and orderly conducting of marriages and burials, the registration of births and deaths, the education of children, the settlement of differences to the exclusion of legal proceedings, were all of them subjects which claimed the attention of these executive bodies, and which continue to do so to the present day.

By far the most important of their functions, however, is the spiritual care of their individual members. This care is especially called forth by certain inquiries respecting the moral and religious state of the body, which are answered periodically, for the information

---

[6] The yearly meeting, like our other meetings for discipline, although, strictly speaking, composed of representatives, is open to any members of the Society—of course, the men and women being convened separately.

of the quarterly meetings.[7] Each little church amongst us is thus brought, at certain periods, to a deliberate view of the condition of its members, and advice is often extended as occasion may require.[8] Again, when

---

[7] The monthly meetings constitute the lowest class of our meetings for the *discipline* of the church. A single monthly meeting, however, often comprehends two or more "preparative meetings," which severally draw up answers to these inquiries. The answers of the monthly meeting itself, are formed from those of its preparative meetings.

[8] These inquiries are as follows :—

I. Are meetings for worship and discipline kept up, and do Friends attend them duly, and at the time appointed; and do they avoid all unbecoming behaviour therein?

II. Is there among you any growth in the truth?

III. Are Friends preserved in love one towards another; if differences arise, is due care taken speedily to end them; and are Friends careful to avoid and discourage tale bearing and detraction?

IV. Do Friends endeavour by example and precept to train up their children, servants, and those under their care, in a religious life and conversation, consistent with our Christian profession; and in plainness of speech, behaviour, and apparel?

V. Is it the care of all Friends to be frequent in reading the Holy Scriptures, and do those who have children, servants, and others under their care, train them up in the practice of this religious duty?

VI. Are friends just in their dealings, and punctual in fulfilling their engagements?

VII. Do Friends avoid all vain sports and places of diversion, gaming, all unnecessary frequenting of taverns and other public-houses, excess in drinking, and other intemperance?

VIII. Are Friends faithful in bearing our Christian testimony against receiving and paying tithes, priests' demands, and those called church-rates?

IX. Are Friends faithful in our testimony against bearing arms, and being in any manner concerned in the militia, in privateers, or armed vessels, or dealing in prize-goods?

cases occur of breaches of morality, or of a departure from our more important Christian testimonies, it is the monthly meeting which must *ultimately* sit in judgment on the transgressor ; and either pass over

X. Are the necessities of the poor among you properly inspected and relieved ; and is good care taken of the education of their offspring ?

XI. Is due care taken, when any thing appears to require it, that the rules of our discipline be timely and impartially put in practice ?

XII. Is there any appearance of convincement among you, and have any been joined to our society on that ground since last year ?

XIII. Is care taken early to admonish such as appear inclined to marry in a manner contrary to the rules of our society ; and in due time to deal with such as persist in refusing to take counsel ?

XIV. Have you two or more faithful Friends, appointed by the monthly meeting, as overseers in each particular meeting ; are the rules respecting removals duly observed ; are the general advices read as directed ; and are the lists of your members revised and corrected once in the year ?

XV. Are Friends annually advised to keep correct and clear accounts, and carefully to inspect the state of their affairs once in the year ?

XVI. Are Friends clear of defrauding the King of his customs, duties, and excise, and of using or dealing in goods suspected to be run ?

XVII. Do you keep a record of the prosecutions and sufferings of your members ; is due care taken to register all marriages, births, and burials ; are the titles of your meeting-houses, burial-grounds, &c., duly preserved and recorded ; are the rules respecting registers and trust property observed ; and are all legacies and donations properly secured and recorded, and duly applied ?

The following ADVICES of the yearly meeting are read, at least once in the year, in the quarterly, monthly, and preparative meetings of men and women Friends ; they are to be read in the men's and women's meetings separately :—

the fault on receiving proofs of repentance, or separate him, for a season at least, from his fellowship with the body.

It is not without meaning that a stress is here laid on the word *ultimately;* for Friends have always

Take heed, dear friends, we entreat you, to the convictions of the Holy Spirit, who leads, through unfeigned repentance and living faith in the Son of God, to reconciliation with our heavenly Father, and to the blessed hope of eternal life, purchased for us by the one offering of our Lord and Saviour Jesus Christ.

Be earnestly concerned in religious meetings reverently to present yourselves before the Lord, and seek, by the help of the Holy Spirit, to worship God through Jesus Christ.

Be in the frequent practice of waiting upon God in private retirement, with prayer and supplication, honestly examining yourselves as to your growth in grace, and your preparation for the life to come.

Be careful to make a profitable and religious use of those portions of time on the first day of the week, which are not occupied by our meetings for worship.

Live in love as Christian brethren, ready to be helpful one to another, and to sympathize with each other in the trials and afflictions of life.

Follow peace with all men, desiring the true happiness of all; and be liberal to the poor, endeavouring to promote their temporal, moral, and religious well-being.

With a tender conscience, and in accordance with the precepts of the gospel, take heed to the limitations of the Spirit of truth, in the pursuit of the things of this life.

Maintain strict integrity in all your transactions in trade, and in your other outward concerns, remembering that you will have to account for the mode of acquiring, and the manner of using, your possessions.

Watch, with Christian tenderness, over the opening minds of your offspring; inure them to habits of self-restraint and filial obedience; carefully instruct them in the knowledge of the Holy Scriptures, and seek for ability to imbue their minds with the love of their heavenly Father, their Redeemer, and their Sanctifier.

upheld the importance of the preceding steps, which ought, if possible, to take place in dealing with delinquents. The first of these is *private admonition.* —" If thy brother shall trespass against thee, go and tell him his fault between thee and him *alone ;* if he hear thee, thou hast gained thy brother!"

"Admonish a friend," said the son of Sirach, " it may be that he hath not done it; and if he have done it, that he do it no more. Admonish a friend, it may be that he hath not said it, and if he have, that he

Observe simplicity and moderation in the furniture of your houses, and in the supply of your tables, as well as in your personal attire, and that of your families.

Be diligent in the private and daily family reading of the Holy Scriptures ; and guard carefully against the introduction of improper books into your families.

Be careful to place out children, of all degrees, with those Friends whose care and example will be most likely to conduce to their preservation from evil ; prefer such assistants, servants, and apprentices, as are members of our religious Society ; not demanding exorbitant apprentice fees, lest you frustrate the care of Friends in these respects.

Encourage your apprentices and servants of all descriptions to attend public worship, making way for them herein : and exercise a watchful care for their moral and religious improvement.

Be careful to make your wills and settle your outward affairs in time of health ; and, when you accept the office of guardian, executor, or trustee, be faithful and diligent in the fulfilment of your trust.

Finally, dear friends, let your conversation be such as becometh the gospel. Exercise yourselves to have always a conscience void of offence towards God and towards man. Watch over one another for good ; and when occasions of uneasiness first appear in any, let them be treated with in privacy and tenderness, before the matter be communicated to another : and Friends, every where, are advised to maintain "the unity of the spirit in the bond of peace." 1791.—1801.—1833.

speak it not again. Admonish a friend, for many times it is a slander, and believe not every tale."[9] The views of this wise, though apocryphal writer, are coincident with those which our Society has always endeavoured to maintain. We consider it to be our individual duty to communicate *in private* with a supposed offender, before we mention his fault to a third person. If we then find that it has not been committed, our care on his account is removed. If, on the contrary, he is guilty of it, our own adherence to an honourable secrecy may greatly increase the efficacy of our endeavours to restore him to the right way.

But important as is the *individual* duty of private admonition, it affords no pretext for the absence, in any church, of an official overseership. It is an essential part of our system of discipline, that as far as circumstances will allow, "two or more faithful friends" should be appointed to this office in each meeting. The proper business of these persons is to exercise a godly care over all the members of the body; to watch against occasions of offence, to settle disputes, and to endeavour to reclaim delinquents, when the evil *first* appears; to strengthen the weak, to rebuke the gainsayers; to reprove the careless; and to maintain, by every means in their power, that purity and harmony in the body, which best adorn our Christian profession. Nor must it be forgotten, that those whom the Holy Spirit raises up to be overseers in the church, ought not only to show, but to

[9] Ecclus. xix, 13—15.

lead the way—to be examples to the flock " in all holy conversation and godliness."

I conceive that the elders and overseers in our meetings—did they fully occupy the place assigned to them—would very nearly correspond in point of authority and function, with the same officers in the primitive church. And it is no less clear, that it is the Christian duty of the younger and less experienced members of the body, to render to them a ready deference and obedience, as to those who watch over their souls, and must give an account of their stewardship. " Likewise, ye younger, submit your selves unto the elder. Yea, all of you, be subject one to another, and be *clothed with humility;* for God resisteth the proud, and giveth grace to the humble."[1]

In communicating with a brother who has been " overtaken in a fault," it will ever be the first endeavour of the truly Christian overseer, to " *restore such an one in the spirit of meekness.*" " The servant of the Lord must not strive, but be gentle unto all men, apt to teach, patient, in meekness instructing those that oppose themselves, if God peradventure will give them repentance to the acknowledging of the truth; *and that they may recover themselves out of the snare of the devil,* who are taken captive by him at his will."[2]

Nor ought the effort of the church, to reclaim her wandering members, to end with the kindly offices of the overseers. When the third step commanded by

---

[1] 1 Peter v, 5. [2] Tim. ii, 24—26.

our Saviour has been taken, and the collective body is informed of the offender's fault, repeated visits should be made to him by persons selected for the purpose, and every endeavour used to bring him to repentance. Such, I trust, is the usual practice of our monthly meetings. Yet I believe there is often a danger lest our care over transgressors should cease after disownment has taken place. Where there is any love for the truth in the disowned party, or any open door for continued efforts on his account, his separation from the body ought surely to be regarded as merely temporary; and it is our bounden duty, with all diligence and prayer, to seek his restoration. "Sufficient to such a man," said the apostle Paul on an occasion of this kind, "is this punishment which was inflicted of many. So that, contrariwise, ye ought rather to forgive him, and comfort him, lest, perhaps, such a one should be swallowed up with overmuch sorrow."[3] To conduct our discipline with impartiality and vigour, and steadily to maintain its *integrity*, is indeed of essential importance to the welfare of the body. Yet the main characteristic of Christian discipline is love—that love which seeks, above all things, the salvation of sinners.[4]

[3] 2 Cor. ii, 6, 7.

[4] The spirit of tenderness, which breathes through the instructions of George Fox, in regard to the treatment of delinquents, is worthy of especial notice, and would, if there were no other, afford ample evidence of the soundness of his Christian character. In one of his early epistles he thus writes : " Now, concerning gospel order, though the doctrine of Jesus Christ requireth his people to admonish a brother or sister twice, before they tell the church, yet that limiteth none, so as that they shall use no longer forbearance.

Although the executive authority rests only with our monthly meetings, provision is made for their help on occasions which require it. Thus, when ministers receive certificates to travel beyond the seas, the authority of the monthly meeting must be confirmed by that of the quarterly meeting, before they are at liberty to proceed.[5] Again, when elders are to

And it is desired of all, before they publicly complain, that they wait in the power of God, to feel if there is no more required of them to their brother or sister, before they expose him or her to the church. Let this be weightily considered, and all such as behold their brother or sister in a transgression, go not in a rough, light, or upbraiding spirit, to reprove or admonish him or her ; but in the power of the Lord and spirit of the Lamb, and in the wisdom and love of the truth, which suffers thereby, to admonish such an offender. So may the soul of such a brother or sister be seasonably and effectually reached unto and overcome, and they may have cause to bless the name of the Lord on their behalf, and so a blessing may be rewarded into the bosom of that faithful and tender brother or sister who so admonished them. And so keep the church order of the gospel, according as the Lord Jesus Christ hath commanded ; that is, 'If thy brother offend thee, speak to him betwixt thee and him alone ; and if he will not hear, take two or three, and if he will not hear two or three, then tell it to the church.' And if any one do miscarry, admonish him gently in the wisdom of God, so that you may preserve him and bring him to condemnation, and preserve him from further evils, which it is well if such do not run into, and it will be well for all to use the gentle wisdom of God towards them in their temptations, and condemnable actions; and, with using gentleness, to bring them to condemn their evil, and to let their condemnation go as far as their bad action has gone, and no farther, to defile the minds of Friends or others; and so to clear God's truth and people, and to convert the soul to God, and preserve them out of further evils.—So be wise in the wisdom of God." See *Introduction to the last edition of the Book of Extracts.*

[5] When a minister from England is about to visit Ireland, this rule is not *imperative.* On the other hand, when the service

be nominated, the quarterly meeting appoints a committee, to assist a committee of the monthly meeting, in proposing names for the consideration of the latter body. In general, it devolves on the quarterly meetings[6] to extend help, as required, either by advice or deputation, to their subordinate bodies; and of this duty they are, from time to time, reminded by the following inquiry:—" Are you careful to give to your monthly meetings that assistance which your place in the body and their state require ?"

This inquiry, together with twelve of those which are answered by the monthly to the quarterly meetings, is answered by the quarterly meetings to our annual assembly, which is thus enabled to form a correct view of the state of the Society. The care of the yearly meeting itself over the Society seldom fails to be evinced, by written advices, as well as by a printed general epistle; and when any quarterly meeting, under circumstances of trial and difficulty, applies for assistance, a deputation is, for the most part, appointed for the purpose. Occasionally, indeed, the yearly meeting has set apart a large committee, for a general visit in Christian love to all its inferior meetings; and many can testify that these labours have been blessed both to those who paid the visits, and to those who received them.

which he has in view lies in *foreign parts*, he must obtain the sanction of the yearly meeting of ministers and elders, or of its subordinate body, (called the morning meeting,) as well as that of his monthly and quarterly meetings.

[6] In some parts of the kingdom the meetings answering to the quarterly meetings are held only *three times*, and in Scotland only twice in the year.

There exists, moreover, a standing committee of the yearly meeting, consisting of numerous friends of London and its vicinity, and of correspondents in the country, which sits at least once a month, during the intervals between one yearly meeting and another. It is the duty of this important body—called "the meeting for sufferings" — to extend advice and assistance to the Society, or to any part of it, under the exigencies which may arise; to provide supplies of the standard books of Friends; to watch the proceedings of the legislature, as far as they affect the Society; to exercise a friendly care over ministers who are travelling abroad; to correspond with Friends in foreign parts; and to protect the interests of the body at large.

Thus is our little church assisted and edified, under the cherishing hand of our holy Redeemer, by the mutual care and sympathy of its component parts.

It is satisfactory to reflect on the unbroken regularity with which the system now detailed has been maintained in our Society, for more than a century and a half. From year to year, and from generation to generation, Friends have kept up their monthly, quarterly, and yearly meetings, and have never found occasion materially to alter the plan so wisely laid down for them by their predecessors. This plan has been, from the beginning, remarkable for that simplicity on the one hand, and that precision on the other, which, under providence, could alone insure its usefulness and stability; and it affords a clear evidence that there was nothing in the religious views of the early Quakers, opposed to the principles of Christian *order*. Some persons, indeed, there were, under our name, of a wild and ungoverned spirit, who refused to submit to these wholesome provisions; but, by the Society at large, they were embraced with gladness, and have ever since been found easy to apply; and salutary in their operation.

While we cannot reasonably doubt, that, in constructing this plan, George Fox and his coadjutors were favoured with the gracious aid of the Holy Spirit, it is evident that their attention was closely fixed on the pattern of discipline presented to them in the *New Testament*. Their system was indeed more developed than that of the primitive believers is known to have been, especially as it regards the subordination of one class of meetings to another; but with regard to main principles, as well as in many distinct particulars, the views and practices of Friends, with respect to church order, appear to be the *same* as those of the primitive Christians.

The acknowledgment of Christ as the only Head and Priest of his people—the direct dependence upon him as the present Ruler of the church—the divine origin of the gift of the ministry, and the absence of all human restriction, as to the persons who might exercise it—the voluntary support of the poor—the appointment, in every church, of deacons to manage the funds raised for that purpose, and of elders and overseers to watch over the flock of Christ; all being distinct, in their official characters, from the prophets or preachers—the settlement of disputes, not before the magistrates of the land, but by the arbitration of brethren—the private admonition of offenders as the first step in discipline—the care extended over women by overseers of their own sex—the select conferences of preachers and elders—the making of rules, the choosing of officers, the disownment and restoration of offenders, by the *assembled* believers—are points which distinguish the simple religious polity of the earliest Christians; and all these points are steadily maintained in the Society of Friends.

In conclusion, however, there are two subjects connected with our view of church government, which appear to claim *especial* notice. The first is the *absence of all ecclesiastical domination*, or of any distinction between a priesthood in power, and a laity in subjection. No such distinction appears to have been known among the immediate followers of Jesus, in the first and purest age of Christianity—and none such exists among ourselves. Our views on this point are indeed by no means opposed to the just influence of the most experienced members of the church, or to the proper authority of appointed overseers; but we consider ourselves to be brethren, possessed of equal rights; and we conceive it to be the duty and privilege of the *church*, to conduct its own affairs, and govern itself. And here there is no place, on the part of individuals, for a proud independence, or impatience of restraint; because, so far as Christian discipline extends, every single member is subjected to the control of the body at large.

Now it is very obvious, as has been already observed, that such a form of church government can be safe and salutary, only while we maintain a still higher principle — that of the supremacy and perpetual superintendence of Christ himself. This is a doctrine on which Friends have at all times delighted to dwell. Often have they been led to call to mind the glowing words of the prophet—" Unto us a child is born, unto us a son is given, and the *government shall be upon his shoulder*, and his name shall be called Wonderful, Counsellor, The Mighty God;"[7] often have they found occasion to recur to the doctrine of the apostle, that God hath put " *all things*" under the feet of Jesus, and given him to be Head *over all things* to the church."[8]

What then is the agency by which Christ conducts his reign, and orders the affairs of his universal people? Scripture and experience alike declare that it is *the agency of the Holy Spirit.* It is by his Spirit that he brings his children into subjection to his will, qualifies them for their respective offices in the body, and guides them individually and collectively, in their course of duty.

The second point to which I was anxious to allude is this—the belief of Friends, that a manifestation of the Spirit is given to every man to *profit withal;* and that the living members of the church, in their endeavours to promote the religious welfare of others, will not fail to receive, as they humbly seek it, his gracious aid and *guidance.* Whether in such endeavours, we act as private individuals, or in the official character of overseers of the flock, it is still in dependence on our Divine Master, and in obedience

[7] Isaiah ix, 6. [8] Eph. i, 22.

to the government of his Spirit, that our duties ought to be performed. We believe that it is thus, and thus only, that we can with confidence offer up the prayer of the psalmist, " Establish thou the work of our hands upon us; yea, the work of our hands establish thou it." [9]

But further—when Christians meet in their corporate capacity, for the purpose of regulating the affairs of the church, and of promoting the cause of religion, Christ is their *rightful president*. And it is our firm belief, that as they reverently wait upon him, they will find him present to assist their deliberations, to prompt their efforts, and to direct their decisions.

That such was the happy experience of the primitive believers has already been shown from Scripture; and there is surely no good reason why Christians, in the present day, did they fully rely on God, should not enjoy a sufficient measure of the same blessed privilege.

We, therefore, consider it to be our duty to conduct all our meetings for discipline, with immediate reference to the government of Christ and to the guidance of his Spirit. Whether we are engaged in appointing officers, in acknowledging ministers; in deliberating on their prospects of service; in admitting members; in dealing with delinquents; in extending advice to subordinate meeetings; or in discussing propositions made with a view to the welfare of the body—whatever subject, indeed, connected

[9] Psal. xc, 17.

with religion and morality may occupy our attention —we believe it to be right, humbly to wait for divine direction, and to yield to that judgment, on the subject before us, which appears to be most consistent with the mind *of Christ.*

On the general maxim, that of every question which can arise in the church, there must be some *right* conclusion, and in the further belief, that as they diligently seek his counsel, Christ will lead his dependent followers into that conclusion, we admit, in our meetings for discipline, of no division of members—of no settlement of any point by majority. Neither have these assemblies, any more than our meetings for worship, a human president. The clerk collects and records the judgment of his brethren, and it is his duty, during the course of every discussion, to take care that proper order be preserved. But he has no personal authority over the assembly—no power to put any subject to the vote—no casting vote of his own.

That this is a principle worthy of our Christian profession, and eminently conducive to the welfare of the church, cannot with any reason be denied; and although its *full effect* may often be prevented by the infirmity of our nature, we are bound to acknowledge that it works well in practice. I am not aware that a single instance has occurred in this country, of the settlement of any question in a meeting for discipline —monthly, quarterly, or yearly—by the division of its members. Have we not then much cause for thankfulness to Him who raised up our forefathers by his power, that he still condescends to preserve us, as a people, in some degree of practical dependence on his own authority; that he still brings us, from time to time, into the same judgment; that he still enables us, when our opinions differ, to condescend one to another *in love?*

Certain it is, that the more we are weaned from the eagerness of the carnal mind, and brought to wait patiently on the Lord, the better we shall be prepared to receive and follow his counsel; the more eminently we shall enjoy the UNITY OF THE SPIRIT, IN THE BOND OF PEACE.

THE END.

Discipleship course?
→ Jason & Tabitha
→ Jeff & Lisa
→ Butch & Crystal
→ English's?
→ Earnhardts
→ Connie